W9-BXL-032

STUDIES IN EDUCATION

Recent Titles

A SYSTEM FOR ANALYZING LESSONS
John Herbert

PROGRESSIVES AND URBAN SCHOOL REFORM
Sol Cohen

FORUM AND FOCUS FOR THE JUNIOR COLLEGE MOVEMENT
Michael Brick

THE LEADER IN THE GROUP
Alfred H. Gorman

FRINGE BENEFITS FOR PUBLIC SCHOOL PERSONNEL
Jack H. Kleinmann

SOCIAL INTEGRATION IN URBAN COMMUNITIES
Robert B. Knapp

THE EMERGING EVENING COLLEGE
Ernest E. McMahon

EDUCATION AND SOCIAL INTEGRATION
William O. Stanley

GUIDANCE: AN INTEGRATING PROCESS IN HIGHER EDUCATION
May A. Brunson

CASES IN COLLEGE ADMINISTRATION
Ronald C. Bauer

THE DEVELOPMENT OF SCIENTIFIC CONCEPTS IN A YOUNG CHILD
John Gabriel Navarra

THE NEGRO WOMAN'S COLLEGE EDUCATION
Jeanne L. Noble

THE LIBERAL AND TECHNICAL IN TEACHER EDUCATION
Merle L. Borrowman

Colonel Francis W. Parker

The Children's Crusader

Jack K. Campbell

Teachers College Press
Teachers College, Columbia University, New York

Library of Congress Catalog Card Number: 67–20114

Manufactured in the United States of America

Acknowledgments

It seems more difficult to write a life than to live it. At least, one person cannot adequately research all that remains of another human existence. This biography of Colonel Parker would not have been possible without the contributions, small and great, of many people. The work started out as a dissertation at Teachers College, Columbia University, under the sponsorship of Lawrence A. Cremin. It was cosponsored by R. Freeman Butts, and Professors A. W. Spieseke and R. F. W. Whittemore were also on the committee which examined and approved the study. I have since then, however, shortened and revised the biography so that any shortcomings are of my own doing.

In the course of research there was the help and assistance of librarians from all the special collections cited in the bibliography. Considerable assistance came from Miss Elizabeth Faries of the Dayton and Montgomery County Public Library and from Mrs. Herbert Kellar of the McCormick Collection, Wisconsin State Historical Society. R. L. Scott, editor of *The Carrollton Gazette–Patriot* (Carrollton, Illinois), made generous efforts in opening up the old files of the *Carrollton Gazette.* He and members of his family thereby helped uncover a little known period in the Colonel's life. Arthur W. Lang, Jr., of the Lang Funeral Home in Pass Christian, Mississippi, and John B. Lanyon, Jr., of The House of Lanyon Undertakers in Chicago, Illinois, both went out of their way to search for old records in their files.

When research led to Helen F. Topping of the Parker Foundation, I found a living memory of Colonel Parker and the same kind of crusading spirit. She provided some letters, manuscripts, and documents which she had collected through the years. This "Topping Collection" will either go to Miss Topping, now in Japan, or to the Chicago Historical Society where it will become part of "The Flora J. Cooke Papers." (This special collection of Flora J. Cooke materials was not available when the author was at research in Chicago.)

I could never forget the many delightful interviews, mentioned in the bibliography, which this study entailed. The late Perry D. Smith, of Winnetka, Illinois, had especially colorful memories of the Colonel, and A. Gordon Melvin could recount his contribution to the Parker Movement in most insightful ways. Inspiring as well as informative, Edna Parker Shepard [Parker's stepdaughter] and Sadie Tolman [Parker's "favorite" niece by marriage] established the best living link to the past. Both women, then in their nineties, have since died, but they represented the enduring qualities of body and spirit and mind. The hospitality of the Francis Parkers and Newton Tolmans at Tolman Pond, New Hampshire, will never be forgotten.

My parents, Helen and Donald J. Campbell of Downers Grove, Illinois, made invaluable contributions. They were especially helpful in researching newspapers of Carrollton, Illinois, and assisting the author in reading through the many newspapers of Dayton, Ohio. My wife's parents, Marion Decker Eschenlauer and the late Arthur Eschenlauer of Cranford, New Jersey, helped their son-in-law with some of the important proofreading, and my wife, Susan Eschenlauer Campbell, accompanied and sustained me on the many trips involved in research. It was, indeed, the help and encouragement of many people which made this book possible. No life can be written, or lived, alone.

JACK K. CAMPBELL

March, 1967

Contents

I

The Road to Education

In the summer of 1859, when slavery troubled the soul of the nation, Francis Wayland Parker tore himself away from family roots in New Hampshire and set out for the heartland of Illinois.[1] This meant leaving behind a widowed mother and three unmarried sisters, but Parker was twenty-one and ambitious. Insecure, and practically an itinerant schoolmaster in New Hampshire, he was promised the principalship of the only district school in Carrollton, Illinois.

Frank Parker, as he was called in those days, had a long way to go. The distance in miles was nothing compared to all he would have to learn. Though he was then considered a promising teacher, genial but strict, he later looked back on himself as "lank" and "pale" and "long-haired," but especially "green." At five feet nine, he had reached his full height but carried only 130 pounds, half his mature weight. He was still beardless and wore his brown hair combed straight back behind his ears. He may have been spare, even emaciated, but to some of the girls back in New Hampshire he was an "Apollo."[2]

Parker had left a different world behind. Traveling by rail as far as Alton, on the Illinois side of the Mississippi River, nothing impressed the young New Englander on his journey more than the endless fields of corn until he saw what he called the "Father of Waters."[3] Beyond this great river stretched the vast open spaces of Indian and buffalo country. Meeting ground of East and West, this river town was also a border between North and South. Described as a "chip off the old New England block," Alton was nevertheless joined to the slave culture downstream by the Mississippi River. Even this far north, slavery was an unsettled matter. Only the year before, large crowds from Missouri, in addition to those from Alton, had gathered to hear Lincoln and Douglas debate the slavery question.[4]

The slavery issue may not have seemed so pressing to Parker at that time as the prospects of his new job. Such anxiety could have brought on the dyspepsia which troubled him as he set forth on the last leg of his journey. It was only thirty miles by stagecoach from Alton to Carrollton, but the road was unpaved. A recent rain had turned it to mud. The prairies of Greene County were shrill with the sounds of birds and insects as the coach bumped along the rutted road. Parker's eye, sharpened by years on a farm, must have marveled at the sea of flowers and the well-wooded countryside, studded with clumps of bass, linden, maple, and cottonwood.

When the stagecoach rolled into Carrollton, Parker had his first look at this thriving county seat. He would never forget his impression of the "old square" that surrounded the courthouse. It was at John Headrick's Hotel where he initially took up lodgings. Next door was Temperance Hall. Down the street and around the square could be found the blacksmith shop, the barber shop, the bakery and restaurant, the livery stable, the shoe shop, the tin shop, the law office, the dry goods store, and the hatter's establishment. Built by public subscription, the new plank sidewalk joined all buildings on the square and extended as far as the schoolhouse, a block to the west. The schoolhouse was a plain, two-story frame structure, with a little square belfry on top. It had green blinds and a white exterior. According to Parker, it was "dirty and comfortless inside."[5]

Already dismayed with the schoolhouse, Parker was even more disappointed to learn that his yearly salary of $600 was to be paid in wildcat scrip, worth only 70 per cent of hard cash. He also learned that his school was definitely a "rough house." One of his predecessors had been threatened with a knife; another had been pelted and driven off with mud.[6]

At that time the citizens of Carrollton were becoming uneasy about the discipline of the younger generation. One of the local newspapers, *The Carrollton Gazette,* devoted to "Agriculture, Literature, and Morality," warned its readers early in September 1859 that the town was full of children and that, whether parents would believe it or not, many were unruly and "even worse than that." The editor believed the parents should train their children or employ good teachers to do it and pay them "good prices." He was then a candidate for school director and lamented the fact that the electorate was so uninterested in education that it never brought out more than half its members for school elections.[7]

As it turned out, the editor was elected later that September by a very good turnout, and he promptly lent the columns of his paper to a notice which proclaimed the hiring of "Mr. F. W. Parker, principal." Miss Gilchrist, Miss Charlotte Jones, and Miss Haggard were reported as assistants. "We feel confident," the editor wrote, "that better teachers have never been engaged in Carrollton. . . ."[8]

Parker had come a long way for this principalship in Carrollton, Illinois. The journey was more than a thousand miles, rougher than a ride over unpaved roads. It had taken all his life.

Even before he was born, there was destiny at work in the name "Francis Wayland" which his parents had chosen in hopes of having a son to model after the president of Brown University. He was born on October 9, 1837, in the village of Piscatauquog, town of Bedford, New Hampshire.[9] In that same year, the great leveler, Andrew Jackson, had stepped down as President of the Republic, and Horace Mann had moved up to the post of Secretary to the Massachusetts State Board of Education. Born under these two stars, it was little wonder that this boy would grow up to associate democracy for all men with education for all men. A widespread panic and depression in the same year served notice that his life would not be easy.

The prominent feature in his ancestry, he would learn, was "as many as five strains of ministers."[10] These strains had all come together in the marriage of Mille Rand and Robert Parker at a simple church wedding in Goffstown on October 29, 1829.[11] It would be almost eight years before this union would produce a son, but in the meantime a daughter, Mary, was born in 1833, and another, Philinda, in 1835.*

Frank's father, Robert Parker, was a cabinetmaker by trade. Born

*For this and subsequent references to births, marriages, and deaths, see Section X (Vital Statistics) in the Bibliography and the following: *History of Bedford, New Hampshire, Being Statistics, compiled on the occasion of the One Hundredth Anniversary of the Incorporation of the Town, May 19, 1850* (Boston: Printed by Alfred Mudge, No. 21 School Street, 1851), pp. 174, 235–239, 266–267, 270, 323, 326–327; *History of Bedford, New Hampshire from 1737, Being Statistics on the occasion of the One Hundred and Fiftieth Anniversary of the Incorporation of the Town, May 15, 1900* (Concord, N. H.: The Rumford Printing Company, 1903), pp. 1024, 1027, 1029, 1105; Ezra S. Stearns (compiler), *Genealogical and Family History of the State of New Hampshire,* Vol. I (Chicago: The Lewis Publishing Company, 1908), pp. 227–229; Augustus C. Parker (compiler), *Parker in America, 1630-1910* (Buffalo, N. Y.: Niagara Frontier Publishing Company, n.d.), p. 475; "The Harris Estate," *Daily Mirror and American* (Manchester, N. H.), September 29, 1871; grave markers in Piscatauquog Cemetery, next to the Congregational Church on South Main Street, West Manchester, Manchester, N. H.; "Cemetery Inscriptions of Manchester, New Hampshire" (unpublished, compiled by W.P.A., 1938, New Hampshire Historical Society, Concord, N. H.), pp. 91, 92, 99, 101–102, 106, 110.

in the town of Bedford on May 13, 1797, Robert Parker was partially deaf and never a well man. Although considered a skilled cabinetmaker, he apparently needed his father's help in going into business. Thus, the cabinetmaker's shop was set up next to William Parker's general store. William Parker's prosperity contrasted starkly with his son's lack of success. A shoemaker when he first settled in Bedford, William bought his first acre with a pair of boots and went on to exploit the wilderness and found the village of Piscatauquog, later to become part of Manchester. By the time he died in 1819, he owned not only the store and the cabinetmaker's shop, but a "Tavern House," the ferry and toll house on the Merrimack River, a half-interest in the saw mill, and numerous shares in both the Union Canal and the Cotton and Woolen Manufactory in Goffstown. He also collected rents from many small farm properties as well as from the "Homestead Farm," with its 130 acres, mansion house, barns, and sheds, on the Mast Road to Boston.[12]

When these vast holdings were finally probated in 1824, Robert Parker, one of ten children, inherited almost $2,000 in cash. He also acquired eight acres of good land and about twenty-five acres suitable for pasture.* It may have been the prospect of such a bequest that led Robert Parker to venture into matrimony, for he had married Charlotte Chamberlin of Pembroke, New Hampshire, on December 31, 1822. No record of her death may be found in New Hampshire, but it must have occurred after the birth of a son in 1827 and before her husband's remarriage in 1829. Their first son, named rather ambitiously after George Washington, was born on August 16, 1823. A daughter, Ann, was born in 1825. The youngest son, Robert, named—less ambitiously—after his father, was born on August 6, 1827. He probably died in infancy. The daughter survived to marry and spend her life in Bedford. The older son went into farming and later moved to New York. None of these children remained in the household, so they could not have made much impression on the early memories of Frank Parker.

It was probably the influence of his mother that started Frank Parker on the road to education. Born on April 29, 1795, daughter of a Bedford clergyman, Mille Rand had not only assisted at the education of successive brothers and sisters (seven in all), but had become a teacher and practiced her skill with "ways of her own."[13] Unmarried until she was thirty-four, she was thus an experienced as well as an original teacher. From her, Frank inherited the blood of a Harvard librarian, John Rand, Harvard contemporary of John Adams and John Hancock, as

* For this and subsequent references to the material holdings of William, Robert, and Nabby Parker, see "Probated Estates," in Section X of the Bibliography.

well as the spirit of the Indian fighter, Colonel John Goffe. Colonel Goffe was believed to be the descendant of Judge William Goffe, who had sentenced Charles I to death and then fled to America upon the restoration of Charles II.[14] With William Goffe as an antecedant, Frank Parker would have come naturally by his instinct for passing judgment on tradition whenever it smacked of tyranny.

Great hopes must have been wrapped up in this little October baby who was born in the late harvest time of his parents' lives. His father was already forty years old and his mother forty-two. They both came from well-established families and no doubt began their marriage with high aspirations; but their present circumstances were not promising. Shortly before his son was born, Robert Parker had to borrow money from his sister's husband, James Walker. A few years later he had to mortgage part of the homestead to his neighbor, Frederick G. Stark. He was finally reduced to borrowing money from his widowed mother, a situation that continued as long as he lived. Young Frank would come to know his father as a poor and sickly man, but the boy was not neglected. He was taught his "letters" before he began school. He learned most of the "pieces" then in vogue and could recite them on command. He was considered "quite a famous declaimer in all the country around," but this early pressure to receive praise developed into extreme self-consciousness. He would be bothered by it the rest of his life.[15]

Frank Parker's first distinct memory was of climbing up to the window in their "log house" to watch a political procession for William Henry Harrison. This would have been in 1840. It was that same year that his youngest sister, Emily, was born. He could never remember the day when he did not want to be a teacher. Nor did he ever forget the impression made by his first day of school when he walked, led along by his two sisters, clutching a Leonard spelling book, which he kept dropping; each time his sisters would pick up the book and hand it back to him.[16]

There had been a public school in Bedford, off and on, as far back as 1753 when the town first voted to keep a school. It was part of the Puritan tradition that education, at least Bible-learning, was necessary for personal salvation. For Frank Parker, education would always be a matter of salvation, but social as well as religious. He retained the spirit, if not the letter, of Puritan doctrine, and would hold to nonsectarian lines for the accomplishment of his educational ends. His parents, it was said, were Baptists—at least they had named their son after the Baptist president of Brown University—but Frank Parker claimed that his religious training was simply "Hard work, responsibility and piety—real, sound, honest, rigid piety." The only preaching he remembered was a hard sell for "fire insurance," or rather, advice on how to avoid Hell. When he was disciplined in school, he remembered that "every whack" on his hand with a "ferrule" felt like an "expiation for sin."[17]

Death and the "Day of Doom" were to become only too real for the young Parker. His ailing father died on September 9, 1844, just as another school year was beginning. His mother had very little with which to provide for the children. She had a plow but no horse. Much of the land was mortgaged. The personal property, assessed down to the last bushel of "corn in the ear," was worth about $200.

Robert Parker's brother, John, was a lawyer and he assumed the responsibility of administering the estate. James Walker, married to Robert Parker's sister, Betsy, was an influential farmer, merchant, and surveyor. He agreed to accept the guardianship of the children. Frank and Emily, both under seven years of age, were boarded out because they were not old enough to earn their keep. A few weeks later, when Frank was seven and legally old enough to be put to work, James Walker was relieved of the expense of boarding the boy. Those four weeks, however, cost the father's estate $2, just the value of the eight silver spoons which represented the only mark of gentility Robert Parker had left his family.

While the inestimable loss of a boy's father seemed to be counted in dollars and cents by all the uncles and aunts, young Frank Parker saw the family furniture and real estate sold at public auction. Perhaps of greater loss to the bewildered boy was the threat of losing his "teacher-friend" who was being transferred from the local school to the newly established academy in Piscatauquog. The teacher, said to be crippled, grumpy, and a disappointed man, was nevertheless a good scholar and had apparently come to fill an important place in the life of the fatherless boy. At that time the village school was too crowded and some of the older boys were being transferred to the academy. Frank thought he knew a great deal more than those older boys, and his "teacher-friend" vouched for his ability. Frank "cried" his way into the academy, but one of his uncles was on the school committee and his grandmother owned a share in the new academy, all of which might have helped as much as the tears.[18]

Decisions about Frank's future were postponed while his father's estate was probated. Part of the trouble in settling the estate was the lingering on of Frank's grandmother, Nabby Parker. She held several of Robert's notes of indebtedness, notes which she did not press but which would have to be paid, with interest. At the same time, her will promised a division of her dower, and Robert Parker's creditors probably thought they could wait until the old woman died.

Nabby went right on living, however, until 1846, surviving Robert by two years. By that time, her dower had dwindled with the years and would not afford much substance for any of her numerous heirs. She could better bestow treasured stories, one after another, upon her grandson. She could tell him he was the seventh generation of Parkers to stem from Captain James Parker, who came from England two centuries earlier. She could tell him about the various "strains of ministers" from which he was descended on the Parker side, including one who was a little too liberal in his views and "turned out" at Newburyport. She knew all about the Parkers because she was born one herself. Her Father, Captain John Parker, was an uncle of her future husband. Both men served the Revolution at Bunker Hill. Born in 1765, Nabby was a full ten years younger than the cousin she would marry.

Nabby Parker could boast of at least one ancestor whom her husband, William Parker, could not claim. That was John Cotton, whose catechism for children, *Spiritual Milk for American Babes Drawn Out of the Breasts of Both Testaments for Their Souls Nournishment,* had taught that the child was corrupt in nature. What would Nabby Parker have thought if she knew the little boy who had just "cried" his way into the academy would grow up to lead a revolution of children against the artificial restraints and educational impositions of their elders?

Most likely, Nabby Parker, who could only sign her will by tracing her name over the handwriting of someone else, never saw academic potential in her grandson. She apparently did not protest when young Frank's guardian, James Walker, decided to apprentice the boy to a farmer. It was a year after Robert Parker's death and even Mille Parker could not protest against the plan to take her boy out of school. Walker said he knew a good farmer near Goffstown, William Moore, who was willing to take the boy. The papers were drawn up, and the eight-year-old boy was bound out until the age of twenty-one.[19]

It was the middle of winter, young Parker remembered, when he made the ten-mile journey to the Moore's farm. A few school books and his father's desk were all he had to take with him. His room was in the garret, with such a low ceiling he could touch the rafters as he lay in bed. The sound of rain on that roof would linger in his memory.

Life went on. Parker thrived on fried pork and pumpkin pie. He worked hard on the farm, but he would always pause to listen for the approach of a wagon or buggy, because he knew that if company came, he would have hot biscuits. Although he also hungered for school, the Moores felt he should remain at home and tend to farming. They relented, however, after the summer chores were done. When he got to school he said he was in the "first class," which, although it had meant the highest class in Piscatauquog, referred to the lowest class here in Goffstown. He was so humiliated at being placed in the lowest class that he took the advice of the Moores and stayed home to work during the rest of the term. After this, though, he did put in about eight weeks of schooling each winter, but the school was poor and he later wondered how he ever learned anything. One master chewed tobacco and spit all around the room. The teaching was apparently even more casual.

Frank longed for someone to love and understand him, but he found a teacher who would meet him at the door and command, "Go in, you little imp of iniquity, go in and I'll show you how to behave!" The little imp was able to fight back. One time he told the teacher in the swallow-tailed coat with brass buttons that "You are not doing right; you don't teach as they do down in Squog."[20]

The years went by, and Frank watched the seasons come and go from his garret window that overlooked the orchard. One time he put his impressions on paper. He put his heart into it, writing about the trees in the orchard, their shining bark, then the buds bursting out until there was one great "snowbank of beautiful appleblossoms." He showed his writing to Mrs. Moore, who had once been a schoolmistress. She glanced at the scrap of brown paper and said that if she could not write better than that she would not try. Mrs. Moore must have come to mean a great deal to the young apprenticed boy because he said he could never be compelled to write a composition again, except when he went to the Academy, and he blamed his inability on this incident with Mrs. Moore.[21]

But he did read. There were almanacs dating back to 1794 in the cupboard, and he read straight through those seasons of history. He read and reread the Bible, Bunyan's *Pilgrim's Progress,* and *Life of Judson* by his namesake, Francis Wayland.[22]

He dreamed of a great deal under the old butternut tree or while he was on the end of a saw. What should he become in life? He would dream of being a statesman, but he couldn't think of anything higher than President of the United States. He would dream of being a soldier, but what would be left for him after he had command of an army? Out of these dreams Parker sensed that teaching was the only profession with endless challenge and possibility.[23]

Parker would one day consider those years on the farm as one of the best preparations for his career as a teacher. He believed there was no place as conducive to elementary education as a farm, because that is one place where a child can be made responsible for something important and learn good work habits while surrounded by a comparatively simple environment. He could learn dependence on the laws of nature as well as personal power in modifying that nature.[24]

Parker found that on the farm the word "study" did not apply to book learning only. He studied geography by observing the hills, valleys, and brooks on the old rocky farm. Topography was discerned in the neatly divided fields, pastures, and patches of woods. He studied geology and minerology in the soil he worked. He observed the effect of sunshine, draught, drainage, and fertilization. He studied botany with the hoe and his bare hands while he learned the name and characteristic of every weed and plant. He knew the trees by name—the best ones to climb, the best for lumber, fences, or firewood. He studied zoology. The animals of the farm were his subjects. He helped to break steers, kill hogs, hunt for eggs, and feed and clean the animals. He knew the wild animals, too, and the insects that "scurried away" when he turned over a stone. He knew the birds—the wrens that nested in the barn, the partridge that would die for her young. And he studied meteorology, learning the signs of different weather. The steady breezes from the east would bring the rain, and rain gave him a day off to go fishing. He knew the lack of shadows meant the noon hour and dinnertime. Most of all, the farm taught him how to be alone with himself and how to observe, investigate, and draw inferences.

The farm was a good school. It lacked only the personal contacts with society outside the home. Five years had been passed with the Moores in Goffstown and the farm could no longer satisfy his hunger for knowledge. He was thirteen and ready to graduate to higher things, to higher knowledge. Perhaps he was only dimly aware that since he had been on the farm there had been a war with Mexico and the nation had expanded to the Pacific coast. He did know that there were things he could only learn in school, and he was determined to get a secondary education. Mr. Moore, to whom he was bound, was not unsympathetic, although he thought it would be best for the boy to stay on the farm. He insisted that Frank talk the problem over with his guardian.

It would appear from Frank Parker's own accounts that his guardian was never in sympathy with him. Parker reports years later that James Walker told him, in a "savage" manner that he was "a lazy brat and did not want to work," that this was the real reason he wanted to leave the farm and go to school. Walker ordered the thirteen-year-old boy back to the farm.[25]

James Walker may have had the best of intentions. He had nothing against education. He had allowed his wards, Mary and Philinda, to continue their education in preparation for teaching. It was still a prevailing notion that teaching was a woman's business. There was certainly no future in it for a widow's son who would have to make his own way in the world. It is also possible that Frank Parker was not the easiest boy to handle. Parker even described himself as a "little, fat, squabble of a fellow," and it was probable that he squabbled with his guardian. He was the kind of boy who would talk back to his teachers if he thought they were doing something wrong. And no other boy dared talk back to him, since he had successfully tested his strength against all the boys who tried him out.[26]

Frank Parker defied his guardian's order to stay on the farm. He broke his apprenticeship and marched off to the nearby academy in Mt. Vernon, where one of his sisters and a cousin were already enrolled.[27]

A resolute young adolescent, Frank Parker earned his way by sawing wood, painting, and varnishing boxes. He farmed in the summers. In this way he labored for three years while pursuing the classical academic course of study. He desperately needed money to finish his last term at the academy. It was his impression that his father had left him an estate of $200 in the trust of James Walker. Actually, after the sale of his father's estate and the payment of his debts, there had been little more than $200 for the whole family. That Parker had been drawing on this account is evidenced by his belief that $40 remained. He went to James Walker again but apparently did not get another cent. Walker told him there were already too many teachers and he suggested that he get a job working on the road for $11 a month.[28]

Parker did not finish his last term at the academy. That winter he was offered his first school, at Corser Hill. He told his students that they must work hard but that there would be time for play. He said he liked to play but had never had much time for it. Many of his pupils were older than himself, and he believed he only made it through that first winter of teaching because of the students' "love and sympathy."[29]

In all his country school teaching, as far as Parker could remember, he simply followed the line he had been taught. His only gift was being able to get along with the students. He said he seldom punished. By boarding around the district he got acquainted with the parents and gained the good will and respect of the children.[30]

Corser Hill paid only $15 a month and "boarding around." He was apparently offered another year at the school, but during the summer he learned there was an opening in Auburn. He walked about ten miles through the woods and fields to make inquiries and found the school committee husking corn. He sat down and husked and talked and bargained. He got the job at $17 a month, with an extra dollar if he "proved himself." He did.[31]

By the time he was twenty, Frank was so successful that he was called to the school in Hinsdale after the boys there had violently "turned out" the master. After that he accepted a position at the grammar school in his home town.[32]

Successful as he was, the teaching profession in New Hampshire was uncertain and unpromising. School committees could hardly afford not to elect the younger and cheaper teachers who were continually coming through the ranks. At best, a master could only count on a "hedgerow" career, farming between the winters of Greek and Latin.

Several of Parker's classmates and friends had gone westward and settled around Carrollton, in Greene County, Illinois. According to Parker, it was Miss Jennie Gilchrist, a former classmate, who suggested his name to the Carrollton School Board. She had accompanied her brothers to Illinois several years earlier and assisted one of them while he was principal of the school in Carrollton.[33] Just why Charles Gilchrist was no longer interested in the position did not seem to worry Parker. His life had been directed toward an educational career. It had not been an easy road to follow. As principal of his own school, however, it might be said that he had arrived.

NOTES

[1] Secondary accounts of Parker's life are divided between 1858 and 1859. Parker himself cited both years at one time or another. There are no official school records for those years in either Piscatauquog or Carrollton. A careful survey of *The Carrollton Gazette* (Carrollton, Ill.). makes it certain that Parker's arrival was in 1859. The very first mention of Parker's name was in *The Carrollton Gazette,* September 10, 1859, when his appointment was announced.

[2] Parker established his height and the color of his hair when he applied for an "Invalid Pension" in July, 1892. "Parker, Frank W., Soldier's Certificate," Can number 17835, Bundle number 22, the National Archives, Washington, D.C. Parker compared his 130 pounds in 1859 with his current 235 pounds when he was interviewed by a reporter for *The Carrollton Patriot* (Carrollton, Ill.) in 1887. "We Claim Him . . . Local Reminiscences of the Prince of Pedagogues," Parker Scrapbooks, 1887, Archives, Harper Library, University of Chicago. See also Francis W. Parker, "Autobiographical Sketch," appendix in William M. Giffin, *School Days in the Fifties* (Chicago: A. Flanagan Co., 1906), p. 121. It was Mary E. Dearborn, a student of Parker's in Auburn, N. H., who remembered his physical and educational attractions. Mary E. Dearborn, "A District Schoolmaster," *Journal of Education,* 51 (April 26, 1900), 259.

[3] "We Claim Him. . . ."

[4] Francis Grierson, *The Valley of Shadows* (Boston: Houghton Mifflin, 1948), pp. 2; 194–201. [Grierson lived in Alton, Ill., until 1859 when he moved to St. Louis.]

[5] "We Claim Him . . ."; Francis W. Parker, *op cit.*, p. 121. A description of the school, and a blueprint of the public square in 1857 was drawn from memory by John Dick and published in *The Patriot Souvenir Edition* (Carrollton, Ill., September, 1896), pp. 19; 35.

[6] "We Claim Him . . ."; Francis W. Parker, *op. cit.*, pp. 121–122.

[7] "Election of School Directors," *The Carrollton Gazette,* September 3, 1859.

[8] "Election of School Directors," *The Carrollton Gazette,* September 10, 1859.

[9] Francis W. Parker, *op. cit.*, pp. 111, 116. Parker's birth is officially recorded in *The New Hampshire Regimental Descript Book, Fourth Infantry,* p. 10, Records Division, National Archives, Washington, D.C.

[10] Francis W. Parker, *op. cit.*, p. 110.

[11] Record of marriage of Robert Parker and Mille Rand, Bureau of Vital Statistics, New Hampshire State Department of Health, Concord, New Hampshire. For subsequent references to such vital statistics as births, marriages, and deaths, see Section X (Vital Statistics) in the Bibliography.

[12] Estate of William Parker, file number 0 7109, Probate Court, Nashua, Hillsborough County, New Hampshire. For subsequent references to the material holdings of William, Robert, and Nabby Parker, see "Probated Estates" in Section X of the Bibliography.

[13] Francis W. Parker, *op. cit.*, pp. 110–111.

[14] *Ibid.*, p. 110.

[15] *Ibid.*, pp. 111; 119–120.

[16] *Ibid.*, p. 111.

[17] *Ibid.*, p. 136; "The Old School House at the Cross-Roads," Parker Scrapbooks, 1898; "A Success at Quincy, Sketch of Col. Parker and His Grand Educational Work," *The Quincy Patriot* (Quincy, Mass.), April 21, 1900.

[18] Francis W. Parker, *op. cit.*, p. 111; Flora J. Cooke, "Colonel Francis W. Parker, His Influence on Education," *Chicago Schools Journal, 19* (March 1938), 146.

[19] Francis W. Parker, *op. cit.*, p. 112.

[20] *Ibid.*, pp. 114–115; "The Old School House at the Cross-Roads."

[21] Francis W. Parker, *op. cit.*, p. 113.

[22] *Ibid.*, p. 116.

[23] *Ibid.*, pp. 116–117.

[24] *Ibid.*, pp. 114; 117. Further elaboration on the educational aspects of the farm are suggested by Francis W. Parker, "The Farm as the Center of Interest," *Journal of Proceedings and Addresses, National Educational Association, 1897,* pp. 527–536. Parker makes similar observations in "The Child," *Journal of Proceedings and Addresses, National Educational Association, 1889,* pp. 479–482.

[25] Francis W. Parker, "Autobiographical Sketch," pp. 117–118.

[26] *Ibid.*, pp. 112–113; 116.

[27] *Ibid.*, p. 118.

[28] *Ibid.*

[29] *Ibid.*, pp. 118–119; Flora J. Cooke, *op. cit.*, p. 147.

[30] Francis W. Parker, "Autobiographical Sketch," p. 120.

[31] *Ibid.*

[32] *Ibid.*

[33] *Ibid.*, pp. 120–121; newspaper clipping, Parker Scrapbooks, 1887.

II

The New Hampshire Yankee in Southern Illinois

It was probably the roughest school in which he had ever taught, and the emaciated, spare young man trembled a little at his first encounter with the hundred-odd youths of Carrollton. He began his teaching without a threat or a rule on September 5, 1859. He put on a smile and read a chapter in the Bible. Then he looked up and told the gawking pupils that his idea of a good school was a place to have "a first class time," and that they must all take hold and work together. His first assistant, Jennie Gilchrist, was so surprised by this show of camaraderie that she felt sorry Parker had come such a long way to become a failure. The children of the frontier, however, responded much the same as had the backwoods youngsters of New Hampshire. Parker could command their good will. The first assignment, simple, constructive, close to the experience of the children, was to clean up the school grounds. They turned out the rooting hogs, repaired and whitewashed the fence, pulled the weeds, and planted grass and flowers.[1] It was a lesson in keeping busy, cooperating, and assuming responsibility.

All that time Parker was still teaching the rules of grammar and spelling in the traditional manner, but his dramatic instinct and natural understanding of children were such that he could make the school the children's town meeting. Unconscious of theory or system, he achieved conventional results through the impact of his own personality. He also believed, in the conventional way, that children should be trained to perfect obedience to him, but he never had to strike a conventional blow in school to achieve it. He "walloped one fellow outside."[2]

Parker was soon gaining the good will of the whole community. He found more congenial lodgings at the boarding house of Adam Engleman, where Mrs. Engleman tried to "kill him" with good food. He even became a prominent member of Carrollton's Sons of Temperance, who met every Tuesday evening. He also lectured his students against the evils of tobacco, but if the privacy of his room at the Engleman's were disturbed, he could generally be found "enveloped in a cloud of smoke."[3]

Just before his first Christmas in Carrollton, the Greene County Teachers, an important local organization, elected him president.[4] A few months later, on March 30, 1860, the Carrollton District School celebrated its tenth anniversary and Parker was in charge of the ceremonies at the courthouse. Entertainment included student declamations and recitations on such themes as "Lulu Is Our Darling Pride" and "The Summer Days Are Coming." "William Tell" and "The Troubled Schoolmaster" were dramatized, between songs by the Four Little Boys.[5]

Not until 1850, when over ten thousand people could be counted throughout the valley of Greene County, had the citizens seen fit to establish a public school. Those were the days of the "Great Compromise" on the slavery issue, however, and Carrollton's very first teacher had apparently held such strong antislavery views that he had to be discharged. The school prospered under less controversial teachers. In 1852 it was enlarged to include two rooms on the ground floor and one room above. The school was still ungraded, much in the manner of an academy, and had a special department for girls. "Patrons" residing in the district were admitted on the "school fund," but the school found it necessary to advertise for outside students. Such students could study orthography, reading, and writing for one dollar per school quarter; arithmetic, English, grammar, geography, and United States History cost two dollars. Natural philosophy, political economy, chemistry, geology, algebra, rhetoric, and physiology were offered for three dollars; and Latin, Greek, French, geometry, and surveying were available for four dollars.[6] It would appear that there was very little emphasis on primary education.

In 1855 the Carrollton District School was organized on a graded system. In the same year the state authorized a direct tax for the support of any school kept six months out of every year. This greatly augmented the "school fund," handled by a commissioner of school lands who had charge of the monies accruing from rent or sale of the sixteenth section of each congressional township. Parker probably found the schools of Greene County better supported than those he left behind in the more settled state of New Hampshire. On February 2, 1861, the editor of *The Carrollton Gazette*, pointing out that Greene County had paid $4.42 for the education of each of its pupils in 1860—a dollar more per pupil than was paid in a neighboring county, suggested that the teachers take note of this and give evidence that they had earned the "surplus."

Near the end of Parker's first year, however, *The Carrollton Gazette* was reporting that visitors of the local school exhibition were so pleased by the "masterly manner" in which it was carried off that they congratulated themselves on the selection of their principal and teachers. They hoped the "present prosperous state of things in the school" would continue. At the end of his first school year in Carrollton, Parker was rehired at an increase of $50 per year.[7]

Parker and a "chum" spent the next eight weeks exploring the Mississippi River and tramping as far north as the new state of Minnesota. They walked right through their shoes and were reduced to such a "ragged pair" that they had a "bandit-of-the-mountain look" when they returned. There were rumors that the school had had to send $50 up to Shakope to finance Parker's transportation back to Carrollton.[8]

Beginning his second year in Carrollton, Parker found that, as the heat of summer wore off, the heat of the presidential election grew warmer. There were "fire-eaters" in those days on both sides of the slavery issue in Carrollton.

Many people of Carrollton were from Virginia and Kentucky, although the population also included strains from New England. It was said that the citizens of Greene County were a mixture of Cavalier and Puritan—"warm-hearted" southerners merged with "hard-headed" Yankees.[9] The election of 1860 was dividing the people to the bone.

Parker was a Republican at heart, although he had been a Free Soiler, opposed only to the expansion of slavery. He held his thoughts in check, because he knew his school directors sided with the Democrats and believed that people in the territories should decide the slavery issue.[10]

When the election came in November, Parker, who had just turned twenty-three, cast his vote for Lincoln. News of Lincoln's national triumph, however, would not be well received a few days later in Carrollton. The great majority of votes in Greene County had gone to Stephen A. Douglas. The Democrats had also taken the local educational offices.[11]

Secession of the Cotton States came with the snow that winter. There was even local talk that Greene County should also secede from the union. At least many people in Carrollton feared Lincoln's inauguration would bring the abolition of slavery and ruin to the South.[12] Such concerns, grave as they were, did not completely dominate the community. Friends of the Carrollton Literary Society were invited to fill the house for the January meeting in order to hear F. W. Parker talk about the training of youth.[13] Parker continued his public appearances for the Literary Society later, taking the affirmative in a debate on whether the common school system should be sustained.[14] Younger than the union, the common school, too, was not unanimously supported.

One of the chief supporters of the common school in Illinois was Ninian W. Edwards, first State Superintendent of Public Instruction. In support of the direct tax for education in 1855, he had argued that it was cheaper to sustain schools than poorhouses, courts, and prisons.[15] Such an idea was not new. Men of the previous generation, such as Bronson Alcott, Ralph Waldo Emerson, Theodore Parker, had urged the "socialization of Christianity" through prison, school, and other social reforms. These sentiments were alive in the West, if not in the words of New England sages. Frontier evangelists had caught the spirit. In his own way Parker was an evangelist, preaching salvation through education. Only free schools could make free men.

If the South had built up public instruction on the scale that Jefferson had advocated, it might have peopled the West with teachers as well as settlers. Instead, it was the North, which Horace Mann and his normal schools put to seed, that scattered "Yankee schools" throughout the territories. In areas like Greene County, which were said to hang to the union "by a thread," a generation of Yankee teachers might have spun the tenuous line of loyalty.

It is probable that Parker and his assistants did not plant partisan ideas in the minds of their pupils. They did teach students to think and act for themselves. When the children were made to see the need for a library, for instance, they formed a committee and launched a campaign in the community for the collection of books.[16] The students also had their own ideas about the conditions in Kansas. There had been fighting there since the territory had been opened up a few years earlier. In the race to people the area with "northern" or "southern" sentiments, the Civil War had already begun. Parker's students wrote letters to people in Kansas. They gathered old clothes for their relief. *The Carrollton Press,* created especially to give a voice to the new Republican party, praised "the zeal with which these pupils engage in the cause of humanity." The Republican editor shamed the adults by reporting that the children were moved by pity and did not stop to inquire into the political faith of the "recipients of their bounty."[17]

By the time *The Carrollton Press* had taken notice of what Parker's students were doing, Kansas was already in the union as a free state. Political events were moving rapidly. While a locomotive on the Jacksonville, Alton, and St. Louis Railroad was thrown off the track by a cow, a more sinister plot to throw the Washington-bound presidential train from the track was reported in Carrollton.[18]

The "deliberate conspiracy" to murder the President-elect was appalling news in *The Carrollton Press.* "Let every citizen who does not wish to see the sun of American liberty set in anarchy, pray God that his life be spared," the editor published, on March 1, 1861.

From *The Carrollton Gazette,* which expressed the Democratic point of view, came the sad note, on March 2, 1861, that "Congressional interference is, we fear, the only truthful epitaph that can be placed on our national tombstone." While there was talk of murder and war, the Democratic paper argued that the people of the South could be "overmatched" but not "subdued." "Does anyone believe," its editor asked, "we can exterminate the people of the South?"

At the same time, *The Carrollton Gazette* hailed the defeat of a military bill in Illinois as salvation from an unnecessary tax for war purposes. It saved the state from "shameful display of barbarous pomp." Through all this Parker remained at the command of his school, but after the shots at Fort Sumter he saddled his pony and rode off to enlist in a cavalry company that some of the men of Carrollton were organizing. Lack of funds, however, prevented the Governor from outfitting the company, and Parker was saved from "barbarous pomp" in an Illinois uniform.[19]

Parker stayed on at the district school, where he was so popular that the directors did not dare dismiss him. The anniversary exercises, in April of 1861, were again well attended, and the public was reported to be delighted by the exhibition.[20] Now that he had so brazenly declared himself a "Union man," the directors, sympathizing with the South, proposed to cut the principal's salary by $100, payable as usual in wildcat scrip. Such paper money was not accepted even for taxes at that time in Carrollton.

It is not likely that Parker gave notice of resignation after he drew his last school order for salary on June 21, 1861. He did, however, return to New Hampshire and await events there.

Parker returned to Piscatauquog to find that his uncle by marriage, Lewis F. Harris, had died on June 29. Owner and president of a bank in Savannah, Georgia, he had been caught in the South at the time of secession. Coming north to rejoin his wife in New Hampshire, he got as far as Ohio before being fatally stricken with dysentery. Hostile armies were now mustering between Parker's widowed aunt and much of her inheritance.[21]

The "war spirit" still gripped Parker, but his sisters pleaded with him not to go to war, as "he was the only son, and the only hope of the house." This argument put him off during the summer. In the meantime he received a telegram from the directors of the high school in Alton, Illinois. They offered him a position there, if he did not wish to return to a reduced salary in Carrollton. He accepted, but before he could leave, the disaster at Bull Run convinced Parker that the war would not be over before his services were needed. He found it harder to resist the impulse to take a hand in the war or to ignore the tide of local patriotism.[22] Even the Democratic newspaper of nearby Manchester, the *Weekly Union*, came out firmly in defense of the Union and the Constitution. The "present civil war," it proclaimed to its "fellow democrats," on July 30, 1861, had been forced on the United States.

Early in August the Manchester members of the New Hampshire First Volunteers, having served their three months, returned to the sound of "Hail Columbia" and "Yankee Doodle." Excitement was in the air. Other regiments were forming. The New Hampshire Third was already too full and a fourth regiment was to be assembled in Manchester.[23] About that time Parker was told that if he helped Captain Newell form a company he would be elected lieutenant. Parker's mother never said a word against his going, and he rather gathered, from the way she acted, that he had better enlist. His sisters gave up their opposition, since he would be receiving a commission. He signed up.[24]

The Manchester *Weekly Union* was advertising for "more good and true men who will stand by the old flag and each other." Such men were to apply for three-year enlistments at the recruiting office above the saloon on Elm Street.[25]

While the regiment was being raised, the textile mills in Manchester were running low on southern cotton. By September 3, 1861, the Manchester *Weekly Union* observed that the schools should be unusually full that fall due to the suspension of the manufacturing works and consequent depression in other branches of business. It was supposed that the unemployed children would take advantage of the opportunity to attend school.

Parker was going to be schooled in self-discipline and the management and leadership of men.

NOTES

[1] Francis W. Parker, *"Autobiographical Sketch,"* appendix in William M. Giffin, *School Days in the Fifties* (Chicago: A. Flanagan Co., 1906), pp. 119, 121. Parker corroborated and augmented his story when interviewed in 1887 for *The Carrollton Patriot* (Carrollton, Ill.). "We Claim Him . . . Local Reminiscences of the Prince of Pedagogues," Parker Scrapbooks, 1887, Archives, Harper Library, University of Chicago. The date for the beginning of school was reported in *The Carrollton Gazette* (Carrollton, Ill.), September 10, 1859.

[2] Francis W. Parker, *op. cit.*, p. 122; "We Claim Him . . ."; "The Old School House at the Cross-Roads," Parker Scrapbooks, 1898.

[3] "We Claim Him . . ."; "Sons of Temperance—Carrollton Division No. 29 . . . ," *The Carrollton Press* (Carrollton, Ill.), March 1, 1861.

[4] "Teachers' Institute," *The Carrollton Gazette,* December 31, 1859.

[5] "Anniversary Exercises of the Carrollton Public School, F. W. Parker, Principal, March 30, 1860," a printed program, Parker Scrapbooks, 1860.

[6] *History of Greene and Jersey Counties, Illinois* (Springfield, Ill.: Continental Historical Co., 1885), p. 595; *History of Greene County, Illinois: Its Past and Present, Illustrated* (Chicago: Donnelly, Gassette and Loyd, 1879), p. 339; *Patriot Souvenir Edition* (Carrollton, Ill.: Patriot Press, 1896), pp. 34–35.

[7] "The School Exhibition," *The Carrollton Gazette,* April 7, 1860; Francis W. Parker, *op. cit.,* p. 122; "We Claim Him . . . ."

[8] "We Claim Him . . . ."

[9] Francis W. Parker, *op. cit.,* p. 121; *History of Greene and Jersey Counties, Illinois,* p. 567; Francis Grierson, *The Valley of Shadows* (Boston: Houghton Mifflin, 1948), p. 2.

[10] Francis W. Parker, *op. cit.,* p. 122; "We Claim Him . . . ."

[11] Francis W. Parker, *op. cit.,* p. 122; *History of Greene and Jersey Counties, Illinois,* pp. 656–657.

[12] "Editorial," *The Carrollton Press,* March 1, 1861; Francis Grierson, *op. cit.,* p. 223.

[13] "Local Matters," *The Carrollton Gazette,* January 5, 1861.

[14] "Literary Society," *The Carrollton Press,* March 1, 1861.

[15] John Williston Cook, *Educational History of Illinois* (Chicago: Henry O. Shepard Co., 1912), p. 55.

[16] "School Library," *The Carrollton Gazette,* February 16, 1861.

[17] "Letter to Mr. F. W. Parker," and "Kansas Relief," *The Carrollton Press,* March 1, 1860.

[18] "An attempt to throw the Presidential train from the track," *The Carrollton Press,* March 1, 1861. *The Carrollton Gazette* reported on March 2, 1861 that there was slight damage when a locomotive was thrown off the track by a cow.

[19] Francis W. Parker, *op. cit.,* p. 122; "We Claim Him . . . ."

[20] "Anniversary Exercises," *The Carrollton Gazette,* April 6, 1861; Francis W. Parker, *op. cit.,* p. 122; "Notice to Tax-Payers," *The Carrollton Press,* March 1, 1861.

[21] "Death of Mrs. Harris," *Mirror and Farmer* (Manchester, N. H.), September 30, 1871.

[22] Francis W. Parker, *op. cit.,* p. 122; "We Claim Him . . ."; "Arrival of the Fourth Regiment . . . The Troops were raised at a time when the volunteering spirit ran high . . . ." *Daily Mirror and American* (Manchester, N. H.), August 30, 1865; "History of the Fourth New Hampshire Volunteers," *Mirror and Farmer,* November 11, 1865.

[23] *Weekly Union* (Manchester, N. H.), August 13, 1861; Francis W. Parker, "Fourth Regiment, New Hampshire Volunteer Infantry," *Revised Register of the Soldiers and Sailors of New Hampshire in the War of the Rebellion, 1861–1866* (Concord, N. H.: Ira C. Evans, Public Printer, 1895), p. 153.

[24] Francis W. Parker, "Autobiographical Sketch," pp. 122–123.

[25] "Fourth Regiment," *Weekly Union,* September 3, 1861.

III

The Lessons of War

The young schoolmaster's lessons of war began in September of 1861, when the Fourth Regiment of New Hampshire Infantry went into camp near Manchester and was officially mustered into the service of the Union amid roll and tap of drums and exhortations by the Governor and other politicians. More than a month before the regiment received its colors, however, Frank Parker was attached to Newell's company and engaged in its recruitment. Since he was not appointed first lieutenant of Company E until the regiment went into camp, he had actually been initiated to military life in a noncommissioned status.[1]

Before the end of September, the hastily thrown-together regiment was packed off in freight cars and shipped to Washington. The men of the New Hampshire Fourth were then issued Belgian rifles and attached to the Expeditionary Corps of General Thomas W. Sherman at Annapolis. Frank Parker celebrated his twenty-fourth birthday under hasty preparations for some kind of amphibious expedition. On October 20, 1861, the regiment was embarked on the steamer *Baltic* and joined a fleet of warships and transports moving slowly down the Chesapeake. Life between decks was cramped and the days must have rolled around as monotonously as the paddle-wheel, at least until the end of October when the fleet butted out into the open sea off the Virginia capes.*

On the second day out the *Baltic,* following lighter draft ships, was

* For this and subsequent references to the activities of the 4th New Hampshire Regiment, see Francis W. Parker, "Fourth Regiment New Hampshire Volunteer Infantry," *Revised Register of the Soldiers and Sailors of New Hampshire in the War of the Rebellion, 1861-1866* (Concord, N. H.: Ira C. Evans, Public Printer, 1895), pp. 153–157, 189; John G. Hutchinson, *Roster: Fourth Regiment New Hampshire Volunteers* (Manchester, N. H.: John B. Clarke Company, 1896); Frederick H. Dyer (Editor), *A Compendium of the War of the Rebellion* (Des Moines, Iowa: The Dyer Publish-

hung up on a shoal and thrashed its side-wheel until the sea was frothy and mudstained. It got safely underway again, only to be hammered by wind and waves off Cape Hatteras. Parker would never forget the "severe fright" of this first sea voyage.[2]

On November 7, 1861, the ships were over the bar at Port Royal, South Carolina, and in position to shell the two forts which dominated the mouth of the Broad River. During the bombardment, Parker and the men of the Fourth "clustered like bees" around the masts and rigging of the *Baltic* and watched the thundering impact of naval ordnance. The forts were abandoned and the New Hampshire Fourth helped to secure the island of Port Royal without a fight.

The expeditionary force then proceeded to pluck the whole cluster of "sea islands" which clung to the mainland except for a little tidewater. The New Hampshire Fourth set up headquarters at Hilton Head Island and settled down to the pick and shovel duty of fortifying the place and making it part of a fleet of islands to blockade the inlets of the great inland waterway of the South. Later that winter, Parker was promoted to Captain during the February expedition against Warsaw Island off Georgia. He was then in command of Company E.[3]

After securing Warsaw Island, which the men of the Fourth considered unfit for dogs or coons, the regiment was involved in the Florida expedition and the capture of Jacksonville, Fernandia, and St. Augustine. These objectives, too, were taken without firing a shot, except for a little skirmish around the picket lines in Jacksonville.

Parker remained in garrison duty at St. Augustine until September of 1862. The regiment was then relieved and returned to the sea islands around Port Royal. Preparations were underway for attacking the mainland. The object was to destroy the railroad bridge across the Pocotiligo River and thereby cut communications between Savannah, Georgia, and Charleston, South Carolina.

Only about thirty miles from Savannah, Parker must have thought about his aunt, Mary Parker Harris. She was said to be in Savannah where her late husband had owned a bank. Earlier in 1862, an agent of her husband's estate in Georgia had been allowed to escort Mrs. Harris through the lines of two warring armies.[4] Parker and his men never got

---

ing Company, 1908), p. 1348; Consolidated Morning Reports of 4th Regiment of New Hampshire Volunteers (October 4, 1861 through May 9, 1865), New Hampshire 4th Volunteers (box file) Circulars, New Hampshire 4th Infantry Regimental Order Book, New Hampshire Regiment Descript Book, Regimental Letter Book, New Hampshire 4th Infantry, in National Archives, Washington, D.C.; "History of the Fourth New Hampshire Volunteers," *Mirror and Farmer* (Manchester, N. H.) November 11, 1865.

much closer to Savannah. The expedition up the Pocotiligo River ran into stiff resistance and the regiment was forced to withdraw into its island defenses off the coast. This was the first time the regiment had really been under heavy fire in its more than twelve months of active duty. The regiment remained for the rest of the winter at Port Royal in drill and picket duty.

Early in April of 1863 the regiment was thrown into an expedition against Charleston, South Carolina. The regiment captured Folly Island without much difficulty and dug in. The Confederates were in strength on Morris Island, separated from Folly Island by a narrow creek. For a time the pickets on both sides politely agreed not to fire on one another and they sometimes exchanged coffee for tobacco. Here the men of the Fourth could plainly see the harbor of Charleston from the tops of tall pine trees. It was said that ladies from Charleston would peer at the "Yanks" through field glasses to see if they had horns growing out of their "frontal bones."[5]

Both sides soon brought up heavy guns and exchanged fire throughout that hot summer. Fort Wagner on Morris Island was finally captured in September, but Charleston itself remained impervious to the assaults of ironclads. The siege went on, but fighting was over for the Fourth. At that time Parker appealed for leave to go home. His request noted that he had not absented himself from the regiment, except for four days on official business, since September 15, 1861. He was granted twenty days of leave, which commenced that December.[6]

Parker's leave was up on the last day of 1863, but at that time he was detained for duty by the Superintendent Volunteer Recruiting Service in Concord, New Hampshire. In the meantime he was reported as absent without leave from his command on Morris Island. Parker was thirteen days overdue when he got back to his regiment, but the proceedings of a military commission, which met in February of 1864, found that he had been detained by proper authority and he suffered no inconveniences or loss of pay.[7]

It is possible that Captain Parker had volunteered his services at Concord at the last minute in order to extend his holiday in New Hampshire. He may have been courting Josephine E. Hall. This young schoolmistress was to become his bride within the year. In any event, Parker was soon back again in New Hampshire. He re-enlisted for "three years, or the war," and received a thirty-day furlough as a bonus. When he got back this time he found Manchester was in financial trouble, and the city fathers were unable to turn his re-enlistment bounty into much cash.[8] The golden days of furlough, however, were quickly spent. Parker and the other re-enlisted veterans returned to their regiment at Gloucester

Point, Virginia, across the river from Yorktown. The regiment was now attached to the Army of the James under General Benjamin F. Butler. It is likely that the regiment which had weathered the war on the sea islands was not up to the spit and polish of the Army of the James. On April 30, 1864, the New Hampshire Fouth was ordered to parade for review in heavy marching orders, with shelter tents, knapsacks, woolen and rubber blanket rolls. After the review a special circular was issued to order every man to wear shoes!

Grant's "Grand Campaign" began a few days later in May. The New Hampshire Fourth was embarked and transported by steam up the James River to establish a surprise landing at the peninsula of Bermuda Hundred, between the James and Appomattox rivers. The army moved cautiously up the peninsula to Drewry's Bluff, about eight miles from Richmond. The New Hampshire Fourth, part of the line of advanced skirmishers, bore the brunt of a counterattack. Caught without flankers, the regiment was temporarily cut off but managed to escape capture. When the smoke cleared, Parker could muster little more than half his company.

The Army of the James was pinned down, but the New Hampshire Fourth was pulled off the peninsula by transports and thrown into Grant's Army of the Potomac in time for the engagement at Cold Harbor. The bloody work of a frontal assault on Richmond, where Lee's forces had coagulated into a hard knot then flowed off in a series of marches and countermarches of maneuver. It all came down to a siege of Petersburg, and the war settled into the trenches.

As the days of June died off, the trenches, at some points within twenty feet of Confederate outposts, were shored up with logs and lumber, but the spirit of the army was caving in. The New Hampshire Fourth, its ranks filled to overflowing when the thaw came that spring, was now melting away. Men and mud of the spring were pounded into the dust of June. Sunstroke added to the perils of those days thundering with mortars, siege-guns, and other fieldpieces.

For weeks during July the "trench talk" had it that a tunnel was being dug under the Confederate positions. On the night of July 29, the New Hampshire Fourth was one of the regiments pulled back from the front and massed behind the "covered way leading to the mine." The next morning the mine was touched off. One eyewitness felt the earth tremble under his feet and he saw an "immense mushroom" rise up in the air, along with rocks and timbers and bleeding bodies, which quickly came "raining" back down.[9] He saw Union columns advancing into the crater rather than around it. Brigades got mixed up. Paralysis seemed to take hold of officers and men who moved as though in a dream. When the Confederate forces recovered from the shock, they poured out a stream of fire in which the New Hampshire Fourth was caught. Men were dropped so quickly that they "lay dead, as if in ranks." There was the sound of "forty-four Fourths of July rolled into one."[10]

The Federal forces not swallowed up in the crater were now in full retreat. Colonel Bell of the Fourth took command of a brigade. A captain was left in command of the Fourth but he was quickly cut down, and Captain Parker temporarily succeeded to command of the regiment.[11]

The regimental colors were said to have been hauled back with as many as fifty-five holes. The regimental ranks were as badly riddled. Parker led the regiment back to reserve duty at Bermuda Hundred. While at rest, with only every third day for picket duty, the regiment was put back together. Only a few hundred men in all could be mustered.

On August 13, the pieced-together regiment, now part of the Tenth Corps, was ordered across the James River at Deep Bottom. Skirmishing around Malvern Hill became a general engagement by August 16. Parker was by then the ranking officer in a whole brigade and took that command at the very moment he found his position overextended and the brigade almost cut off. He fell back to the rifle pits that had recently been captured and disposed of his brigade to receive a countercharge.

"I stood upon a stump and directed the fire as the enemy charged upon us twice," Parker remembered, and "during the third charge, I received a bullet, cutting through my chin and crushing my wind pipe . . . ." He fell to the ground and blood was seen to rush from his mouth.[12]

In the frenzy of that third Confederate charge, hands somehow reached out and pulled the crumpled body of Parker out of the line of fire. A minnie ball was removed from the flesh of his neck by the regimental surgeon before he was shipped down the Chesapeake to the U. S. General Hospital at Fort Monroe.[13]

As the pieces of reality fitted back together, one at a time, Parker awakened to the painful absence of home. Through a civilian agent from New Hampshire, he appealed to the Adjutant General in Washington for leave. The agent reported that Parker was "very desirous to visit his friends in New Hampshire . . . ."[14]

The request came to nothing, but Parker was soon ordered to a camp near Annapolis for light duty. At that time a surgeon certified that he would be unfit for active field service for at least thirty days. Parker's request for a transfer to a camp in Concord, New Hampshire, was denied, but he did manage to get orders to the Commanding Officer,

Draft Rendezvous, New Haven, Connecticut.[15] In late September of 1864 he was on his way back to New England.

Parker left only the military war behind. A political war was being waged at home over the re-election of Lincoln. That Parker was a Lincoln man must have been clear to the political forces in New Hampshire. That he was a hero who had risen to the command of the New Hampshire Fourth and even to a whole brigade was in the record. He bore the fresh scars of his sacrifice for the Union, and a dashing mustache gave evidence that like the President he had allowed his whiskers to grow. It is not certain what political strings were pulled but, even without an official leave of absence from his post in New Haven, Parker was soon back in New Hampshire and scheduled to make a round of political appearances and speeches for Lincoln during the last week of October.[16]

Parker was granted a fifteen-day leave on November 1, 1864.[17] He was scheduled to speak at the "Last Union Rally" on Monday evening, November 7, 1864, but the Honorable N. B. Bryant spoke so long to an overflowing crowd in Smyth's Hall that the other speakers decided it was too late in the day to open their prepared speeches.[18]

The subsequent re-election of Lincoln was heralded in the Repubclian newspaper of Manchester, but its opposition paper insisted that it would continue to "interpose a strong protest against the wickedness of the national administration, and a strong barrier against the threatened despotism." The Democratic paper also charged that army commanders had taken men into their quarters if they were for McClellan and had got them to change their votes. It also scored the furloughing of large numbers of soldiers so they could come home and vote.[19]

It was no secret that Governor Gilmore of New Hampshire was a Lincoln man and had worked through the state agent in Philadelphia to have orders issued to furlough New Hampshire men in hospitals.[20] On October 26, 1864, the *Daily Mirror and American,* the Republican paper of Manchester, argued that "Surely no one else has a better right to say who shall be president than the brave, true-hearted boys who have given up everything to defend our homes."

Although Parker's leave had expired by the middle of November, he was away from his post again on December 1, 1864, when he married Josephine ("Phenie") E. Hall in Bennington, New Hampshire.[21] This was a "leap year" but there is nothing to suggest that Phenie initiated the proceedings, except that Parker had not chosen to marry during his fifteen days of leave in November. She was almost as old as Parker, and perhaps, at twenty-five, she was simply tired of waiting.

One person who knew Parker in later years had believed that Phenie was "a beautiful young woman."[22] Another such friend reported that Parker had known Phenie as a child, that he remembered her in school as she sat "on a bench, demure and still, with a little shawl folded tightly about her." She was also said to have been a teacher and a faithful correspondent during Parker's frequent and long absences from New Hampshire.[23]

Whatever Phenie was really like, she seemed to fit into her husband's life as naturally as the air he breathed. She hardly received special mention in the autobiography he spontaneously dictated many years later. He said: "I came home and was detached as Adjutant General of the rendezvous at New Haven, Connecticut, and took an active part in the second Lincoln campaign. I stopped in New Hampshire for three or four weeks, and was married to Phenie E. Hall of Bennington, New Hampshire, went back to New Haven . . . ."[24]

Perhaps Phenie accompanied her husband back to New Haven and shared life as much as possible with him, but in any event, she was already pregnant and a new life beginning in her. It was little more than a month after the marriage when the governor of New Hampshire appointed Parker to the rank of Lieutenant-Colonel.[25] In order to be mustered into the service at this rank he would have to rejoin his regiment. Two days later, on January 5, 1865, he made his decision and requested to be relieved from the temporary duties in New Haven.[26]

During his absence, the New Hampshire Fourth had been pulled out of the lines around Petersburg and employed in the naval and amphibious expedition against Fort Fisher on the coast of North Carolina. When he left New Haven, Parker was probably unaware that he was to become a father. When he was reported at muster again with his regiment on February 11, 1865, he was very much aware of death. Fort Fisher had fallen. The massive earthworks, twenty-five feet high and extending more than a half a mile, were still surrounded with broken shells and balls and bodies. He had returned to bury the commanding officer, Colonel Bell, as well as other comrades. Now in command of the regiment, he had to restore its battered morale as well as lead it against the next objective—Wilmington. Bad weather and dank swamps were about the only defenses left to that city, and it was easily taken. After that, the regiment, now attached to the Army of the Ohio, pushed on to Goldsboro and formed a junction with Sherman's army coming up from its expedition in Georgia and South Carolina. The two armies held up at Goldsboro for refitting, and all the while Parker's men were detailed to the guarding of railroad communications being restored between Goldsboro and the coast.

Except for roving bands of enemy, the Confederate forces, under the command of General Joseph E. Johnston, now held positions on the other side of the Roanoke River. While further action was impending, North Carolina newspapers fell into Federal hands and could not disguise the fact that there were hunger, inflation, despair, and dissension in the Southern camp. A correspondent with Sherman's armies even claimed there was a civil war in the South itself and that the Confederacy was a "gone goon."[27]

Just as the armies under Sherman were prepared to resume the offensive, news confirming the fall of Richmond set off guns to honor the victory rather than win a new one. Bands played and Negroes encamped nearby were said to caper to the music as though "bit by tarantulas."[28] But, even as Hallelujas were raised to "Father Abraham," the President was about to die by an assassin's bullet.

On the front page of the *New York Herald,* Saturday, April 15, 1865, the staggering news of Lincoln's assassination filled column after column. On the back page, the *Herald* correspondent in the field in North Carolina reported that Lieutenant-Colonel Parker and a squad of nineteen men were captured by a rebel cavalry force at Burgan, near Goldsboro, on April 9. A quarter of a century later, Parker claimed that he and his adjutant were captured by a squad of Wilber's Cavalry when they made a detour. He said one of the rebels took his boots and he was marched barefooted through Raleigh.[29] Parker seems to have experienced remarkably bad luck in being captured on the very day Lee was making his historic surrender at Appomattox Court House.

His treatment by the "rebels" left a scar quite different from the one in his neck. Many years later, at an army reunion, he said that he did not harbor bitter feelings toward the South but that he was bitter about the home guards, "the cowardly ruffians who abused our prisoners —but let that pass."[30] It is possible that several "cultured southern ladies" advocated his immediate hanging on the night of his capture and that he was imprisoned in an old smoke house, together with a man covered with smallpox.[31]

Parker was caught up in the Confederate retreat toward Greensboro when Johnston asked for a truce on April 14. About this time, Parker was paroled under truce, and although not allowed to return to his command, he probably suffered no further humiliation. He had to wait until April 26, 1865, when Johnston submitted to unconditional surrender. When Parker rejoined his regiment, now stationed in Raleigh, his first order, on May 6, was for companies to furnish him with a complete list of pay and clothing for all paroled or exchanged prisoners.[32]

After several months of occupation duty in Raleigh, North Carolina, Parker led his regiment back to New Hampshire in triumph. Parker said he had gone to war for the preservation of the democratic ideal.[33] He would have to go on fighting for that ideal the rest of his life. He had seen the "horror of war in all its forms." All through the conflict he wondered how humanity could be saved from such "barbarism" and from another "fratricidal war." He concluded that the only way was to educate the children into true freedom through the common schools. The war taught Parker that "the hope of the world" and even "perpetuating the Republic" depended on the schools. He resolved to continue his work in the field of education.[34]

When asked what part of his education he valued most, Parker cited his five years on the farm and his four years in the army. The army, he said, gave him some measure of self-control, though not very much, he added. He gained just enough discipline to "steady" himself.[35]

The education in self-discipline began with his first day of army life. To accept former schoolmates or neighbors as superiors or inferiors, to live in a fixed and uniform way, he said, was a "violent wrench." He found it was "a long step from a democracy to a perfect despotism." He later learned to live in the trenches and splinter proofs of Folly Island and Petersburg, with shells exploding and dropping all around. Waking to find "a mate dead by his side" required "an endurance, a constant command of self." Parker knew that "sinking of heart" and the "awful trembling and shrinking" that preceded a battle, but "after the first fearful struggle with cowardly self," he said, "excitement bears one through danger and even the agonies of death itself."[36]

It was in the summer of 1864, pinned down in the trenches around Petersburg, that he wrestled with the greatest fear, a fear worse than death for Parker, the "agonizing thought—*if we should fail!*"[37] As in all lessons of life the fear of failure is the most injurious to success. Perhaps Parker held this lesson in mind when he one day determined to rid the school of report cards and the fear of failure.

Parker learned to control himself, but the most valuable lesson of war for an educational reformer may have been the ability to control others. His qualities of leadership were not conspicuous in the beginning of his military career. In fact, they were decidedly lacking.

On April 18, 1862, when the regiment was garrisoned in St. Augustine, Florida, seventy-nine men of Parker's Company E put their names on a petition for his removal. The petition charged that Captain Parker was "hurtful for the service and for the honor of Company E." By way of more specific details, the men charged Parker with "abusing his men by striking and choking them." They accused him of being drunk a good deal of the time and giving whiskey to men on duty. Moreover, they found him not fit to hold command of a company.[38]

The muster rolls show Parker "present in arrest" from April, 1862, until August 8, 1862, when he was brought before a General Court Martial. Charges that he was drunk on April 2, 1862, while on a "scout," and again drunk while Officer of the Day on April 19, 1862, were dropped on a technicality, because the charges were not properly made out according to the Articles of War. Parker was tried on the charge of "Conduct prejudicial to good order and military discipline," with the specifications that he gave intoxicating liquor to sentinals on duty the night of April 7, 1862, and that he was unable to perform his duties on the same occasion.[39]

One enlisted man overheard Parker telling other officers on the night in question that his "boys" would follow him "to hell if he insisted upon it." This witness said Parker talked loudly and was not in proper uniform. In fact, he was disheveled in appearance and seemed in need of support. Another witness said Parker "reeled" and "stumbled" up the stairs to his quarters that night. Glasses were heard rattling above, along with "silly expressions." Next morning it was said he couldn't talk plainly and the men laughed about it for a long time. The Sergeant of the Guard on that April 7 testified that Parker offered him and his companion a bottle of "Scotch ale."

Parker handled his own defense. In cross-examining the Sergeant of the Guard he asked, "Did you notice anything peculiar before you came up?"

"I noticed that he was talking and laughing different than I heard before," the Sergeant replied.

"Isn't Captain Parker apt to talk and laugh pretty loud?" Parker asked.

"I do not think he is."

"Did you ever see Captain Parker in a state of intoxication previous to that time?"

"Do not think I ever did."

"Have you ever seen him in a state of intoxication since?"

"Don't think I have."

"How much ale do you know him to have drunk?" asked a member of the court.

"Only that we three drank a bottle."

Parker began his own defense with the testimony of Lieutenant Wiggins, who had been himself under arrest for some time and the recipient of a court martial. He testified that he shared the same room with Captain Parker and did not notice him being intoxicated. Lieutenant Edgerly, who had brought charges, could no longer remember that Parker was unable to perform his duties on the night of April 7. He could only remember one time when the accused was drunk and that was on a later occasion, not the time cited in the specification.

When the court reconvened on August 11, 1862, it found Parker not guilty. His acquittal was promulgated on September 3, 1862. If the court appeared lenient with Parker, it was no less lenient in its hearings of similar cases at that time.[40] The regiment was about to be pulled out of garrison duty in St. Augustine. Perhaps it needed every officer.

There seems to be no doubt that Parker had done some drinking. One of Carrollton's Sons of Temperance, he may not have known much about drinking or how to hold his liquor. The real issue was why the men in his company had believed he was hurtful for their honor and why they charged he was not fit to hold command. It is doubtful if the honor of a company of red-blooded New Hampshire enlisted men could be besmirched by an officer who might have gotten drunk or offered to share his "commissary" with them.

There may have been some political spite in the action taken by the men. Parker recalled that his regiment was mostly made up of Democrats.[41] He was, of course, a Republican. The Democrats were becoming dissatisfied with the conduct of the war. The men of the Fourth had earlier registered disgust with the policy of the army not to use the captured slaves on Hilton Head Island. There was grumbling and complaining among the men that "many a noble soldier died from the effect of hard work which the Negro might easily have done.[42] During that cold, damp winter on Hilton Head, "the slow, sad music of the funeral march was daily heard." Discipline had deteriorated. When a soldier was reprimanded for a dirty rifle at inspection, he dared snap back that he had the "brightest shovel."[43]

It was shortly after the regiment landed in Florida that its commanding officer, Colonel Thomas J. Whipple, resigned his commission and went home. It was said that he left, much to the regret of the men, without reason. His resignation may have reflected political dissention. Whipple was a Democrat who viewed the Republicans as the cause of the war.[44] If the men had come to associate the Republicans with the cause of the war and their present unhappy circumstances, Parker was a likely target for their wrath.

More likely, the men were striking out blindly at the harsh discipline of a military life which was a torment to them. Parker admitted that he was "by nature a Martinet," and that he was noted in the army for his discipline.[45] Up to that time the regiment had never been engaged in heavy fighting. The men may not have appreciated what seemed like unnecessary harshness simply for the sake of army regulations. Whether a victim of politics or of his own harshness, Parker must have learned that he would have to look out for the welfare of his men and win their respect rather than to demand it by nature of his office. The next time he got into trouble, it was when he tried to put the welfare of his own men before the interests of the army.

It was August 10, 1863, at Folly Island, within sight of the harbor where war had begun in the humiliating loss of Fort Sumter. Just keeping the men in food, cartridge boxes, cap pouches, and such petty items as haversacks, canteens, camp kettles, and mess pans required the exertion of enormous energies. Everything had to be unloaded from ships. Already the heavy work, along with intense heat and brackish drinking water, had thinned the ranks.[46] Captain Parker was detailed to the command of a fatigue party that included more than a hundred men. His men had unloaded supplies that August morning until noon. At that time Parker went into the Quartermaster's office to inquire about a whiskey ration and dinner for his men. He was given an hour and a half but told to be back at half past one o'clock.[47]

Parker marched his men back to camp, but he gave them more rest than was allotted. When the detail got back to the fleet landing, Captain J. A. Burns of the Quartermaster Department called Parker into his office and demanded to know why he was late. According to Burns, Parker simply said he "supposed the only reason was that he didn't get there any sooner."

Burns told him that this was only one of several instances in which fatigue parties had been late. He said he would have to prefer charges. Parker, a captain himself at this time, was alleged to have muttered something about not caring what happened and that it was "tough" to take orders from a captain.

Parker was put under arrest and brought before a General Court Martial four days later. He was charged with disobedience of orders and neglect of duty. The high command was not wasting time about making this a test case, especially since the delay on August 10 made the steamer *Escort* miss the tide.

The testimony of Captain Burns made up the case for the prosecution. Parker began his own defense with the testimony of the Assistant Surgeon of the New Hampshire Fourth. He said that Parker had an "impaired condition of the digestive organs . . . . It seemed to be the result of heat and a torpid condition of the liver." The Assistant Surgeon said that Parker could have been excused from duty that day but had chosen to fall in with his men.

Other testimony established that when Parker got back to camp for dinner that day he entered his tent without food and fell face down on his bed. Other witnesses testified that the fatigue party had returned before three o'clock, the time of return on the charges and specifications. (Parker had already learned the importance attached to the specific wording of charges.) It was also established by witnesses that the steamer *Escort* was fully unloaded by three-thirty, and a civilian-government pilot testified that the tides were such that day that the *Escort* could have gotten over the bar at four o'clock.

In spite of this persuasive defense, the court found Parker guilty and sentenced him to be reprimanded in public by the Commanding General. Parker wrote an appeal in which he reviewed the evidence and added that he believed white men could not work in July and August in such a climate, that walking half a mile, eating dinner, and returning, all in an hour and a half, was unreasonable. He wrote that the "lives of men should be sacrificed only when necessity requires." He finally added: "I certainly tried to do my duty . . . . I can hardly imagine that the result of such a day's work—contending as I did against physical disability . . . should end in my disgrace."

Nevertheless his punishment was carried out. Parker learned the meaning of humiliation, but he had fought for his men and they were soon to fight for him. Shortly thereafter he was leading his company against the Confederate forces on the neighboring Morris Island. "The bugle sounds," he remembered, and the men fell in, formed their lines hurriedly and silently, columns advanced. The "rattling of minnie balls, the hurtling crash of shell," Parker said, told the men that the enemy was ready. They advanced, "all eyes fixed in their sockets . . . . Men fall here, there, everywhere. Forward! *double-quick!* Like a flash the deadly paleness changes to a ruddy glow, the blood leaps and dances in the veins, death is nothing now, let it come!"[48]

Parker had become a leader of men. After the fall of Morris Island, Parker was appointed Recruiting Officer for the regiment. Hundreds of veterans re-enlisted for another three years.[49] Parker had become not only a soldier, but a soldier's soldier. No officer whose men still wanted his removal would be appointed to seek their re-enlistment. Parker had learned how to command men and their respect. This was one of his first lessons of war.

Parker had learned that men respond best to orders when they understand the reason for them. When he had been court-martialed in 1863 for failing to return his fatigue party on time, he had apparently not known that a short delay would hold up the sailing of a ship. When Captain Burns told him what his tardiness had cost, he said he would have been back a little sooner if he had known. Captain Burns remarked that he didn't consider it necessary to explain "to every man with whom

I transacted business, all the necessities of its being promptly done . . . ." The lesson, "if I had only known," stuck in Parker's mind.

Keeping a regiment of young, strapping New Hampshire boys in strict military harness, while on occupation duty in Raleigh after the war, was a task of no ordinary proportions, especially since the ranks were filling up with recruits who had never seen action. His orders then were carefully construed to explain their reasonableness. When he requested company commanders to instruct their men according to the regulations of packing knapsacks, slinging haversacks, canteens, and the general mode of dress, he tempered the order by explaining that "the adoption of a correct style is fully as easy as the adoption of an incorrect style . . . " and that only by a "perfect uniformity" could the regiment be pronounced in good order.[50]

He also ordered that the men pay careful attention to the cleanliness of their persons, clothing, tents, and cookeries. He even ordered that underclothing must be changed at least once a week. In so ordering he was careful to explain that cleanliness was important in avoiding "diseases of Southern climate."[51]

When it came to his attention that some of the men were pillaging neighboring gardens, he advised the men that he had sought to make their duties as light as possible, "consistent with good discipline in this hot, sultry climate, but if such a course is persisted by a few thieves in the regiment, a guard of thirty men will have to be detailed each day and not a man can be allowed out of camp, which would be very unpleasant." He also mentioned that the reputation of the regiment was at stake and that it might be assigned to a less pleasant post for occupation duty.[52]

If Parker had been too severe in his discipline at the beginning, his last reprimand from the army was that his discipline was too lax. While still stationed in Raleigh, after the war, Parker learned that the Brigade Inspector had made some statements which were derogatory to his character and to the general reputation of the whole regiment. These statements, in the form of the June Inspection Report, would be reviewed by higher commands and bring discredit to Parker and his men. He immediately requested a Board of Inquiry to investigate the "implied Charges . . . ."[53]

The charges, it appeared, were to the effect that he held a rather loose rein on the men and that something of a disorderly house was kept near the east corner of the camp. Evidence was brought before the board that the "house" in question was occupied by several Negro families, that officers and men of the New Hampshire Fourth frequented the house to have their washing done. On one occasion a Negro woman was drunk there and contributed toward a disturbance of the peace. The Provost Marshal had to send out the Patrol Guard to restore order.

The investigation, however, showed the other inmates of the house were not disorderly. Evidence was produced to show that when Parker was advised of the incident he had reprimanded some of the officers at Dress Parade. When all the evidence was in, the board found that the "house" in question was not a "house of ill fame." It found the discipline of the Fourth good, the morals of the officers and men "as good as regiments generally." The opinion of the board was that there should be no cause for any derogatory remarks in the Inspection Report.[54]

These findings were promulgated on August 15, 1865, shortly before the regiment was to leave for home. It was a final victory for Parker and his men. The war taught him how to fight injustice as well as to hold command.

Beyond the lessons of war, Parker's military experience made him a leader in war and he would remain a leader throughout the "war generation." The army gave him a title of leadership that would be honored all his life. On June 22, 1867, the War Department appointed Parker to "Colonel by Brevet in the Volunteer Force, Army of the United States, for faithful and meritorious service . . ."[55] For the generation that fought the war, and for the next generation that honored the heroism of its fathers, the title of "Colonel" would open many doors. Such a title might hold more weight with the public and with some boards of education than the title of high academic degrees. At least, it was the title of a fighter, and Parker would be a fighter the rest of his life.

NOTES

[1] "Company Muster-in Roll as checked in December 1891 for pension," and "Letter of certification from A. D. Ayling, Adjutant General, State of New Hampshire, Concord, March 18, 1893," and "Letter from F. W. Parker to Lt. Col. Ed. W. Smith, Morris Island, South Carolina, November 24, 1863," Document File, Francis W. Parker, Record and Pension Office, War Department, Record Group Number 94, National Archives, General Search Room, Washington, D.C. New Hampshire Regimental Descript Book, 4th Infantry, Records Division, Army and Air Corps Branch, National Archives, Washington, D.C.; Francis W. Parker, "Fourth Regiment New Hampshire Volunteer Infantry," *Revised Register of the Soldiers and Sailors of New Hampshire in the War of the Rebellion, 1861–1866* (Concord, N. H.: Ira C. Evans, Public Printer, 1895), p. 153; John G. Hutchinson, *Roster: Fourth Regiment New Hampshire Volunteers* (Manchester, N. H.: John B. Clarke Co., 1896), p. 93; "History of the Fourth New Hampshire Volunteers," *Mirror and Farmer* (Manchester, N. H.), November 11, 1865.

[2] Francis W. Parker, *op. cit.*, p. 153; Francis W. Parker, "Autobiographical Sketch," appendix in William M. Giffin, *School Days in the Fifties* (Chicago: A. Flanagan Co., 1906), p. 123.

[3] "General Order Number Fourteen, Head Quarters of the Fourth New Hampshire Volunteers, Warsaw Island, Georgia, February 13, 1862," New Hampshire 4th Infantry Regimental Order Book, Records Division, Army and Air Corps Branch, National Archives, Washington, D.C.

[4] "Death of Mrs. Harris," *Mirror and Farmer*, September 30, 1871.

[5] "History of the Fourth New Hampshire Volunteers."

[6] Parker's request for leave, dated November 24, 1863, with Colonel Bell's endorsement, final approval on November 27, 1863, and leave papers, Special Orders Number 626, Department of the South, Headquarters in the Field, Folly Island, S. C., December 1, 1863, with the endorsements of passage on the U.S.S. *Fulton*, arrival in New York Harbor on December 11, 1863, Document File, Francis W. Parker.

[7] "Proceedings of a Military Commission which convened at Morris Island, South Carolina, February 5th, 1864 . . ." and "Special Orders Number 25, Head Quarters, Superintendent Volunteer Recruiting Service, Concord, New Hampshire, December 31st, 1863," Document File, Francis W. Parker.

[8] "A year ago this month . . . ," *Daily Mirror and American* (Manchester, N. H.), November 28, 1864; "A Note from Col. Parker, Quincy, Mass., Sept. 8, 1879," newspaper clipping, Parker Scrapbooks, 1879, Archives, Harper Library, University of Chicago; John G. Hutchinson, *op. cit.*, pp. 14, 16; Francis W. Parker, "Fourth Regiment New Hampshire Volunteer Infantry," p. 154.

[9] General Regis de Trobriand, in Otto Eisenschiml and Ralph Newman (Eds.), *The Civil War, The American Iliad as Told by Those by Those Who Lived It*, Vol. I (New York: Grosset and Dunlap, 1956), p. 592.

[10] "History of the Fourth New Hampshire Volunteers."

[11] *Ibid.;* Parker's name appears on General Orders issued on August 1, 1864, and thereafter until he is wounded, New Hampshire 4th Infantry Regimental Order Book.

[12] Frank W. Parker, letter to Hon. Wm. Lochran, Com. of Pensions, Washington, D.C., March 24, 1894, and Samuel D. Marckres [a former private in the 4th New Hampshire Volunteers], affidavit, Soldier's Certificate, Francis W. Parker, Can no. 17835, Bundle no. 22, National Archives, Washington, D.C.

[13] Samuel D. Marckres, *op. cit.;* "Declaration of Original Invalid Pension," Francis W. Parker, Can no. 17835, Bundle no. 22.

[14] Parker claimed he was "delirious for some time," in F. W. Parker, letter to Hon. Wm. Lochran; "L [not clear] Mason, N. H. Agent to Adjutant General Townsend, Washington, D.C., September 6, 1864," Document File, Francis W. Parker.

[15] All requests and orders, with endorsements thereto, are found in Document File, Francis W. Parker.

[16] "Hon. Samuel Upton, and Capt. F. W. Parker, will speak at . . . ." *Daily Mirror and American*, October 26, 1864.

[17] "Special Orders No. 377, November 1st, 1864," Document File, Francis W. Parker.

[18] "Last Union Rally!" *Daily Mirror and American*, November 7, 1864;

"Our Union loving Citizens had a Splendid Gathering," *Daily Mirror and American,* November 8, 1864.

[19] *The Daily Union* (Manchester, N. H.), November 9, 1864, November 14, 1864, November 18, 1864.

[20] "Gov. Gilmore for Lincoln," *Daily Mirror and American,* Ocotber 27, 1864; "New Hampshire Soldiers Coming Home," *Daily Mirror and American,* October 26, 1864.

[21] Record of Marriage: Groom, Francis W. Parker; Bride, Josephine E. Hall . . . . State Department of Health, Bureau of Vital Statistics, Concord, N. H.

[22] Flora J. Cooke, "Colonel Francis W. Parker: His Influence on Education," *Chicago Schools Journal,* **19** (March 1938), 148.

[23] Marion Foster Washburne, "Col. Francis W. Parker: The Man and Educational Reformer," *Francis Wayland Parker: His Life and Educational Reform Work, Souvenir Issued in Honor of the Silver Anniversary of the Quincy Movement* (New York: E. L. Kellogg and Co., April, 1900), p. 14.

[24] Francis W. Parker, "Autobiographical Sketch," p. 124.

[25] Parker's appointment was certified, from original documents, by the Adjutant General's Office, New Hampshire, on March 18, 1893, for pension purposes. Document File, Francis W. Parker.

[26] "F. W. Parker to Head Quarters, Draft Rendezvous, New Haven, Connecticut, January 5, 1865," and "Special Order No. 31, Draft Rendezvous, New Haven, Connecticut, January 31, 1865," Document File, Francis W. Parker.

[27] "Mr. D. P. Conyngham's Despatch, Newbern, N. C., April 11, 1865," *The New York Herald* (New York, N. Y.), April 15, 1865.

[28] *Ibid.*

[29] Francis W. Parker, "Autobiographical Sketch," p. 125.

[30] Newspaper account of Parker's address at a soldier's reunion, 1879, Parker Scrapbooks, 1879.

[31] Newspaper clipping quoting Mr. John P. Hodgman, member of Company E, Fourth New Hampshire Volunteers, on the occasion of a reunion in 1880, Parker Scrapbooks, 1880.

[32] "Circular . . . By order of F. W. Parker, Lt. Col., 4th N. H. Vols., May 6, 1865," Box File, Volunteer Army of the Civil War, New Hampshire 4th, Regimental Papers, National Archives, Washington, D.C.

[33] Francis W. Parker, *Talks On Pedagogics, An Outline of the Theory of Concentration* (New York: E. L. Kellogg and Co., 1894), p. 451.

[34] Francis W. Parker, "Discussion on the South and Its Problems," *Journal of Proceedings and Addresses, National Educational Association, 1894,* pp. 586–587; Francis W. Parker, "Autobiographical Sketch," pp. 125–126.

[35] *Ibid.,* p. 117.

[36] Newspaper account of Parker's address at a soldiers' reunion, 1879, Parker Scrapbooks, 1879.

[37] *Ibid.*

[38] "A Petition of the Members of Co. E. 4th N. H. Regiment for the removal of Captain Parker from said company, April 18, 1862," Document File, Francis W. Parker.

[39] "Record of a General Court Martial held at St. Augustine, Florida, commencing July 30, 1862, case of Francis W. Parker" (KK260), Records

Division, Army and Air Corps Branch, National Archives, Washington, D.C. Subsequent references to this trial and testimony therein are all from this record.

[40] See cases of Lt. V. B. Richardson, Lt. F. Kendall, Captain G. Granger tried about the same time by this court. Records Division, Army and Air Corps Branch, National Archives, Washington, D.C.

[41] Francis W. Parker, "Fourth Regiment New Hampshire Volunteer Infantry," p. 153.

[42] "History of the Fourth New Hampshire Volunteers."

[43] *Ibid.*

[44] *Ibid.;* Reverend Stephen G. Abbott, *The First Regiment New Hampshire Volunteers in the Great Rebellion* (Keene, N. H.: Sentinel Printing Company, 1890), p. 41.

[45] Francis W. Parker, "Autobiographical Sketch," p. 134.

[46] "History of the Fourth New Hampshire Volunteers"; basic needs are noted a shortage order, December 14, 1863, New Hampshire 4th Infantry Regimental Order Book.

[47] "Proceedings of a General Court Martial Convened at Morris Island, South Carolina, August 5, 1863 . . . . Case 14, Captain Frank W. Parker" (File NN383), Records Division, Army and Air Corps Branch, National Archives, Washington, D.C. Subsequent references to this trial, testimony, and appeal, are all from this record.

[48] Newspaper account of Parker's address at a soldier's reunion, 1879, Parker Scrapbooks, 1879.

[49] "General Orders Number 3, Head Quarters, 4th NH Vols, Morris Island, S. C., January 15, 1864," Document File, Francis W. Parker. The number of re-enlistments vary according to sources, but the lowest figure is 288 and the highest 400. John G. Hutchinson, *op.cit.,* p. 16; Francis W. Parker, "Fourth Regiment New Hampshire Volunteer Infantry," p. 154; "A Note from Col. Parker, Quincy, Mass., Sept. 8, 1879," newspaper clipping, Parker Scrapbooks, 1879.

[50] "Circular . . . By order of F. W. Parker, Lt. Col. Commanding, Head Quarters, 4th N. H., Raleigh, N. C., May 11, 1865," Box File, Volunteer Army of the Civil War, New Hampshire 4th.

[51] "Circular . . . By order of F. W. Parker, . . . May 13, 1865," Box File, Volunteer Army of the Civil War, New Hampshire 4th.

[52] "Circular . . . By order of F. W. Parker, . . . June 15th, 1865," Box File, Volunteer Army of the Civil War, New Hampshire 4th.

[53] "F. W. Parker, Lt. Col. 4th N. H. Vols., Commanding Regiment, Headquarters 4th N. H. Vols., Raleigh, N. C., June 20, 1865, to Captain E. Church, A.O.G.G. Brig.," Document File, Francis W. Parker.

[54] "General Orders No. 3, by order of Brevet Major General Ames, Headquarters District of Raleigh, Raleigh, North Carolina, August 15, 1865," Document File, Francis W. Parker.

[55] "General Order No. 65, dated War Department, Adjutant General's Office, June 22, 1867." [Rank to date from March 13, 1865] Document File, Francis W. Parker.

IV

The Soldier Schoolmaster of Manchester

The return of the New Hampshire Fourth was keenly anticipated in Manchester all through the summer of 1865. For Parker's pregnant wife, Phenie, the delay must have been difficult to understand, even though there were reports in Manchester that there was a "perfect reign of terror" in those areas of North Carolina where no troops were stationed.[1] Imposing "peace" on the South must have been harder to understand than waging war. It is possible that Governor Smyth of New Hampshire put pressure on his fellow Republicans in the War Department to get the boys back home.[2]

The Manchester *Mirror and Farmer* reported on August 26, 1865, that the Secretary of War directed troops of the Department of North Carolina to be mustered out. By the time the people of Manchester had received this news, the New Hampshire Fourth was already two days on the road. It had left Raleigh, North Carolina, by rail on August 24th. On August 25th the train ran off the track near Petersburg, Virginia. The men were severely shaken up and one "substitute" from Philadelphia was reported killed.[3]

The City Government of Manchester appointed a committee to make arrangements for a proper reception of the Fourth. When a telegram was received that the regiment would soon be home, the mayor and reception committee stayed up all night and had a brass field piece polished up to salute the regiment as soon as its train came into sight. At four o'clock on the morning of August 29th, the field piece was fired off four times before the reception committee discovered that the approaching train carried cattle instead of soldiers.[4]

Later that morning, at ten o'clock, the regiment finally arrived and received its triumphant salute. The men were formed into columns by companies and marched off through Canal Street and up to Smyth's Hall, where eight tables had been laid out the entire length of the assembly room to serve the heroes. After the refreshments, Lieutenant Colonel Parker called on the veterans gathered there to remember "the scenes . . . they had passed, and the faces they had left behind . . . ."[5]

About a week after Parker came out of the army, his little girl came into the world. When Ann E. Parker was born in Manchester on September 9, 1865, her father recorded his occupation as "teacher," although, in fact, he was an unemployed war hero.[6]

The Manchester schools had resumed on the last Monday in August, just before Parker's return.[7] The next term would not begin until December, and even then, Parker had no assurances of a job. He said his friends were disgusted with his resolve to remain a teacher.[8] One can almost see James Walker, his former guardian, shaking his head in disappointment. Here was a widow's boy who had made good in the army, and now, with a wife, a child, and without security, he was searching for a job which, at best, most people considered only temporary for a man. To make matters worse, from a businessman's point of view, the Manchester mills were being supplied with raw cotton again, and business opportunities were never better.[9]

Parker liked to remember, years later, that he was looked upon by his friends as "a young man who had succeeded very well," and that he had a commission in the regular army or a clerkship in Washington offered to him. In fact, he said of himself that "nothing was too good" for him in those days.[10]

A political career was in the offing. Parker was hardly out of the army before he was appointed a "councillor" by the Grand Veterans League of New Hampshire to help establish a home for indigent and disabled soldiers.[11] Later he was elected president of the Manchester Soldiers' Association.[12] Parker said, however, that he did not want to go into politics. The political climate was actually not suited for one who was tired of war. There was talk of war with France to dislodge Maxmillian from Mexico. There was war between Republicans and Democrats over the politics of peace. Much in the manner of Lincoln, Parker preached "reconstruction and reconciliation." He said, "the war is over, the Southern people have done the best they can, now let us shake hands and make up."[13] This sentiment would hardly endear him with the radicals that had taken over his own party.

The unemployed war hero withdrew across the river from Manchester to his hometown of Piscatauquog. He and his wife and daughter boarded with his mother and sisters at the house on Amherst, near High Street.[14]

Parker's sister Mary was teaching in Piscatauquog. Philinda Parker taught in the Manchester school system. The youngest sister, Emily, did not live with the family at this time. She was also a teacher in Manchester. Both she and Philanda earned less than $300 a year in the Manchester system.[15] This was a school system which the *Daily Mirror and American* of Manchester had heralded on November 17, 1864, as the best in the state, even unsurpassed in Massachusetts.

The schools were organized in classes of "ungraded," "partially graded," "primary," "middle," "intermediate," "grammar," and "high school." The ungraded and partially graded classes pertained only to small districts. A child could enter the primary level at age four and the middle level, of two years' duration, whenever he had mastered the prerequisite studies. The intermediate grade was for those who could not attend regularly or who had some mental or physical disability. A four-year course of study was prescribed for the grammar grades, and the high school offered both classical and "English" programs, that is, a college preparatory and a terminal curriculum. Measures for governing the children were said to be "mild and persuasive" as far as possible, and teachers were required to keep a record of "corporal punishment."[16]

In 1866, Manchester had eleven school districts, fifty-two schools, and about 4,500 pupils.[17] It was into such a school system that Frank Parker was finally admitted. James O. Adams, Superintendent of Public Instruction, noted in his report for 1865 that there was an interruption in the North Grammar School when principal W. W. Colburn resigned. Apparently Lieutenant Colonel Parker, formerly principal of the only school in Carrollton, Illinois, was not the first choice. The superintendent reported that the school committee was not successful in its first effort at securing a suitable replacement. He said that they finally had obtained a "gentleman who has the ability of adjusting himself to the position . . . ."[18] That gentleman was Frank Parker.

It was as principal of the North Grammar School, serving about 135 pupils, that Parker resumed his teaching career late in 1865.[19] The retired Lieutenant Colonel began to whip his school into a regiment, with battalion drill and regimental devotion to duty. His efforts were successful and a new high for attendance and deportment was soon attained.[20]

The general impression of his superintendent was that Parker's discipline was little short of perfection. He said the order in the school was characteristic of the military, in some cases too severe, but on the whole a disciplinary system which "commends itself to universal approbation." The only danger he saw in Parker's militaristic methods was that their prominence might render "proper mental discipline entirely a subordinate requirement . . . ."[21]

Parker believed this was the first time in his life that he had departed from conventional teaching. He developed a system of "ranking," based on emulation and incentive, rather than strictness and punishment. This system put each pupil into a particular rank in class, dependent on attendance, deportment, and scholarship. This rank would be altered frequently by "negligence, or misdemeanor, unnecessary absence or tardiness, or by failure in recitation . . . ." [22]

Although Parker increased the amount of time in school devoted to physical education and he concentrated on achieving good order and morale, he was equally concerned with academic training. He complained that eleven out of twelve pupils entered high school without decent handwriting or a "thorough knowledge of any common school branches." In his very first year in the Manchester system, he had the impertinence to address such complaints, along with suggested remedies, to his superintendent.[23]

Parker blamed a lack of system for poor learning. He might have used the military "chain of command" to illustrate his point, but he chose the machine shops of Manchester. He argued that in such shops each man has one particular part of a complex machine to make. To that end the worker bent all his energy and was responsible for the slightest flaw. The master workman would inspect each part before it went into the machine. Parker argued that such specialization and supervision was needed in teaching. He pointed out that the master of a grammar school had little control beyond his own "division." There was no uniformity in what the various teachers, preparing students for the grammar grades, were doing. If there were one master, as in a machine shop, Parker believed each teacher would be assigned a particular task and know it was done well. "Would it not be wise," he wrote in his report, "to apply a little of the wisdom which shapes for use the hard iron and steel—to the education of immortal minds—so malleable that a blow light as breath will leave a mark for eternity?" [24]

Parker was not successful in capturing the whole school system and imposing the supervision of the military or machine shop. He was rehired, however, for a second year, and his salary was increased from around a thousand dollars to eleven hundred.[25] Joseph G. Edgerly replaced James Adams as superintendent at that time, but he was just as enthusiastic about Parker's work as his predecessor had been. In his first report, Edgerly noted the attention being paid to a new method of writing used in the schools, especially in the North and South grammar schools. He called the method "systematic," which had a ring of Parker to it. The superintendent said "progress has been truly surprising compared with former years . . . . I know the system is condemned by many, yet *results* show that it is successful, and I know of no better criterion by which to judge." [26]

Whether or not Parker was responsible for initiating this systematic system of writing, he was using it in his school and apparently getting results. He was surely defending this new approach, along with the superintendent, or he would not have tolerated it in his school. It may have been at this time, while defending a new technique, that he became convinced that educational doctrine was more deeply entrenched in New England than Puritan dogmatism, Noah Webster more revered than Jonathan Edwards.[27]

About this same time he was taking a devout but nonsectarian turn in religion himself. He was active in establishing the first Young Men's Christian Association in New Hampshire. The initial convention for this purpose met in Manchester in 1868 and he was elected president.[28] The link between education and nonsectarian Christianity would become as firmly fixed in his thinking as the link between education and the preservation of the democratic ideal, but at the very moment he was achieving a good reputation in Manchester, he was becoming uneasy. Something was wrong with education. He observed how unhappy little children worked at their letters. He saw them dangling their legs in weariness. He wondered if God intended this "mournful process" for the development of the "embryonic man."[29]

Whatever God intended, the results were not good. Parker found that in the grammar grades a child was exposed to more than three thousand half-hour lessons in spelling without being able to write a common letter. He began to realize that the methods of cramming were only making the child's mind "stultified." Each grade had its prescribed number of pages to be memorized.[30]

It is not certain when Parker began to search for a new position, but he must have felt constrained in his old home town. Perhaps he felt especially harassed by those who believed the schools of Manchester were too good for any reforms.

Whatever efforts Parker began to exert to find a new job were not dictated by a sense of failure. On the contrary, he must have been excited by the results he was getting and by his own plans for creating a new departure in education. There was no need to move on. He had been elected to serve for another year, through March of 1869.[31] Nevertheless, he probably longed for more freedom to experiment. As he had already experienced in Illinois, the west was less encumbered by the laws of tradition.

Parker said he did not like the idea of playing politics, but he approached Governor Smyth. Smyth owed him a political debt for his work in the election of 1864. Smyth suggested Dayton, Ohio, where he had recently helped to establish the Soldiers' Home.[32] Dayton, close to Antioch College where Horace Mann had removed himself from the conservative constraints of Boston, must have sounded good to Parker.

It was soon reported in Dayton that Governor Smyth, as well as other "distinguished" citizens of New Hampshire, had recommended Parker as "one of the best educators in New England." In July of 1868, the Dayton School Board elected Parker to the principalship of the First District School.[33]

Parker's departure from Manchester was mourned, at least by the superintendent of schools. In his next annual report the superintendent complained of the inefficiency and lowering of rank at the North Grammar School after Parker had left. The trouble was blamed on the change in leadership. Parker was said to have been so popular with the children that the new principal could hardly be expected to give satisfaction for his first term.[34]

Perhaps Parker's military methods of discipline could only work with a Colonel in command. Parker's personal touch had always worked magic, but he was now in search of a universal touch. For the second time in his life he was going west to seek his educational fortune.

NOTES

[1] "From Lieutenant A. W. Hahn, Raleigh, North Carolina, August 21, 1865," *Daily Mirror and American* (Manchester, N. H.), August 30, 1865.

[2] "History of the Fourth New Hampshire Volunteers," *Mirror and Farmer* (Manchester, N. H.), November 11, 1865.

[3] "The Fourth Regiment, Lt. Col. F. W. Parker, commanding, arrived in New York last evening . . . ." *Daily Mirror and American,* August 29, 1865.

[4] "Arrival of the Fourth Regiment," *Daily Mirror and American,* August 30, 1865.

[5] *Ibid.*

[6] Birth Certificate, Ann E. Parker, Bureau of Vital Statistics, New Hampshire State Department of Health, Concord, N. H.

[7] "Schools," *Daily Mirror and American,* August 26, 1865.

[8] Francis W. Parker, "Autobiographical Sketch," appendix in William M. Giffin, *School Days in the Fifties* (Chicago: A. Flanagan Co., 1906), p. 125.

[9] "Business is reviving everywhere," *Mirror and Farmer,* September 23, 1865.

[10] Francis W. Parker, *op. cit.*

[11] "Grand Veteran League of New Hampshire," *Mirror and Farmer,* September 16, 1865.

[12] "The Manchester Soldier's Association," *Mirror and Farmer,* March 31, 1866.

[13] Francis W. Parker, *op. cit.*

[14] *Manchester Directory, 1864* (Manchester; N. H.: Adams, Sampson and Co., 1864), pp. 121–122; *Manchester Directory, 1866* (Manchester, N. H.: Sampson, Davenport and Co., 1866), p. 109.

[15] "Eleventh Annual Report of the Superintendent of Public Instruction

being the Twentieth Annual Report of the School Committee of the City of Manchester, 1865," *Manchester School Reports* (Manchester, N. H.: Henry A. Gage, 1866), pp. 5, 12; *Manchester Directory, 1869* (Manchester, N. H.: Sampson, Davenport and Company, 1869), p. 119.

[16] *Regulations of the Public Schools in the City of Manchester, Adopted by the School Committee, March 22, 1865* (Manchester, N. H.: Printed by Charles F. Livingston [unclear], 16 and 17th Smyth's Block, 1866), pp. 13–14, 23–29.

[17] *Manchester Directory, 1866,* p. 158.

[18] "Eleventh Annual Report of the Superintendent of Public Instruction . . . ," p. 18.

[19] The North Grammar School opened in August of 1865 with 135 students. *Daily Mirror and American,* August 29, 1865.

[20] "Twelfth Annual Report of the Superintendent of Public Instruction and Reports of sub-committees and Teachers, constituting the Twenty-first Annual Report of the Board of Education of the City of Manchester, 1866," *Manchester School Reports* (Manchester, N. H.: William H. Fisk's Job Printing Establishment, 1867), p. 46.

[21] *Ibid.*

[22] Francis W. Parker, *op. cit.,* p. 126; "Twelfth Annual Report . . . 1866," p. 13.

[23] "Twelfth Annual Report . . . 1866," pp. 46–47.

[24] *Ibid.,* pp. 48–49.

[25] *Manchester Directory, 1866,* p. 159; William Little, *A Brief History of the Schools of Manchester, New Hampshire* (pamphlet material in the Public Library, Concord, New Hampshire), p. 148; "Thirteenth Annual Report of the Superintendent of Public Instruction, being the Twenty-second annual report of the Board of Education of the City of Manchester, 1867," *Manchester School Reports* (Manchester, N. H.: John B. Clarke's Book and Job Printing, 1868), p. 6.

[26] "Thirteenth Annual Report . . . 1867," p. 27.

[27] Francis W. Parker, "The Quincy Method," *American Journal of Sociology,* **6** (July 1900), 115.

[28] George Winch, *Outline History of State Work of the Young Men's Christian Associations of New Hampshire, 1852-1908* (Manchester, N.H.: Stratton, 1908), p. 26.

[29] Francis W. Parker, "Autobiographical Sketch," pp. 126–127; Amalie Hoffer, "The Chicago Normal Training School—A Dream Come True," *Kindergarten Magazine,* **9** (November 1896), 175.

[30] "Twelfth Annual Report . . . 1866," pp. 47–49.

[31] "Thirteenth Annual Report . . . 1867, p. 78.

[32] "The Soldiers' Home," *Dayton Journal* (Dayton, Ohio), October 27, 1870. [This article was the occasion of an annual visit of the Board of Managers of the National Asylums of Veterans. Governor Frederick Smyth then said he took more pride in this institution than any other.]

[33] "Personal," *Dayton Journal,* September 7, 1868.

[34] "Fourteenth Annual Report of the Superintendent of Public Instruction, being the Twenty-third annual report of the Board of Education of the City of Manchester, 1868," *Manchester School Reports* (Manchester, N.H.: Henry A. Gage, Printer, 1869), p. 43.

V

Reconstruction in the Schools of Dayton, Ohio

When the Parkers moved to Dayton in the summer of 1868, the city claimed a population of 30,000 or 40,000 and a reputation of considerable importance in manufacturing. The school census showed 9,214 white and 151 colored children between the ages of five and twenty-one, but a total of only 4,213 were enrolled in school and less than 3,000 were in actual daily attendance.[1] Thus two out of every three children in Dayton were not availing themselves of a public education. Making the schools serve the needs and interests of all classes in the community was recognized by the board of education as its most challenging problem.[2]

In this regard, the *Dayton Journal,* a Republican party organ, criticized the school system because it neglected the education of the "masses." The subject matter was considered impractical and the methods of rote teaching too dull.[3] The *Daily Ledger,* spokesman for the Democratic party in Dayton, considered the schools an important element in the forming of society, but it called the "crying evil" of the schools the "cramming process" and the "hot house" haste with which little children were pushed ahead in their studies. The common schools should be for the common people but they were accused of actually hindering the wishes of the working families who wanted to fit their children for practical professions. The "expense of time" was added to the "expense of books" to make an education too costly for the majority. Although the Democratic paper found the prescribed course of study inappropriate for the common people, the paper held firmly to the belief that the common schools were for the common benefit, as essential as street lamps, police, fire engines, or courts.[4]

The President of the Board of Education granted that there was no controversy over the support of common schools, but he insisted that the schools were "of and for the people," and instruction was free from any partisan or sectarian interference.[5] Political control, if not interference, was definitely an issue in Dayton. The Town Council and the Board of Education were both dominated by the Republican party. Political competition was keen. The Republican newspaper cautioned party leadership, on March 12, 1869, to be careful in the consideration of nominations for the council and school board since Republicans could only remain in the majority by electing good officers. The Democratic newspaper found the worst fault of the schools was in their "guardianship."[6] Both papers, however, were spokesmen for various school reforms. Parker would find Dayton much more receptive to innovation than Manchester.

In was a happy coincidence for Parker that he came to Ohio at a time when the *Dayton Journal* proclaimed a general "educational revival."[7] Moving into the hub of a growing urban complex, the Parkers established residence at 460 Third Street, in downtown Dayton, not far from the classic columns of the old courthouse.[8] On September 7, 1868, the *Dayton Journal* reported "Colonel F. W. Parker" among "recent valuable accessions to the Dayton Society." He was said to come highly recommended from New Hampshire, as well as from his "faithful service in the Army." It was with the title of Colonel that Frank Parker arrived. He would be more and more referred to as "the Colonel" during his Dayton days, possibly as an easy way to distinguish him from Caleb Parker, a prominent member of the Board of Education. The title would stick with him the rest of his career.

Caleb Parker, no relation of the Colonel's, was a retired Dayton industrialist. His influence on the board of education was enormous, and he had for a long time strongly recommended that the board employ a "General Superintendent." It was then being argued that members of the school board were businessmen and could not devote sufficient time to the "minute details" in the management and modes of instruction in the schools.[9] Even before the Civil War the office of superintendent had been established, over the opposition of the local teachers and the public plea for economy. The office was soon abandoned. In 1866 there was again so much concern about a businesslike administration of the schools that Caleb Parker accepted the duties, but without monetary compensation. An attempt to bar his re-election to the Board of Education in 1867 was interpreted by the *Dayton Journal* as a means of abolishing the idea of a school superintendent. Caleb Parker was elected to the board again, but he did resign as acting superintendent in April of 1868, and no one replaced him.[10]

Colonel Parker, champion of a superintendency in Manchester, thus came to a city that had just renounced such an office. At that time there were six autonomous school districts in Dayton, although the school for the sixth district was still being constructed. There was a separate high school. Germans and Negroes in Dayton had their own schools. The total public school properties were worth around $195,000, just a little more than the value of the Presbyterian church and a little less than the water works.[11]

It was to the principalship of the graded school in the first district that Parker had been called, at a salary of around $1,600 a year.[12] This would be his first theatre of action in Dayton and the stage on which he would mount his educational designs. His school had an enrollment of nearly seven hundred students, four hundred of whom were six to ten years in age. Most of the rest ranged from ten to fifteen. There were very few older students.[13]

It was fortuitous for the Colonel that the Board of Education, at Caleb Parker's insistence, was turning its attention at this time to the work of the primary grades. This level had long been neglected by the board. Rooms were most crowded in the early grades and it was said that the harried teachers had to "hurry and even *worry* from day to day and from hour to hour."[14]

Parker had not worked with primary-grade children since his days in the country schools, but he said he was especially happy to work with them again, in compliance with the board's interest. He said the primary teachers asked for his help, but he had to tell them he did not know anything about primary teaching. He promised the teachers he would learn. Setting his mind to this matter he was astonished to find that teachers themselves did not study their profession. Parker was also astonished that almost no "juvenile books" were published. He had to work something out on his own. His first efforts, he conceded, were "crude."[15]

There had been some attempt to introduce new methods into the primary grades, even before the advent of the Colonel. In 1867, the acting superintendent, Caleb Parker, reported that the children in the primary grades were being taught "a progressive" course in "object teaching," which meant the cultivation of the perceptive faculties before the exercise of the reasoning powers. This technique may have been influenced by the schools of the German community, whose members undoubtedly had immigrated with some notions of the methods employed by Pestalozzi and Froebel. Regardless of its source, this technique had to be defended against traditional rote learning. Caleb Parker had fought for "object teaching" by explaining that it was not new and had always been employed by good teachers.[16]

Similar to the "ranking" system that Frank Parker had initiated in Manchester, the schools of Dayton had established a "new register," which took account of each student's standing in "attendance, recitation, and deportment." To this competition a "roll of honor" was added which Caleb Parker believed had brought up attendance from 85 to 90 per cent.[17]

In terms of school discipline, efforts had already been made in Dayton to modify the "iron rule" of achieving good order. This was quite an innovation in a state where it could be reported that a child must "assume but one position" while seated all day in school.[18]

Light gymnastics had even been introduced into the school program and it was said that such physical exercise had "relieved the *ennui* of the schoolroom, rendered the recitation more prompt and satisfactory, and secured a more abiding interest on the part of the pupils." In order to alleviate the monotony of teaching through a single text, the Board of Education had worked to make a public school library available to the students through cooperation with the Dayton Library Association.[19]

In spite of all these innovations, Parker found that education in Dayton was still based on the examination plan. The whole idea of "per cents" was related to cramming and unnatural methods of learning. On examination days, Parker said, the various neighboring cities "went wild" and even telegraphed each other to compare per cents. This whole procedure, Parker argued, "was to learn words and recite them, and then write them down in the examination stiff and strong."[20]

Parker began the teaching of reading on a "phonetic plan," but he soon introduced the "word method," which stressed the whole word or idea rather than its meaningless parts. He said he changed little in the teaching of arithmetic and geography at first, but he dropped the study of technical grammar. In general, he continued the system of ranking that he had developed in Manchester and that had already been started in Dayton.[21]

Parker also inherited a system of grouping and coeducation, which had been inaugurated in the First District School shortly before his arrival. Coeducation had crept into the Dayton schools as an incident to reforming the instruction at the primary grade level without added cost. Caleb Parker had wanted to provide for individual differences in ability. Each grade had two teachers—one for boys and one for girls. Integrating boys and girls in either section A or section B according to achievement rather than sex achieved his purpose without requiring the services of another teacher.[22]

Parker put such innovations, as well as his own, successfully to the test. In spite of cold weather in December, just prior to the Christmas holidays, there was a large group of parents and board members on hand for his first closing exercises. On Christmas Day, 1868, the *Dayton Journal* reported that these exercises "proved a success worthy of the name of a genuine exhibition." The editor reminded his readers that the credit was due to the new principal. The same day, the opposition paper, the *Daily Ledger,* reported the closing exercises with the same enthusiasm and remarked in conclusion that Colonel Parker and his corps of assistants were making the First District School a "model."

Rather than oppose new or unconventional methods which the Colonel was applying, the *Dayton Journal,* on January 29 of the New Year (1869), took a page from the Colonel's new text on teaching by reporting that principals should all be held responsible for any "glaring defects" in the schools, and they should insist on practical results, not mere exhibitions of memory, cramming, and "wonderful feats of parrot-like recitations."

In December of 1868 the *Dayton Journal* had hesitated to praise Colonel Parker too highly for fear of causing dissention among the other principals. By the January 29 article, however, the *Journal* was compelled to come right out and accuse one district school of not graduating one pupil out of a hundred with a "decent hand writing." The success of the First District School was shown as an example of what could be done with new methods. What was going on in the Colonel's school could be inferred from the *Journal*'s editorial which claimed that a schoolroom should be pleasant and agreeable, that "a teacher's ability should be measured by his capacity to train up thoughtful, earnest and honest men and women, not in gaining *per cents* . . ."

If all seemed to be going well, at least with the press, there was soon to be a clash between the Colonel and his board. It came about the same time that President Andrew Johnson, after his helpless vetoes and impeachment trial, was coming to the end of his clash with Congress. On March 5, 1869, the *Dayton Journal* dismissed the former president with the notice that "Andy Johnson vetoed the Inauguration procession yesterday. He refused to ride in it, and wouldn't go to the capitol to be mustered out." In the same edition a local notice to parents read: "The introduction of the new and expensive Slate into the First District School has been against the direct vote of the Board of Education . . . ."

Three days later the *Dayton Journal* announced that there seemed to be a little "unhappiness" between the board members of the First Ward and Colonel Parker of the First District School. That "unhappiness" was over the Harper's Writing and Drawing Slate which the Colonel had apparently required of his students. Parents were said to be humoring their children but grumbling about the expense. While the *Journal* commended the board's rejection of the slate on account of expense, the editor hoped the incident would "simmer down," because Colonel Parker's services were highly valued.

In same edition of the *Dayton Journal,* however, two board members paid for a notice in order to make it clear that the board was not responsible for "inflicting a *change and* expense" upon the parents. This notice informed the public that Colonel Parker had required the slates in defiance of the board. Some members of the board, it was said, were even insulted by Principal Parker when they endeavored to learn from him by what authority he was acting. One of the men who brought this to the attention of the public was a Democrat. The issue may have been infused with politics. At least the Democrats had long opposed the expense of books as a burden on the poor, although they had not been opposed to change. Parker believed a "great book house by its agents" was responsible.[23] It is possible that board members were influenced, if not corrupted, by publishers or other business concerns that had interests in the school. It is certain that the very board member who complained the most about the slates was a recipient of school funds. He owned a construction company which received school contracts for "privy vaults."[24] It is to be wondered if he would have opposed change in such contracts, or even innovation in plumbing, as much as change or innovation in education.

The board made an official inquiry into the matter and it came out that the controversial slate had actually been tentatively approved by the board several months earlier. The Committee on Text-books opposed the recommendation on account of expense and the board then dropped its approval.[25] Parker definitely had gone ahead on his own authority.

Years later, Parker thought that the newspapers of Dayton had "poured out the vials of their wrath" against him.[26] There is no such evidence. By the end of his first year, the First District School was even highly praised by the press. It received a commendation by the president of the board. Should there be any doubt about rehiring the wilful Colonel for another year, the board had a petition of more than forty names which asked that Parker be retained.[27]

The board and press, however, did pour forth venomous wrath against the deficiencies in the lower grades. In 1869, the annual examination of applicants for admission to the high school revealed how poorly they had been prepared. The board officially announced that the examination was not a credit to the common schools. Certain exceptions, however, were established. Out of the eight applicants from Parker's First District School seven were found fully qualified. This was contrasted with one district school where only fifteen out of thirty-two were qualified, or to another school where only three out of eleven were able to achieve the minimum requirements.[28]

The *Dayton Journal* blamed a lack of uniformity in the preparation of students for this deplorable condition. On July 5, 1869, it argued that if all students had the benefit of such teaching that went on in the First District School there would have been much better results. The board believed part of the problem resulted from the lack of a superintendent and a uniform system in the schools.

The question of a superintendent was a sore point. The *Dayton Journal* found opposition centered among the teachers who did not want to be "superintended," and among certain members of the board who did not want to abdicate any power and influence. The editor believed that the "little uneasiness" between the board and Colonel Parker over school slates would not have happened if there had been a superintendent to whom all questions of policy could have been referred. The editor also brought to the attention of the public that there was hardly a village in Ohio at that time which did not have a superintendent.[29]

The poor showing on the June examinations only brought matters to a head. A month earlier the board had actually resolved on the appointment of a superintendent. It was argued that, with a payroll of almost $40,000 for teachers' salaries alone, no businessman could argue against the expense of a superintendent.[30]

As it turned out there was no opposition from the Democratic press, although it suggested "respectfully" that, in making a selection of candidates, "home talent" should not be overlooked.[31]

One of the local candidates was considered by the board at its mid-July meeting, but a motion was raised instead to elect W. E. Sheldon of Boston at a salary of $3,500 per year. The "rambling debate" which followed resulted in a postponement of election for two weeks. It is not certain whether the deadlock was political, educational, or even financial, but by the middle of August the board came up with a Mr. Alex H. Gow of Evansville, Indiana, at a "salary not yet fixed."[32]

Mr. Gow made an appearance in Dayton a few days later and spoke at the City Teachers' Institute. He made a good impression, after which Colonel Parker drilled the teachers on rhetorical selections. Unaccountably, except for "private reasons," he later declined the position. The board wired him to reconsider, but he declined emphatically, a fact which "seriously embarrassed the board of education."[33] It was almost time for school to begin for another year and the matter of a superintendent was dropped.

Unsuccessful in its attempt to improve the preparation of students through a system-wide supervision, the board was more successful in efforts to improve the quality of teaching. It had inaugurated what the *Dayton Journal* called a "fruitful era" by effecting the City Teachers' Institute. At the "auspicious" opening of this institute in April of 1869, Colonel Parker had led a group of teachers in techniques of geography teaching. The May meeting of the institute found the Colonel holding forth on "writing." In August the president of the board lectured the teachers on securing good order by kindness rather than harshness. Parker conducted exercises in arithmetic, demonstrated the usefulness of maps, and challenged the teachers to resign when they ceased to make their profession a subject of daily study.[34]

More ambitious than the institute was the proposal to establish a normal school in Dayton. The plan had been reported to the president of the board as early as May 13, 1869, at the same time that proposals for a superintendent were being entertained. The supply of teachers, as well as their quality, was possibly an issue in this proposal. The Annual Report of the State Commission of Common Schools for the year 1868 had found the pay of teachers in Dayton the lowest in Ohio for any city its size.[35] A normal school could be advocated as an economy if it would increase the supply of teachers and thereby hold down the wages they could demand.

At a special meeting of the board on August 19, 1869, the Committee on Buildings reported that the proposed normal school could be housed in a new school that was just nearing completion. It was also resolved that the normal school should be in the charge of the principal for that district school and that a committee on "Normal School and Teachers' Institute" should be established to supervise the course of study, selection of textbooks, tuition, and general administration. The length of training was proposed for one year, part of which time would be devoted to the theory of teaching and the rest to its actual practice. The training was to be free for "all qualified females of the age of sixteen and upwards," if they were residents of Dayton and agreed to teach two years in the local system. Nonresidents would be admitted for a fee of $60. In addition to these plans for a normal school, the board required all teachers to attend the City Teachers' Institutes, which, incidentally, met on Saturdays or other holidays, and teachers who were absent or tardy would be docked twice as much in wages as was usual for absence or tardiness on regular school days.[36]

It is not certain what influence the Colonel had in these developments, but he was called "the father of our Normal School" when he chose to leave Dayton several years later.[37] It is certain that, as soon as the board adopted a motion to locate the normal school in the new Sixth District school building, it approved the Colonel for its principal. The appointment of Miss Emma Brown as assistant teacher, as recommended by the Colonel, provoked one board member to fear that the normal school would become "Parkerized."[38]

The Colonel was now indeed in position to "Parkerize" the whole school system. He was principal of the normal school as well as the Sixth District School in which it was housed. The building, incidentally, was fitted for steam heat and furnished with "single" desks of black walnut. It was the pride of the community and therefore represented the confidence the board had in Parker.[39]

Before the normal school was formally opened on September 15, 1869, it had twenty-one applicants, ten of whom were graduates of the Dayton Central High School.[40] Parker was almost immediately engaged in recruiting better faculty for his staff. One candidate invited him to observe her at work in one of the schools of Lima. When he got there he was ordered out by a local official, Judge Hughes. Parker argued that he had been invited there, and the public schools were opened to anyone. The judge struck him, after being incensed by what he called Parker's insolence in words and actions.[41] The Colonel was restrained by other parties to the altercation or the judge would have been "polished off"—at least this was the opinion of the *Dayton Journal* which published the whole report on October 7, 1869. The judge, it said, was lucky to get off with "a whole skin," because the Colonel was adept in the "art of self-defense."

The incident typified the Colonel as a man of temper. No man could oppose him without expecting an open fight, but for the children he always had a "kindly smile and cordial greeting" at the door each day. It was said that he even knew all the children in his school by name. Parker's method of governing, according to the memory of former students, was based on "self-control." It was a common practice in the Sixth District School for teachers to leave their classes at times and allow the children to pursue their work unwatched—a practice considered extremely unusual to educators generally in those days.[42]

It was with the "old guard" principals and traditionalist teachers that Parker frequently lost his own self-control. Such a fracas was reported at the City Teachers' Institute in October of 1869. There was the "usual diversity of opinion," but, over the question of "object lessons" and attractive displays in schoolrooms, real "agitation" was reported. Parker battled for the children's right to think, to learn through the senses, and to have an attractive classroom.[43]

Parker later thought that all the teachers said he was wrong in his teaching.[44] He may have exaggerated. During his efforts to work out a new kind of teaching at the normal school, however, he had a good press. By 1870, early in January, the first normal school examinations were held and the *Dayton Journal* reported, on January 12, that "several very efficient teachers" were transferred thereby to positions in the district schools.

The advent of the "Gay Seventies" was said to have brought a renewal of religious faith to Dayton, as well as educational reform.[45] The Colonel would bring this faith and educational reform together. In February of 1870, a group of citizens, including Frank Parker, petitioned the pastors of the evangelical churches in Dayton to call a public meeting for the purpose of forming a Young Men's Christian Association.[46]

Parker's interest in this organization had already been developed in Manchester. For a generation that was pulling up roots and leaving the farm for the city, there was a special need for guidance. Since public education had to be nonsectarian, the Young Men's Christian Association was ideally suited to combine moral training with education. Parker's whole educational philosophy was gravitating toward a kind of religion with the school at the center of worship and salvation.

At this time Parker's own religious development appeared devout but nonsectarian. In May of 1869 he had lectured at a Sabbath School Convention, which happened to meet in a Lutheran church. He approached the teaching of the Bible as he would approach any literature. His text was the Gospel of Mark, chapter ten. He read the verses to the demonstration class. Asking that all Bibles be closed he then inquired of each member of the class what fact stuck out in his memory. He proceeded to bring out geography by asking about the positions of Jericho and Jerusalem. He asked about the purpose of Jesus' journey. He asked about the blind man, Bartimaeus, and wondered if the students could compare the blind man with sinners who were blinded with wickedness.[47] This demonstration revealed his methodology of drawing ideas from the students, then making them think about purposes, relationships, and comparisons.

In that same chapter of Mark, Jesus said: "Suffer the little children to come unto me, and forbid them not . . . . " In these words, Parker might have found a text for his whole career as a teacher.

What part Parker played in creating citizen interest in a Young Men's Christian Association is not known. A large "audience" did assemble at a public meeting in the Lutheran church on February 13, 1870. Initial steps were there taken for the formation of the "Christian Institute" and Colonel Parker was chosen secretary. It was Colonel Parker who suggested the formation of a committee from each religious congregation in the city to solicit membership.[48]

At the first regular meeting of the new society on March 1, 1870, Robert W. Steele was elected president. He was also a member of the Board of Education. At the same meeting, Frank Parker was elected vice-president, and Board of Education President, E. Morgan Wood, was elevated to the office of corresponding secretary.[49]

The newly created Young Men's Christian Association established a "reading room" in the *Dayton Journal* building. Thus Colonel Parker now had the ear of important members of the school board as well as the Republican press of Dayton.

It would be difficult to assess just how much Parker's energetic leadership in the Young Men's Christian Association helped to carry out his educational reforms. The personal contacts alone and his heightened stature in the community must have strengthened his cause immeasurably. The Young Men's Christian Association represented all "sects and persuasions" in the city except the Catholics. It had been liberally subscribed to by local citizens, and the *Dayton Journal* reported on March 19, 1870, that it would become the leading institution in Dayton.

It may have been only coincidence, but shortly after the Colonel and the president of the board were associated together in the Young Men's Christian Association, Parker's influence was extended from the student teachers to all the teachers in the school system. Until a superintendent could be found, the Committee of the Normal School was authorized to hold monthly meetings for the instruction of teachers.[50]

E. Morgan Wood, President of the Board of Education, claimed to be a strong supporter of Parker long before his connection with him in the Young Men's Christian Association. He said he helped to bring Parker to Dayton in the first place. In retrospect, Wood observed that Colonel Parker's methods in the Dayton schools were in advance of the general theory of education at that time. "I am very glad," Wood said, "that he impressed me with value of them and that I was able to stand with him in resisting the attacks upon his work . . . ."[51] It is quite likely that Parker was better able to impress the board president in those days through the informal contacts in the Young Men's Christian Association.

Whatever the opposition or attacks upon his work, Parker seemed to thrive on such agitation. In April of 1870 he became a member of the executive committee for the South-Western Ohio Teachers Association, which he may have helped to organize.[52] Back home, the benefits of the normal school were reported to be "daily becoming more apparent, especially in that these practice teachers could substitute in regular classes when teachers were ill." Observers were marveling that "not a scratch was visible upon the desks" of Parker's Sixth District School.[53] This seemed to be mute testimony for the effectiveness of Parker's unorthodox methods in governing a school.

By the end of the first year, the new Sixth District School was rated a "first class institution" by a group of visitors. They observed that "old chaps," who had been educated thirty to fifty years earlier, would find it hard to realize all the improvements effected by the Colonel. The school was actually attractive and the instruction was pleasing. Children even liked school. School was not the "irksome task" it used to be.[54]

In June of 1870 there was no sign of battle over Parker's reappointment. In July the focus of attention was the outbreak of the Franco-Prussian War in Europe. The effect on the weather of heavy cannonading was soon the topic of conversation in Dayton, as well as the educational merits of the French and Prussian schools. It was generally believed that the secret of the sweeping Prussian successes over the French was that the armies of Louis Napoleon lacked discipline and education.[55]

While the Second Empire of France was falling apart, Parker's personal life was going to pieces. "It was here," he said in his autobiographical sketch, "that my wife died and left me with a little girl."[56] That is all he said about the woman who had quietly shared his life since 1864. That is all he said about the little girl he brought into the world. It must have been painful for him to summon up the memories of that sorrowful season of life.

Phenie Parker died in Minneapolis, Minnesota, on December 6, 1870.[57] Why she went to Minneapolis is a mystery, but the place was so engraved in Parker's mind that he had it etched on her tombstone. He must have left Dayton to share with Phenie the last few months of her life in Minneapolis. There is no mention of him in Dayton at the City Teachers Institute which began in September. His absence from school was only casually reported in October when the board was called into session to raise the salary for Emma Brown while she was "acting as Principal of the Sixth District School." In November the board was asked to make a temporary appointment until the return of Colonel Parker.[58] On November 29, 1870, the *Dayton Journal* gave a long account to the meeting of the South-Western Teachers Association and Parker's name was conspicuous by its absence.

It was not until February 24, 1871, that the *Dayton Journal* reported Parker's activities in town again. There was still no accounting for his absence or a note of sympathy for his personal loss. It would almost seem that no one knew he had a wife, or that he and Phenie had been so long separated that the papers circumspectly avoided mention of her. This was unlikely. There is no question about Phenie following her husband to Dayton. As she lay dying in Minneapolis she gave Dayton as her place of permanent residence.[59] While she and her husband were out of town in November of 1870 a letter addressed to Phenie E. Parker was reported in the list of unclaimed mail at the Dayton Post Office.[60] It is curious that the letter was not properly delivered, but the fact that it was not addressed to both her and her husband or simply to Mrs. F. W. Parker might account for the mistake. Since her name was not on the subsequent "letter list" friends must have claimed the letter and even may have forwarded it to Minneapolis.

The obscurity of Phenie may be partly social and partly personal. It was customary in those days for wives to keep in the shadow of their husband's public lives. In addition, Phenie's health was delicate. She died of pulmonary consumption, and the symptoms of exhaustion, loss of weight, and coughing must have forced her into a special kind of retirement long before the final stages of the illness.[61] Parents might even have opposed the retainment of Parker if they had known his wife suffered from such a fearful and contagious disease. It is likely that Phenie went to Minneapolis for reasons of health, but it might also have been a better place for a Dayton teacher's wife to die. Parker's great love for his wife is marked by the tombstone of towering marble which he erected over her grave in Manchester, New Hampshire.

Annie was barely five years old when her mother died. She had probably been placed in the care of relatives long before her mother's wasting away reached the final agony. It is probable that there were no such relatives in Dayton so that only Parker's closest friends may have known he had a daughter. Nothing is known of Phenie's family except that it must have been from New Hampshire. Some relative might have gone to Minneapolis and thereby account for Phenie's presence there.

It is quite possible that the little girl was returned to New Hampshire even several years before her mother's death. Annie's first three years had been in a home shared with her aunts, Mary and Philinda. Mary Parker had since married John Cayzer and Philinda was wed to Nehemiah T. Folsum. The Folsum's infant son—Wayland Parker Folsum—did not survive his first year, 1870, and Annie would have been a great consolation for the grieving young parents.[62]

In any event some permanent arrangements had to be made for the little girl after her mother's death. The Colonel may have wanted to find a housekeeper and raise the child in Dayton, but he probably acquiesced to the arguments of relatives who had already become attached to Annie. They could provide a better home, and, as a school teacher, he would have long vacations in which to visit the child. It is almost certain that Annie did not live with her father. The Colonel returned to take up residence at the leading hotel in Dayton—the Beckel House. The hotel was noted for its conveniences and its "water closets" on every floor, but its four-story labyrinth of two hundred rooms was hardly suitable for a motherless child.[63]

During Parker's absence, a question had arisen in the press as to whether the public schools had perhaps been diverted, gradually, from their proper function. The legitimate object was to "impart instruction only" and not the "ornamental, or scientific branches of education." There was also some question about the broadening operations of the schools, now undertaking night classes for older students and adults.[64]

As far as Parker was concerned, the public schools were being "diverted" *too* gradually. Tradition had one of its strongest defenses in the laws which covered teacher certification. Teachers were given periodic examinations for renewal of their certification to teach. The tests were rigid, formalized and admitted only rigid and formalized teachers into the classroom. The tests were the same for teachers in the primary and secondary levels, obviously working a hardship on the primary school teachers who had not been exposed to as much rote learning as those in the high schools. It would be difficult to determine the qualifications of either a primary or secondary teacher for anything but rote teaching when examination questions went something like this:

Question: What race of men inhabit the South Sea Islands?
Answer: The Sandwiches; they have the Gospel preached to.
Question: Of what is the earth composed?
Answer: Of land and water.[65]

In March of 1871 the Colonel balked at such tests and refused to take his regular renewal of certification exam. Perhaps this was only another example of his fearless stand for what he believed was right; or he might have put his job on the line because his career in Dayton was of less importance to him now that it separated him from his little daughter. Nevertheless, Parker's action led to a special meeting of the board in order to issue an order for his salary. The board believed it could pay him without a suspension of its rules, but it did not approve an authorization to waive the requirement for the two-year certificate issued by the Board of Examiners.[66]

It is not known whether the Colonel was later forced to take an examination, but he had the satisfaction of hearing President Wood defend his action. Wood explained to the public that under the present laws all teachers must obtain certificates from the County Board of Examiners, and he called for better laws in the certification of teachers.[67]

Rejecting tests for himself, the Colonel also rejected tests and grading for the students. Later that same March he refused to use the prescribed cards of attendance, deportment, and recitations, as instructed by the board. It took another board meeting to direct him to conform.[68]

The normal school, under its recalcitrant principal, continued to get a good word from the press. It was even receiving commendations from visiting educators.[69] Special attention was drawn to the "Kindergarten," which was called a "philosophical playroom." Instruction was through "sport and trifles." It was based, according to the *Herald,* June 27, 1871, on the "celebrated German system, but has been Americanized."

The second year of the normal school closed in June of 1871 with an exhibition of "object lessons," as well as other innovations. Such methods were reported by the *Dayton Journal,* on June 29, 1871, to be a puzzle to "old fogies" but a grand invention for children. The next day the president of the board confided, in the *Dayton Journal,* that when the normal school had been proposed there were some members of the board who thought this new branch of the school system would be an "expensive luxury." The president now could reveal that the board was convinced no mistake had been made.

Before the school year was quite completed, the board was again seeking a superintendent. The office of "Supervising Principal," however, was agreed upon and a candidate determined. Colonel Parker was the unanimous choice of the board to fill this new position at a salary of $2,000.[70]

As "Supervising Principal" Parker began his fourth school year in Dayton. His duties began early in August of 1871 at the County Teachers' Institute. He was one of the directors. It was at this time that he learned Warren Higley, formerly a high school principal in Cleveland, Ohio, had been elected Superintendent of Dayton schools.[71]

After the sessions of the County Teachers' Institute, the City Teachers' Institute convened in Dayton on September 4. At that time the Colonel introduced the new superintendent to the gathering of about one hundred teachers. On the last day of the institute, when Superintendent Higley presented a list of resolutions he hoped to carry out, Colonel Parker sprang to his feet and moved for their adoption. He said that, of the three years he had labored in Dayton, this day had given him the greatest satisfaction.[72]

It was either a happy coincidence or a matter of design that the board had found a superintendent with educational slants that parallelled those of Parker. To the principals and teachers of Dayton, many of whom must have ridiculed and opposed the Colonel's ideas, the new superintendent said that Parker's methods were now "accepted by the foremost educators of the age."[73]

The superintendent and supervising principal worked well together and Parker may have benefited greatly from the experience of his superior officer, even though the Colonel operated mainly at the management and examination of the lower grades while Higley concentrated on the upper.[74]

These efforts at reconstructing the school system of Dayton had hardly begun when Parker got word of an inheritance which would equal two and a half times his annual salary. His aunt, Mary Parker Harris, died in Manchester on September 23, 1871. She was sixty-five and had long been confined to her house with dropsy. Her death must not have been a surprise to Parker, but the $5,000 she bequeathed to him, with a like amount going to each of his sisters, was probably unexpected. She had been the wealthy widow of a banker and had no children of her own, but it had been generally believed that she would leave everything to her husband's side of the family because he had earned the money.[75]

While the Colonel was no doubt rejoicing over this good fortune, Dayton was going wild over the visit of President Ulysses S. Grant. On October 3, 1871, the President and his family registered at the Beckel House where the Colonel was in residence. It was here that a "levee" was held for the President, with a grand reception, which ended in a delegation of "school ma'ams." Although it was said that "everyone was there," no mention was made of a meeting between the Colonel and the General under whom he had served at the battle of Cold Harbor.[76]

The bitter controversy of political "Reconstruction" was then at its worst and Parker may have wanted to avoid taking sides. He must have realized by then that the public schools could best be served by those who were not aligned, either in politics or in sectarian religion.

On October 7, 1871, the *Herald* charged that Grant's visit in Dayton was only to meddle in local politics. It also took the occasion to blame Grant for running a corrupt political machine in Washington. The *Herald* had replaced the *Daily Ledger* in Dayton and was just as "radically Democratic in principle." C. L. Vallandigham had been the publisher of the *Daily Ledger* which characterized its rival newspaper as the "dirty Journal," representative of "lawlessness, dirt, indecency and disorganization." It was Vallandigham who had been such a dangerous "copperhead" during the Civil War that he had to be arrested. Dayton was so full of people with similar sentiments that a riot followed and the office of the *Dayton Journal,* Republican newspaper, was destroyed.[77]

While the *Dayton Journal* supported the military reconstruction of the South, the Democratic newspaper opposed it and even considered the "Loyal League" more dangerous than the "Ku-Klux bogy."

It is obvious that the Colonel would want to keep himself and the schools out of such bitter controversy. He did not even make his opinions known when the Democratic paper exhorted its readers in October of 1871 to vote against any man who would send their children to school with Negroes. It is true that some radical Republicans had campaigned for integration of the schools, but, although the Republicans were in control of Dayton, the Negroes had their own separate school. When the average attendance of that school was as low as twenty, the Board even recommended that it be closed. It is not certain whether the board intended to integrate these Negro children or to neglect their education completely. This recommendation was put on file and apparently forgotten as a later report accounted for forty-one colored students enrolled and a 91 per cent attendance.[78]

It is unlikely that the Colonel took any stand on the racial integration of schools, but he may have worked at making the curriculum more practical and attractive for the Negro children, thus increasing attendance at their school. Parker had been intimately acquainted with integration from the beginning. He had gone to school with a Negro child in New Hampshire.[79] He was on Port Royal Island when the Emancipation Proclamation, freeing the slaves in the disloyal states, was read to the troops on the first day of 1863. The fires of New Years' Eve were smoldering in the pits, the roasted beeves of celebration were consumed to the bone, and the war which had been a rebellion on the night before was now a social revolution. "My country, 'tis of thee . . . ." rang out among the Negro troops stationed on the island with Parker. Even then, Parker may have been convinced that education was the only salvation for the Negro people. He probably noticed the attempt of one Negro regiment on Port Royal to have a schoolhouse. He may have observed the eagerness with which the Negroes sought the spelling book.[80] Later, he saw the valor of these Negro troops in the battles for Fort Wagner and Petersburg.

On March 16, 1869, Parker must have read the "Penalties of Rebellion—From Wealth to Utter Poverty—the surviving family of the Greatest Slaveholder of the South in a Poor House," which appeared in the *Dayton Journal.* Hilton Head Island had been owned by this "greatest slaveholder of the South," and he escaped to the mainland just before Parker and the New Hampshire Fourth captured the island in 1862. For the slaves left behind it seemed "de judgment day." That there was something revolutionary in the air, along with the Negro hosannas to liberty, must have struck Parker as early as 1862. Now, in 1869, he read that the former owner of Hilton Head had died. One of his sons was killed in the war, his wife and daughter-in-law were now in a Charleston almshouse and his surviving son was only a driver on one of the Charleston street cars. An age had passed. Parker and his men on Hilton Head had helped to bury it. In Dayton, Parker saw that the future of the Negro in American society was still unsettled. Whatever Parker's beliefs about racial integration at that time, the radicals in the Republican party were losing the peace that followed their successful war to free the slaves. The appeal for school integration at home may have especially weakened them. By 1871 the Democratic newspaper in Dayton could report that the *Dayton Journal* was one of the very few "trooly loil" radically Republican papers left in Ohio.[81]

Although the Democratic and Republican newspaper inveighed against each other over the reconstruction of the Union, there was no such division in regard to the reconstruction of the common schools. Both newspapers led sacred cows of traditional education to slaughter in the attempt to make common schools more amenable to an industrial society. While the Republican newspaper supported Parker's reforms, the Democratic newspaper concurred and even suggested more radical changes. It called especially for "craft-schools" in order "to remedy this unfitness for life with which our education leaves our youth." It argued that a blacksmith should be able to drive home a "horse-nail" as well as an argument in metaphysics, and that a dentist should extract molars as well as "hidden Greek roots."[82] The Democratic press also questioned the propriety of "marks, prizes, and awards."[83] The *Daily Ledger* argued, on November 21,1871, that play was useful in instruction and that toys could be good teachers. To what extent Parker influenced such newspaper remarks or was influenced by them is unanswerable, but the keel was laid in Dayton for much of the new education which Parker was about to launch for the whole nation.

His days in Dayton were now numbered. In November of 1871 he interrupted his work and set out for New Hampshire to attend his mother's illness. She died on November 30, shortly after his arrival. He was back in Dayton within a week, and the sympathy he received in the press at this time makes absence of such concern for his wife's death the previous December all the more extraordinary.[84] He was probably back in New Hampshire for the Christmas vacation. In January of 1872 he acquired title to a cemetery lot in the graveyard where his parents lay.[85] This, as well as the extravagant marble monument for his wife's final resting place, was probably financed through his recent inheritance. It may have been at this time that he decided to bury his past in Dayton and seek a new life and career elsewhere.

On January 18, 1872, it was reported in the *Dayton Journal* that Parker would remain at his post as supervising principal only until the close of the school year. It was added that this announcement disappointed his students, and let some of them to defer graduation from January to June.

Precisely why Parker wanted to leave Dayton, which was just beginning to accept the reforms for which he had been fighting, is a matter of conjecture. His rising fortunes there may have even inspired him to seek greater worlds to conquer. That he had confidence in himself—perhaps a little too much—was the considered opinion of E. M. Wood, President of the Board of Education.[86]

Parker's immediate objective in resigning was to free himself for study in Germany at the University of Berlin. He had always wanted to go to college and had been preparing to do so at the time the Civil War interrupted his plans. When the war was over, he had family responsibilities and could not go.[87]

E. M. Wood believed Parker chose a German education in order to compare his own theories with those of Froebel. He believed it was the opposition Parker received in Dayton that made him want to pursue an academic degree.[88]

Parker himself said he feared, at least inwardly, that he might be wrong in his teaching theories. He sought confirmation. He was also sensitive to the taunts of teachers and principals who had drawn attention to his poor educational background. They had, in fact accused him of being an "illiterate man."[89] If it mattered more where a man matriculated than what he advocated, Parker's decision to leave Dayton was probably largely motivated by a desire to get his academic credentials in order. He could find no better source of educational prestige than in Germany.

Parker was not the only one to be leaving the school system. The teacher turnover was always a problem. The Colonel pictured the "terrible distress" of his "school teacheresses" which made them "marry to get out of their misery." This way of leaving the labors of the schoolroom, Parker cracked at a meeting of the County Teachers' Association in March of 1872, was like jumping into the water to get out of the rain.[90]

At the same time Parker described his work as the "Educational New Departure." He stressed that parents should be "made of more" by the teachers in the effort to win approval of this new and better method of teaching. He indicated that it was only a minority which delighted in "pulling down" the progress of schools. Teachers, he said, could count on the right judgment of the people if the community were only properly addressed.

Before the "new departure" was even fully articulated it was time for the Colonel to depart for Germany. The board marked the end of his stay with a "private and confidential" meeting. It was also reported in the *Dayton Journal* on June 29, 1872, that the Colonel would be missed, not only for his educational efforts but for his "religious and benevolent labors" as well. The *Journal* reflected on the Colonel's hard fight to overcome the prejudices which "attached like barnacles to the older methods," but Parker's "indomitable energy and enthusiasm" were said to have "carried the day." It was mentioned, however, that he would leave enemies behind.

The "new departure" had a long way to go, but as Parker set sail for Germany he let it be known that he believed he would live long enough to see his theories "universally acknowledged."[91]

NOTES

[1] *Dayton Public Schools—Annual Report of the Board of Education for the School Year Ending June 30, 1872* (Dayton, Ohio: United Brethern Publishing House, 1873), p. 35; *Dayton Public Schools—Annual Report of the Board of Education for the School Year Ending August 31, 1867* (Dayton, Ohio: Journal Book and Job Rooms, 1868), p. 29; *Dayton Directory, 1870–71* (Dayton, Ohio: A. Bailey, Publishers, 1870), p. 5; A. W. Drury, *History of the City of Dayton and Montgomery County, Ohio,* Vol. I (Chicago: S. J. Clarke Publishing Co., 1909), p. 443.

[2] *Dayton Public Schools—Annual Report . . . August 31, 1867,* p. 3.

[3] "The School Question," *Dayton Journal* (Dayton, Ohio), March 19, 1868.

[4] "Editorial," *Daily Ledger* (Dayton, Ohio), November 16, 1868.

[5] *Dayton Public Schools—Annual Report . . . August 31, 1867,* p. 3.

[6] "Our Common Schools," *Daily Ledger,* December 22, 1868.

[7] "Union Schools," *Dayton Journal,* May 4, 1869.

[8] *Dayton Directory, 1870–71,* p. 205.

[9] A. W. Drury, *op. cit.,* p. 614; *Dayton Public Schools—Annual Report . . . August 31, 1867,* p. 3.

[10] *Dayton Public Schools—Annual Report of the Board of Education for the School Year Ending August 31, 1875,* (Dayton, Ohio: Journal Book and Job Rooms, 1876), pp. 14–15; A. W. Drury, *op. cit.,* p. 443; "The School Question."

[11] *Dayton Public Schools—Annual Report . . . August 31, 1867,* frontispiece; "Estimated value of Church, School, Asylum, and other public buildings . . . in Dayton," *Dayton Journal,* September 27, 1870.

[12] Francis W. Parker, "Autobiographical Sketch," an appendix to William M. Giffin, *School Days in the Fifties* (Chicago: A. Flanagan Co., 1906), p. 126.

[13] "Dayton Public Schools," *Dayton Journal,* July 24, 1869.

[14] *Dayton Public Schools—Annual Report . . . August 31, 1867,* p. 11.

[15] Francis W. Parker, *op. cit.,* pp. 127–128.

[16] *Dayton Public Schools—Annual Report . . . August 31, 1867,* p. 12.

[17] *Ibid.,* p. 18.

[18] *Ibid.,* p. 30; "The Deportment Question in the Public Schools," *Dayton Journal,* March 8, 1871.

[19] *Dayton Public Schools—Annual Report . . . August 31, 1867,* pp. 31, 37.

[20] Francis W. Parker, *op. cit.,* p. 127.

[21] *Ibid.,* p. 128.

[22] *Dayton Public Schools—Annual Report . . . August 31, 1867,* p. 9.

[23] Francis W. Parker, *op. cit.,* pp. 127, 128.

[24] "Notice," *Dayton Journal,* July 29, 1869.

[25] "Board of Education," *Dayton Journal,* March 12, 1869; "City Matters: Proceedings on the Slate," *Dayton Journal,* March 29, 1869.

[26] Francis W. Parker, *op. cit.,* pp. 127, 128.

[27] "Board of Education," *Dayton Journal,* July 3, 1869.

[28] "Our Public Schools," *Dayton Journal,* July 5, 1869.

[29] *Dayton Journal,* July 9, 1869; February 18, 1869; March 8, 1869.

[30] *Dayton Journal,* May 13 and 14, 1869.

[31] "The Superintendent Question," *Daily Ledger,* July 19, 1869.

[32] *Ibid.; Dayton Journal,* July 20, 1869, and August 13, 1869.

[33] "School Matters," *Daily Ledger,* August 25, 1869; *Dayton Journal,* August 19, 1869, and August 25, 1869.

[34] *Dayton Journal,* April 19, May 24, August 14, and August 17, 1869.

[35] *Dayton Journal,* May 7 and 14, 1869.

[36] "City Matters," *Dayton Journal,* August 29, 1869.

[37] "Colonel F. W. Parker," *Dayton Journal,* June 29, 1872.

[38] *Dayton Journal,* August 20 and 26, 1869.

[39] *Dayton Journal,* March 17, 1868; February 22, 1869; April 9, 1902.

[40] "City Summary," *Dayton Journal,* September 8, 1869.

[41] "The Other Side of a Personal Matter," *Dayton Journal,* October 25, 1869.

[42] "Parker . . . Memorial Meeting," *Dayton Journal,* April 9, 1902.

[43] "Teachers' Institutes and Teaching," *Daily Ledger,* October 30, 1869; "City Matters," *Dayton Journal,* October 28, 1869.

[44] Francis W. Parker, *op. cit.,* pp. 128, 129.

[45] Charlotte Reeve Conover (Ed.), *Dayton and Montgomery County, Resources and People* (New York: Lewis Historical Publishing Co., 1932), p. 135.

[46] "Young Men's Christian Association," *Dayton Journal,* February 11, 1870.

[47] "City Matters, Sabbath School Convention," *Dayton Journal,* May 17, 1869.

[48] "Young Men's Christian Association," *Dayton Journal,* February 14, 1870.

[49] "Young Men's Christian Association," *Dayton Journal,* March 2, 1870.

[50] "City Matters, Board of Education, End of Ancient Regime," *Dayton Journal,* April 15, 1870.

[51] "Parker . . . Memorial Meeting."

[52] "South-Western Ohio Teachers' Association Meeting in Hamilton, Butler County," *Herald* (Dayton, Ohio), April 25, 1870.

[53] "City Matters, Sixth District School," *Dayton Journal,* April 2, 1870.

[54] "Sixth District School," *Dayton Journal,* June 18, 1870.

[55] *Dayton Journal,* July 9, 1870; October 13, 1870; October 18, 1870; "Why the Prussians Beat the French," *Herald,* December 28, 1871. Parker's reappointment had been listed in the *Herald* on June 23, 1870. The *Dayton Journal* apologized on June 25, 1870, for omitting Parker's name on the list of reappointed principals published on June 23, 1870.

[56] Francis W. Parker, *op. cit.,* p. 128.

[57] "Certificate of Death, E. Parker," City of Minneapolis, Division of Public Health, Vital Statistics, Vol. I, registered no. page 10.

[58] *Dayton Journal,* October 7, 1870, and November 11, 1870.

[59] "Certificate of Death, E. Parker."

[60] "Letter List, Official Publication," *Dayton Journal,* November 2, 1870.

[61] "Certificate of Death, E. Parker."

[62] *History of Bedford, New Hampshire from 1737, Being Statistics Compiled on the Occasion of the One Hundredth and Fiftieth Anniversary of the Incorporation of the Town, May 15, 1900* (Concord, N.H.: The Rumford Printing Co., 1903), p. 1027; Augustus G. Parker (compiler), *Parker in America, 1630–1910* (Buffalo, N.Y.: Niagara Frontier Publishing Co., n.d.) p. 475; "Cemetery Inscriptions of Manchester, New Hampshire" (unpublished, copied by W.P.A., 1938), New Hampshire Historical Society, Concord, N.H.

[63] *Williams' Dayton Directory for 1871–1872* (Dayton, Ohio: Williams and Co., Publishers, 1871), p. 220; *Dayton Journal,* August 5, 1869 and September 27, 1870.

[64] "The Schools Again," *Dayton Journal,* December 15, 1870; "Opening of the City Night Schools," *Herald,* November 4, 1871.

[65] "Teachers' Examinations," *Dayton Journal,* February 6, 1869.

[66] "Important to Teachers," *Dayton Journal,* March 14, 1871.

[67] "Report from E. Morgan Wood: Need for a New Law," *Herald,* April 14, 1871.

[68] "Board of Education," *Dayton Journal,* March 24, 1871.

[69] "Normal School," *Dayton Journal,* April 14, 1871.

[70] *Dayton Public Schools—Annual Report of the Board of Education for the School Year Ending June 30, 1872* (Dayton, Ohio: United Brethren Publishing House, 1873) p. 157; "Important Action of the Board of Education," *Dayton Journal,* June 23, 1871.

[71] *Dayton Journal,* August 4 and 7, 1871.

[72] *Dayton Journal,* September 5 and 9, 1871.

[73] "Board of Education," *Herald,* October 28, 1871.

[74] "The Supervising Principal," *Herald,* October 28, 1871. Parker later claimed he "stole" some of his ideas from "Cleveland" in remarks at the National Educational Association. See *Journal of Proceedings and Addresses, 1880,* p. 49.

[75] "Death of Mrs. Harris," *Mirror and Farmer* (Manchester, N.H.), September 30, 1871; "The Harris Estate," *Daily Mirror and American* (Manchester, N.H.), September 29, 1871.

[76] "Grant Reception in Dayton," *Herald,* October 3, 1871; "President

Grant registered himself and family at the Beckel House yesterday," *Dayton Journal,* October 4, 1871.

[77] "Grant Meddling with an ordinary state election," *Herald,* October 7, 1871; "Editorial," *Daily Ledger,* July 1, 1868; Louis W. Koenig, "The Most Unpopular Man in the North," *American Heritage,* **15** (February 1964), 82.

[78] *Herald,* October 3, 1871; March 23, 1872; February 23, 1872; June 17, 1872.

[79] Francis W. Parker, *op. cit.,* p. 115.

[80] Thomas Wentworth Higginson, *Army Life in a Black Regiment* (Boston: Beacon Press, 1962) pp. 23–25. [Higginson was on Port Royal Island at the same time Parker was stationed there.]

[81] "Editorial," *Herald,* March 15, 1871.

[82] "Craft-Schools Wanted," *Herald,* April 26, 1872.

[83] "School Reform," *Daily Ledger,* March 2, 1869.

[84] "City Matters," *Dayton Journal,* December 8, 1871; "Cemetery Inscriptions of Manchester, New Hampshire."

[85] Estate of Francis W. Parker, Box 65–297, No. 81, May 1902, Probate Court of Cook County, Chicago, Illinois.

[86] "Parker . . . Memorial Meeting."

[87] Francis W. Parker, *op. cit.,* p. 129.

[88] "Parker . . . Memorial Meeting."

[89] Francis W. Parker, *op. cit.,* p. 129.

[90] "Montgomery County Teachers' Association," *Herald,* March 30, 1872.

[91] "Colonel F. W. Parker—at the private and confidential meeting held by the Board of Education on Monday night," *Dayton Journal,* June 29, 1872.

VI

The Student Pedagogue in Bismarck's Germany

The Berlin to which Parker came in 1872 was the capital of the German Empire, hammered together only two summers earlier on the battlefields of France. In those days of national triumph under William I, it is little wonder that Parker thought he had come to study at the "University of King William in Berlin."[1] Actually, he was at the University of Berlin, founded several generations earlier during the reign of Frederick William III of Prussia.

Admission to the university did not require the *Testimonium maturitatis* of a German gymnasium, although admission without it would not guarantee the right of state examinations or entrance to the learned professions of Germany. More interested in a foreigner's passport than in his academic credentials, the "Secretariat" of admissions would not be concerned about Parker's sketchy academic background. One simply paid his fees and received a certificate of matriculation.[2]

Although students were allowed freedom in choosing courses and professors, it was customary to pursue a special field of study. Parker's selection of courses must have appeared irregular to the university officials. No evidence remains to indicate what specific courses Parker chose, but he was told that they did not lead to any degree. "But they do lead to the children of America," Parker is alleged to have said.[3] This was surely his sentiment, whether he ever expressed it in so many words. What remained of his inheritance would not provide for the three to five years of study generally required for a degree.[4] He could only afford to follow an education motivated by genuine interest. Such freedom to learn, unburdened with marks and degrees, was what Parker had been advocating in America. The idea of "forced study" was also inconceivable to the Germans at the university level, where *Lernfreiheit,* the freedom of the learner, was built into the system.[5]

Parker could have sampled the geography of Müller, the history of Ranke, the physics of Helmholtz.[6] It is probable that he did study psychology and history, as well as philosophy and pedagogics.[7] He must have been especially attracted to Friedrich Harms, one of the last Hegelian professors at Berlin in those days. Harms believed philosophers should turn to the understanding of education, which, he said, was the greatest of all human endeavors.[8] At least it is known that Parker studied with a "direct pupil of Hegel."[9] Although it was said that Parker had a "markedly un-Hegelian type of mind," there was something of Hegel's World Spirit which ran through Parker's belief that God was working out man's character through the school. Parker also viewed history as the struggle between two ideals. One ideal, the thesis, was rule of the many by the few. The antithesis was the ideal of society ruling itself. The conflict between these two ideals was basically an educational conflict—the education of what Parker called "limitation" against the education of "freedom."[10]

An education of "limitation" was to make people believe they were educated but at the same time leave them unable to question or think freely. This was achieved by the method of "Quantity" teaching, through word-cramming, memorizing textbooks by the page, keeping the mind from "looking outside a certain definite circle." Colleges set the standards by demanding quantity. They asked of applicants, "But how many pages have you learned? Have you read Virgil? Xenophon? Homer? Come in and learn more words."[11]

The education of "freedom" was achieved by what Parker called "Quality" methods, based on "self-effort" and "original inference." Object-lessons, investigation, experiment, liberty to think, all were such techniques of Quality teaching. It was this kind of teaching which Parker believed was developing the "perturbed spirit." This spirit was the real spectre haunting Europe.[12] Marx had borrowed from Hegel the material concepts of development. Parker had borrowed the concepts that eternity is quality, as well as growth and change.[13] Unlike Marx, who considered class cleavage to be the *result* of exploitation, Parker saw it as the *means* of exploitation. The method was simply to divide and conquer, to shut groups within themselves in cultural stagnation. This was achieved through separate channels of education. "Class isolation," Parker argued, had been fixed by "class education."[14]

Even while Parker studied Hegel at the University of Berlin, the younger generation there was beginning to look at Hegelians as though they were "old fossils."[15] There were competing philosophies. There was a questioning of absolutes. It was probably due to the work of Herbart and his disciples that Parker found pedagogics treated as a science in Germany.[16] He discovered that in the "zeal for true methods, and in contempt for mere book-cramming," Germany was far ahead of America.[17] By the time Parker matriculated the disputation and lecture were still standard procedures, but the seminar, stressing student activity rather than that of the teacher, was beginning to take their place.[18] The Germans had experienced such methods of self-activity in the elementary schools where the influence of Pestalozzi and Froebel had reached.

Perhaps it was in pursuit of some seminar project that Parker investigated the miracle of child gardening in Berlin. He said he became quite familiar with the work of the kindergarten there, and he may even have visited Frau Froebel who was still living.[19] Through the study of Froebel, at least, he learned of "the harmonious development of the human being; body, mind, and soul."[20] He also gained a new dimension in the understanding of "object teaching." From the German term, *Anschauungsunterricht,* literally "seeing teaching," he found there was more to object teaching than simply bringing objects before the child's senses. Teaching must present objects to the reference of the child's "mental sight."[21]

Parker's first lessons in Germany, however, were probably not in the university or kindergartens of Berlin. They were on the parade grounds of Spandau, a few miles west of Berlin. It was there, early in September of 1872, which must have been shortly after his arrival, that he saw "twenty-five thousand Prussians in the field, reviewed by three emperors."[22] Francis-Joseph of Austria-Hungary and Alexander II of Russia were then in Berlin on state visits. The glittering of bayonettes and brass buttons may have impressed the royal visitors of William I, but they did not blind Parker to the harsh military subordination of the individual. Parker had been a soldier himself, and, although he looked back with pride on his military career, he knew it was not an "education."[23] It appeared to Parker that a Prussian officer was "generally a perfect illustration of trained precision—stiff, ungainly, and abnormally precise—a machine rather than a man."[24]

It seemed to Parker that large standing armies were more of a means to suppress the personal right of choice than to defend the nation against foreign foes.[25] The army was a school for training the automaton that Parker saw parading in review.

One lance-corporal, who was lost in the pageantry of plumes and gold braid that day on the parade grounds of Spandau, was Friedrich Paulsen. In a matter of three years he would be teaching at the University of Berlin. That night he marched off to a supper of boiled mutton and carrots that was "dished up in large milk tubs." He fell asleep amid straw in a sheep barn. If Parker and Paulsen ever met personally, the American would not have found this young Prussian "a machine rather than a man." Parker, however, would have wondered why a man of such education could remain a "monarchist." Of "monarchial rule and military authority" Paulsen was always convinced, even when he dazzled the intellectual world with his lectures and seminars on philosophy and pedagogy. Although Paulsen said he leaned toward democracy, his concept of it was simply a paternalistic kind of sympathy for the people.[26]

Parker never doubted that the best psychology and the best pedagogy came from Germany.[27] He did wonder why these superior methods of teaching did not produce advocates of democracy and equality. Why was the individual suppressed in Germany? Parker searched for an answer. He found German authoritarianism was fixed in their history and in the organization of their schools.

During the revolutions that jarred the monarchies of Europe from the fall of the Bastille to the fall of Napoleon, Parker found German schools were being used as a "regenerating force." The teachings of Pestalozzi were accepted and Quality teaching was admitted into the schools. By the time Napoleon was safely exiled, however, the aristocrats discovered that the people were actually thinking. The people even thought they were the equals of the aristocrats. The Prussian minister of education was then instructed to return the schools to what Parker called "Quantity" teaching. After the liberals tried unsuccessfully to restore freedom in 1848, even the kindergarten was interdicted as subversive. From "first to last," Parker learned, "the education of Prussia has wavered between autocracy and democracy, between quantity and quality . . . ."[28]

It was Bismarck who finally lifted the restrictions on Quality teaching, and Parker believed it was the impact of this education that gave the Germans their recent victories over the French. Bismarck was, Parker said, the greatest statesman of the day, even though he was an absolute monarchist.[29]

If Quality teaching allowed the individual to seek truth for himself, how could Bismarck maintain a rigid autocracy? Parker believed the explanation was not in methods alone but in the state system of education. The Germans were superior to the Americans in their Quality teaching but not in their system. It was not from Germany that America got the "common school," Parker said. The "common school" was born of democracy. Germany had its compulsory mass education, but the lower classes had separate schools. Even though the university did draw from various social classes, Parker found that "class" or "sectarian" feeling was too strong to change by the time a student reached the university level.[30]

Parker saw that German schools also isolated the sexes. He said there was no education possible for free men without coeducation. Coeducation was one of the few educational innovations which Parker said did not come from Germany.[31]

The form or structure of the educational system was thus more important than its methods of instruction. Perhaps this was the most significant lesson of all that Parker learned in Germany. He saw that the democratic ideal could triumph only through the education of all children together.

He probably brought the superiority of the American "common school' to the attention of his German acquaintances. At least he said that Americans were generally noted for their "boasting propensities" and he tried not to speak about how much better things were in America. He was also distressed that the Europeans saw America only through "Mrs. Trollope's Travels," or "Cooper's Indians," or through the "Tammany rings, Credit Mobilier, and railroad accidents."[32]

One evening at a supper for boys in Berlin, however, he was not taken for an American at all. The boys stood up when he entered because they mistook him for Bismarck.[33] Such a mistake was not unreasonable. Like the Iron Chancellor, Parker was balding, mustached, and was similar in massive features. He, too, created the impression of a "colossal" man.[34] This resemblance to Bismarck might have made him feel more at home in Berlin, but he was not always at home there. He visited the schools of Switzerland, France, Italy, and Holland. He singled out the schools of Switzerland and France as superior to those in America.[35]

In late September of 1873 he visited the much celebrated Vienna Exhibition where he spent eight days "looking" until his eyes grew tired. The exhibition, he said, was the "World illustrated," and "a world in miniature." It was what he called "object teaching of the highest and best kind." He said that books failed and history was meagre compared to these concrete illustrations.[36]

His greatest disappointment was with the American exhibit. "Oh! Ye Gods . . ." was his comment when he sent back a report to the *Dayton Journal* in Ohio. "One could not blame a sharp observer," he said, "if he decided, after carefully inspecting our department, that we are occupied mostly in killing hogs and making sewing and mowing machines and soda fountains." He found no order or taste in the American exhibit. It was more like "a bachelor's clothes closet." He was also appalled at the dominant materialism and the sales pitches that seemed to put price-tags on everything. The railroads, especially, had taken advantage of the exhibition to attract immigrants and sell the undeveloped land through which their tracks ran.

In his correspondence with the *Dayton Journal,* published on October 14, 1873, Parker said the school exhibition was the best part of the American show, although it failed to convey the one great contribution of American education—its system of common schools for all, without a cent of tuition.

Parker had undoubtedly made the arrangements for submitting examples of student work to this show even before leaving Dayton. At least the Vienna Exhibition had been heralded in Dayton for many months before he left.[37] It was now the main purpose of his correspondence with the *Dayton Journal* to report to the children that their "examination papers" had received a "mark of honor" at the Vienna Exhibition. He added that seeing those papers made him recall "the bright eyes and happy faces of the writers."

Parker must have been yearning for home. He said that every day made him prouder of his own country.[38] Nevertheless, he stayed on another year and booked passage for home in the winter of 1874–1875, after more than two years abroad. He could now return with confirmation of some of his theories regarding natural methods of education. He brought back questions about the relation of education to democracy. Most of all, perhaps, he brought back a "suspicion *(eine Ahnung)* of the truth."[39]

NOTES

[1] Francis W. Parker, "Autobiographical Sketch," an appendix to William M. Giffin, *School Days in the Fifties* (Chicago: A. Flanagan Co., 1906), p. 129.

[2] Friedrich Paulsen, *The German Universities, Their Character and Historical Development* (New York: Macmillan, 1895), p. 176; Lincoln Steffens, *An Autobiography of Lincoln Steffens* (New York: Harcourt, Brace, 1931), pp. 132–133.

[3] Francis W. Parker, *op. cit.,* p. 137.

[4] In addition to the length of time generally required for a degree, it was estimated that expenses ran between $250 and $500 for each term. Friedrich Paulsen, *op. cit.,* p. 186.

[5] *Ibid.,* pp. 201–202.

[6] *Ibid.,* pp. 215–216; Friedrich Paulsen, *An Autobiography* (New York: Columbia University Press, 1938), p. 214.

[7] Marion Foster Washburne, "Col. Francis W. Parker: The Man and Educational Reformer," *Francis Wayland Parker: His Life and Educational Reform Work, Souvenir Issued in Honor of the Silver Anniversary of the Quincy Movement* (New York: E. L. Kellogg and Co., 1900), p. 17.

[8] Nicholas Murray Butler, "Foreword," in Friedrich Paulsen, *An Autobiography,* p. vi.

[9] Parker told this to Amalie Hoffer in her article, "The Chicago Normal

Training School—A Dream Come True," *Kindergarten Magazine,* **9** (November 1896), 176.

[10] Marion Foster Washburne, *op. cit.,* p. 17; Francis W. Parker, *Talks on Pedagogics, An Outline of the Theory of Concentration,* (New York: E. L. Kellogg and Co., 1894), pp. 25, 348–349, 401; Col. F. W. Parker, "The Conflict of the Two Ideals," Parker Scrapbooks, 1884, Archives, Harper Library, University of Chicago.

[11] Francis W. Parker, *Talks on Pedagogics,* pp. 408, 440.

[12] *Ibid.,* pp. 408, 409, 414.

[13] *Ibid.,* p. 398.

[14] *Ibid.,* pp. 405, 406.

[15] Friedrich Paulsen, *An Autobiography,* p. 215.

[16] Amalie Hoffer, *op. cit.,* 176.

[17] F. W. Parker, "European Correspondence," *Dayton Journal,* Dayton, Ohio, October 14, 1873.

[18] Friedrich Paulsen, *The German Universities,* p. 141.

[19] Francis W. Parker, "Autobiographical Sketch," p. 129; Francis W. Parker, "Froebel's Life Work," Parker Scrapbooks, 1891 [probably Dec. 20.].

[20] F. W. Parker, "Froebel's Idea of Education" [Talk II], unpublished manuscript, p. 1, Topping Collection, 1325 Stonybrook Lane, Mountainside, N.J.

[21] F. W. Parker, "The Schoolroom as Workshop," *New England Journal of Education,* **5** (January 18, 1877), 32.

[22] F. W. Parker, "Order" [Talk IV], unpublished manuscript, p. 6, Topping Collection.

[23] *Ibid.*

[24] Francis W. Parker, Talks on Pedagogics, p. 265.

[25] *Ibid.,* p. 404.

[26] Friedrich Paulsen, *An Autobiography,* pp. 221–222, 230.

[27] Francis W. Parker, "Discussion of Prof. Richard Jones' German Methods of Using the Mother Tongue," *Journal of Proceedings and Addresses, National Educational Association, 1894,* p. 483.

[28] Francis W. Parker, *Talks on Pedagogics,* pp. 410–414.

[29] *Ibid.,* p. 414; Col. F. W. Parker, "The Conflict of the Two Ideals."

[30] Francis W. Parker, "Discussion of Prof. Richard Jones' German Methods of Using the Mother Tongue," p. 483; Francis W. Parker, *Talks on Pedagogics,* p. 406; Friedrich Paulsen, *The German Universities,* p. 111.

[31] Francis W. Parker, "Discussion of Prof. Richard Jones' German Methods of Using the Mother Tongue," p. 483.

[32] F. W. Parker, "European Correspondence."

[33] John Williston Cook, *Educational History of Illinois* (Chicago: The Henry O. Shepard Co., 1912), p. 269.

[34] Bismarck is well described in Kappel S. Pinson, *Modern Germany* (New York: Macmillan, 1954), p. 126.

[35] Francis W. Parker, "Autobiographical Sketch," p. 129; F. W. Parker, "European Correspondence."

[36] *Ibid.*

[37] "Universal Exhibition of Commerce and Industry in Vienna in 1873," *Herald* (Dayton, Ohio), January 20, 1872.

[38] F. W. Parker, "European Correspondence."

[39] Francis W. Parker, *Talks on Pedagogics,* p. 400.

VII

The Education of the Quincy Adamses

While Parker was widening his educational vision in Germany, the reality of educational inefficiency was coming into focus in Quincy, Massachusetts. Headed by John Quincy Adams, II, grandson of the President for whom he was named, the Quincy School Committee reported in 1872 that many of the town's schools were operating without maps, blackboards, globes, and other aids to teaching. It was argued, in the businesslike sentiments of the times, that "to drag along in these days, in order to save a small immediate outlay, without the best instruments of education, is as uneconomical as to manufacture with old-fashioned or worn-out machinery."[1]

It was in that same year, 1872, that Charles Francis Adams, Jr., younger brother of the chairman, was elected to membership in the School Committee. Influenced by a reading of Horace Mann, he brought a reformist's attitude to the committee.[2] He believed what had happened to American schools was what was happening to American society. Americans were an organizing people. They had a "constant tendency toward the uniform and the mechanical—to what is known in politics as 'the machine'." He believed Americans were organizing their schools to meet the confusion of new immigrants and new bodies of knowledge, but the intellectual subjects were becoming more and more diffused and being handled mechanically, that is, without intellectualism. The schools, then, had become "mechanical educational machines" which were a combination of the "cotton mill" and the "railroad," with the "State-prison" as a model.[3]

According to Adams, school committees had become boards of directors, running the schools of the nation on a timetable. Children were "so much raw material." They must move in step, and exactly alike. Any deviation from this semi-military method was sternly repressed as a breach of discipline. All knowledge was a vast accumulation of facts, rules, and definitions that were laboriously committed to memory. Thus the teacher sat in his chair, "a sort of lone fisherman on the great ocean of things known, and he hooked up out of it now a rule, and now a fact."[4]

Formerly, the day of public examination for each school in Quincy was conducted by the teacher. Parents and friends crowded into the vacant places while the members of the School Committee sat on a platform in dignified silence. With Charles Francis Adams, Jr.,* on the committee, the examinations were taken out of the hands of the teachers in 1873. Each member of the committee questioned the students on a different branch of study. The classes went to pieces. The children could only respond to memorized questions and answers prepared by their teachers. They had no real understanding of their studies or of the process of thinking for themselves. It was also found that—in the ten years between 1863, heart of the Civil War, and 1873, at the onset of the national panic and depression—the current students could do no better on similar tests. In spite of this the cost of education in Quincy had more than doubled in those years.[5] The financial panic and need for economy undoubtedly had a great deal to do with the long hard look the School Committee was beginning to give to the educational system.

As Charles Adams "dragged wearily" through the school inspections of July 1874, he also observed the differences between the "lowest" and the "highest" type of child in Quincy, the lowest type being confined to a particular local school.[6] Below the hill in Quincy, on which the Adams dynasty of statesmen had been founded, lay a valley rapidly filling up with proletarians. The traditional education for the highest type of child was not as easily learned by the lowest.

The changing character of Quincy was also putting strain on the old town-meeting style of government, because of the need to provide greater civic services. As a suburb of Boston, Quincy was losing its rural character and separate identity. It had even come to be recognized as a "bedroom" town by the well-to-do-members of the School Committee who commuted to Boston.[7] The business leaders still ruled, although there was competition developing among the Irish stone cutters who had established their own subcommunity around the granite quarry.

It was at the town meeting of March 1875 that the Irish had a "field-day," according to Charles Adams. Adams was then re-elected to

* For purposes of brevity, Charles Francis Adams, Jr., will hereafter be referred to as, simply, "Charles Adams."

the School Committee by "the skin of his teeth." The prospect of being turned out by an "Irishman" prompted Adams to write "altogether disgusting," in his diary.[8]

The contest for a seat on the School Committee was more than a struggle between the ruling gentry and the rising new class. It was a contest between the old mechanical modes of education and the hope of something better. Ironically, it was the old gentry that was suggesting educational innovations. The School Committee had raised the issue of educational waste and inefficiency. The opposition agreed that something was wrong with the schools, but a change of committee membership rather than system was said to be the only needed reform.[9]

The School Committee proposed both educational *excellence,* and *economy*. Hiring more teachers and reducing the size of each class was considered too expensive, but the committee decided to hire one man, especially trained in education, and give him the responsibility of working out a better system.[10] The re-election of Charles Adams was only one issue in that March town meeting of 1875. The other issue was over the proposed appropriation of $2,000 to hire a superintendent of schools.

Although Adams believed committeemen were involved in business and not equal to the task of specializing in educational matters, he argued for the appropriation on the grounds that a rise in taxes would mostly come out of his own family coffers. This argument, more than the public concern for a superintendent, may have helped to carry the appropriation, but it was said by an opponent that the wealthy would simply shift the burden of taxes on the lower classes through higher interest on loans and through higher rents and prices.[11]

Finding a trained superintendent proved to be more difficult, however, than getting the appropriation for his salary. Charles Adams considered this one of the "inexplicable facts of the day," in that men would be especially trained to care for children's bodies and teeth, and even their souls, but it was not considered necessary to spend more than "a half hour" to train someone to care fo the child's mind.[12]

The School Committee advertised in the Boston papers. There were enough applicants but none was considered qualified. James H. Slade, a new member of the committee, was entrusted with the details of selecting the right candidate. The chairman, John Quincy Adams, II,* who often went fishing with Slade, kept inquiring if there had been a "nibble" in the "superintendency sea." Slade had just about decided on one candidate, more or less out of desperation, when a heavy-set man strolled into his Boston office one afternoon and asked to be considered for the position.

* To be referred to hereafter as "John Adams."

Slade remembered him as a most unlikely candidate. Among other things, he was wearing the "worst hat" Slade had ever seen. He was about to say the job was taken when he caught a certain glint of intensity in the candidate's eye. The man was granted an interview and in a few minutes Slade was captured by the man's enthusiasm and credentials. After the candidate was brought around to the chairman's office, John Adams took Slade aside and said this was no orinary nibble in the superintendency sea. "Slade," he said, "you have landed a whale."[13]

That "whale" was Francis W. Parker. Since returning from Europe that winter, he had spent several months at his home in Manchester, New Hampshire. He wanted to remain in New England, especially around Boston where he thought there were better opportunities and more advantages for continued study. During those months he experienced what he called "several failures" in his family.[14] This may have reflected the hard times brought on by the depression following the financial panic of 1873. He might have been referring to the death of his former guardian, James Walker, a pillar of the Parker clan.[15] In any event, he had offered his services again to the schools of Manchester, but there was no opening. He claimed he was not even wanted in Boston as a "sub-master."[16] It is probable he was therefore discouraged and even despondent about his career when he came to answer the newspaper advertisement about the superintendency in Quincy.

The recommendation of Slade and the elder Adams was apparently enough to convince the School Committee of Parker's worth. His name was submitted on April 7, 1875, and Charles Adams, although he had never seen Parker, moved successfully that the candidate be unanimously chosen to serve as superintendent for one year, commencing on April 20th.[17]

About to start an educational revolution, Parker stopped off at Lexington, Massachusetts, on his way to Quincy. He participated on April 19, 1875, in the centennial celebration of the first shots fired for American independence.[18]

It was on the next day, Tuesday morning, April 20, with the mercury hovering at 25°, that the Colonel was greeted by the whole School Committee of Quincy.[19] Parker was immediately charged with devoting his full time to the examination and improvement of the schools. He was cautioned, however, not to move too fast. The committee emphasized "gradual remodeling," and warned that "reorganizations take time."[20]

Parker was placed in charge of seven schools, which included primary, intermediate, and grammar grades, as well as a high school. The enrollment was about sixteen hundred, including almost a hundred students at the high school level. He met the teachers at the Lyceum Room on the evening of April 21, and the next day he made the round of schools with Charles Adams. Adams recorded in his diary that it was a "useful and happy day."[21]

Parker was quick to find a special need for a common, continuous, and systematic plan of work for all the schools in Quincy. He was appalled that children came to school after five or six years of "vigorous development" in "Nature's great methods, object teaching and play," only to find "imagination, curiosity, and love for mental and physical activity" destroyed by "dull, wearisome hours of listless activity upon hard benches." It was no wonder, he declared in his first report to the committee, that the love for school was so often crushed out of the "little innocents." Even the desks, he observed, seemed to have been "invented to torture the little ones."[22]

In spite of the fact that Parker believed the schools of Quincy were better than the average when he came there, he found children mouthing words mechanically, without understanding the ideas they represented. It was difficult for teachers, Parker said, to get rid of the idea that "words in themselves have some mysterious power of creating ideas" or that memorizing rules and definitions and acquiring a great mass of "disconnected facts" did not produce useful learning.[23]

Parker expressed wonder that a nation of prolific inventiveness was still moving in the "stagecoach of educational methods" and following the old worn ruts of rote teaching. He said "schoolkeepers" were like retired clerks who had "closed and balanced their accounts with learning:" He proclaimed that his job as superintendent was to be a teacher of teachers. This would have to be accomplished though teachers' meetings. Teachers would be also encouraged to visit each other, to note special strengths and weaknesses of their colleagues. All principals of the district schools were organized into a council or supervisory board to assist him in these endeavors.[24]

While Parker set out to forge the forty or so teachers of Quincy into a faculty for the study of education, he claimed that in the process he got more from these teachers than he gave. He said he taught a little in every class, not because he thought he was a model but because he wanted to learn to teach.[25] Starting at the lowest primary room, Parker could take over a class and become a child without being childish. He could then go from grade to grade and be childlike no longer but a growing boy. It was said he could reach rapport with any group of children within five minutes after entering a class.[26]

Parker got permission to use the recitation room at one of the schools in order to give demonstration lessons and lectures to his teachers at the end of school days. At the first such session, he must have surprised as well as exhausted the faculty with his rapid fire of questions.

"Education, what is it?" he would ask. "Why it is necessary?" "How shall we begin to educate?" "Why?" "What new notions about Education have come to you within a week? Illustrate." "Are you a growing teacher?"[27]

In later sessions he gave model lessons, supplied books on teaching theories. "See, Say, Use," were the favorite words he put on the blackboard. "Give your knowledge a body," he would say, "Make it an organic whole." "Help me fill in this skeleton of a map with flesh and blood; in other words to give it life."[28]

Giving each member of the faculty various books to study in preparation for succeeding sessions, he would then question them on their reading. One of the school principals soon came to understand what Parker was trying to do, especially after he had read his assignments in Erasmus, Comenius, Montaigne, Froebel, and Pestalozzi. Parker was trying to seek unity in the schools without uniformity. He was giving his teachers complete freedom while he led them to "build up a cooperative system of teaching founded upon simple, solid, and normal scientific educational principles." This young principal found that the teachers were not imitating Parker as much as they were catching his spirit, "absorbing his views of truth and *becoming his disciples.*"[29]

The principal of the Washington School, Isaac Freeman Hall, was at first impressed by the size of the Colonel. He had expected to find the new superintendent a noisy, bold, and aggressive figure, but to his surprise, the Colonel was "quiet, reticent, and unassuming." Hall said Parker often kept his eyes closed while observing classes, but when he opened them, there was a flash of penetrating, thoughtful, and farseeing alertness. Though not yet forty, Parker looked at this young principal in a fatherly way. Parker would later consider Hall one of his "boys."[30]

The School Committee, catching Parker's spirit, too, approved and adopted his schedule for the next year as soon as the July school examinations were over. The new schedule called for a reduction in the primary and grammar grades from nine to eight years. The school year was also reduced from forty-three to forty weeks and divided into three terms. Children were grouped according to their achievement rather than age.[31]

The autumn term of 1875 brought forth the first notice of "F. W. Parker" to the readers of the *Quincy Patriot*. His office hours, from eight to twelve o'clock on Mondays and Saturdays in the office of the Honorable John Quincy Adams, 96 Hancock Street, were publicized in in the *Quincy Patriot* on September 4, 1875. Parker was by then boarding nearby with John H. Gilbert, physician, who lived on the corner of Hancock and Faxon.[32] The same issue of the *Quincy Patriot* reported that there would only be a half session of school that Monday so the teachers could meet with the superintendent in regard to the new course of study.

The old course of study had been discarded. Starting at the lowest level, some features of the kindergarten were to be introduced. Songs and plays would be stressed. Blocks and colored sticks for weaving would be provided, altogether with freedom of movement for the child and shortened lessons in order to avoid weariness. Parker said the child's first years of schooling generally fixed his whole future course in education. The first years must be made into a "pleasant, cheerful home," Parker argued, where the "little folks play, sing, read, count objects, write, draw, and are happy under the direction of very faithful and efficient teachers." He believed the "Object Method" or "Mother's Method" of showing an object or picture of an object must come before the teaching of the name. He abolished the "ABC's" at the lower grades. Reading was approached through the "word method." Parker explained that children should learn the whole word rather than its parts, as they had learned to speak the language. Rules of grammar were replaced by exercises and drill in constructing sentences, letter writing, and short compositions. All writing was designed to describe activities that were real and meaningful to the child's experiences.[33]

Spelling was taught through exercises in writing rather than through what Parker called "numberless exercises" and "common recitation." Good spelling was developed by acquiring "mental pictures" of the whole words and the things they represented. Words of the child's own vocabulary were stressed. Parker found that words commonly misspelled were not the "jaw-breakers" but the simple words like "which" and "those." He emphasized the simple and useful words first, and then the "ornamental."[34]

Charles Adams soon observed the success of these measures. He said the children were learning to read as they had learned to walk, in a natural manner. The alphabet was "robbed of its terrors and stole upon them unawares," he said, while the spelling and copy books were thrown out.[35]

Although technical grammar was discontinued in the early grades, Parker believed it should be taught later when proficiency in speaking and writing had been acquired.[36]

Arithmetic was also overhauled. Meaningless numbers were as bad to Parker as meaningless words. He observed that through the old methods of teaching arithmetic a majority of grammar students, even high school students, could not solve a simple mathematical problem.

He also observed that an "intelligent stone worker" in Quincy could teach his son to measure stone in a few months. Arithmetic, he believed, should be taught in the same way, by teaching one definite thing at a time, and teaching "things" with figures as their representatives.[37]

Parker was reversing the logic of proceeding from rules and definitions to the problems. As with spelling and grammar, he also believed arbitrary principles of mathematics should be taught at the higher levels.[38] In other words, the children could better learn the rules when problems made them seek rules or generalizations.

Beyond the three R's, geography had a special fascination for Parker. Opposed to the textbook catechism of questions and answers about the earth, he insisted on field trips where he could direct the children in making sketches and mud models of what they saw. He argued that the beautiful landscapes and sea views of Quincy contained in miniature every form of land and water on earth. Imaginary constructs, he believed, of the unseen world could be better learned through the physical surroundings of Quincy than through the unconnected mass of statistics and facts in the geography books.[39]

In all, children were being taught to read, write, spell, and think all at the same time. They were taught to "talk" with their pens, Parker said, as they had already learned to talk with their tongues, by using them.[40]

Not all children responded with equal facility to these innovations. A very large percentage, according to Parker, of children entering the Quincy schools belonged to the class called "dull Pupils." Some had minds which had developed more slowly, others were strictly limited by nature or had inherited mental defects by bad training at home. Under the old system, these children were made to feel their dullness, were scolded and even "driven into hopeless stupidity." Parker believed that under his new system, which was built on a recognition of nature's individuality rather than uniformity, the children whose minds developed slowly were accelerated by contact with objective methods of teaching. The timid children were stimulated by kindness and homelike atmosphere in the classroom. The children with defective minds were treated as "a physician treats a chronic disease," and their weak powers were constantly strengthened through special activities.[41]

The concern with individuality was reflected in the new order of discipline. Parker insisted that "the school should be made like a miniature and a model democracy."[42] In this way, self-control and self-government could be developed.

Above all, the school must be made more attractive. Parker demanded that "sunshine" be let into the classrooms. Although he could not reconstruct the buildings, which generally had small windows, he could equate sunshine with "good wholesome, normal instruction, a mild, firm government and a proper amount of exercise."[43]

Teaching children to think before the tools of thinking were properly memorized aroused suspicion and opposition. Parker retorted by saying that those educators who believed little children could not reason were blinded by their own unreasoning methods. He said, "Having by our methods induced helplessness, we straightway made helplessness a reason for our method."[44] Attempts at broadening the curriculum were also attacked. The teaching of sewing, for instance, was satirized in the local newspaper by acknowledging that it would at least protect girls in the future from being "fleeced by conscienceless dressmakers."[45]

Nevertheless, Parker was free to work out his theories under the political protection of the powerful Adamses. The annual town meeting of March 1876 approved the appropriation of his salary for another year. The same meeting raised $600 for the celebration of the Fourth of July.[46] It was the Centennial of American Independence. The Centennial Exhibition in Philadelphia was then underway, and Parker must have taken advantage of the special $11 round trip by train and steamer between Quincy and Philadelphia. He later mentioned the free kindergarten exhibit there which was conductd by Miss Ruth Burritt.[47] It was this same 1876 exposition that introduced the revolutionary methods of manual training, developed in Russia, to American audiences. Parker may have been as much influenced by this as President John D. Runkle of the Massachusetts Institute of Technology.[48]

On the Fourth of July, 1876, Quincy was awakened at half past four in the morning by a ringing of bells. The festivities continued throughout the day with various children's entertainments, a band concert, and fireworks. In one of the tents unfurled for the occasion, Parker took the platform to present a history of the public schools in Quincy. His words went over so well that they were later printed on the front page of the *Quincy Patriot,* July 15, 1876. Free schools, independence, and democracy were all mutual partners, he had said. "Throughout the centuries of Quincy's history," Parker concluded his remarks, "its people have ever manifested a deep interest in education, and I believe," he said, "that I am right when I say that at no time in the past has that interest been greater than it is in this the first year of the new century [of Independence]."

Parker was not exaggerating. Not only in Quincy, but in Boston as well, people were discussing what was coming to be known as the "Quincy System." It was a conversation piece. "Is Colonel Parker a crank or a genius?" "Will it be possible that our children can be played into an education?" Parents who discovered that their children could not repeat the letters of the alphabet were surprised that they could read and write. Still, the older generation sensed something was not quite right.[49] It is possible that nothing except the summer campaigning of Hayes and Tilden for the presidency was of more concern in Quincy.

Another school year with the new and controversial system of education was inaugurated in the fall of 1876, although the subsequent confusion in the Electoral College, after the national elections in November, probably diminished the concern over what was happening in the schools. The disputed election was resolved, and after the Electoral Commission declared Louisiana for Hayes, the *Quincy Patriot* reported on February 24,1877, that there "appears to be only a few now, who doubt Hayes will be declared elected, and that he will be peaceably inaugurated as president."

It was not so certain, however, whether Parker would be peaceably retained as superintendent. One item set up for a vote in the town meeting of March, 1877, was whether the town should instruct the School Committee to discontinue the services of the superintendent. Another item was to stop the appropriation of funds alloted for the purchase of school library books. (With what books he had, Parker had been hiring a carriage to move them around from school to school.)[50]

As though the novel approaches to education which Parker represented were not enough to condemn him, there was even a rumor circulating that he was making money out of contracts for coal and for transportation of pupils. John Adams squelched this maliciousness through an indignant letter to the *Quincy Patriot* on March 3, 1877. He explained that Parker had nothing to do with such contracts, that these matters were the responsibility of the School Committee. He said the records of contracts were public and open to review.

Before the town meeting, however, the School Committee was divided over Parker. School Committeeman Edwin W. Marsh, unlike James H. Slade, for instance, who had little respect for the past or its traditions, was considered a "veteran of the old system" and was always suspicious of innovation. Now he had dug up something on Parker to discredit him. The official minutes of the committee meeting for March 10, 1877, simply noted that the matter of teachers' salaries was tabled. Charles Adams, however, recorded in his diary that the meeting had been "very unpleasant." Marsh, it seemed, was "after Parker" and had called him a "libertine." What he found out about Parker is not known. Nothing of this nature was mentioned in the newspapers. The issue over Parker, however, was not educational. It was moral. Charles Adams met with Parker by appointment on Monday, March 12, 1877, and had a talk with him about his "character."[51]

Whether there was any truth in the matter, whether the alleged offense was grave or merely an indiscretion, can only be left to speculation; but even a whisper of moral scandal would have ruined Parker and his work in the Quincy of those days. At that very time the Women's Christian Temperance Union was battling for legislation in Quincy to halt the sale of alcoholic beverages. The issue was drawn in terms of black and white, between "morality and religion on the one side and vice and crime on the other."[52] Even a breath about Parker's drinking episode in the army might have been enough to wither his reputation with the mothers of the Quincy children.

The reformation of the Quincy schools was now hanging on some charge of moral character. On Sunday, March 18, Charles Adams walked down to his brother John's house and discussed the "Parker case." They both resolved to "stand by him."[53] The moral issue therefore remained buried, but the educational issue was very much alive.

The town meeting, with Parker's job at stake, opened in March, with John Adams as moderator. The Republicans were in firm control but the school issues were so deadlocked that a special meeting had to be called for a later date in March.[54] It would appear that the School Committee was in real trouble, even though its Republican support was as strong as ever in the community. Business had not yet recovered from the depression of 1873, and there is no doubt that the high cost of education was as of much concern as the controversial superintendent.

Parker believed that the "unflinching front" of the School Committee was usually too much for the enemies of the "new-fangled notions," but the recent slash of wages had aroused the stone workers who labored in the quarries of Quincy. Parker said it was impossible to reason with these "unreasoning" men. At the special town meeting on March 26, 1877, these stone workers began to crowd out the friends of the school, and Parker counted them as his enemies. He remembered that special meeting as "a battle royal for the little ones."[55]

The *Quincy Patriot,* on the other hand, reported the special meeting as "harmonious," with probably not more than twenty people speaking. Those who strongly advocated economy and dismissing the superintendent were counted in the minority.[56] Parker remembered the cheers following the motion to reduce appropriations and to eliminate the office of superintendent. He would never forget the argument of a "socialistic leader" who sprang to his feet and said: "Shall we day laborers work for less than the school teacher? Shall a superintendent, who has nothing to do but ride around in a carriage and draw his salary at ten dollars a day—shall he take the bread out of the mouths of our children? The honest hearted quarry workers see their children starving because a lazy superintendent must live."[57]

Parker's support came from the aristocrats of Quincy. He remembered how Charles Adams had defended him and the new system. Adams replied to the "socialistic leader" by calling his remarks the poorest and weakest arguments ever devised to degrade the minds of men. "Because I get one or two dollars a day no one else should get more! Such foolishness," Adams said, "robs men of ambition . . . sinks them to the lowest level." He addressed the stone cutters and asked them what they were voting away. He answered that they were voting away the only means by which their children could better themselves. "Better deprive yourselves of every comfort in life; better go hungry; better send your little ones supperless to bed than to take from them the most valuable thing it is in your power to give them—an education." He added that other places were waiting for the superintendent, should he be dismissed, but the children must remain, to be taught by the poorest teacher that one or two dollars a day will hire.[58]

It appears that Adams had the last word. Even the appropriation for $500 to buy library books was carried, and the motion to discontinue the office of superintendent was "indefinitely postponed."[59]

The following year there was no issue whatsoever about retaining Parker. He had even become safe enough for the Republican Caucus of Quincy to nominate as a trustee for the public library. He was also in the running for one of the two openings in the management of the Adams Academy.[60] This academy had been founded only a few years earlier in order to prepare students for college. Charles Adams believed boys who wanted to go to college could better prepare themselves at this academy than at the public high school.[61]

Parker was in sympathy with the idea that the public high school should serve the public interest and the private schools could better serve the interests of higher education. Let the "Grammar School" be the "People's College," he believed, and make its aim "to give the masses the best preparation for life's work." The high school in Quincy would be more profitable to the town, according to Parker, if its entire time were given over to the "common sciences" or to those subjects which were more practical than "Latin."[62]

Parker ran fourth in the balloting for trustee of the public library by collecting only 671 votes. He received just two votes for a place in the management of the Adams Academy.[63] Unsuccessful in his political endeavors, Parker was nevertheless considered so successful in his professional capacities that the neighboring town of Milton proposed that the two towns should consolidate their school systems under the superintendency of Parker.[64] No formal action, however, was ever taken by the School Committee of Quincy. Perhaps the members would have liked to share the expense of Parker with the town of Milton, but they probably did not want to share the notoriety which the Quincy school system was beginning to gain. Leading journals of the day had begun to send correspondents to Quincy in order to find out about the educational innovations.

The *School Journal,* published in New York City, claimed to be the first to hear of the "magnificent work" in Quincy and dispatched a professor to investigate and "let the world know."[65] In 1879 a series of "Quincy Letters," from Mrs. S. C. F. Hallowell appeared as far away as the Philadelphia *Ledger.*[66] In the same year Parker's name was mentioned at the convention of the National Educational Association as an example of the "new teacher."[67]

Whether Quincy was an educational Mecca or a Babylon of childhood indolence was a subject of pilgrimages from all over the country. Said one visitor of the Quincy schools: "This is very noisy." The teacher's reply was, "Precisely, madam, this is a workshop, not a funeral."[68] The *New York Tribune* went so far as to credit the Quincy system as being the "starting point in the reorganization of the deplorable American system."[69]

The claim that thirty thousand visitors descended on the Quincy schools between 1878 and 1880 is probably an exaggeration.[70] As early as 1878, however, the School Committee had been concerned about the increase in expenses for carriage hire. Parker then explained that a large number of visitors from "abroad" wished to visit some of the schools more remote from the center of town.[71] The *Quincy Patriot,* on February 8, 1879, accounted for 6,396 visitors during the previous year alone. By 1879 it was necessary for the School Committee to draw up some rules for limiting such visitations. Requests for teachers to give special exercises to exhibit the new system were said to be completely disrupting school routine.[72]

The Quincy system had become famous, much to the surprise of Parker. He said he was the most astonished man in the world when the schools of Quincy were "written up in all the papers," and thousands of visitors came pouring in. He believed the "notoriety" resulted from the radical changes he introduced in the East, rather from the merit of his work.[73] In this the editors of the *New England Journal of Education* concurred. They said the leading educators in the middle and western states had been working on the same ideas for the last twenty years. They were obviously surprised about the "prodigious excitement in New England" over the Quincy system. It seemed, to the *New England Journal of Education,* that the Quincy School Committee had "drawn up old Quincy in a bucket from the bottom of a deep educational well," and that, finding themselves above ground, the members of the committee "issued a bulletin announcing the discovery of a new educational universe." The unfortunate truth, according to this journal, was that New England had all "too many of the same kind of old, dry wells."[74]

By the time the news of Quincy reached England, through some educational pamphlets of Charles Adams, a London journal dismissed the whole development as nothing more than a realization of Froebel's theories. The London journal was impressed, however, with the system of administration in Quincy. The journal complained that English schools were still organized and administered by "amateurs."[75]

Parker himself indicated that there never was a Quincy method or a Quincy system, unless one agreed to call the method "a spirit of study" and the system "everlasting change."[76] Charles Adams agreed that there was no "system," that the educational efforts in Quincy were "marked throughout by intense individuality."[77] What happened at Quincy was basically a protest against the educational institutions of that time, institutions which had become rigid and formal, general and abstract.

The cardinal principle of the new educaton, according to Adams, was that teaching should be a science, that *a priori* knowledge should be replaced by inductive research.[78]

Parker believed the fundamental lesson of Quincy was its rejection of traditional teaching, its breaking through the "very thick crust of conservativism and conceit." It was a search for natural methods of teaching.[79]

As far as this development was concerned, Parker credited the two Adamses, along with Slade, the man who discovered him, and strangely enough, Marsh, the man who almost destroyed him, as the four men to whom the "New Departure" in education was mainly due.[80] Charles Adams, however, gave Parker full credit for the educational developments in Quincy, except for the idea that the number of courses should be reduced as part of the process of simplification.[81] Nevertheless, some people equated the Quincy system with Adams rather than with Parker. As late as 1900 a superintendent of schools addressed the National Education Association and credited Charles Adams with the "Quincy discovery."[82]

On the whole, Adams and Parker should probably share in the fame which came to the Quincy system. Adams at least contributed to the publicity. His lectures and pamphlets on the educational experiments were said to have stirred "a hailstorm."[83] His name was a mighty influence, but as he said himself, the radical ideas and theories were Parker's, although they supported the "less clearly defined ideas" of the committee.[84] As for education, he once said he knew a little about several subjects, but nothing about teaching.[85] Adams did make it possible for

Parker to get a hearing. He helped to make Quincy the showcase in which Parker got a national audience. Otherwise, Parker's work, as in Dayton, would probably have gone largely unnoticed.

Parker had found a School Committee which was "disgusted and dissatisfied," a committee that had reached the conclusion that the whole educative system was wrong, "a system from which the life was gone out."[86] Without such a committee, representing or at least shaping public opinion, no teacher or group of teachers could have successfully protested against the formalized educational system which was more interested in its own being than in that of the child's.

Association with the Adams name and reputation, however, had some disadvantages. Wendell Phillips, the great humanitarian, described the Quincy system as a "pet scheme of the Adamses" to undermine the common school foundation of the republic. Phillips said the system was "begotten by a brain so confused by aristocratic prejudices that it cannot apprehend facts." He said the philosophy was unsound and that no reform ever came down from the upper classes of society.[87] He was one who confused Adams and Parker in the development of the Quincy system, but he missed the point that these newer methods were opposed to the forces of conservativism.

It is true that Adams was an aristocrat. He was not without his own sense of class consciousness. He hated crowds. He was not above the use of such terms as the "torpid and uninformed stratium," or "born and bred in the habitation of labor," or the "inchoate mass," and "dollar and dollar-and-a-half a day people."[88] There is no evidence, however, that he feared the rise of the masses or that he sought to use the schools as a lever of the rich to hold down the poor. He only feared that the lack of a good education would bring out the animal in men, would lead to the rise of the brute. The aim of education for Adams was not to indoctrinate and enslave but to free the mind of man. He believed the purpose of the common school should be to prepare children for the important work of continually educating themselves. It was for such a goal—self-education—that he had also helped to establish the public library in Quincy.[89]

Parker considered Adams a Republican "in the highest sense of the word, without a spark of undemocratic aristocracy."[90] He was on intimate terms with Adams. On several occasions they dined together and passed away the evenings. He even went sailing with this grandson and great-grandson of presidents.[91] Perhaps it was more than educational interests which brought them together. They had the war in common. Adams had also served in the islands off South Carolina and in the siege of Petersburg.[92]

The School Committee, as well as Charles Adams, nevertheless was not always in agreement with Parker. The spring examinations of the schools had come to be known as the "Examination of the Superintendent." The members of the committee often raised questions and doubts about Parker's methods. Sometimes, Parker admitted, he could defend himself successfully. Some questions led to doubts in his own mind, but he said he never changed in the slightest unless he was thoroughly convinced. Had he done so, the committee would have followed the usual precedent and he would have been the "football of six resolute men." He claimed that the servile, abject attitude of superintendents and teachers before school authorities degraded the profession. School authorities, from Parker's angle of vision, took pleasure in seeing their employees cringe, even though they despised them for it. Parker did not argue for obstinacy or pigheadedness, but he exhorted teachers to a "courageous adherence" to truth when they thought they had found it.[93]

Charles Adams said that Parker was lacking in business methods and could not always "accommodate himself to circumstances in dealing with men. His practical judgment was often bad. He was apt to do the right thing at the wrong time. He was impatient of opposition." On the other hand, Adams credited Parker with being "possessed with an idea, and he was indefatigable in his efforts to put it in practice."[94] He said there was no real conflict between the superintendent and school authorities. The most important contribution of this educational revolution in Quincy, as far as Adams was concerned. consisted in the recognition by the School Committee that it needed a competent and intelligent executive officer.[95]

It was Parker who believed one of the "profound mysteries" of the world was the "marvelous psychological change that comes over respectable, intelligent, and otherwise wise laymen when they are elected by their fellow-citizens to serve on school committees." They would never dream of superintending an electric plant or building a bridge, but they felt fully competent to "mold society into right living, and shape the destinies of a nation by means of common education."[96]

In Quincy, however, Parker had been given almost "unhampered" support by the School Committee. He was held accountable to "results" alone. As far as results were concerned, Charles Adams was satisfied that there had been improvement—and at lowered cost, that children could use nouns, adjectives, and verbs even if they did not know what they were. He was satisfied with the improvement in attendance and with the whole "change in spirit."[97] Before the National Educational Association in 1880 he hailed the Quincy results. He said the experiments were so successful that they should be followed throughout the country. He based his argument on the George A. Walton report of 1879. This report, which was included in the forty-third annual report of the Massachusetts Board of Education, contained the results of school examinations in Norfolk County. On the basis of these state tests, Quincy was distinguished by the highest percentages in everything except mental arithmetic.[98]

That Parker's methods had created an educational millennium in Quincy, however, is hardly consistent with some of the private remarks in Adams' diary. Almost three years after Parker had begun his work in Quincy, Adams found the examination in one of the schools "shocking." He said not one child in six could read a common book at sight.[99]

Parker's methods had not worked miracles, but Adams' salary guide for teachers had not allowed Parker to hold all the teachers he had so laboriously tried to train. Quincy salaries had fallen below the average market price in the county and this made it difficult to retain good teachers, especially after the Quincy schools had become renowned and other systems would bid for them. Parker accused the School Committee of false economy. He said Quincy paid for the training of teachers and other towns reaped the rewards.[100]

The depression, however, had caused a general reduction of wages in Quincy. In 1877 the School Committee made a studied effort at readjusting teachers' salaries and saving school expense. Charles Adams found that the whole body of Quincy teachers was renewed on the average every four or five years. He therefore recommended lowering salaries of beginning teachers only.[101]

Parker also blamed the teachers themselves for their low wages. He said it was difficult to raise the salaries of all teachers at once, but if he tried to raise the compensation of any outstanding teacher, the others cried out against it. This "Trades Union plan of uniform salaries," Parker believed, was as much responsible for low salaries as the resistance of the School Committee itself. It would only follow, he reasoned, that if they concentrated on raising individual salaries, one at a time, the other salaries would soon follow.[102]

Parker was actually on the verge of resigning in 1878. An informal discussion of the School Committee on January 6, 1879, centered on the problem of retaining Parker beyond the expiration of his "present engagement."[103] Parker did stay on and was promptly reelected by the committee on April 5, 1879. His salary, however, remained the same.[104] His task soon became greater. In July, the committee authorized him to establish a "Training School" for the preparation of teachers.[105]

Parker finally gave notice on March 24, 1880, that he had been elected as one of the Supervisors of Schools in Boston and that he intended to accept.[106]

On the whole, Parker had not been completely happy about the results of his work in Quincy. He believed that the work of the primary grades could only be termed "fairly a success," and that of the grammar grades "by no means a failure." Nevertheless he had given so much more attention to the lower level that the work of the higher grades was not fully developed. In fact, he complained that the result of his work beyond the primary schools had become something of a compromise between the natural methods and book cramming. In the final analysis he believed he had succeeded in making school more pleasant for children. He considered the best effect of all his efforts was the "more humane treatment of little folks."[107]

Parker's resignation, especially in lieu of the unfinished work at the grammar school level, was naturally a blow to the School Committee. Within a few weeks of Parker's announced intention to leave, Charles Adams submitted his own resignation to the committee. He was offered an appointment on the State Board of Education, but he excused himself from Quincy affairs on the basis of "business engagements."[108] A great educational team had broken up, but it had aroused the interest of the country.

Parker's resignation was accepted with thanks for "his kindness and courtesy . . . his long, arduous, and invaluable service in the interests of the Schools of Quincy."[109]

The system Parker planted in Quincy continued to flourish. A teacher who had trained under Parker—a Mr. Sylvester Brown—was elected to succeed him.[110] Lelia Patridge visited the Quincy schools the following September and published a long account of the Parker heritage. She described such features as "the joyous life" of the schools, and the comradeship of teachers and pupils. She told of the "grouping" according to ability and the individual instruction. She hailed the marked attention given to "dull students." She noted the variety of activities and the constant use of drawing as a means of expression. She marveled at the use of supplementary reading materials and at the tests which were aimed at the children's "power to do" rather than their power to memorize.[111]

While Miss Patridge thought Parker's spirit had descended in Quincy, the School Committee marked the passing of Parker with regret bordering on panic. The committee reported that Parker had "breathed life, growth and happiness into our schoolrooms," but they asked, "Where were we to look for it when he should go?"[112]

The committee had recognized that Parker's great work was the "Emancipation from arbitrary rule." This could not be sustained without "persistent and vigilant intellectual exertion," because the "temptation to lean upon formulas is almost irresistible." The retention of a system or a method was not considered enough. In its report for 1880 the committee found the old ways were creeping back. "We detect it everywhere; in the mechanical aping of liberty no less than in service obedience to forms." The committee thought itself fortunate to have the services of Sylvester Brown, but it realized his task was a difficult one, that "it was no child's play to make good the place of his predecessor."[113]

And the problem was made worse as a result of their own false economies. The members of the committee complained that no less than thirteen teachers, some of them the "most valuable of the corps" left in that first year after Parker's departure. They left, it was explained, to accept the "greater inducements which wealthier or more lavish employers were glad to offer."[114]

After a few years Mr. Brown left also. It was said that he would rather teach than to serve "in a slavish way the average School Committeeman."[115] The Quincy system was thus left to struggle on in the place of its birth because it lost the vitality of its leader. The Quincy system was Colonel Parker himself, his physical force, his personality. As a set of ideas or a course of study, it was a body without a soul when Parker left.

It was for a younger member of that Adams generation to sum up. Henry Adams sensed that "American society had outgrown most of its institutions," and that "the generation that lived from 1840 to 1870 could do very well with the old forms of education; that which had its work to do between 1870 and 1900 needed something quite new."[116] That something new had been made known to the whole country as the "Quincy System." It would go on growing with Parker.

NOTES

[1] *Annual Report, School Committee, Town of Quincy, 1871–1872,* p. 16.

[2] Edward Chase Kirkland, *Charles Francis Adams, Jr., 1835–1915, The Patrician At Bay* (Cambridge, Mass.: Harvard University Press, 1965), p. 144; Charles Francis Adams, Jr., Diary, June 1, July 9, 10, 1872, Massachusetts Historical Society, Boston, Mass.

[3] Charles F. Adams, Jr., "Scientific Common-School Education," *Harper's New Monthly Magazine* (October 1880) 936–937.

[4] *Ibid.,* pp. 937–938.

[5] Charles Francis Adams, Jr., "The New Departure in the Common Schools of Quincy," *Elementary School Journal,* **35** (March 1935), 496–498.

[6] Charles Francis Adams, Jr., Diary, July 14, 1874.

[7] Edward Chase Kirkland, *op. cit.* pp. 142–143; *Annual Report, School Committee, Town of Quincy, 1874–1875,* p. 4.

[8] Charles Francis Adams, Jr., Diary, March 1, 1875.

[9] "For the Patriot: Our Schools," *Quincy Patriot* (Quincy, Mass.), March 13, 1875.

[10] *Annual Report . . . 1874–1875,* pp. 4, 12, 109; Charles F. Adams, Jr., "The New Departure in the Common Schools," pp. 496–498.

[11] *Ibid.,* p. 499; "On Taxation," Quincy Patriot, March 27, 1875.

[12] Charles Francis Adams, Jr., "Scientific Common-School Education," p. 939.

[13] James H. Slade, "The Finding of Colonel Parker," *Journal of Education,* **51** (April 26, 1900), 260. Isaac Freeman Hall recalled a similar story except that he mistakenly thought Charles Francis Adams, Jr., had discovered Parker. Isaac Freeman Hall, *In School from Three to Eighty* (Pittsfield, Mass.: The Eagle Printing and Binding Co., 1927), p. 169.

[14] Francis W. Parker, "Autobiographical Sketch," an appendix to William M. Giffin, *School Days in the Fifties* (Chicago: A. Flanagan Co., 1906), p. 129. It appears certain Parker returned from Europe in late 1874. He claimed to have spent six months at his home in New Hampshire before going to Quincy. Frank W. Parker, letter to William Lochran, Com. of Pensions, Washington, D.C., March 24, 1894, Francis W. Parker, Soldier's Certificate, Can No. 17835, Bundle No. 22, The National Archives, Washington, D.C.

[15] James Walker, 1789–1875, Piscatauquog Cemetery, West Manchester, N.H.

[16] Francis W. Parker, "Autobiographical Sketch," pp. 129–130.

[17] *Record of the General School Committee for the Town of Quincy,* April 7, 1875; *Annual Report, School Committee, Town of Quincy, 1875–1876,* p. 117.

[18] "The Parker-Quincy Celebration," *Journal of Education,* **51** (April 12, 1900), 168.

[19] Charles Francis Adams, Jr., Diary, April 20, 1875.

[20] *Annual Report . . . 1875–1876,* pp. 109–110.

[21] *Ibid.,* p. 6; *Record of the General School Committee for the Town of Quincy,* March 6, 1875; Charles Francis Adams, Jr., Diary, April 21–22, 1875.

[22] *Annual Report . . . 1875–1876,* pp. 117, 123–124; *Annual Report, School Committee, Town of Quincy, 1878–1879,* p. 174.

[23] *Annual Report . . . 1875–1876,* p. 124; *Annual Report, School Committee, Town of Quincy, 1877–1878,* p. 132.

[24] *Annual Report . . . 1875–1876,* p. 123; *Annual Report . . . 1877–1878,* p. 131; Francis W. Parker, "A Sketch of the Work in the Quincy Schools from 1875 to 1880," V, *School Journal,* **30** (August 1, 1885), 69.

[25] Francis W. Parker, "The Quincy Method," *American Journal of Sociology,* **6** (July 1900), 117.

[26] Isaac Freeman Hall, *op. cit.,* p. 170.

[27] *Ibid.,* pp. 170, 172.

[28] *Ibid.,* pp. 173–174.

[29] *Ibid.,* pp. 173–174.

[30] *Ibid.,* pp. 169–170, 186.

[31] *Annual Report . . . 1875–1876,* p. 117.

[32] *Quincy Weymouth and Braintree Directory, 1878–1879* (Boston: C. W. Calkins and Company, 1878), pp. 84, 53.

[33] *Annual Report . . . 1875–1876,* pp. 121–124; *Annual Report, School Committee, Town of Quincy, 1876–1877,* p. 125.

[34] *Annual Report . . . 1875–1876,* p. 128; *Annual Report . . . 1876–1877,* p. 125.

[35] Charles Francis Adams, Jr., "The New Departure in the Common Schools," p. 500.

[36] *Annual Report . . . 1875–1876,* p. 128.

[37] *Ibid.,* pp. 128–129.

[38] *Annual Report . . . 1876–1877,* p. 127.

[39] *Annual Report . . . 1875–1876,* p. 129; Francis W. Parker, *Outlines of How to Study Geography* (New York: D. Appleton and Co., 1893), pp. 13–19.

[40] Francis W. Parker, "A Sketch of the Work in the Quincy Schools from 1875 to 1880," V, p. 122.

[41] *Annual Report . . . 1878–1879,* pp. 171–172.

[42] *Annual Report . . . 1877–1878,* p. 130.

[43] *Annual Report . . . 1875–1876,* p. 121.

[44] *Annual Report . . . 1876–1877,* p. 127.

[45] "Sewing in Public Schools," *Quincy Patriot,* March 4, 1876.

[46] "Town Meeting," *Quincy Patriot,* March 25, 1876.

[47] "Trip to Philadelphia, Centennial Exhibition," *Quincy Patriot,* May 20, 1876; Francis W. Parker, "Froebel's Life Work," Parker Scrapbooks, 1891, Archives, Harper Library, University of Chicago.

[48] Lawrence A. Cremin, *The Transformation of the School* (New York: Alfred A. Knopf, 1961), pp. 23–26.

[49] Ella C. Wilson, *Pedagogues and Parents* (New York: Henry Holt, 1904), p. 39; Edwin W. Marsh, "My Dear Mr. Lull," *Quincy Patriot,* April 21, 1900.

[50] "Town Meeting," *Quincy Patriot,* March 3, 1877; Francis W. Parker, "The Quincy Method," p. 118.

[51] Charles Adams, Jr., "Letter to Mr. H. W. Lull," *Quincy Patriot,* April 21, 1900, *Record of the General School Committee for the Town of Quincy,* March 10, 1877; Charles Francis Adams, Jr., Diary, March 10, 12, 1877.

[52] "The Woman's Christian Temperance Union," *Quincy Patriot,* February 24, 1877.

[53] Charles Francis Adams, Jr., Diary, March 18, 1877.

[54] "Town Meeting," *Quincy Patriot,* March 10, 1877.

[55] Francis W. Parker, "A Sketch of the Work in the Quincy Schools from 1875 to 1880," II, *School Journal,* **29** (June 13, 1885), 374; Francis W. Parker, "The Quincy Method," p. 115.

[56] "Report of Adjourned Town Meeting held on Monday last," *Quincy Patriot,* March 31, 1877.

[57] Francis W. Parker, "A Sketch of the Work in the Quincy Schools from 1875 to 1880," II, p. 374.

[58] *Ibid.*

[59] "Report of Adjourned Town Meeting held on Monday last."

[60] "Republican Caucus," *Quincy Patriot,* March 2, 1878; "Town Meeting," *Quincy Patriot,* March 9, 1878. There was also one "F. A. Parker," possibly a misprint of F. W. Parker, who received one vote for manager of the Mount Wollaston Cemetery. *Ibid.*

[61] "Adams Academy," *Quincy Patriot,* March 3, 1877.

[62] *Annual Report . . . 1876–1877,* pp. 119–120; *Annual Report . . . 1878–1879,* p. 174.

[63] "Town Meeting," *Quincy Patriot,* March 9, 1878.

[64] *Record of the General School Committee for the Town of Quincy,* May 6, 1878.

[65] "Colonel Parker," *School Journal,* **32** (September 25, 1886), 168.

[66] Lelia E. Patridge, *The Quincy Methods* (New York: E. L. Kellogg and Company, 1885), p. xi.

[67] Rev. A. D. Mayo, "The New Teacher in the New America," *Journal of Proceedings and Addresses, National Educational Association, 1879,* p. 63.

[68] "Our Schools," *Quincy Patriot,* February 14, 1880.

[69] "Our Schools: From the *New York Tribune," Quincy Patriot,* January 24, 1880.

[70] "A Success at Quincy, Sketch of Col. Parker and His Grand Educational Work," *Quincy Patriot,* April 21, 1900.

[71] *Record of the General School Committee for the Town of Quincy,* February 8, 1878.

[72] *Ibid.,* April 5, 1879.

[73] Francis W. Parker, "A Sketch of the Work in the Quincy Schools from 1875 to 1880," V, p. 69.

[74] "Editorial," *New England Journal of Education,* **11** (January 1, 1880), 8.

[75] "An American Experiment," *The Journal of Education, A Monthly Record and Review,* London, England, No. 164—No. 61, New Series (March 1, 1883), 91–92.

[76] Francis W. Parker, "The Quincy Method," p. 117.

[77] Charles Francis Adams, Jr., "The New Departure in the Common Schools of Quincy," p. 500.

[78] Charles Francis Adams, Jr., "Scientific Common-School Education," pp. 937–938.

[79] Francis W. Parker, "A Sketch of the Work in the Quincy Schools from 1875 to 1880," V, p. 70.

[80] Francis W. Parker, "A Sketch of the Work in the Quincy Schools from 1875 to 1880," I, *School Journal,* **29** (June 6, 1885), 357.

[81] Charles Francis Adams, Jr., "The New Departure in the Common Schools of Quincy," p. 502.

[82] Aaron Gove, "The Trail of the City Superintendent," *Journal of Proceedings and Addresses, National Educational Association, 1900,* p. 217.

[83] "Editorial," *New England Journal of Education,* **11** (January 1, 1880), 8.

[84] Charles Francis Adams, Jr., "The New Departures in the Common Schools of Quincy," p. 499.

[85] Isaac Freeman Hall, *op. cit.,* p. 155.

[86] Charles Francis Adams, Jr., "The New Departure in the Common Schools of Quincy," p. 499.

[87] Wendell Phillips, "Wendell Phillips on the Quincy System," *Journal of Education,* **12** (December 16, 1880), 403.

[88] Adams confided in his diary, June 17, 1875, that he "kept far from the maddening crowd." Class derogatory remarks were attributed to Adams by Seth Dewing, Jr. "Town Meeting," *Quincy Patriot,* March 27, 1880. Adams believed in equality of men before the law, but not in social equality. Edward Chase Kirkland, *op. cit.,* p. 141.

[89] Charles Francis Adams, Jr., *The Public Library and the Public Schools* (Boston: Estes and Lauriat, 1879), pp. 5–8.

[90] Francis W. Parker, "A Sketch of the Work in the Quincy Schools from 1875 to 1880," I, p. 357.

[91] Adams mentions dining with Parker in his diary, November 28, 1875, April 23 and May 29, 1876, March 31, 1878, November 23, 1879, February 29, 1880. Parker went sailing with him on July 2 and 4, 1878. In all this time Adams mentioned no one else dining with him except Dr. Dimmock on May 29, 1876, and February 10, 1878. His brother, Brooks, dined with him on June 1, 1879.

[92] Edward Chase Kirkland, *op. cit.*, pp. 25, 29.

[93] Francis W. Parker, "A Sketch of the Work in the Quincy Schools from 1875 to 1880," I, p. 357.

[94] Charles Francis Adams, Jr., *History of Braintree, Massachusetts (1639–1708), The North Precinct of Braintree (1708–1792) and The Town of Quincy (1792–1889)* (Cambridge, Mass.: Riverside Press, 1891), p. 303.

[95] Charles Francis Adams, Jr., "The New Departure in the Common Schools of Quincy," pp. 499, 504.

[96] Francis W. Parker, "The Quincy Method," p. 114.

[97] Charles Francis Adams, Jr., "The New Departure in the Common Schools of Quincy," pp. 503–504.

[98] Charles Francis Adams, Jr., "The Development of the Superintendency," *Journal of the Proceeding and Addresses, National Educational Association, 1880,* pp. 61–76; Francis W. Parker, "A Sketch of the Work in the Quincy Schools from 1875 to 1880," II, p. 374; Francis W. Parker, "The Quincy Method," p. 119.

[99] Charles Francis Adams, Jr., Diary, February 7, 1878.

[100] Francis W. Parker, "A Sketch of the Work in the Quincy Schools from 1875 to 1880," V, p. 70.

[101] *Record of the General School Committee for the Town of Quincy,* September 15, 1877.

[102] Francis W. Parker, "A Sketch of the Work in the Quincy Schools from 1875 to 1880," V, p. 70.

[103] *Record of the General School Committee for the Town of Quincy,* January 6, 1879.

[104] *Ibid.,* April 5, 1879.

[105] *Ibid.,* July 7, 1879.

[106] *Ibid.,* March 24, 1880.

[107] Francis W. Parker, "A Sketch of the Work in the Quincy Schools from 1875 to 1880," V, p. 70; Francis W. Parker, "The Quincy Method," pp. 117–118.

[108] *Record of the General School Committee for the Town of Quincy,* May 1, 1880; Charles Francis Adams, Jr., Diary, April 30, 1880.

[109] *Record of the General School Committee for the Town of Quincy,* March 24, 1880.

[110] *Record of the General School Committee for the Town of Quincy,* April 12, 1880.

[111] Lelia E. Patridge, *op. cit.*, pp. xi–xiii.

[112] *Annual Report, School Committee, Town of Quincy, 1880–1881,* p. 191.

[113] *Ibid.,* pp. 191–193.

[114] *Ibid.,* p. 193.

[115] Isaac Freeman Hall, *op. cit.*, p. 194.

[116] Henry Adams, *The Education of Henry Adams* (New York: Random House, 1931), p. 26.

VIII

Up to Boston!

Boston was the Mecca toward which all New England teachers set their faces, and Parker believed there was no higher praise than to be called there to teach. In addition to praise, he was to receive almost double his Quincy salary.[1]

The Boston schools, which Parker considered among the best in the whole civilized world, then enrolled around fifty thousand students. Parker was to be supervisor of forty-two primary schools in eight of the school districts of Boston. There were more than four hundred teachers for him to supervise, and each teacher had an average of fifty pupils.[2] It was a big job, but Parker was heralded in Boston as a man of powerful physique and robust health. Moreover, he was said to have a "boundless good humor." His Quincy reputation, of course, had preceded him, and one newspaper claimed that he would effect a mighty revolution in a few years.[3]

The revolution in Boston had started the year before Parker's appointment. Indeed, if there had not been a change of superintendent and policy in 1879, Parker might never have cracked the select circle of Boston supervisors. John D. Philbrick had been the superintendent of schools in Boston for many years when he was replaced in 1879. At that time the Boston School Committee instituted what it called a "radical change."[4] Philbrick had been a "conservative." Parker respected him, however, and he was sorry that "bitterness shaded the last years of his life."[5]

One of the most radical moves of the School Committee had been to separate the primary schools from the control of the grammar school masters. The committee reported some opposition to this change but believed resistance had "nearly ceased" by the end of the 1879–1880 school year. Actually, the committee had to admit two years later that this move had kept the Board of Supervisors "practically divided" all that time.[6]

The *Annual Report* of the Boston School Committee for 1880 did not reveal any controversy over the advent of Parker. It was simply stated that the radical development in that year was the institution of the "new departure" in education. What is this new system? The committee answered its own question by saying: "To experts in education, it is sufficient to say simply, the 'Quincy Method.' To the outside public, we desire to say that in the sphere of instruction, it is easier and simpler, because more natural . . . . In a word it may be said regarding the whole system, the pupil is treated less like a machine, and more like a child . . . ."[7]

Parker began to impose his system with characteristic vigor. Meeting his teachers for the first time in an assembly, he said: "I expect to see a great many things I don't like, and I mean to tell you of it. I expect some of you will shed a great many tears; but out of these tears I expect you will become better teachers."[8]

Parker could handle the tears of primary school teachers who were women of limited educational training. Primary grades had traditionally been assigned to inferior teachers and were dominated by the masters of the grammar schools.[9] Such masters would be much harder to deal with. Parker was probably counting heavily on the recent revision of supervision which separated the primary and grammar grades.

It was said to be a "bitter pill for Boston to swallow," when the schools of its little suburb had gained prominence under the leadership of an unknown educator. Boston "masters" considered that they knew all there was to be known about education, and it would be difficult for an outsider to influence them, especially an outsider who found fault with the schools.[10] Even when Parker's fame in Quincy had reached the national level, and teachers from all over the country were flocking there to see how Parker was shepherding the little children, at least one prominent Boston "master" denied knowledge of Parker. Indifference was also mixed with outright hostility. When the Massachusetts Teachers Association had met in Boston during December 1879, the "Quincy Method" was compared to patent medicine such as "hop Bitters."[11]

Colonel Parker happened to be present at this session of the Massachusetts Teachers Association, and he retaliated by asserting to the members, as proof of their conservatism, that their organization had been originally formed to oppose Horace Mann. This assertion was hotly denied by the younger members. By this time Horace Mann had achieved a certain amount of respectability. Older members, however, admitted under pressure that there was truth to Parker's charge. They claimed, however, that Horace Mann had great faults. He tried to crush those who opposed him.[12]

Now the Boston conservatives would have to crush Parker. The "masters" were armed with intellectual slings that bore the rock of ages. The "new" education had to first defend itself from the "unpardonable sin of being young." Rather than oppose the weight of centuries, Parker defended the "new departure" by claiming it was old, that there was nothing new in the "Quincy Method." He said this method was indebted to all the great teachers of the past. Parker laughed at the "tender-footed" educators who could not advocate anything until it was found traditional.[13]

After arguing that his ideas were old, Parker had to defend himself against the charge that he had stolen all his theories. He replied that these charges were the "solid truth." He said he stole from Aristotle, Pestalozzi, Spencer, from the schools of Cleveland and Cincinnati, and he said everyone else ought to steal all he could. Even then there was not half enough for the famished minds of children.[14]

After arguing that he stole some of his ideas from schools in the West, Parker had to fight against Boston's "crime of locality." This meant that nothing good could come out of the west. Boston had once questioned Lincoln and Grant because they had come out of Illinois.[15]

Not only would Boston, which Parker called the "Athens of America," resist anything new, or stolen or from the West, it would oppose any person lacking in proper Bostonian amenities. Perhaps Parker had gotten rid of that awful hat which had so impressed James H. Slade of the Quincy School Committee. Perhaps he heeded the advice of Charles Francis Adams, Jr., that he would have to get a new suit and a tall hat if he wished to succeed in Boston. It was definitely reported, however, that on one of his first supervising visits to a school in Boston he was mistaken for a plumber![16] Bold, zestful, unconventional in his personal as well as professional life, Parker had the courage, according to one critic, of being "crude."[17]

Without formal academic degrees Parker must have been regarded as a barbarian in Boston. It was reputed that he even said, "I am going to have a hard fight here, and I am going to be beaten, but I shall make it easier for the next man." He did say that "the blood of a few martyrs would be the seed of true educational freedom."[18]

At least he had the full support of the School Committee. He even had another Adams—Brooks, younger brother of the Quincy School Committeemen—on the Boston School Committee. This Adams was chairman of the Subcommittee on Primary School Instruction.[19] The committee in Boston was even prepared, in some respects, to go farther down the road of reform than Parker. It was at this time that the committee considered doing away with corporal punishment, but the proposal was finally voted down when it was argued that not a single large town or city in the United States, or anywhere in Europe, had students governed in any other way than through such punishment. Parker himself was reported to be in favor of retaining corporal punishment, "if circumstances demanded it." He volunteered the opinion that he would have no rule on the matter. He believed the way to rid the schools of corporal punishment was to place an excellent teacher in every room.[20]

When teachers gathered in those days, the great theme that ran through their discussions was the "probable effect of engrafting Colonel Parker on Boston." This theme dominated the fifty-first annual meeting of the American Institute of Instruction, which met at Saratoga Springs, New York, in July of 1880. Boston teachers, it was reported, were never out in greater force.[21]

In his opening address at the convention, Dr. B. Northrup, Secretary of the Connecticut State Board of Education, praised the work of Parker and the "Quincy Method." He said that the schools of Quincy were "manifestly inferior," when he visited them just prior to the coming of Parker. Since then they had become models for the nation. He then introduced the Colonel to the members of the American Institute of Instruction as the "best-known educator in the United States."[22]

The Colonel said he had come to Saratoga Springs for his health and not to talk. He had only finished his fourth glass of the famous spring-water when he came across the program for the convention. When he saw that the "Quincy Method" was going to be discussed, he said he came to the convention because he was anxious to know something about it. Then, in a clear and modest tone, speaking without notes, he was reported to have made the best impression he had yet achieved with educators in any public address. He built his talk around the word "freedom." He said his system meant freedom for teachers as well as for children. Teachers must be artists, following an ideal, not artisans with a pattern. He went on to insist that his methods were not a bag of tricks, not mere "teaching technicalities." The teacher, he said, must know the subject matter, but also the mind, and how to adapt the two.[23]

William T. Harris followed Parker to the platform. He had been superintendent of schools in St. Louis and was now associated with the Concord School of Philosophy. Already an imminent educator, he would one day be the United States Commissioner of Education. At this time he praised Parker but implied that the "work in Quincy" had only brought out "formal activity" and may have neglected "substantial activity." By "substantial activity" Harris meant the world of the mind.[24]

For several days after the opening session, the "hotel talk" centered on the "new departure in Boston." Then the opposition hit the convention floor in what was reported as "the liveliest day perhaps in the history of the Institute." Dr. John D. Philbrick, former superintendent of Boston schools, took the lead in attacking the "new departure." He argued that "dropping all systematic study of language" was a "great mischief." He defended the importance of Latin and Greek in the curriculum. Parker got some applause when he objected to holding the children's noses to the grindstone. William E. Sheldon, of the *Journal of Education,* however, got more applause when he said he favored substantial work, even if it were "grindstone" work.[25]

A "spirit of quiet, chafing criticism" of Parker began to sweep the convention. The Colonel was reported as "excited to a high degree." He took the platform and tore into his opponents in a "personal" way. With words and arms flying in all directions, everyone would remember his actions, but no one could quite remember exactly what he said.[26]

Parker recovered his composure sufficiently enough to join the National Educational Association and address its members at Chautauqua, New York, later that summer of 1880.[27] Among many educators, at that time, there was talk that the Colonel would not last long. His influence was ascribed to the enthusiasm which he had been able to generate.[28]

Boston gossip soon had it that the teachers "from the High School down" were "out of sorts" and "disgusted with the present management."[29] Opposition centered on the Board of Supervisors. In its *Annual Report* for 1881, the School Committee even had to justify the existence of such a board. It said people had attempted to underrate the whole system because they found fault with some of the "details of its execution." It was a "delicate matter," the committee added, to go into the "personal constitution" of the board. The committee did not impute any shortcomings to individual members or "echo any vague and indefinite complaints."[30]

Parker was probably not surprised at this resistance, but he may have been finding that the power of his personal touch was less effective in such a big school system. "Quincy Methods," it seems, could not be achieved in a day or a year, simply because the School Committee had directed that such radical changes take place. A revolution from above could not be immediately effective, and it was obvious that the "Quincy Methods" had not taken hold in all the lower grades in Boston. It was in the fall of 1880 that G. Stanley Hall, then a lecturer in psychology at Harvard and Williams, began actual experiments in the Boston schools on "the content of children's minds." Hall determined that all children were absorbing a "chaos of half-assimilated impressions, half right, half wrong." He pointed out, for instance, that after the methods of cramming, children knew much about a cow, but they were sure it was no bigger than a small mouse because of the pictures of it in their books.[31]

It would be a long time before G. Stanley Hall would be influential enough to lead educators down the path of "Child Study," and, in the meanwhile, Parker, without the support of experimental science, had to drag the teachers along with him.

By the summer of 1881, Parker complained that he was in need of much rest, but he agreed to give three weeks of his summer vacation to the Martha's Vineyard Summer Institute. It was only a short distance from Boston by ferry. His class in "didactics," beginning in July, was not well advertised and his pupils numbered only about fifty, but the island of Martha's Vineyard turned out to be a haven, well removed from the battles in Boston. The island was noted for its hotels and plank walks, its pure water and healthy sea breezes.[32] Parker even found romance in the air.

Mrs. Frances Stuart, of the Boston School of Oratory, was a lecturer in elocution at the Institute. She immediately caught the playful attention of the Colonel, but he soon discovered that she did not like to be called a "yell-ocutionist."[33]

Described as a "splendid, big boy, and a wise, good man in one skin," the Colonel could not help but appreciate the charms of Mrs. Stuart. She was exquisitely feminine, at the same time having the intellectual interests and capacities of a man. This rare combination was manifested in her large eyes and sensitive mouth, overshadowed by a broad, intellectual brow.[34]

Parker was in the susceptible period of his early forties. Mrs. Stuart, ten years younger, was not only attractive but keenly interested and insightful about the business of education. She was also a striking example of a "liberated" woman, wedded to the cause of liberty and equal rights for all her sex. Having long since discarded her given name of "Mary," she had even reduced her middle name of Frances to Frank. It was probable that "Frank" met "Frank" on equal terms on the "piazza of the Sea-View Hotel" that summer of 1881.[35]

The Colonel made it a point to learn more about "Mrs. Stuart." She had resumed her maiden name after liberation from the bondage of an unfortunate marriage, but she had to begin life again with two young daughters. Mabel had been born in 1865 and Edna in 1868, both before their mother was twenty-one. The Colonel, however, insisted on calling his new friend "Miss Stuart," which might indicate that he saw no barrier to a more intimate friendship. Mrs. Stuart told him she had one daughter taller than herself and another daughter who would be attending one of Parker's schools in the fall. Apparently their discussions then turned to the teaching of spelling, and Mrs. Stuart was quite interested in Parker's ideas on the matter.[36]

No sooner was the summer over than Parker found an excuse to seek out this young woman who taught elocution at the Boston School of Oratory. He said he wanted to smooth out his "rough sounding" voice. It had bothered him since he was wounded in the neck during the war. He even complained that when he lectured very long his voice would break off into a "hoarse whisper." That he made "progress in his manner of public speaking" would soon be noticed by educators who had previously thought of Parker on the platform as a "bull in a china closet."[37]

Mrs. Stuart had begun her career by studying at the Boston University School of Oratory under Lewis B. Monroe. She was coached by the Shakespearian critic Henry Hudson and the great Shakespearian reader Robert Raymond. She studied articulation and visible speech with Alexander Graham Bell. When the Boston School of Oratory was established as a separate institution, Mrs. Stuart served Professor Raymond in the Department of Voice and Delsarte System of Gesture.[38] She was, indeed, a remarkable woman.

Mrs. Stuart established lodgings in Boston that fall, at 7 Beacon, house 935 East Fourth. It was therefore more convenient for her to meet the Colonel, and her daughter, Edna, recalled that Parker's residence at 150 Tremont Street was soon familiar ground.[39]

It is quite probable that Parker's own daughter, Annie, was going to school in Boston at this time and enjoying the companionship of her father. The *Boston Directory* included a "Miss Annie Parker," boarding at 6 Burroughs Place.[40] She was sixteen years old, the same age as Mrs. Stuart's daughter, Mabel.

Parker must have been reaching the stage of suitor during the fall of 1881. Neither he nor Mrs. Stuart had ever remarried, possibly because their careers would admit no rival. Now it may have occurred to both of them that marriage would not inhibit but enhance their careers. Parker especially needed the *savoir-faire* which Mrs. Stuart could offer. She was "aristocratic to the fingertips by birth." If Parker was to succeed in teaching Boston how to teach, perhaps Mrs. Stuart was needed to teach Parker how to live as a Bostonian. It was soon observed by educators that after Mrs. Stuart came into Parker's life, at least his necktie was "kept straight."[41]

Parker's position in Boston, however, was still too insecure for him to make any commitments in the way of marriage. The crisis passed in March of 1882 when he was re-elected to another term on the Board of Supervisors. Charles Francis Adams, Jr., immediately wired his congratulations. At last, he said, the "new model" could be fairly introduced. "Time and patience," he noted, "these are all you want; and now, if you only stick to it, you are destined to revolutionize the common school education of Massachusetts, and through it of America. . . ."[42]

Though Parker's position was somewhat more secure, at least for another year, the Board of Supervisors was no less opposed and divided. The School Committee, in its report for 1882, warned the Supervisors that they ought to be a "homogeneous" rather than a "heterogeneous" body. The committee believed that the methods of the board should be the same for all, not just for one supervisor. Perhaps the committee favored the methods of Parker, but it had come to the conclusion that "Whatever tends to divide the Board of Supervisors so that it cannot profitably sit together in counsel, robs it of an important means of usefulness and efficiency."[43]

Although Parker continued to hold power on the Board of Supervisors, those powers were being circumscribed. The School Committee found that the supervisors, most likely Parker in particular, had been doing the work of principals as well as their own. The powers and duties of the supervisors and the principals were therefore being carefully defined and separated. In addition to limiting the duties of the supervisors, the committee recommended, probably under pressure, that the responsibility of the primary schools should revert once more to the principals of the grammar grades.[44]

With the individual powers of principals restored, and especially with the "masters" of the grammar schools in control of the primary schools again, Parker must have felt that the hope of reaching the teachers and effecting a revolution in education was greatly diminished. Nevertheless, by the summer of 1882, he was undoubtedly happy to be making a return engagement at the Summer Institute of Martha's Vineyard. Here he could teach teachers, and it was said that his classes attracted 150 people from Canada and as many as twenty-three states. His students included forty-seven principals or heads of departments and seven superintendents.[45]

Now Parker could indulge himself in the pleasure of Mrs. Stuart's company, after her lectures on "The Delsarte Method—Its Uses and Abuses." Love was the headiest vintage of Martha's Vineyard. Parker was in love, and Mabel, the eldest daughter of Mrs. Stuart, found romance with George Rolfe, son of the Summer Institute president. They, too, would soon marry.[46]

Love for the Quincy Methods also brought Lelia Patridge to Martha's Vineyard. She was also planning to publish a book on these methods which she had observed in Quincy just after Parker's departure. Now, at the suggestion of the editor of New York's *School Journal,* she took "copious" notes at all of Parker's lectures. When she showed them to him and asked permission to publish them, he said the notes were her's to do with as she liked. He did insist on revising them if he was to endorse their publication. Miss Patridge confessed that his revisions turned out to be his own "re-writing."[47]

These notes, subsequently published as *Talks on Teaching,* sold more copies than any other educational book of the times. It was adopted by most state reading circles. Commissioner of Education, William T. Harris, later claimed that the book was more helpful in stimulating student motivation than any book on pedagogy ever published. *Talks* was reissued in 1891 as the twelfth edition. A fifteenth edition was brought out in 1903, after the Colonel's death.[48]

While Parker had been spinning out these talks on teaching at Martha's Vineyard, probably under the inspiration of Mrs. Stuart, he also made important converts. One of these was Alice H. Putnam, of the Chicago Froebel Society.[49] She was to become especially important in the days ahead, when Parker would be making Chicago the center of the new educational departure.

Parker received a call to take over the principalship of the Cook County Normal School, near Chicago, shortly after he returned to his Boston post in the fall of 1882. He immediately wrote Mrs. Putnam to inquire about the "general status of the educational work there." She warned him of the battles he might expect with the board of education there, but she indicated that Chicago was in a very "plastic" condition educationally. The idea that Chicago was ready to "grow rationally," apparently greatly impressed the Colonel.[50] He may also have contacted his cousin, Charles Irving Parker, who was then a principal of a suburban high school near Chicago. At least he would have one advocate among the principals of that city. His cousin was said to entertain the advanced ideas that the Colonel advocated.[51]

It was a time of decision for Parker. It had already been settled that he and Mrs. Stuart would marry, but he was apparently unhappy with his position in Boston and his future bride had her roots there. She might not be happy elsewhere. It was his future happiness, as well as his career, that was being risked. On September 27, 1882, Parker "opened his heart" in a letter to A. H. Champlin, chairman of the Committee on Teachers and Salaries, County Board of Education, Cook County, Illinois. He wrote:

> Dear Sir: Your letter in regard to the Cook County Normal School is at hand. I must frankly confess that the position is in many ways a tempting one. The one great desire of my heart is to teach directly; the more I supervise the more that desire increases. I am convinced that theory can only be kept within its proper limits by constant practice. . . . This work, Principal of a Normal School, would give me an opportunity to study the science of teaching and all that relates to it. In supervising, my forces are scattered. On the other hand, my position in Boston is an excellent one. I was re-elected last spring without the slightest effort on my part. The future here looks exceedingly favorable; indeed, unless I signally fall, I can stay here all my life. I have been urged very strongly by very influential persons in Philadelphia, members of the School Board, and others, to take the superintendency of that city. I prefer to stay in Boston; still, if the conditions are favorable to success there, I could not refuse. I have thus presented the selfish, personal side of the matter. The only question should be, "Where can I do the most good?" *In some sense I am or have been made responsible for the success of a reform in teaching. Where can I best push such a reform, in supervising or training teachers?* My success in training teachers leads me to incline to the latter. Still I am in doubt. Under the proper conditions, with a free hand to work out slowly my ideal, a life spent in building up a great Normal College may be the most economical use of my time . . . . So you see it is a terribly solemn question with me, this matter of changing the base of my operations. I am forty-five years old (forty-six next month), in splendid health, and capable of much hard work. I shall be married (D.V.) in a short time to a lovely woman. She is called (and of course I think she is) the best teacher of elocution (the Delsarte system) in this this country . . . .[52]

A. H. Champlin hastened to reply that he considered Parker the one man for the job. "Do not frighten us by naming too high a salary," he wrote. He added that Mrs. Putnam had been in correspondence with him and that she said great things in an educational way were in store for Cook County if Parker's services could be obtained.[53]

Parker replied on October 5, 1882, that "There is one great inducement for me to take a Normal School, and that is to work out my ideal face to face with my own pupils . . . . Yet a mistake now for me would be fatal . . . . As to salary, I certainly want enough to keep me out of the Soldiers' Home in my old age . . . ." He admitted that in his struggle for better teaching he had never allowed money to enter into his plans. As a result, he said, he was poor. He felt strongly constrained, however, to accept the offer, if made, for no less than $5,000 in salary.[54]

Such a salary was much more than the $3,750 he was then drawing in Boston, but his future wife was making almost that much at the Boston School of Oratory and they would lose that income if they moved to Chicago.[55]

Parker, reportedly, had been offered $6,000 as superintendent of schools in Philadelphia. It is certain there was an earnest effort there to secure a competent man for that job. It remained open until March of 1883, when James McAlister, possibly recommended by the Colonel, accepted the position.[56]

As it turned out, the Cook County Normal School met Parker's demands. Even Mrs. Stuart encouraged him to accept.[57] Parker himself, in retrospect, was not really sure why he accepted the offer, unless it was a stroke of "Divine Providence."[58] At any rate, the Colonel submitted his resignation in Boston on November 22, 1882, to take effect on the first of December.[59] He could not even wait this out. On November 29th, he married Mrs. Stuart, and it was reported that they left the same afternoon for Virginia.[60]

Parker's departure from the educational scene in Boston was therefore as abrupt as it was probably unexpected. Though he was rushing into a honeymoon, he had no reason to believe that his career in Chicago would be of such unmixed bliss. A. M. Kellogg, editor of the *School Journal* and considered an "insider" on school politics, had warned Parker about the Cook County Normal School as soon as he heard of the Colonel's decision. He begged him not to go there.[61] Parker must have been unsettled by this warning and he wrote again to Dr. Champlin about the promises made. He said his friends would not forgive him if he took the position under any shadow of uncertainty.[62]

It was too late to turn back, regardless of assurances, and Parker's move was hailed, even in the *School Journal,* where it was said that Parker's resignation was a serious loss to Boston. It was suggested that Parker had never felt at home there. Boston's *Journal of Education* took exception to its New York rival and claimed to be at a "serious loss" to know what would be the "serious loss" to Boston.[63]

Boston had lost the revolution. Parker expected the decisive educational battlefield would be in the West, and he wanted to be in the thick of the fight. Chicago, he also believed, was the "storm centre" of American civilization.[64] American civilization and the new education were inseparable in Parker's view, but he probably had no idea that he was headed into such a storm.

NOTES

[1] Francis W. Parker, "A Sketch of the Work in the Quincy Schools from 1875 to 1880," III, *School Journal,* **29** (June 27, 1885), 407; F. W. Parker, letter to Dr. A. H. Champlin, October 5, 1882, as printed in "The History of Col. Parker's Normal Connection," *Chicago Sun* (Chicago, Ill.), July 5, 1887.

[2] *Annual Report of the School Committee of the City of Boston, 1880* (Boston: Rockwell and Churchill, City Printers, 1881), pp. 219; 272; *Annual Report of the School Committee of the City of Boston, 1881* (Boston: Rockwell and Churchill, City Printers, 1882), pp. 37, 41, 329.

[3] "Col. Parker," Parker Scrapbooks, 1881, Archives, Harper Library, University of Chicago.

[4] Francis W. Parker, "A Sketch of the Work in the Quincy Schools from 1875 to 1880," III, p. 407; *Annual Report . . . Boston, 1880,* p. 16.

[5] Col. F. W. Parker, "John D. Philbrick," *School Journal,* **31** (June 5, 1886), 357.

[6] *Annual Report . . . Boston, 1880,* p. 16; *Annual Report of the School Committee of the City of Boston, 1882* (Boston: Rockwell and Churchill, City Printers, 1883), pp. 17, 18.

[7] *Annual Report . . . Boston, 1880,* p. 17.

[8] "From the *Boston Home Journal,*" *Quincy Patriot* (Quincy, Mass.),

[9] *Annual Report . . . Boston, 1882,* p. 17.

May 29, 1880.

[10] "Colonel Parker," *School Journal,* **32** (September 25, 1886), 168.

[11] "Colonel Parker," p. 168; "Massachusetts Teachers Association Met Monday Evening in the Girls Normal High School," *School Journal,* **16** (January, 1880), 3.

[12] *Ibid.*

[13] "Professor Payne, of Anne Arbor, thinks that the creed of the new education is expressed in the text: We learn to do by doing," newspaper clipping, Parker Scrapbooks, 1885; Francis W. Parker, "Discussion," *Journal of Proceedings and Addresses, National Educational Asociation, 1880,* p. 49.

[14] *Ibid.*

[15] "Professor Payne, of Anne Arbor . . . ."

[16] "Boston Gossip, Boston, November 1, 1881, The Doughty Colonel," newspaper clipping, Parker Scrapbooks, 1881; "Mistaken in the Person," *Quincy Patriot,* May 9, 1880.

[17] Francis W. Parker, "A Sketch of the Work in the Quincy Schools from 1875 to 1880," V. *School Journal,* **30** (August 1, 1885), 69.

[18] Boston Gossip, Boston, November 1 . . ."; Francis W. Parker, "A Sketch of the Work in the Quincy Schools from 1875 to 1880," I, *School Journal,* **29** (June 6, 1885), 357.

[19] *Annual Report . . . Boston, 1881,* p. 327.

[20] "Corporal Punishment," *Journal of Education,* **12** (December 2, 1880), 379.

[21] "From the *Boston Traveller,* 'The Quincy Method';" *Quincy Patriot,* July 17, 1880.

[22] "Education in Council at Saratoga," *Journal of Education,* **12** (July 15, 1880), 77, 84.

[23] *Ibid.,* p. 84; "From the *Boston Traveller,* 'The Quincy Method'."

[24] *Ibid.*; "The Concord School of Philosophy," *Journal of Education,* **14** (July 21, 1881), 76.

[25] "From the *Boston Traveller,* 'The Quincy Method';" "Education in Council at Saratoga," p. 90.

[26] "From the *Boston Traveller,* 'The Quincy Method'."

[27] Col. Francis W. Parker, "Discussion," *Journal of Proceedings and Addresses, National Educational Association, 1880,* pp. 49–50; *Journal of Proceeding and Addresses, National Educational Association, 1900,* p. 739.

[28] A. M. Kellogg, "Col. Parker at Quincy and Chicago," *Francis Wayland Parker: His Life and Educational Reform Work, Souvenir Issued in Honor of the Silver Anniversary of the Quincy Movement* (New York: E. L. Kellogg and Co., April 1900), p. 43.

[29] "Boston Gossip, Boston, November 1 . . . ."

[30] *Annual Report . . . Boston, 1881,* p. 21.

[31] G. Stanley Hall, "The Content of Children's Minds," in Charles Edward Skinner, Ira M. Gast, and Harley C. Skinner (Eds.), *Readings in Educational Psychology* (New York: D. Appleton, 1926), pp. 484–485.

[32] Lelia Patridge, "Introduction," to Francis W. Parker, *Talks on Teaching,* reported by Lelia E. Patridge, memorial edition (New York: A. S. Barnes Co., n.d.), p. 5; "Martha's Vineyard," *Quincy Patriot,* August 19, 1876.

[33] Alice H. Putnam, "A Reminiscence," *Frances Stuart Parker, Reminiscences and Letters* (Chicago: privately printed by C. L. Ricketts, 1907), p. 36.

[34] "Our Superintendent," *Quincy Patriot,* December 13, 1879; *Frances Stuart Parker, Reminiscences and Letters,* p. 18.

[35] *Frances Stuart Parker, Reminiscences and Letters,* pp. 36, 57–58, 61, 123; "Mrs. Frank Stuart Parker," *Journal of Proceedings and Addresses, National Educational Association, 1899,* p. 246. George R. Hall, Administrator of Parker's estate, testified that Mrs. Frances Stuart Parker disliked the name of Mary. In the matter of the estate of Francis W. Parker, deceased, dated, Chicago, April 23rd, A.D. 1902, In the Probate Court of Cook County, File 17–1379, Docket 65, Chicago, Ill.

[36] Marriage certificate, Francis W. Parker to Mary F. Stuart, November 29, 1882, Boston, Mass., Division of Vital Statistics (Vol. 336, p. 205, no. 3677), State House, Boston, Mass.; Cora Wheeler, "Early Life, Boston," *Frances Stuart Parker, Reminiscences and Letters,* pp. 11–12; Death Certificate, Frances Stuart Parker, April 1, 1899, Chicago, Illinois. Bureau of Vital Statistics, 130 North Wells Street, Chicago 6, Ill.; Department of the Interior, Bureau of Pensions, Cert. N. 869791, Francis W. Parker, Soldier's Certificate, Can No. 17835, Bundle No. 22, The National Archives, Washington, D.C.; Frances Stuart Parker, letter to Mabel, dated August 7, 1881, Cottage City, *Frances Stuart Parker, Reminiscences and Letters,* pp. 13–14.

[37] Martha Fleming, "Family and Home Life, Chicago," *Frances Stuart Parker, Reminiscences and Letters,* p. 22; Parker's claim for a disability pension in 1894, Department of the Interior, Bureau of Pensions.

[38] Cora Wheeler, *op. cit.,* pp. 13–14; "Mrs. Frank Stuart Parker."

[39] *The Boston Directory, No. 78, 1882* (Boston: Sampson, Davenport, and Company, 1882), pp. 813, 990; Interview with Edna Parker Shepard, October 14, 1962.

[40] *The Boston Directory, No. 78, 1882,* p. 812.

[41] Martha Fleming, *op. cit.*, pp. 23, 26.

[42] Charles Francis Adams, Jr., letter to F. W. Parker, dated March 29, 1882, as printed in "The History of Col. Parker's Normal Connection."

[43] *Annual Report . . . Boston, 1882,* p. 20.

[44] *Ibid.*, pp. 23–24.

[45] Lelia Patridge, *op. cit.*, p. 5.

[46] *Ibid.;* Cora Wheeler, *op. cit.*, p. 12; George Harvey Genzmer, "Rolfe, William James," *Dictionary of American Biography,* **16**, edited by Allen Johnson (New York: Charles Scribner's Sons, 1943), pp. 118–119.

[47] Lelia E. Patridge, "Introduction," *The Quincy Methods* (New York: E. L. Kellogg and Company, 1885), p. xiv. [Although Miss Patridge took notes for this book in 1880, she believed the notes taken at Martha's Vineyard, from Parker's own lips, should precede the book on actual practice of the Quincy Methods.]

[48] "E. L. Kellogg and Co., New York and Chicago, Advertisement for Parker's *Talks on Teaching,*" in Thomas T. Tate, *The Philosophy of Education, or the Principles and Practices of Teaching* (New York: E. L. Kellogg and Co., 1885), p. 21; *School Journal,* **31** (February 20, 1886) 118; W. T. Harris, letter to Colonel Parker, dated September 1, 1894, Department of the Interior, Bureau of Education, Washington, D.C., included in *Biennial Report of the* [*Cook*] *County Superintendent of Schools from July 1, 1892, to June 30, 1894* (Chicago: J. M. W. Jones Stationery and Printing Company, 1894), p. 42; *A Catalog of Books Represented by Library of Congress,* Vol. 114 (Ann Arbor, Mich.: Edwards Brothers, 1945), p. 227.

[49] Alice H. Putnam, "A Memorial Letter from Alice H. Putnam," *Kindergarten Review,* **12** (March 1902), 501.

[50] *Ibid.*, p. 502.

[51] John Williston Cook, *Educational History of Illinois* (Chicago: The Henry O. Shepard Co., 1912), p. 673. Charles Irving Parker was the principal of the suburban high school in Oakland and a disciple of his cousin, according to a newspaper clipping in Parker Scrapbooks, 1883.

[52] F. W. Parker, letter to A. H. Champlin, dated September 27, 1882, as printed in "The History of Col. Parker's Normal Connection."

[53] A. H. Champlin, letter to Col. F. W. Parker, dated October 2, 1882, as printed in "The History of Col. Parker's Normal Connection."

[54] F. W. Parker, letter to Dr. A. H. Champlin, dated October 5, 1882.

[55] *Ibid.*

[56] *Ibid.;* Editor's note in "The History of Col. Parker's Normal Connection"; Marion Foster Washburne, "Col. Francis W. Parker: The Man and Educational Reformer," *Francis Wayland Parker: His Life and Educational Reform Work, Souvenir Issued in Honor of the Silver Anniversary of the Quincy Movement* (New York: E. L. Kellogg and Co., April 1900), p. 21; "The New Superintendent of the Philadelphia Schools," *Journal of Education,* **17** (March 22, 1883), 184.

[57] A. H. Champlin, letter to F. W. Parker, dated October 10, 1882, as printed in "The History of Col. Parker's Normal Connection"; "Mrs. Frank Stuart Parker."

[58] Frances W. Parker, "Autobiographical Sketch," appendix in William M. Giffin, *School Days in the Fifties* (Chicago: A. Flanagan Co., 1906), p. 132.

[59] Francis W. Parker letter to Phineas Bates, Jr., Secretary, Board of Education, dated November 22, 1882, as printed in a newspaper clipping called "Resignation of a Supervisor," Parker Scrapbooks, 1882.

[60] Marriage certificate, Francis W. Parker to Mary F. Stuart, November 29, 1882; "Col. Francis W. Parker, a supervisor of the Boston Public Schools, who has accepted the principalship of the Cook Co. (Chicago) normal school, was married, last week to Mrs. M. Frances Stuart, of the School of Oratory, and started for Virginia in the afternoon," newspaper clipping, Parker Scrapbooks, 1882.

[61] Editor's note and A. M. Kellogg, letter to F. W. Parker, dated November 6, 1882, as printed in "The History of Col. Parker's Normal Connection."

[62] F. W. Parker, letter to Dr. A. H. Champlin, dated November 11, 1882, as printed in "The History of Col. Parker's Normal Connection."

[63] "Editorial," *Journal of Education,* **16** (December 7, 1882), 360.

[64] Marion Foster Washburne, *op. cit.,* p. 21; "A Success at Quincy, Sketch of Col. Parker and His Grand Educational Work," *Quincy Patriot,* April 21, 1900.

IX

The "Normal" Life in Chicago

Colonel Parker was to assume the principalship of the Cook County Normal School on the first of January, 1883.[1] The school was not then within the city limits of Chicago, nor did it serve the educational system of that city. It was incorporated in the village of Englewood, town of Lake, Cook County, Illinois. Englewood would be annexed to Chicago in 1889, but the Normal School would not come under the Chicago Board of Education until 1896. Nevertheless, Chicago pervaded the atmosphere of the Normal School from the beginning.[2]

In 1883, Englewood and its Normal School were connected to Chicago by several railroads. Little more than a saloon and "Farmers Rest," however, were at the 61st Street and Halstead railroad station in Englewood to greet the visitor. Open prairies reached to the horizon and cattle were pastured around the Normal School by the local "cow puncher."[3]

When the school had been brought to Englewood in 1869 and established on a twenty-acre campus just seven or eight miles south of Chicago' courthouse, no one dreamed that the city would ever extend so far south.[4] The metropolis, however, was now rapidly approaching the outskirts of Englewood. Chicago had burgeoned from an unincorporated village in 1837 to an industrial and transportation center of half a million people by the time Parker arrived. Even this booming community was to triple in population during Parker's tempestuous stay there.[5]

The Cook County Normal School to which Parker came was originally instituted by John Eberhart for the preparation of "country" teachers. Eberhart was elected school commissioner in 1859 and commenced his circuit supervision of the Cook County schools at precisely the same time Parker began teaching in Carrollton, at the other end of the state. Eberhart was soon appalled by the lack of preparation he found among the county teachers. Many were without educational credentials of any kind. Some were simply on the payroll for political reasons and did not even teach. Eberhart blamed the inadequate and corrupt condition of the schools on the territory's large population of "squatters" and renters, most of whom were foreign born and were said to have little interest in the schools.[6]

In his efforts toward reform, Eberhart focused on improving the training of teachers. He even succeeded in convincing the Cook County Board of Supervisors that they should finance a "Teachers Institute" in 1860, but the idea of a normal school was out of the question. Even the term was unfamiliar in those parts, where, at best, "training departments" in some of the high schools prepared young women to teach.[7] Seven years later, however, Eberhart won out, and the county authorized a provisional normal school. It was advertised as a training school for both sexes, with free tuition for county residents.[8]

The railroads—powerful economic and political forces in those days—apparently assisted in putting teacher training on a professional track. The Chicago and Rock Island Railroad offered free passes to students, and old freight cars were even provided as temporary classrooms.[9] The first classes, with Daniel S. Wentworth as teacher and principal, were held in the village of Blue Island, but the school announced plans to make its permanent home in whichever community offered the most to its support. A normal school would attract business; therefore, there was considerable competition among the local villages. Englewood, with only two hundred citizens, won the prize by offering twenty acres, then valued at about $800, and a lump sum of $25,000 in cash.[10]

The contract for the school building was let out in June of 1869 and the cornerstone laid that September, amid parades that included the plumed members of the local Grand Lodge. Community pride must have been dampened, however, by the ridicule which the Chicago newspapers heaped upon the location of such a school. Englewood was said to be a "frog pond," an inaccessible swamp.[11]

Scandal, as well as ridicule, marked the school from the beginning. Budgeted at $25,000, the building ended up costing six times that amount by the time it was completed in September of 1870. In answer to charges of "swindle," Principal Wentworth argued that the excessive expense was wholly chargeable to the "system of doing public business." The community could be proud, however, in housing its Normal School in what was called one of the finest buildings west of Philadelphia. Although the building had the novelty of steam heat, it was said to have no sanitary equipment and no water except for a surface well.[12]

Even this expensive physical plant was quick to fall into decay, and by the time Parker assumed the principalship, the school's famous heating apparatus was in such bad condition that the coils were continually bursting, often forcing classes to be dismissed during the winter months.[13]

By Parker's time, the school property was actually described as dilapidated. There was "no library to speak of," and no science laboratories or a gymnasium at all. The faculty, it was said, "was an equal mixture of competence and politics."[14] Although the Cook County Normal School had been allowed to run down financially and deteriorate materially, it was not educationally stagnant or decadent when Parker took over. Its former principal, Daniel S. Wentworth, was thirteen years older than Parker but a farsighted advocate of the new education. Parker considered him his "honored predecessor" and even believed that Wentworth was in a direct line from Horace Mann.[15]

The Normal School would not have survived through the years at all without the powerful leadership and sacrifices of Wentworth. The school was generally strangled for want of appropriations. Even the residence hall, with its gabled roof, had to be financed out of Wentworth's own funds and credit, although such a hall was desperately needed to accommodate the young girls from the country. Wentworth was also attacked every step of the way in his efforts to establish sound foundations for professional teacher training in Cook County. Nevertheless, he succeeded in holding the school together and retaining the principalship, except for one year, since the school had been founded in 1867.[16]

Wentworth was generally recognized as an important civic as well as educational leader in Englewood, and some credit for the rapid development of the village was given to him. During those years, however, there had been a general "exodus" from the confines of Chicago, especially after the great fire in 1871. The establishment of the stockyards in the town of Lake (though several miles from the Normal School) also contributed to the development of the community.[17] While Englewood was mushrooming in population, the Cook County Normal School did not enjoy such growth. It never graduated as many as forty students in any one year during Wentworth's tenure.[18]

Wentworth's failing health in 1882 brought the Normal School to the prospect of a lingering or even sudden death. It was claimed that the school had only survived because Wentworth lived. In the fall of 1882, Wentworth died in Denver, Colorado, where he had gone for his health. His remains were returned to "lie in state" at the front hall of the

"Normal." The Masons contributed to an impressive funeral, and the Chicago and Rock Island Railroad, which had helped in the early beginnings of the school, now provided nine coaches to accommodate the mourners to Wentworth's final resting place in Rosehill, Illinois.[19]

It was discovered that Wentworth would have died penniless, except for an insurance policy which had been subscribed for him by friends. He had always sacrificed his own interests for those of the school. Now, however, he left a widow (a former teacher at the school) and two small children without much substance. It is possible that his death, so lavishly commemorated, was as important as his life in securing financial support to carry on the work of what was really his school. The conscience of the community was touched. There was now a willingness to keep Wentworth's work alive, even if it meant securing the greatest educator that money could buy. Colonel Parker was thus engaged as Wentworth's "natural, his perfect successor."[20]

When Parker assumed the principalship of the Cook County Normal School in 1883, the school consisted of three departments. One was the Professional Training Class. A second was the elementary school of eight grades that constituted one of the district schools of Englewood. A A third included the four grades of the high school. Upon the annexation of Englewood by Chicago, in 1889, the high school was removed to other quarters and the Cook County Normal School was strictly a professional training school for elementary grade teachers.[21]

When Parker took over, the "practice" department of the Professional Training Class consisted of only two rooms and one regular teacher. He quickly brought six rooms and six teachers to this service. The Professional Training Class was then divided into three divisions, according to the differences in knowledge and progress of its members. Candidates for a diploma were admitted at any time of the year if they were graduates of high school or college. A 90 per cent average in four years of academic high school work exempted candidates from an entrance examination. Three years of successful teaching were considered the equivalent of a high school diploma for purposes of matriculation.[22]

There was no tuition for residents of Cook County, including Chicago, but nonresidents were charged $75.[23] Before 1896, when the Normal School was still controlled by the county, it was ignored by the Chicago Board of Education and no credit given to city teachers for training there. It therefore drew fewer students from Chicago than would otherwise be the case. Parker, of course, attracted students from all over the country. Nevertheless, there were never more than ninety-five students in any one class between the years 1883 and 1896. The average graduating class during those years numbered sixty-eight.[24] This was still a considerable increase over the average enrollment prior to Parker's principalship.

The prescribed course of study for the Professional Training Class was forty weeks. Parker did not consider this nearly sufficient, but no Cook County or Chicago Board of Education would extend the requirement until 1899, by which time the Colonel had moved on from the Normal School.[25] Parker did manage to get around the board's limitations by offering graduate work. Some of his most devoted students chose to stay on longer than the required year. They were offered "elective" courses in kindergarten training, physical education, elocution, history, geography, literature, science, manual training, mathematics, art, modeling, printing, drawing, music, and hygiene. Extension courses were also available through cooperation with other colleges, such as the University of Chicago.[26]

The work of the Professional Training Class, as well as that of the children in the elementary department, was continually changing. Parker had no final answers to the problems of teaching. He was continually experimenting. He did not fear making mistakes, even though he was hounded by community pressure and forced to defend everything he did. "The road to success," Parker said, "is through constant blundering.[27]

A certain style of educational experimentation, however, persisted. Each member of the Professional Training Class studied with a special departmental teacher as well as with a "critic" teacher at the grade level assignment. "Practice" teachers spent at least one hour a day throughout the year in observing the critic teacher at work and in teaching the class themselves. In addition, to observation and practice at the various grade levels, the student teachers were given intensive instruction by departmental teachers in the various subject-matter disciplines. Techniques of projecting each subject of study were employed, with emphasis on the need to carefully plan and prepare all lessons. What Parker called "illustrative teaching" was the over-arching technique to be mastered. This technique relied heavily on the use of pictures, models, field trips, and all kinds of concrete examples and specimens. The purpose was to direct children to observe things closely, to see relationships, and to describe them orally and in writing. Models and apparatus for much of this teaching were made by the teacher and students in the manual training shops. Such shops, as well as the library and museum, were organic parts of the whole school, around which lessons were planned.[28]

The whole faculty, departmental as well as critic teachers, cooperated with the "practice" teacher in preparing the outlines of subject matter and the "illustrative" methods and devices for adapting the material to the age and attainment of the children. These outlines were usually laid out a month in advance. When the outlines and plans were put into practice, the whole faculty was involved in the critique and evaluation.[29]

After completion of the forty-week course of study, members of the Professional Training Class who met the standards of the school were granted a diploma qualifying them for vacant positions in the schools of Cook County. Candidates for the diploma were evaluated on satisfactory evidence of professional attitudes as well as skills. Candidates were not only judged on their ability to "govern" and teach a class "fairly well," but on their courage to fight for the ideals of the new education.[30]

The elementary department, in which this practice took place, included eight grades and a kindergarten. The kindergarten had been initiated with hesitation by Wentworth in the last years of his life. Miss Matilda H. Ross of Columbus, Ohio, a pupil of Susan E. Blow, had been engaged for the year 1880-1881. It was Parker, however, who gave full support to the kindergarten as the very foundation of the new education. He immediately set up a class in 1883 with Mrs. Alice H. Putnam as the teacher. It was partially financed by the Chicago Froebel Association.[31]

The curriculum for the kindergarten and eight grades was gradually remodeled from separate and discrete subjects into an integrated whole that would later be known as a "core" curriculum.[32] The methods were similar to those developed in Quincy.

Parker not only smashed the traditional subject matter patterns of curricular organization and the methods of harsh mental discipline but the whole system of artificial rewards. This reform, he remembered, brought "a delegation of mothers" to him in the spring of 1883 with an "urgent plea for the retention of the monthly report card." Parker turned their opposition into support when he showed them what he considered the true test of a child's progress in school—the improved "character" and happiness of the child.[33] Parker was quick to organize "mothers' meetings" and parents' associations in order to spell out the work of the school to the community at large.[34]

Parker's success in overthrowing traditional education depended on a tightly knit, disciplined party of teachers. Parker's faculty at the Cook County Normal School was exactly that. From the first he had insisted on a free hand in the selection of teachers. He weeded out instructors who were inflexible in their methods or who were strictly political appointees. Although he had recommended no changes during his first term in 1883, he thereafter acted with dispatch. The Cook County Board of Education was still under his spell and elected only Parker candidates for the vacant teaching positions. Only four of Wentworth's original staff remained after the first year of Parker's administration.

One of the four was William C. Dodge, a Cook County Normal School graduate of 1871 who had filled in as principal between the regimes of Wentworth and Parker. Emily J. Rice, graduate of Edward Sheldon's Oswego Normal School in New York, was also retained, as well as Helen R. Montfort, graduate of Albany State Normal School, and Eleanor Worthington, who attended the Oswego Normal School and gone on to study with Louis Agassiz. Mrs. Daniel S. Wentworth, widow of the former principal, remained as "matron" of the boarding house.[35]

Half of the old guard left over from Wentworth's regime were graduates of the Oswego Normal School, which Parker credited as being the "pioneer" of the science of education in the United States.[36] It was through the school's founder, Edward Sheldon, as much as any single individual, that the theories of Pestalozzi and Froebel had been introduced into American pedagogy. As early as 1861 Sheldon saw the importance of understanding the "infant mind" and the natural order of succession in the development of the mind. He believed the kindergarten would be the "emancipation" of children.[37]

With such zealots of the Oswego movement as a nucleus of his staff, Parker went on to appoint Cora Wheeler from the Boston School of Oratory, Lelia E. Patridge, who had done so much to introduce Parker to the reading public, and Alex E. Frye, who had been a schoolboy in Quincy when Parker began his work there. He brought in another student of Sheldon's in Professor H. H. Straight. By no means the least of his new appointments was his wife, Mrs. Frank Stuart Parker.[38]

Parker went on to seek out his teachers with care. For the work on manual training he brought I. M. Carley from the Boston Sloyd School.[39] For the work on natural sciences in the elementary schools, he enticed Wilbur S. Jackman from Harvard's Natural Science Department.[40] William M. Giffin, who became vice principal of the Normal School in 1889, came with a master's degree from Lawrence University.[41] For the latest thinking in psychology, Parker sought out Collin E. Scott from G. Stanley Hall's psychology laboratories at Clark University. Parker said "Dr. Scott" was always explaining what people *really* meant when they said something at faculty meetings.[42]

Perhaps Parker's favorite teacher was Zonia Baber. An 1885 graduate of the Cook County Normal School, she soon became a part of the faculty as well as a special part of Parker's life.[43] One time she was forced to leave the school and travel South on account of health. "I trust you are fully aware of your great sins against yourself," Parker wrote, "and will never attempt overwork again, no matter how interesting geography is." Later he wrote that he was teaching a little geography himself. "I don't go deep down into the bowels of the earth as you do," he wrote, "but only skim along the surfaces like a swallow, and I am quite sure one swallow don't [sic] make a summer."[44]

Miss Baber was still absent in the spring of 1897 when the board made appointments for the following year. Parker assured her that she would be elected "without a murmur," unless, he added, "your friend Mr. C. S. Thornton gets in his deadly work and pops us all out. Then we shall travel together, form a variety show and go around the world." (Thornton was Parker's "deadly" enemy on the Chicago Board of Education, but at the time of this letter Thornton had just retired. Parker could therefore use his name in jest.) He told Miss Baber that as long as he was principal she would head his geography department. She was told to put that in her pipe and smoke it.[45]

In mock tones, Parker once wrote his "beloved sister" that she must "seize hold of the everlasting truth" and realize that she was not sick. He insisted that she had no stomach or liver, that the earthly body was simply a fiction. "The trouble with you," he said, "is that you have been believing that you have a body and also that you have red hair. You have neither. It is all your mortal mind." It is obvious from these remarks that Parker was influenced by the "Christian Science" of his contemporary, Mary Baker Eddy. Although he seemed to be satirizing the revelations of Mrs. Eddy, satire was his usual style in attempting to amuse and cheer up his ailing teacher. In the same letter, he told Miss Baber that he and the other teachers were shocked "beyond all comprehension" at her "awful wickedness" when they learned she had attended a cockfight on Sunday. He said they all mourned and passed an hour together in silent meditation.[46]

Parker's playfulness also came out in a postscript when he wrote that "Mrs. Parker sends you a kiss—I do not dare." He even indicated that his wife thought this had "gone far enough."[47] Mrs. Parker was also very fond of Miss Baber. Calling her "Dearly Beloved," she once added a postscript to one of the Colonel's letters, saying there was a good argument for marriage—grandchildren. By 1896, when she was writing, Mrs. Parker had already been enjoying the children of her oldest daughter, and she told Miss Baber to pick out a man in a hurry because it would take "twenty-four years at best" to produce a grandchild.[48]

It was Zonia Baber who brought Flora J. Cooke to the attention of the Colonel. Miss Cooke, perhaps more than any other member of Parker's family of teachers, would carry on his work in the next generation. Born Flora Julietta Hannum in 1864, less than a year before the birth of Parker's own daughter, she also lost her mother when she was five. Like Annie's father, Mr. Hannum was unable to care for the children. The brothers and sisters were successfully placed, but Flora went in and out of six homes within a year. Considered an unruly child, she grew up to prove Parker's thesis that there never was a bad child—only bad homes, bad habits, and bad conditions.[49]

The little girl was finally adopted by her mother's closest friends—Luella and Charles Cooke of Youngstown, Ohio. She began teaching in a rural school when she was only nineteen and transferred to the public schools of Youngstown the next year. There she came under the spell of the new principal, Zonia Baber.[50] Miss Baber was later called back to her alma mater, the Cook County Normal School, to take up teaching there, and she prevailed on the Colonel to send for the gifted Miss Cooke. It was said that Parker agreed to hire the young lady without an interview, if Miss Baber would take full responsibility for the success of her "protégé."[51]

When Flora J. Cooke took up her duties in 1889 at the Cook County Normal School, she was so shy that she thought she would die or resign before speaking up at faculty meetings. She remembered that Parker told her to decide quickly what she would do, because, if she stayed, she must contribute to the thinking of the faculty. He said "that is the only way you can learn and grow, and that's what we're all here for.[52]

Parker made enormous demands of his teachers. He insisted that they take part in the club and community life of Englewood in order to further the interests of the school.[53] He insisted that they devote themselves to the new education and work together for a "perfect unity of action." In order to see the work of the school as a whole, there were morning exercises in which everyone participated. Parker never quite abandoned the regimen of the military. Each day, after the morning exercises, he appointed an "Officer of the Day" from the ranks of the faculty. Lieutenants were daily elected from the Professional Training Class. The lieutenants visited as many of the classes as possible and reported "all that was good" to the "Officer of the Day." This report, in turn, was submitted to the Colonel.[54]

The kind of teaching Parker advocated was not easy. It required the understanding of children as well as of subject matter, the understanding of the nature of learning as well as the things to be learned. He was no easy task-master. Moreover, one of his teachers insisted that he was feared by the staff and "practice" teachers, that he struck real terror to their hearts.[55] Even Parker's devoted young disciple, Flora J. Cooke, found the Colonel "impetuous, impatient of obstacles, a ruthless champion of children, very human."[56] Parker was accused of yelling and bellowing at his teachers. One time when he found a teacher giving report cards, in spite of strict orders to the contrary, he was said to have actually "roared" and to have torn up the cards in front of the children.[57]

One teacher defended the Colonel by saying he never "bellowed" angrily. She remembered how he would enter a room and shout questions at the children as though giving commands to a company, but this was to gain the attention of the class. When he was unduly severe, one witness insisted, there was good reason for it.[58] Parker may have been talking about himself when he said that those who have a brusque manner and are loud-voiced suffer from timidity. They are really self-conscious, he said, and afraid.[59]

It was more as a strict father than an oppressive disciplinarian that Parker worked with his teachers. He did attempt to "control, govern, direct" them, but his main insistence was that each teacher focus on the development of every child. It was in this way that Parker made his school a family where all were interested in the welfare and progress of each.[60]

The Parker home was always open to his teachers. Every Sunday night, the "old maids," as he playfully called his female teachers, met informally at the house, and Mrs. Parker charmed these sessions with her readings of poetry. The Parker house, at 6640 Honore Street in Englewood, was more than a mile from the Normal School but it was very much a part of the school. It was the social center for his teachers. It was also the headquarters for planning educational strategy. The library, which was the Colonel's pride, opened into the spacious entrance hall on the first floor. It was was wainscotted with bookshelves bearing several thousand volumes. One end was devoted to the works of pedagogy, including all the writings of Horace Mann and what was reputed to be an "original Rousseau." Parker's workshop, on the second floor, was littered with current publications on education. It even had a "fad corner" in spite of his denial that he was an educational faddist. One of his chief "fads" was learning foreign languages. He prided himself on reading the Bible in various languages.[61]

The Parkers had purchased title to this acre of property when they first arrived in Cook County and, shortly thereafter, built the two-story frame house on it. Although the property was originally part of a new development, the city began closing in around the Parker home as the years went by. The frame house, however, remained shut off from the street by a fence, a wide expanse of lawn, and a garden plot. The open porches around the house were veiled in summer by "a mass of vines and clinging greens."[62]

It was to this house that his daughter, Annie, came to die in 1885. She had been suffering for about fourteen months with the same pulmonary tuberculosis that claimed her mother. Just twenty years old,

Annie had only two more weeks to live when she reached the new home of her father and stepmother.[63]

Why Annie had not joined her father in Chicago at an earlier time is not known. She had not married but was probably well established elsewhere. There may have been some jealousy regarding her father's new family ties. Only a flicker or two of memory survives to recall her life at all. She was remembered as a "very bright girl," a "lovely girl," and as a "big girl, who was good with little children." It was said that a photograph of Annie, now lost, was always in her father's study.[64]

Attended by Parker's friend from the Cook County Board of Education, Dr. Champlin, Annie died on October 27, 1885. Funeral arrangements were made through the House of Lanyon Undertakers. Her final resting place, however, remains unknown. Her death certificate placed interment in Manchester, New Hampshire, although no stone or other marker recalls her memory in the Parker plot.[65] It is possible that she was buried beside her mother, and that the intention of erecting a monument for her was never carried out. That Parker went to Manchester about this time is evidenced by the meeting of the "Parker Veteran's Club," made up of survivors of Company E, New Hampshire Volunteers of the Fourth Regiment, which met in Manchester at the City Hall on November 7, 1885.[66]

Personal tragedy, which Parker had lived with in childhood as well as manhood, probably increased rather than depressed his drive to create a better world through education and nonsectarian Christianity. The very next year after Annie's death a Young Men's Christian Association appeared in Englewood, probably due in no small part to Parker, who later was elected to its board of managers.[67]

If Parker had not been able to give the love and devotion to his own child which he had showered on all children, it was probably the fault of circumstances rather than design. He was always "adopting" people and helping friends and relatives. He was especially concerned about his New Hampshire nieces and nephews. He tried to arrange for each of them to spend a year with him in Chicago. Bertha Mille Cayzer, daughter of Parker's sister, Mary, graduated from the Cook County Normal School in 1892. She later married a Chicago boy and settled in Oak Park, Illinois. Her husband would one day be the administrator of Parker's estate.[68]

Percy and Blanche Folsum, the children of Parker's sister, Philinda, also lived and studied with the Parkers. They both went into teaching.[69] Wayland Parker Tolman, son of Parker's younger sister, Emily, left the farm near Keene, New Hampshire, for the life in Chicago. He reported back to the farm that Mrs. Parker was more of a career woman than homemaker. He thought she was quite a "spender," especially in regard to the table she set. On the other hand, when the Parkers sent old clothes to the Tolman farm, Emily wondered how her brother's family could wear clothes so long. Wayland Parker Tolman did not become a teacher, but his bride was put through cooking school by the Colonel.[70] The Parkers were always generous when it came to education.

Edna, the youngest daughter of Mrs. Frank Stuart Parker, was also trained at the Cook County Normal School, but she never became a teacher. Officially adopted by the Colonel in 1895, Edna Frances Glazier became Edna Stuart Parker.[71] In a sense, all children were adopted by Parker. He had appointed himself their educational guardian.

NOTES

[1] *Biennial Report of the County Superintendent of Schools from July 1, 1882 to June 30, 1884* (Chicago: J. M. W. Jones Stationery and Printing Co., 1885), p. 36.

[2] *Biennial Report of the County Superintendent of Schools from July 1, 1888 to June 30, 1890* (Chicago: J. M. W. Jones Stationery and Printing Company, 1890), p. 15; *Biennial Report of the County Superintendent of Schools from July 1, 1894 to June 30, 1896* (Chicago: J. M. W. Jones Stationery and Printing Co., 1896), p. 85.

[3] Gerald E. Sullivan (Ed.), *The Story of Englewood, 1835–1923* (Chicago: Foster and McDonnell, 1924), pp. 11, 27, 223.

[4] John F. Eberhart, "An Historical Sketch of the Cook County Normal School," *Chicago Schools Journal,* **17** (Jan.–June 1936), 124–125; Francis W. Parker (Ed.), "Englewood's Schools, Their Rise, Progress and Present Status Graphically Described," p. 7 [typed copy from *Daily Evening Call* (Englewood, Ill.), Special Number, Thursday, October 9, 1890], Historical Files, Chicago Teachers College South; *The Cook County Normal School* (Circular published by the Cook County Normal School Alumni Association, 1871), Historical Files, Chicago Teachers College South.

[5] Statistics supplied by the Superintendent of Schools on the sixtieth anniversary of the incorporation of Chicago. *School Report. Public Schools of the City of Chicago. Forty-third Annual Report of the Board of Education for the Year Ending June 25, 1897* (Chicago: J. M. W. Jones Stationery and Printing Co., 1897), p. 27.

[6] John F. Eberhart, *op. cit.,* pp. 121, 123.

[7] *Ibid.,* p. 122; Edwin G. Cooley, "The Chicago Teachers College," *Dedication of the Chicago Normal School, April 20 and 21, 1906* (Chicago: Chicago Normal School Press, n.d.), p. 41.

[8] John F. Eberhart, *op. cit.,* pp. 128–129.

[9] *Ibid.,* p. 128; "Normal to Honor Memory of Leader on Anniversary," *Southtown Economist* (Englewood, Ill.), November 8, 1939; "Chicago Teachers College History" (Unpublished manuscript, no author), pp. 1–2, Historical Files, Chicago Teachers College South.

[10] John F. Eberhart, *op. cit.*, pp. 124–125; "Chicago Teachers College History," p. 2.

[11] John F. Eberhart, *op. cit.*, p. 125; Francis W. Parker, *op. cit.*, p. 6; Polly Flynn, "The Early History of Chicago Teachers College in Its Relation to the Community" (Scrapbook of newspaper clippings, probably compiled in 1938 or 1939), Historical Files, Chicago Teachers College South; Dr. A. H. Champlin, "Memories of 'Normal'," *Dedication of the Chicago Normal School, April 20 and 21, 1906,* p. 106.

[12] John F. Eberhart, *op. cit.*, p. 124; newspaper clipping, Daniel S. Wentworth Scrapbook, Historical Files, Chicago Teachers College South; "Chicago Teachers College History," p. 2.

[13] "First Witness for the Defense," newspaper clipping, Parker Scrapbooks, 1887, Archives, Harper Library, University of Chicago.

[14] Orville T. Bright, "Address at Memorial Exercises, April 19, 1902," *Education Report, 1901–1902* (U.S. Office of Education, Report of the Commissioner of Education for the year 1902), p. 273.

[15] Francis W. Parker, *op. cit.*, p. 10; Biennial Report of the County Superintendent of Schools *from July 1, 1892 to June 30, 1894* (Chicago: J.M.W. Jones Stationery and Printing Co., 1894), p. 61; *Biennial Report . . . 1894–1896,* p. 95.

[16] Francis W. Parker, *op. cit.*, p. 8; "Chicago Teachers College History," p. 2; John F. Eberhart, *op. cit.*, pp. 127, 129.

[17] Francis W. Parker, *op cit.*, p. 9; Polly Flynn, *op. cit.; Alfred T. Andreas, History of Cook County from Earliest Period to Present Times,* Vol. III (Chicago: A. T. Andreas Co., Publishers, 1886), p. 334.

[18] *Alumni of the Chicago Normal School* (published by the officers of the Alumni Association, 1908–1909), n.p., Historical Files, Chicago Teachers College South.

[19] John Williston Cook, *Educational History of Illinois* (Chicago: The Henry O. Shepard Company, 1912), p. 4; "Obituary," in Polly Flynn, *op. cit.;* "Chicago Teachers College History," p. 4.

[20] "The Normal School," Parker Scrapbooks, 1887; Cora E. Lewis, "Daniel S. Wentworth," *Dedication of the Chicago Normal School, April 20 and 21, 1906,* p. 36.

[21] *Biennial Report of the County Superintendent of Schools From July 1, 1886 to June 30, 1888* (Chicago: J.M.W. Jones Stationery and Printing Co., 1888), pp. 49–50; *Biennial Report . . . 1888–1890,* p. 22.

[22] Francis W. Parker, "An Account of the Work of the Cook County and Chicago Normal School from 1883 to 1899," *Education Report, 1901–1902* (U.S. Office of Education, Report of the Commissioner of Education for the year 1902), p. 251; *Biennial Report . . . 1886–1888,* pp. 49–50.

[23] *Biennial Report of the County Superintendent of Schools from July 1, 1890 to June 30, 1892* (Chicago: J.M.W. Jones Stationery and Printing Co., 1892), p. 109.

[24] *Ibid.*, p. 40; *Biennial Report . . . 1894–1896,* p. 85; *Alumni of the Chicago Normal School.*

[25] Francis W. Parker, "Account of the Work of the Cook County and Chicago Normal School from 1883 to 1899," p. 263; "June 28, 1899," *Proceedings of the Board of Education of the Education of the City of Chicago, July 13, 1898–June 28, 1899* (Chicago: Press of John H. Higgins, n.d.), p. 736.

[26] Mary Agnes Riley, "A History of the Chicago Normal School" (Un-

published M.A. Thesis, University of Chicago, 1914), p. 104; Helen M. Hefferan, "Col. Francis Wayland Parker," *Chicago Schools Journal,* **18** (September 1936), 6, 105; Robert L. McCaul, "Dewey's Chicago," *The School Review* (Summer 1959), 273.

[27] F. W. Parker, "Obstacles in Our Way," *Journal of Education* **15** (May 18, 1882), 315.

[28] *Biennial Report . . . 1882–1884,* pp. 36–37.

[29] Mary Agnes Riley, *op. cit.,* p. 103.

[30] *Biennial Report . . . 1888–1890,* p. 42.

[31] John F. Eberhart, *op. cit.,* pp. 128–129; *Biennial Report . . .1886–1888,* p. 49.

[32] Francis W. Parker, "Account of the Work of the Cook County and Chicago Normal School from 1883 to 1899," pp. 253, 258–261; B. Othanel Smith, William O. Stanley, and J. Harlan Shores, *Fundamentals of Curriculum Development* (New York: Harcourt, Brace and World, 1957), p. 313.

[33] Francis W. Parker, "Account of the Work of the Cook County and Chicago Normal School from 1883 to 1899," p. 254.

[34] Mary Agnes Riley, *op. cit.,* pp. 107–108; Helen M. Hefferan, *op. cit.,* p. 7.

[35] F. W. Parker, letter to Dr. A. H. Champlin, dated November 11, 1882, as printed in "The History of Col. Parker's Normal Connection," *Chicago Sun* (Chicago, Ill.), July 5, 1887; "Thornton's Living Spite, Why the Lawyer Has Hounded Col. Parker of the Normal School for Years," *Chicago News,* (Chicago, Ill.), November 1, 1898; *Biennial Report . . . 1882–1884,* p. 53; "Chicago Teachers College History," *op. cit.,* pp. 3–4; "Normal School," newspaper clipping, Parker Scrapbooks, 1884.

[36] *Biennial Report of the County Superintendent of Schools from July 1, 1892 to June 30, 1894* (Chicago: J.M.W. Jones Stationery and Printing Co., 1894), p. 62.

[37] E. A. Sheldon, letter to Elizabeth P. Peabody, September 27, 1861, as printed in Ruth Markendorpff Baylor, "The Contribution of Elizabeth Palmer Peabody to Kindergarten Education in the United States" (Unpublished Ed.D. dissertation, New York University, 1960), p. 79.

[38] *Biennial Report . . . 1882–1884,* p. 53; "Chicago Teachers College History," pp. 3–4; Isaac Freeman Hall, *In School from Three to Eighty* (Pittsfield, Mass.: The Eagle Printing and Binding Co., 1927), pp. 151, 225.

[39] Amalie Hoffer, "The Chicago Normal Training School–A Dream Come True," *Kindergarten Magazine,* **9** (November 1896), 186.

[40] Flora J. Cooke, "Colonel F. W. Parker As I Knew Him," *Illinois Teacher,* **24** (June 1936), 325.

[41] Amalie Hoffer, *op. cit.,* p. 189; *Journal of Proceedings and Addresses, National Educational Association, 1895,* p. 1042.

[42] Amalie Hoffer, *op. cit.,* p. 187; Francis W. Parker, letter to Zonia Baber, dated March 23, 1897, Topping Collection, 1325 Stonybrook Lane, Mountainside, N. J.

[43] *Alumni of the Chicago Normal School.*

[44] Francis W. Parker, letters to Zonia Baber, dated January 8, and March 23, 1897, Topping Collection.

[45] Francis W. Parker, letter to Zonia Baber, dated February 25 and May 5, 1897, Topping Collection.

[46] Francis W. Parker, letter to Zonia Baber, dated March 23, 1897, Topping Collection.

[47] *Ibid.*

[48] Francis W. Parker, letter to Zonia Baber, dated February 25, 1897, Topping Collection.

[49] Flora J. Cooke, "Colonel Francis W. Parker: His Influence on Education," *Chicago Schools Journal,* **19** (March 1938), 152; Carol Lynn Gilmer, "Flora Cooke: Grand Old Lady of Education," *Coronet* (October 1947), 79; "Funeral Services," newspaper clipping pertaining to Flora J. Cooke, Topping Collection; Sarah Greenebaum (teacher under Miss Cooke), interview with author, April 25, 1962.

[50] "Funeral Services"; Sarah Greenebaum, *op. cit.*

[51] Carol Lynn Gilmer, *op. cit.,* p. 79; "Opportunities and Episodes of a Teacher's Life in America During the Last Half Century—Born 1864—teaching life 1884 to 1934—Present Date, 1941" (typed copy of what purports to be a personal reflection by Miss Cooke), Topping Collection; Sarah Greenebaum, *op. cit.*

[52] Flora J. Cooke, "A Brief Sketch of a Chapter in the Early History of the Chicago Teachers College" (typed copy of a paper delivered by Miss Cooke at the Chicago Teachers College, February 8, 1945), Topping Collection. On another occasion she told the story slightly differently, saying that Parker told her that shyness resulted from selfish pride. Flora J. Cooke, *Colonel Parker* (Chicago: Press of the Francis W. Parker School, 1910), n.p.

[53] Amalie Hoffer, *op. cit.,* pp. 178–179.

[54] Francis W. Parker, "Account of the Work of the Cook County and Chicago Normal School from 1883 to 1899," *op. cit.,* p. 249; Mary Agnes Riley, *op. cit.,* pp. 108–109.

[55] Mrs. W. E. Ludwig, letter to Professor E. P. Wilson, no date, but probably in the 1930's when Professor Wilson was soliciting information about Parker, Topping Collection. [Mrs. Ludwig recalled that Parker was loved by all the children but "seemed to strike terror to the hearts of the teachers in training. His schoolroom manner was horrible . . . ." One morning in class, he said, "Let's have an old-fashioned love feast, like they do in revivals and everyone talk. I want to know why some of you girls never recite for me." In response, he heard that the girls were afraid, and he laughed and assured them his bark was worse than his bite.]

[56] Flora J. Cooke, "Colonel Francis W. Parker: His Influence on Education," p. 150.

[57] Cora de G. Heineman, letter to E. P. Wilson, dated March 4, 1938, Topping Collection.

[58] Adell Walker, letter to E. P. Wilson, dated April 28, 1935, Topping Collection.

[59] Francis W. Parker, *Talks on Pedagogics, An Outline of the Theory of Concentration* (New York: E. L. Kellogg and Co., 1894), p. 274.

[60] Flora J. Cooke, "Colonel Francis W. Parker: His Influence on Education," p. 152.

[61] Francis W. Parker, letter to Zonia Baber, dated March 23, 1897, Topping Collection; Flora J. Cooke, "Sunday Evenings," *Frances Stuart Parker: Reminiscences and Letters* (Chicago: C. L. Ricketts, 1907), pp. 31–33; Amalie Hoffer, *op. cit.,* pp. 174–175; Flora J. Cooke, "Colonel Francis W. Parker,

His Influence on Education," p. 148; *Journal of Proceedings and Addresses, National Educational Association, 1895,* p. 1040. (Parker's home was actually twenty-six blocks due west of the normal school, according to *Chicago Street Map* (Chicago: Rand McNally and Company, n.d.).

[62] "In the Matter of the Estate of Francis W. Parker, deceased," File 17–1379, Docket 65, Probate Court of Cook County, Chicago, Ill.; Amalie Hoffer, *op. cit,* pp. 174–175.

[63] Ann E. Parker, Physician's Certificate of Death, State Board of Health, Bureau of Vital Statistics, 130 North Wells Street, Chicago, Ill.

[64] *Ibid.;* Parker's stepdaughter remembered Annie as a "very bright girl." Enda Parker Shepard, interview with author, in Brookline, Massachusetts, October 14, 1962. The other memories of "Annie" were supplied by Parker's niece by marriage, Sadie French Tolman at Tolman Pond, New Hampshire, October 13, 1962.

[65] Ann E. Parker, Physician's Certificate of Death; John B. Lanyon, Jr. letter to author, dated June 19, 1963; "Cemetery Inscriptions of Manchester, New Hampshire" (Unpublished work, copied by the W.P.A. in 1938), New Hampshire Historical Soceity, Concord, N.H.

[66] "The Parker Veteran Club . . . ." *Mirror and Farmer* (Manchester, N.H.), November 19, 1885.

[67] Gerald E. Sullivan, *op. cit.,* p. 157; Edwin Burrill Smith, John C. Grant, and Horace Mann Starkey, *Historical Sketch of the Young Men's Christian Association of Chicago, 1858–1898* (Chicago: R. R. Donnelly and Sons Co., 1898), p. 74.

[68] Newton F. Tolman, letter to author, dated September 19, 1962; Sadie French Tolman, interview with author, Tolman Pond, Nelson, N.H., October 13, 1962; *Alumni of the Chicago Normal School; Parker in America, 1630–1910,* compiled by Augustus G. Parker (Buffalo, N.Y.: Niagara Frontier Publishing Company, n.d.), p. 475; "In the Matter of the Estate of Francis W. Parker, deceased."

[69] Newton F. Tolman, *op. cit.*

[70] Interviews with Newton F. Tolman and Francis Wayland Tolman, grand nephews of Parker, and Sadie French Tolman at Tolman Pond, Nelson, N.H., October 12–13, 1962; Newton F. Tolman, letter; Newton F. Tolman, *North of Monadnock* (Boston: Little, Brown, 1961), p. 147.

[71] Edna Parker Shepard, *op. cit.;* "In the Matter of the State of Francis W. Parker, deceased." (It is not known why Parker did not adopt both step-daughters. In his application for a government pension, filed July 14, 1892, later revised on January 15, 1898, he claimed to have adopted both of his wife's children. Francis W. Parker, Soldier's Certificate, Can No. 17835, Bundle No. 22, National Archives, Washington, D.C.)

X

The Philosophy of Educational Reform

Unlike so many of his contemporaries, Parker did not equate the movement for public support of schools with education for freedom or democracy. He had seen what public support had done in the German Empire, where he observed that children never learned that they could find truth for themselves. Moreover, Parker argued that the arrangement of subject matter and the methodology of teaching which had been inherited from the past were designed for an aristocratic society. He believed the course of study was only a means to an end. The use of the traditional curriculum could not, therefore, achieve democratic ends. Traditional subject-matter education was aimed at character development of "subject-peoples."[1]

Parker believed that even if educators subscribed to democratic principles, the dead formalism of traditional subject matter and methodology would lead to knowledge for the sake of knowledge, bigotry, pedantry, and ultimate authoritarianism. He criticized the "Humanist" vestiges of traditional education which imposed "empty formulas" and "dead language" on the child. He criticized the useless and ornamental quality of much that was handed down in the traditional school. He attacked the formal study of knowledge which was cut off from universals and devitalized in isolated subject fields where quantity of learning prevented quality of thinking. He reproached the traditional curriculum for dividing and separating the mind from the body of the child, the skills from the content of learning, the humanities from the natural sciences.[2]

Parker considered the methodology of traditional education as slavish in purpose as its arrangement of subject matter. The subject matter was drilled into the children with monotonous repetition, harsh punishment, artificial rewards. The child was deprived not only of the right to question and think for himself but of the right to exercise the slightest liberty of action. These methods were consistent with the purposes of traditional education. They were the methods of aristocracies or of prisons.[3] Such methods were incompatible with democracy. Parker also considered these methods immoral and unnatural.

The methods were immoral because they deprived the child of the God-given right of making moral choices. The use of force and corporal punishment degraded the "soul." The substitution of competitive grades for whips was even more insidious because it taught the social vice of selfishness. Parker did not argue that Puritan predestination held sway in the traditional school, but he did argue that the testing and grading of children rewarded or punished them according to the acts of their ancestors.[4]

Parker found the methods of traditional education unnatural, in that they forced children to memorize abstract facts from books while closing the concrete world of nature to them. Parker could not understand why educators crammed the child with "husks" when, he said, "the bread of life fills every nook and corner of the universe."[5] It was unnatural to deprive the child of the free use of his reasoning powers. The emphasis of traditional methods on "verbal memory" rather than mental reasoning was even holding back the natural "evolution of thought power." In this regard, he continually attacked faculty psychology, which still prevailed and sanctioned the methods of blind drill and memorization. Parker argued again and again that such methods did not discipline or exercise the brain. They only loaded down the mind with "vague word images."[6]

Parker insisted that the real purpose behind the memorization of abstract and isolated subject matter was the prevention of freedom and growth. He did not blame Thomas Jefferson, or later political and educational statesmen, for proposing to put such traditional education at the disposal of all the people through government support. This was the only kind of education that was known. It was now necessary to find educational means to conform to the revolutionary and unprecedented values of democracy.[7]

By the 1890's Parker believed he had discovered and tested the "unifying principles" of a system of education which would unite democratic ends with democratic means. In what he called the theory of concentration, the leading point was that all effort should be centered on the child rather than the subject matter.[8] It might be said that Parker would make the school, as well as the government, the servant rather than the master of the people.

Word knowledge about democracy, learned by rote, was not a subject of study in Parker's curriculum. Democracy, he said, must be lived, must be taught in action. The school must be a model democracy, a "germinal republic, the embryonic nation."[9]

Education for freedom must start with freedom for the child in school. Children must also learn their individual responsibility for the good of the group. Disorder did not result at the Cook County Normal School when artificial restraints were removed from the children. True order, Parker said, was moral. Children were intrinsically moral. They might come to school with "home-made" selfishness, but they could soon learn that the altruistic motive was essential to self-interest. With inherent "interest" as the motive of educative work, and with love as the essence of teaching, Parker believed children could work out God's design of a moral and democratic life. In seeking "Truth" they would be free.[10]

Seeking truth through clear, independent thinking was vital for citizens of a democracy. Since the separation and isolation of subject matter had been the means of frustrating clear thinking in the past, Parker organized a curriculum based on the hypothesis that there was a natural unification of subject matter, just as there was a unity of action and expression in the child, a unity of "mind, body, and soul." Clear thinking, Parker said, was the ability to see relationships, to go beyond the limited "mental horizon" of traditional education, which prevented children from looking outside a "certain definite circle."[11]

Finding and organizing subject matter for the "mental nutrition" of every pupil at each grade level was what Parker considered the "problem of problems." In his theory of concentration, he unified content into what he called the central subjects. These subjects conformed to the unity of nature and were central to the child's experience. Parker believed the "round" of education was begun by the child before he entered school. There was nothing in the college curriculum, Parker said, which was not a matter of investigation for the child. The problem of curriculum development was building on what the child had "spontaneously" and "unconsciously" begun.[12]

The central subjects focused on the natural environment of the child. Motivation was inherent because of the child's natural curiosity about the world around him. In pursuing this interest, the child would learn about the inorganic sciences of meteorology, geography, geology, and minerology. Physics and chemistry would be learned in relation to the continual change discovered in the inorganic world. The inorganic sciences were then studied in connection with what Parker called the life sciences. The life sciences depended on the inorganic sciences as life depended on its physical environment. The life sciences proceeded from a study of botany—simple life forms—to the more complex forms in zoology. Botany and zoology evolved through the curriculum, like the evolution of nature itself, into the more highly developed form of life—man. The study of man was called anthropology, based on the complexities of social relationships which Parker called the study of ethnology. History was the highest form of study in the pursuit of truth, since it demonstrated man's spiritual struggles. History represented the reality of change in the spiritual evolution as chemistry, physics, and physiology represented change in the inorganic and life sciences.[13]

All the central subjects were taught as an "organic, inseparable, interdependent unit," comparable to the universe which presented truth was a unit. They could not be pursued in isolation of one another, since nature itself had no separate classifications. In addition to being bound together through the interdependence of nature, the central subjects were also united through the study of form and number which were found in everything in nature.[14]

Just as there was a unity in all that must be learned, so there was a unity in the method of learning. Knowledge was acquired through the senses. Parker divided the "sense products" into the modes of attention and expression. The modes of attention were "observation," "hearing language," and "reading." Attention meant a stopping of the "continuous flow of conscious states," in order to concentrate the will on certain things or objects. Parker believed that trained observation, especially through field excursions and first-hand experience, was the best mode of attention. Oral language, however, was the most vital part of human environment. Although he was critical of the Humanist tradition, which he believed had buried school children under "dead" words, he granted that language was to the human being what the mind was to the body. He did not go so far as to argue that there would be no thought without language, but he did not question that language was the most prominent factor in human education.[15]

While these modes of attention—observation, oral and written language—were mental, the modes of expression were physical. They were thoughts and emotions manifested through the body. Parker listed nine such modes—gesture, voice, speech, music making, modeling, painting, drawing, and writing. These modes of expression had an indispensable function in achieving the unity of thought and action which Parker considered so necessary for effective learning.[16]

The modes of attention and expression were twin processes of mental and physical learning and had to be developed simultaneously, in conjunction with the central subjects. One mode could not be taught or learned in isolation from another. Reading, a mode of attention, for example, and writing, a mode of expression, were not taught separately but at the same time and in reference to some content in the central subjects. An economy of school time was also effected by teaching skills and subject matter together.

Parker's theory of concentration provided an organizational pattern for the curriculum, but it was also an attempt at seeking the "structure" inherent in the various disciplines of knowledge. Parker believed knowledge had a structure, as God and nature had a design. It would follow that if students learned the structure or design of knowledge, facts would fit together naturally and not fall into a series of meaningless things to memorize. Parker made it quite clear that knowledge was one thing and knowledge arranged pedagogically was another.[17]

The whole theory of concentration was actually a method which sought the design or law of nature. Parker said the finding of such laws was the end and aim of the subjects of study. His theory was not a philosophy, he said, but a science, a tool for the teacher. He acknowledged the experimental sciences, with their methods of induction and observation, as the inspiration of the central subjects. It was such scientific methods, he said, which accounted for the chief success of his work at the Cook County Normal School. He rejoiced that the methods of education were rapidly bringing the teacher in touch with the spirit of the age, the spirit which he said pervaded all sciences—"everlasting becoming." He argued that the methods of the scientists the world over must become the methods of the teacher. Such methodology was founded on the "suspended judgment" and would destroy all "narrowing prejudices" and all beliefs in dogmas.[18]

Parker did not invent democracy or the new methods of pedagogy or the techniques of experimental science. The significance of his educational theory was the way he sought to unite purpose, method, and subject matter. Unity was his passion. He aimed at "unity of body, mind, and soul, unity of educative effort, unity of action, unity of thought, and unity of thought and expression." Disunity was his bane. The disunity or isolation of subject matter, such as "reading by itself," or "arithmetic with an occasional application," "geography without history," "art for art's sake," was what he called "analysis gone to seed." Even worse, such isolation of subjects was the method of aristocracies to keep the people from thinking.[19]

Parker claimed that his first "intimation" of what was to become this theory of concentration came from Delsarte's work in voice and pantomimic expression. Delsarte's demonstrations of the reaction of the body on the mind might have suggested the modes of attention and expression to Parker. Such an "intimation" must have come after Parker's work at Quincy, when intimacy with Frances Stuart of Boston linked him in marriage with one of the nation's greatest exponents of Delsarte. Except for the elaborate unification of purpose, method, and subject matter, however, the theory of concentration appears consistent with Parker's educational practices in Quincy and even as far back as his work in Dayton, Ohio. His struggle for unity, moreover, was probably congenital. He fought for it in the Civil War. He prayed for it in his associations with Unitarianism, Universalism, and the Young Men's Christian Association.[20]

Parker actually gave credit for the theory of concentration to Herbart. The term itself, of course, was definitely taken from Herbart, but Parker believed the Herbartian theory stopped short of the need for complete individual freedom through personal effort. What Parker believed was the most distinguished feature of the "Herbartian pedagogics" was the idea of "movement ahead." The concept of "eternal becoming" was Hegelian, but Herbart introduced the element of possibility which Darwin would later demonstrate in biology. In Herbart, Parker liked the idea that nothing is ever finally worked out, every course of study should be in the process of improvement.[21]

Parker was enormously influenced by Rousseau, whose romanticisms about nature touched off a political as well as a pedagogical revolution, but Parker was critical of Rousseau's advocation of "wild growth." Parker thought Rousseau meant to leave the child alone until a "wise purpose could apply proper conditions." Growth, for Parker, was subject to divine as well as to natural laws. Parker also believed the teacher must know the "immediate needs of life" at every stage and supply "the external condition to the changing internal conditions" of the child.[22]

If not completely "romantic," Parker was, at least, an intuitionist. He said he knew what was right before he had an opportunity to prove it, and he claimed that his educational heroes—Comenius, Pestalozzi, and Froebel—were also intuitionists.[23] Nevertheless, Parker's theory of concentration actually worked itself out experimentally in the classrooms and faculty meetings of the Cook County Normal School. It was put together piece by piece.

One of the teachers contributed to the theory when he complained that nature should not be viewed in "bits and rags," in a leaf or a twig. Nature study needed a larger vision, a vision as large as nature. At other meetings it was observed that number was in all subjects, that the proper place to teach arithmetic was in all subjects. Theories led to practices and practices to theories until the theory of concentration was ready for national consideration. Accompanied by his "corps of assistants," Parker first broadcast the full nature of his theory and experiments at the Teachers Retreat, Chautauqua, New York. It was the summer of 1891 and one Chautauqua newspaper commented that Chicago was now famous for sending out teachers as well as beef and pork.[24]

Parker later delivered the same talks at the Cook County Normal Summer School, Teachers College of Columbia University, and the University of Minnesota.[25] Transferring the spoken word to the written page was always difficult for Parker, but, with the help of his wife on every page, he managed to produce a manuscript which was published in 1894 as *Talks on Pedagogics: An Outline of the Theory of Concentration.* The book was instantly successful. A literary magazine, *The Critic,* received Parker's "Talks" as more than a "*tour de force* concocted for a teachers' institute." The practicality of Parker's work was praised as a theory worked into a practice, and supported by much data.[26]

The theory of concentration provoked considerable discussion among the leaders of the National Educational Association. It was called a "courageous work" and a "noble contribution" by Charles De Garmo, a leading exponent of Herbart in the United States.[27]

B. A. Hinsdale, once a colleague of John Dewey at the University of Michigan, was a powerful opponent of traditional formal discipline, but he was less enthusiastic about "concentration" than was De Garmo. He called for caution. He said there was not yet sufficient authority for this theory. The work of Ziller and Parker, he said, was insufficient.[28] Ziller had followed Herbart in the integration of subject matter but organized all learning experiences around history and religion.[29]

The proponents of traditional education naturally lined up against Parker's theory. They attacked its purpose, content, and method. An education designed for social rather than academic ends was obviously anathema to the academicians. The theory was opposed because it was anti-intellectual in purpose, not because it was anti-aristocratic. Parker had experienced the branding iron of anti-intellectualism in Dayton, and he had set his sails for Germany and academic confirmation of his theories. He had experienced such criticism in Boston, and the masters of the high schools succeeded in isolating and driving him to Chicago. Now, William T. Harris, United States Commissioner of Education, stood in Parker's way. Harris simply could not understand why knowledge should not be the end of education.[30]

Parker was actually as intent as Harris that children should acquire knowledge. He was only opposed to the acquisition of abstract "word" knowledge. He once made it quite clear that "the main difficulty with most teachers is, not failure in the use of natural methods, but ignorance of the subjects taught." Nevertheless, for Parker, knowledge and love of the child ranked above knowledge and love of subject matter.[31]

In clashing with Harris on the purpose of the school, Parker considered education the prime business of government in securing the blessings of democracy for the people. He sought to bring the home into the school, the school into the home. "Give one tithe of the earnestness and enthusiasm to child education (prevention) that is given to reform," he said, "and the blessed work of salvation will be done." It would mean the purification of the "ballot box" and of democratic government. It would mean "equal rights" for all men. It would mean that society would have the essentials for growth as well as the desire for growth toward a "higher life."[32]

Commissioner William T. Harris, on the other hand, believed the school came after the family, church, and state in the formation of character and citizenship. He would not have the school usurp the responsibilities of other institutions. Harris was also opposed to Parker's theory of concentration which focused on the child rather than the society. Harris would place society at the center of the curriculum and correlate children to it. He believed the educator should study the world and then study the child in order to adjust the one to the other. The educator, he believed, must bring the child into a knowledge of the world as it actually was and "a mastery of its appliances."[33]

Parker, resting his purpose of the school on reconstructing society rather than reinforcing it, said, "We do not clearly see that the guide of all education is the present state of society and its needs." He found "the prejudices and traditions of society outside the school make ideal society, as an immediate proposition, impossible." In this sense he objected to "correlating" children to what he considered an imperfect society.[34]

While Parker's social aims were attacked as anti-intellectual or beyond the responsibility of the public schools, his selection of subject matter was found lacking in the humanities. Parker had been so intent on sponsoring the sciences that he was accused of plotting to supplant the ancient verities. Parker ridiculed the charge when it came up at the 1895 convention of the National Educational Association, but he did insist that reading lessons should include passages from science as well as from literature. He even argued that there would be no literature if nature were taken out of it. "The entire universe pulsates," he said, "thrills, vibrates, with the thought and love of one great eternal being . . . whose work is the spiritual growth of man, who reveals himself . . . in every leaf, flower, rift of cloud, blade of grass . . . ."[35]

Parker's curriculum organization was also challenged by those who subscribed to rival systems. As late as 1895 Charles De Garmo pointed out at the convention of the National Educational Association that "co-ordination," "correlation," and "concentration" of studies had not been properly defined as to their likeness and distinction.[36]

William T. Harris, generally considered the most eminent educator of the time, was an exponent of what was called correlation of studies. He defined this as a correlation between student and society along five lines of study that were of parallel rank. These groups of studies, or "windows of the soul," were mathematics and physics, biology, literature and art, grammar and technical study of language, history and sociology.[37] Harris considered correlation a study of the logical order of topics and branches of knowledge, but he also looked at it as a "symmetrical whole of studies in the world of Human Learning." He sought psychological symmetry within the formal discipline concept of exercising the faculties of the mind.[38]

The symmetry of topics and branches of knowledge that Harris fashioned into the theory of correlation was essentially different from Parker's concentration. Concentration involved an organic unity of subjects, while correlation was a mechanical unity of five parallel but not intersecting studies.

Parker had urged that the National Educational Association make a special study of curriculum organization. A Committee of Fifteen was authorized in 1893 to investigate the "co-ordination" of studies. When the report came out in 1895 and William T. Harris reported for the subcommittee on the Correlation of Studies in Elementary Education, Parker's theory of concentration was ignored. Parker rose in anger to object to the "abstract philosophy" in the report. This investigation, he said, was like the play *Hamlet* with Hamlet kicked out. The committee, he added, had not made a careful study of concentration or of the theories developed by Herbart, Ziller, Stoy, or Rein. Parker said he would accept the report respectfully and take it home to study "prayerfully," but he moved that a committee of fifteen be appointed to revise it.[39]

Harris argued in rebuttal that "concentration," as he defined it, had no place in a report on the "co-ordination" of studies. He said Parker's concentration was actually much more than a pattern for organizing the curriculum. It was an "ideal" for working out a whole way of life.[40] An attempt was made by members of the National Educational Association to impersonalize the clash between Harris and Parker. Someone said it was really Hegel and Herbart at variance. It was also said, "We have the Calvinistic theology set over against the Unitarian."[41]

It was indeed a controversy between a rational, *a priori* philosophy of education and an inductive, empirical philosophy. It was even a religious controversy, especially in regard to Parker's methods of learning.

Parker's empirical emphasis of learning through touch and the other senses, as well as through active "doing," was criticized as materialistic and even antireligious. Such accusations resulted in a battle at the Denver meeting of the National Educational Association in 1895. John S. Clark, a Boston teacher and publisher of art books, charged the "whole scheme of experimental psychology" was to "reduce mental phenomena to unmediated physical energies playing through matter, and so to dispense with self-activity in the intellectual life of man . . . ." By way of evidence, he quoted from William James of Harvard and from Parker's *Talks on Pedagogics*. He finally blamed them, as well as Herbart, Hume, and Mill, for constructing a psychology without a soul.[42]

Parker said of himself that he had taught psychology for many years and never dreamed of teaching a doctrine of materialism. He said he had always held there was a transcendental ego, though he admitted there may be insufficient evidence. Beyond that, he made the critic admit from the convention floor that he knew of not a single American educator who held an antireligious philosophy.[43]

Parker went on to observe that such charges sounded like "an echo of old Boston that reached back to the days of Cotton Mather and the Salem witchcraft; a statement made to deftly arouse the suspicion of pietists and dogmatists; and echo of the attacks upon all discoverers in in the realm of truth since the days of Galileo." Parker worked himself into a rage and asserted that one had but to call a teacher a materialist in order to injure and cripple his influence.[44]

John S. Clark readily admitted under pressure that Parker was not a materialist, but he insisted that Parker's philosophy sometimes appeared that way. He said the current interest in psychology gave the materialistic side of Parker's teaching more prominence.[45]

The United States Commissioner of Education also frowned on materialism and the new psychology. William T. Harris was appalled by the attempt to explain the human being through the animal. He was first attracted to the new psychology, he said, but he became quickly hostile to the experiments which undertook to reason from the body to the mind, from the events of the animal life to the human and spiritual life of man.[46] He never went so far as to accuse Parker of materialism, but he chided Parker for his emphasis on the empirical rather than the rational aspects of learning. Harris was especially critical of the new creed in education which glorified "learning by doing." He actually confronted Parker on this point at a meeting of the National Educational

Association in 1901, saying that Parker was all wrong, that the child learned through inhibition rather than by doing. "On the cortical surface of the brain," he said, "the great area is that which is occupied with the function of inhibition. The child gains power by learning to control himself, to refrain from motor action."[47]

Harris was not the only educator to believe learning by doing was "quackery" and that "knowing is the necessary preparation for doing." Parker had come to prefer calling his methods of activism a teaching which leads pupils to investigate for themselves. He said he never advocated "doing without thinking." How can we know what first we do not do? This was Parker's question. How can we know, he also asked, unless there is an activity of the senses? He even went so far as to argue that character is "a bundle of habits." Habit was developed through repeated acts, each repetition being a doing.[48]

Approaching the mind, even the soul, through the body was obviously as much theological heresy as it was educational. The new education could not help but alienate itself from the forces which were then mobilizing against the encroachment of science on religion.

While attacking experimentalism in psychology and education, William T. Harris came to the defense of faculty psychology and argued that only mental discipline could unlock the real world for the child. Disrespect for such discipline, he said, was bad education. "Leave the child free to play games as he will," Harris said, obviously referring to what might be called a creeping kindergartenism, "but do not call it formal education . . . .[49]

Parker had attacked traditional education for its undemocratic, immoral, and unnatural purposes, content, and methods; but traditional educators retaliated by opposing Parker's purposes as anti-intellectual, his content as antihumanistic, and his method as antireligious. It would appear inconceivable that Parker could take over the intellectual centers of the country, even if he had political authority to do so. The classroom was held by the academicians. It would be futile to prescribe new purposes, content, and methods, if teachers were not trained in accepting or using them.

Nevertheless, by the end of the nineteenth century the educational protest groups, of which Parker was a recognized leader, had made such progress against the traditionalists that they were seriously regarded by the National Educational Association. In fact, education and the "new" education had come to be so synonymous at the turn of the century that one eminent educator asked if the "cranks" had changed or if it was the main body of education? By 1895 there actually was agreement among members of the National Educational Association that there should be more teaching and less testing, more observation and less rules to memorize, more supplementary reading and less formal grammar, more teaching of things and less of forms, more freedom and less "cast-iron order."[50]

It was the development of professional teacher training which made this revolution possible. During the twenty-five years since Parker's celebrated work at Quincy, a new generation of educators emerged—a generation that had been exposed to a discipline of education. Even universities had begun to endow chairs of pedagogy. In 1895 Parker rejoiced at the decision of the New York State legislature to license only teachers with at least one year of professional training. By 1901 the National Educational Association was advocating such a requirement for all the states of the union.[51] The academic strongholds had been cut off or breached through the professional schools of education.

Parker's work at the Cook County Normal School was a model for the nation in this rapid development of professional schools for teachers. Parker's inspiration for teacher training was the work of Horace Mann, but the Colonel himself credited E. A. Sheldon of the Oswego Normal School as the most important man in the improvement of teaching methods. Sheldon, on the other hand, said Parker had done more than than any other man in the United States to arouse the people to the fact that there were better ways of teaching, and that "knowledge" was not the "whole of education."[52]

Parker's teacher training was not without intensive study of subject matter. Knowledge in the various academic disciplines was left to the academic centers of higher education, but Parker's teacher training included work in psychology and the natural sciences—subjects still neglected in the colleges—and he put special stress on the history of education. Such a history revealed the truest insight into the process of all human development.[53]

Since Parker held that "unapplied theories" were like faith without works, the observation and practice of teaching were central in Parker's teacher training. In developing the "artist" teacher, Parker sometimes confused or nullified the difference between the science and the art of teaching. He used the word "pedagogic" to indicate the science of education, and "pedagogy" for the art of teaching. Nevertheless, the artist teacher must be trained in the science of education. This did not mean that the teacher should be equipped with lesson plans and formulas to be put into practice. The artist teacher was to be continually creative and in the same process should "incite" the pupils to be creative and to "work out their own salvation."[54]

Parker saw education as a science which required special training.

(Traditionalists had made no special provision for teacher training. The only education thought necessary was a mastery of special subject matter.) Parker also saw special schools for teacher training as a way of liberating prospective teachers from the traditionalists in the colleges. Traditionalists could only be destroyed by cutting them off from the next generation of teachers.[55]

Parker considered the "practice school" in the new education for teachers a proving ground for the new science of education as well as a place for the preparation of teachers. As far as Parker was concerned, the normal school was even more than a place to experiment with educational theories or to train teachers. It was an "object lesson" for teachers, for parents, and for the public in general. It was a "laboratory" for perfecting life, society, and the state.[56]

While teacher training schools were circumventing the academic centers, the academicians were experiencing an intellectual revolt within their own ranks. They were being divided and weakened at the very moment they needed unity and strength in opposing the nonacademic influences creeping into education. No longer would traditionalists face a doughty but rough and self-taught adversary in the person of Colonel Parker. They were now facing professors with the finesse of John Dewey and college presidents with the power of Charles W. Eliot. The academic tradition of intellectual absolutism, determinism, and deductive logic was being challenged on intellectual ground by relativism and inductive and scientific methods of thought.

By the last decade of the nineteenth century, this intellectual insurrection had reached the proportions of what Morton White called a "Revolt against Formalism." It was more than a revolt against the formalism of traditional education; it was a revolt against formalism in philosophy, economics, government, and science. John Dewey was a leader in attacking formal logic. Thorstein Veblen led the way against the natural laws of classical economics. Legal formalism based on logic rather than life was attacked by Justice Oliver Wendell Holmes. William James assaulted the science of psychology which was based on precept rather than experiement.[57]

The leaders of this "revolt" were all influenced by the nineteenth century theories of change and evolution. Even before Darwin gave scientific evidence to support a theory of evolution, the dominant philosophy of the nineteenth century had been that of Hegel, where history was the process by which the "Idea of Spirit" slowly realized itself in the world. Change and evolution, for Hegel, were only means and not ends of Creation, but this philosophy had actually opened the door to revolt by admitting, ever so slightly, the legitimacy of change.[58] After Darwin there was no holding back the flood of scholars who were released from the academic walls of fixed and immutable laws. Parker, in the same stream of thought, sought to open up the schools to these new ideas.

The revolt against formalism had at its center a new philosophy, designed as an "active force in civilization," and based on experience rather than logic.[59] Charles Peirce gave it a name in 1878 when he wrote of "pragmatism" in an issue of *Popular Science Monthly.* A critic of the "pedantic age" which attended more to "words than to things," Pierce was giving a philosophy to what Parker was then doing in Quincy.[60]

Pragmatism was a philosophy which opposed authoritarianism and assumed men could rule their own ideas as well as their governments.[61] As such, it was an intellectual support for Parker's educational purpose of preparing for democratic self-government.

Parker received intellectual backing for his curricular content from the experimental scientists. For a long time the natural sciences had been too new and too closely associated with practical and vocational interests to hold respectable counsel in the courts of higher education. By the end of the nineteenth century, however, the practical application of science had remade the world in the image of science itself. Industrialism had changed the course of life and demanded courses in the education of the young. All along, traditional educators had been losing their battle to hold the subject matter line to the seven liberal arts. As many as 149 new subjects were said to have been introduced at the secondary level alone between 1787 and 1870.[62]

Parker believed this fragmentation and isolation of knowledge in numerous courses had been used by traditional educators to frustrate independent thought. The traditional educators argued that this proliferation of knowledge only made it more necessary to hold the curriculum to the basic prescriptions inherited from the past.[63]

In 1886 President Charles W. Eliot of Harvard shocked the academic world by suggesting the "elective system" as a solution to the problem of fitting an expanding knowledge into a limited curriculum. Parker and the other editors of New York's *School Journal* were among the few at that time to join in Eliot's defense.[64] The idea of allowing students a choice in selecting courses soon tended to divide educators into liberal and conservative factions which finally led to an investigation by the National Educational Association. The Committee of Ten came out for the liberal position in 1894 when it reported in favor of the elective system.[65]

While the sciences, in their many forms, were gaining admittance to the curriculum amid academic controversy, Charles De Garmo told the

National Educational Association in 1895 that the great problem of the day was the slow evolution of "race-ability" and the "rapid evolution in knowledge." He suggested that the only hope was for educators to supply some "unifying organization of studies."[66]

Parker's design for a unified curriculum came, therefore, at an opportune time. It was also in line with the thinking of the new scientists of society. Auguste Comte, who had made science a philosophy and even a religion, found the "isolation of the sciences" wrecked effective teaching. Long before Parker, Comte despaired of European education which was theological, metaphysical, and literary. In attempting to make the methods of science the methods of education, he consolidated the whole of acquired knowledge into one body of homogeneous doctrine; and, like Parker, ended with a unity of method—the method of science.[67]

Herbert Spencer had a greater following in America of Parker's time than any other contemporary thinker. When Parker had been a teacher in the backwoods of New Hampshire, Herbert Spencer pioneered the movement against traditional education. He stood for a less decorative and a more useful education, for a more pleasureable education that would appeal to the child's natural wishes and tendencies. He called for methods that were based on "concrete illustration." Most important, Spencer prepared the reception of Parker's central subjects by organizing and unifying all knowledge. He had argued that the various aspects of evolution as revealed in geology, biology, psychology, astronomy, and sociology, were all part of the same evolution, the component parts of the "one Cosmos." "Unification," Spencer wrote, was the characteristic of developing thought. The theory and practice of education, he said, were the subjects which involved all others.[68]

Parker also received intellectual support from exponents of the new psychology. Faculty psychology, which had been the strongest prop for mental discipline and the drill methods of traditional education, was beginning to be challenged. Even in Parker's time, many who advocated the addition of sciences to the curriculum argued for the superior mental discipline that the sciences would offer.[69] It was not until the twentieth century that the animal experiments of Thorndike scientifically discredited faculty psychology.[70] In the meantime, a school of "associationists," deriving inspiration from the empiricism of Herbart, were denying the rationalist contention that specific mental faculties even existed.[71] Parker was so intrigued by this new psychology that he insisted it was the central basis of the new education.[72] The idea of the association of thoughts in building memory could even have inspired Parker's association of subject matter in the central subjects.

It was not until 1894, after his theory of concentration had gone to press, that Parker became fully aware of the experimental developments of Child Study, an important movement in the new psychology. G. Stanley Hall, at its head, suggested in 1894 that Parker would find confirmation for some of his theories and more effective modes of expressing them if he looked into the Child Study Movement.[73]

Parker quickly found data which did support his theories. He found, for instance, the "law of diffusion of nervous energy" supported his thesis that the child's extremities were the last to be coordinated. Finger exercise in writing at an early age was therefore physically detrimental. He found evidence to support his thesis that there was an organic relation between thought and expression, that mental action depended on bodily health and exercise.[74]

Parker was so enthusiastic that he helped organize the Illinois Society for Child Study in 1894, and two years later the Colonel was elected president of the Child Study Department of the National Educational Association.[75] Parker encouraged teachers to cooperate with Child Study laboratories by watching and reporting the activities of their students. Such efforts were leading to more concern for the health of the child, for diagnosing physical defects as causes for mental difficulties. An appreciation of physical and mental differences was being developed even before the rage of testing and intelligence quotients.[76]

Child Study was in the mainstream of the theories of evolution. Since life developed from the simple to the complex, the study of the child was the logical beginning for the study of man. It is probable that the work of the Child Study Movement, which enjoyed the recognition of scholars in anthropology, as well as psychology and education, turned intellectuals toward Parker's elementary school work. The elementary schools were scientific laboratories for this study of man, and Parker's educational practices therefore became the object of serious scholarly investigation.

Although unity of purpose, content, and method was the foundation of Parker's pedagogy, his philosophy was completely lacking in unity. It was pieced together out of Christian idealism and natural law absolutes, as well as experimental and democratic relativism. He saw development and progress aimed at freedom, but he believed freedom was perfect obedience, submission to natural or divine laws. This contradiction between free will and determinism did not trouble Parker. Its explanation was inherent in the Hegelian dialectic. "Freedom" and "Necessity" were thesis and antithesis in Hegel's logic, but they found synthesis in the "World-Spirit," which was both Freedom and Necessity. Each human being was part of the vast organic state. As such, Hegel had it, as did

Parker, that "Only that will which obeys law, is free; for it obeys itself . . . ."[77]

Parker said he never proposed to scrap Hegelianism. He would accept whatever Hegel had to offer that was good. He liked Hegel's "magnificent spirit of progress," which Parker also attributed to Pestalozzi, Froebel, and Herbart.[78] The philosophic absolutism and rationalism of Hegel, however, could not be squared with pragmatism and empiricism any more than slavery could be reconciled with freedom. One observer of the Cook County Normal School in 1886 observed that Parker's ideal of freedom might be a "pious fraud." There were certain underlying forces which actually directed the child. This observer then said it was doubtful if freedom really meant more than freedom to follow where Colonel Parker led.[79]

Parker's theories were marked with idealism in purpose but pragmatism in methods. He was more at home with the empiricist followers of Herbart, however, than with the rationalists and neo-Hegelians such as William T. Harris. In spite of this, he never joined the Herbartian Club for the scientific study of education. When he addressed its first official meeting in 1895, Parker insisted he was not a Herbartian. He said he did not like the idea of followers in America because it was undemocratic and because it closed off change and progress.[80]

Parker appropriated ideas from both poles of educational thought. He was an exponent of learning through experience, but at some points in his theory of concentration he claimed that there was an automatic genesis of thought, that the "ego" was completely impotent as a force in shaping thought.[81] Although he extolled freedom, he believed the child should only be emancipated from influences which might hinder his inward and automatic development according to eternal law.[82] His frequent use of the term "self-activity," for instance, was ambiguous because it could be interpreted in the Herbartian sense of external interest or in the Hegelian sense of inward "self-effort."[83]

In his passion for unity, Parker tried to join conflicting theories into a new synthesis. There was room in his philosophy for Hegel and Herbart, for absolutism and relativism, for rationalism and empiricism. In this regard, Parker's theory of concentration was not consistent with the "Revolt against Formalism." His work was more of an attempt in synthetic tradition of Comte and Spencer to unite all knowledge. It was also an attempt, in the line of Kant and the Transcendentalists, to unite the two worlds of nature and spirit.[84]

William James was pointing out in the nineties that there were many sciences, not just one. He admitted that most thinkers still believed there was but one science, and James said he looked forward to the time when the growth of sciences would again run into "one body of Truth." But "meanwhile," he said, there were many "beginnings of knowledge" in many fields, and all kept separate from one another for the sake of "practical convenience."[85]

At the same time, while the "new psychology" was coming into vogue among educators, William James warned against deducing any "definite programmes and schemes and methods" for immediate school use.[86] Parker ignored this. When one scientist complained that scientific data on Child Study was inconclusive, that "the Philistines are continually calling for results," Parker replied that "a dying world is calling for results."[87]

Parker's world was indeed dying, but he was helping to bury it by searching for scientific verification for all truth. He retained Christian as well as Hegelian idealism, but he turned more and more to the persuasions of science and behaviorism. He quoted the laws of "motor discharge" and the "organic circuit" of John Dewey, the theory of man as a "reflex animal" by William James, and the "dynamogenesis" of Mark Baldwin.[88] He tended more and more to concern himself with the world of nature and with the theory of Darwin. Like Darwin he never sensed the conflict between religion and science; he never seemed to understand what bothered Dewey about Darwin's theory of natural selection. The theory implied that the creation may have been one of accident rather than of plan. Parker only considered the study of nature the study of God's work.[89]

Despite the fact that inconsistencies were part of the Hegelian dialectic, traditionalists, (generally idealists in the school of Hegelianism) criticized Parker for *his* inconsistencies. The Colonel was also said to be considerably larger in personality than in psychology.[90]

The charge of inconsistency never seemed to bother the Colonel, but by the end of the century he turned over the philosophy of the new education to John Dewey. Dewey, he said, put the ideas into "terse and pregnant words."[91] Parker's concern was more and more directed at the politics rather than the philosophy of educational reform, and his greatest contribution to the new education was probably the way he carried the crusade for the educational salvation of children down to the level of the parents. He forced them, rather than the educational or political bosses, to decide the fate of the common school and of democracy.

NOTES

[1] Francis W. Parker, "Discussion of 'German Methods of Using the Mother Tongue'," *Journal of Proceedings and Addresses, National Educational Association, 1894,* p. 483; Francis W. Parker, *Talks on Pedagogics, An Outline of the Theory of Concentration* (New York: E. L. Kellogg and Co., 1894), pp. 390, 401–410; Francis W. Parker, "The School of the Future," *Journal of Proceedings and Addresses, National Educational Association, 1891,* pp. 85–86; Francis W. Parker, "The Plan and Purpose of the Chicago Institute," *The Course of Study,* **1** (July 1, 1900—June 1, 1901) 18–19.

[2] Francis W. Parker, *Talks on Pedagogics,* pp. 24, 177–178, 404–406, 408–409; Francis W. Parker, "An Account of the Work of the Cook County and Chicago Normal School from 1883 to 1899," *Education Report, 1901–1902,* U.S. Office of Education, Report of the Commissioner of Education for the year 1902, p. 249; Francis W. Parker, "The Plan and Purpose of the Chicago Institute," p. 18; Francis W. Parker, "Discussion of 'The Place of Art in General Education'," *Journal of Proceedings and Addresses, National Educational Association, 1895,* pp. 847–848; Francis W. Parker, "The New Department," *Journal of Proceedings and Addresses, National Educational Association, 1895,* p. 949.

[3] Francis W. Parker, "The Plan and Purpose of the Chicago Institute," p. 9; Francis W. Parker, *Talks on Pedagogics,* pp. 365, 370.

[4] *Ibid.,* pp. 362–369; Francis W. Parker, "An Account of the Work of the Cook County and Chicago Normal School from 1883 to 1899," pp. 252–253.

[5] Quotations by F. W. Parker in *The Practical Teacher,* as collected in the form of newspaper clippings, Parker Scrapbooks, 1884, Archives, Harper Library, University of Chicago. No copies of *The Practical Teacher* could be found. Parker was the editor of this periodical from September 1884 to April 1885 according to W. S. Monroe, "Memorial to Francis W. Parker," *School Journal,* **64** (April 5, 1902), 384.

[6] Francis W. Parker, "An Account of the Work of the Cook County and Chicago Normal School from 1883 to 1899," p. 249; Francis W. Parker, *Talks on Pedagogics,* p. 362. An excellent study of the hold of faculty psychology may be found in Walter B. Kolesnik, *Mental Discipline in Modern Education* (Madison: The University of Wisconsin Press, 1962).

[7] Francis W. Parker, "Art in Everything," *Journal of Proceedings and Addresses, National Educational Association, 1900,* pp. 509–510; Francis W. Parker, "The Training of Teachers," *Journal of Proceedings and Addresses, National Educational Association, 1895,* p. 970.

[8] Francis W. Parker, "Principles of Correlation," *School Journal,* **62** (March 2, 1901), 217–219; Francis W. Parker, *Talks on Pedagogics,* p. 376.

[9] Francis W. Parker (Ed.), "Englewood's Schools, Their Rise, Progress and Present Status Graphically Described," p. 2. (typed copy from *Daily Evening Call* (Englewood, Ill.), Special Number, Thursday, October 9, 1890), Historical Files, Chicago Teachers College South; Francis W. Parker, *Talks on Pedagogics,* p. 346.

[10] *Ibid.,* pp. 337–338, 347–349, 351–352, 359, 391; Francis W. Parker, "The Plan and Purpose of the Chicago Institute," p. 23.

[11] Francis W. Parker, *Talks on Pedagogics,* pp. 26, 46, 394, 408.

[12] *Ibid.,* pp. 16, 23–24, 25–46; Francis W. Parker, "An Account of the Work of the Cook County and Chicago Normal School from 1883 to 1899," p. 250.

[13] Francis W. Parker, *Talks on Pedagogics,* pp. 25–46, 377.

[14] *Ibid.,* pp. 43–44, 377, 379; *Biennial Report of the County Superintendent of Schools from July 1, 1886 to June 30, 1888* (Chicago: J. M. W. Jones Stationery and Printing Co., 1888), p. 51.

[15] Francis W. Parker, *Talks on Pedagogics,* pp. 51–52, 118–119, 161, 173–177, 378–382.

[16] *Ibid.,* pp. 223, 379-381.

[17] *Ibid.,* pp. 42, 349, 373; Francis W. Parker, "An Account of the Work of the Cook County and Chicago Normal School from 1883 to 1899," p. 250.

[18] Francis W. Parker, *Talks on Pedagogics,* pp. 26–27, 46, 373, 453; *Biennial Report of the County Superintendent of Schools from July 1, 1892 to June 30, 1894* (Chicago: J. M. W. Jones Stationery and Printing Co., 1894), pp. 61–62; Francis W. Parker, "Application of Child Study in the School," *Journal of Proceedings and Addresses, National Educational Association, 1895,* pp. 419, 422.

[19] Francis W. Parker, *Talks on Pedagogics,* pp. 26, 394, 405.

[20] *Ibid.,* p. IV; "Pedagogical Works," *The Critic* (new series), **23** (January–June 1895), 402; Francis W. Parker, "An Account of the Work of the Cook County and Chicago Normal School from 1883 to 1899," p. 259. Parker's interest in Unitarianism may only be inferred from his association with the Adamses in Quincy. That he may have attended the Universalist Church in Chicago is suggested by a telegram from his housekeeper to Edna Parker Shepard. A Chrisholm, telegram to Mrs. T. R. Shepard, 5:40 p.m., March 3, 1902, Francis W. Parker, 1837–1902, Telegrams and Memoranda, Collections, Chicago Historical Society.

[21] Francis W. Parker, *Talks on Pedagogics,* p. 399; Francis W. Parker, "Application of Child Study in the School," pp. 420–421, 423.

[22] Col. Francis W. Parker, "Outlines of Pedagogics," *School Journal,* **31** (May 22, 1886), 325.

[23] Amalie Hoffer, "The Chicago Normal Training School—a Dream Come True," *Kindergarten Magazine,* **9** (November 1896), 175.

[24] Francis W. Parker, *Talks on Pedagogics,* pp. III–IV; Francis W. Parker, "An Account of the Work of the Cook County and Chicago Normal School from 1883 to 1899," pp. 248–249, 256, 259–260, 263; "Why Colonel Francis W. Parker Could Not Find a Clean Shirt," newspaper clipping dated July 20, 1891, Parker Scrapbooks, 1891.

[25] Francis W. Parker, *Talks on Pedagogics,* p. III. What Parker referred to as the New York Teachers' Training College was probably Teachers College, Columbia University. At least Parker was known to have lectured there. Lawrence A. Cremin, David A. Shannon, and Mary Evelyn Townsend, *A History of Teachers College, Columbia University* (New York: Columbia University Press, 1954), pp. 23, 288.

[26] Francis W. Parker, "Autobiographical Sketch," appendix to William M. Giffin, *School Days of the Fifties* (Chicago: A. Flanagan Company, 1906), p. 113; Francis W. Parker, *Talks on Pedagogics,* "Dedication." This work was said by Lawrence A. Cremin to be probably the first treatise on pedagogy

to gain international repute. Lawrence A. Cremin, *The Transformation of the School* (New York: Alfred A. Knopf, 1961), p. 134. The review of Parker's work in *The Critic* also credited Herbart's psychology with a "positive advance." "Pedagogical Works," p. 402.

[27] Charles De Garmo, "The Principle upon which the Coordination of Studies should proceed," *Journal of Proceedings and Addresses, National Educational Association, 1895,* p. 87.

[28] B. A. Hinsdale, "Discussion," *Journal of Proceedings and Addresses, National Educational Association, 1895,* p. 110; Walter B. Kolesnik, *op.cit.,* p. 28.

[29] Charles De Garmo, *op. cit.,* p. 94.

[30] "Col. Parker on Education," clipping from *School Weekly,* August 3, 1899, Parker Scrapbooks, 1899.

[31] Francis W. Parker, *Talks on Pedagogics,* p. 338; Francis W. Parker, "Discussion on What to Teach About Alkohol [*sic*]," *Journal of Proceedings and Addresses, National Educational Association, 1900,* pp. 255–256; Francis W. Parker, "The Report of the Committee of Ten—Its Use for the Improvement of Teachers Now at Work in the Schools," *Journal of Proceedings and Addresses, National Educational Association, 1894,* p. 451.

[32] Francis W. Parker, *Talks on Pedagogics,* p. 417; *Biennial Report of the County Superintendent of Schools from July 1, 1884 to June 30, 1886* (Chicago: J. M. W. Jones Stationery and Printing Co. 1886), pp. 49–50.

[33] William T. Harris, "Discussion of the Report of the Sub-committee on the Correlation of Studies in Elementary Education," *Journal of Proceedings and Addresses, National Educational Association, 1895,* p. 350; Merle Curti, *The Social Ideas of American Educators* (Paterson, N.J.: Littlefield, Adams and Company, 1959), p. 345.

[34] Francis W. Parker, "Art in Everything," p. 510; Francis W. Parker letter to the Trustees, dated July 31, 1899, Papers of Anita McCormick Blaine (Chicago Institute Folders), McCormick Collection, Wisconsin State Historical Society, Madison, Wisconsin.

[35] Louis Soldan, "Discussion of What has been Accomplished in Coordination in the Field of History and Literature," *Journal of Proceedings and Addresses, National Educational Association, 1895,* p. 114; Francis W. Parker, "Discussions," *Journal of Proceedings and Addresses, National Educational Association, 1895,* pp. 114, 848.

[36] Charles De Garmo, *op. cit.,* p. 87.

[37] Lawrence A. Cremin, *op. cit.,* pp. 14–15; Merle Curti, *op. cit.,* p. 346; Frank M. McMurry, "Some Applications of Correlation," *Journal of Proceedings and Addresses, National Educational Association, 1896,* p. 529; William T. Harris, "The Necessity for Five Co-ordinate Groups of Studies in the Schools," *Journal of Proceedings and Addresses, National Educational Association, 1896,* p. 287. Harris made some variations on the five groups. Lawrence A. Cremin, *op. cit.,* p. 19.

[38] William T. Harris, "Report of the Sub-committee on the Correlation of Studies in Elementary Education," *Journal of Proceedings and Addresses, National Educational Association, 1895,* p. 287.

[39] William H. Maxwell, "Report of the Committee of Fifteen," *Journal of Proceedings and Addresses, National Educational Association, 1895,* p. 287; Francis W. Parker, "Discussion of the Report of the Sub-committee on the

Correlation of Studies in Elementary Education," *Journal of Proceedings and Addresses, National Educational Association, 1895,* p. 344.

[40] William T. Harris, "Discussion of the Report of the Sub-committee on the Correlation of Studies in Elementary Education," pp. 345, 349; Francis W. Parker, "The Plan and Purpose of the Chicago Institute," p. 23.

[41] Walter B. Hervey, "Discussion of the Report of the Sub-committee on the Correlation of Studies in Elementary Education," *Journal of Proceedings and Addresses, National Educational Association, 1895,* p. 346.

[42] John S. Clark, "The Aims of Art Education in General Education," *Journal of Proceedings and Addresses, National Educational Association, 1895.* pp. 833–834, 852.

[43] Francis W. Parker, "Discussion of the Place of Art in General Education," p. 847.

[44] *Ibid., p. 847.*

[45] John S. Clark, "Discussion of the Aims of Art Education in General Education," *Journal of Proceedings and Addresses, National Educational Association, 1895,* pp. 852, 854.

[46] William T. Harris, "The Danger of Viewing Biological Analysis in Reasoning on Educational Subjects," *Journal of Proceedings and Addresses, National Educational Association, 1902,* p. 215.

[47] William T. Harris, "Discussion on the Object of Instruction in Domestic Science," *Journal of Proceedings and Addresses, National Educational Association, 1901,* pp. 587–588.

[48] Francis W. Parker, "A Sketch of the Work in the Quincy Schools from 1875 to 1880," V, *School Journal,* **30** (August 1, 1885), 122; Francis W. Parker, "Talks on Psychology," V, *School Journal,* **31** (June 26, 1886), 408; Francis W. Parker, "How to Do by Doing," *Journal of Proceedings and Addresses, National Educational Association,* 1887, p. 381.

[49] William T. Harris, "Discussion on the Object of Instruction in Domestic Science," p. 588.

[50] Orville T. Bright, "Changes—Wise and Unwise—in Grammar and High Schools," *Journal of Proceedings and Addresses, National Educational Association, 1895,* p. 278. In the same session, Parker also noted that "not long ago a skirmisher on the advance line was often driven back by the brickbats of contempt.... There is just a little now and then left...." Francis W. Parker, "Discussion," *Journal of Proceedings and Addresses, National Educational Association, 1895,* p. 191.

[51] Francis W. Parker, "Looking Backward," *School Journal,* **59** (August 12, 1899), 118; Francis W. Parker, "Application of Child Study in the School," p. 418; Francis W. Parker, "Discussion," p. 191; "Declaration of Principles," *Journal of Proceedings and Addresses, National Educational Association, 1901,* p. 29.

[52] Francis W. Parker, *Talks on Pedagogics,* pp. 426–431; *Biennial Report of the County Superintendent of Schools from July 1, 1890 to June 30, 1892* (Chicago: J. M. W. Jones Stationery and Printing Co., 1892), p. 27; *Biennial Report... 1892–1894,* p. 62.

[53] *Biennial Report of the County Superintendent of Schools from July 1, 1888 to June 30, 1890* (Chicago: J. M. W. Jones Stationery and Printing Co., 1890), pp. 44, 64.

[54] Francis W. Parker, "An Account of the Work of the Cook County and Chicago Normal School from 1883 to 1899," p. 251; *Biennial Report*

... *1888–1890,* p. 44; Francis W. Parker, *Talks on Pedagogics,* p. 451; Francis W. Parker, "The Report of the Committee of Ten—Its Use for the Improvement of Teachers Now at Work in the Schools," p. 450.

[55] Francis W. Parker, "Sixth Biennial Report of the Cook County Normal School, 1892–1894," Historical Files, Chicago Teachers College South; Francis W. Parker, "The Training of Teachers," p. 970.

[56] *Biennial Report ... 1888–1890,* p. 44; Francis W. Parker, "An Account of the Work of the Cook County and Chicago Normal School from 1883 to 1899," pp. 248, 251.

[57] Morton White, *Social Thought in America: The Revolt Against Formalism* (Boston: Beacon Press, 1959), pp. 11–26.

[58] *Ibid.,* pp. 11–13; Henry D. Aiken, *The Age of Ideology: The Nineteenth Century Philosophers* (New York: Mentor Books, The New American Library of World Literature, 1961), pp. 81–82, 71; G. W. F. Hegel, "Introduction to the Philosophy of History," *Hegel Selections,* edited by J. Loewenberg (New York: Charles Scribner's Sons, 1929), pp. 338–442.

[59] Morton White, *op. cit.,* pp. 174, 11–12.

[60] Morton White, *The Age of Analysis: The Twentieth Century Philosophers* (New York: Mentor Books, New American Library of World Literature, 1955), pp. 143–144.

[61] Henry Steele Commager, *The American Mind: An Interpretation of American Thought and Character Since the 1880's* (New Haven, Conn.: Yale University Press, 1959), p. 95.

[62] Alice Miel, *Changing the Curriculum: A Social Process* (New York: D. Appleton-Century, 1946), p. 3.

[63] Walter B. Kolesnik, *op. cit.,* pp. 20–21.

[64] "Editorial," *School Journal,* **31** (January 23, 1886), 52.

[65] Walter B. Kolesnik, *op. cit.,* pp. 20–21.

[66] Charles De Garmo, *op. cit.,* p. 87.

[67] Henry D. Aiken, *op. cit.,* pp. 134–135, 137.

[68] Richard Hofstadter, *Social Darwinism in American Thought* (Boston: The Beacon Press, 1955), pp. 31–32; Herbert Spencer, *Essays on Education and Kindred Subjects,* with Introduction by Charles W. Eliot (London: Everyman's Library, J. M. Dent and Sons, 1963), pp. vii–xvii, 7, 42, 85; Henry D. Aiken, *op. cit.,* pp. 176–177, 181–182.

[69] Walter B. Kolesnik, *op. cit.,* p. 28; B. A. Hinsdale, *op. cit.,* p. 110.

[70] Walter B. Kolesnik, *op. cit.,* p. 135.

[71] *Ibid.,* pp. 23–25, 135; R. Freeman Butts, *A Cultural History of Education* (New York: McGraw-Hill Book Company, 1947), p. 461.

[72] Francis W. Parker, "The School of the Future," p. 84.

[73] G. Stanley Hall letter to Mr. Bright, dated May 21, 1894, as printed in *Biennial Report ... 1892–1894,* p. 41.

[74] Francis W. Parker, "Application of Child Study in the School," pp. 424–425.

[75] *Ibid.,* p. 427; "Francis W. Parker," *Encyclopaedia of Biography of Illinois, Vol. III* (Chicago: The Century Publishing and Engraving Co., 1902), p. 407; "Department of Child Study, Committee upon Nominations," *Journal of Proceedings and Addresses, National Educational Association, 1896,* p. 836.

[76] Francis W. Parker, "Application of Child Study in the School," pp. 424–427; R. Freeman Butts and Lawrence A. Cremin, *A History of Educa-*

tion in American Culture (New York: Henry Holt and Co., 1953), p. 439.

[77] Francis W. Parker, *Talks on Pedagogics,* pp. 261, 883, 389; G. W. F. Hegel, *op. cit.,* p. 389.

[78] Francis W. Parker, "Discussion," p. 191.

[79] "Chicago and Vicinity," newspaper clipping, Parker Scrapbooks, 1886.

[80] Francis W. Parker, "The Report of the Committee of Ten—Its Use for the Improvement of Teachers Now at Work in the Schools," p. 447; "Round Table of National Herbart Club," *Journal of Proceedings and Addresses, National Educational Association, 1895,* pp. 959–960; Francis W. Parker, "Application of Child Study in the School," p. 419; Francis W. Parker, "Discussion of the Comparison of the Educational Theories of Froebel and Herbart," *Journal of Proceedings and Addresses, National Educational Association, 1895,* p. 549.

[81] Francis W. Parker, *Talks on Pedagogics,* pp. 142, 383.

[82] Francis W. Parker, "A Discussion," *Journal of Proceedings and Addresses, National Educational Association, 1880,* p. 49; Frances W. Parker, "Application of Child Study in the School," p. 420.

[83] G. W. F. Hegel, *op. cit.,* p. 435; Walter B. Kolesnik, *op. cit.,* p. 14; Francis W. Parker, *Talks on Pedagogics,* pp. 16, 25, 256, 261, 389.

[84] There is some controversy in regard to Kant's uniting the worlds of nature and spirit. One position has Kant joining the two worlds. Harold Hoffding, *A History of Modern Philosophy: A Sketch of the History of Philosophy from the Close of the Renaissance to Our Own Day,* B. E. Meyer (trans.), Vol. II (London: Macmillan, 1935), pp. 104–105. Another position holds that Kant made a "dual legislation." John Dewey, *German Philosophy and Politics* (New York: Henry Holt, 1915), p. 20.

[85] William James, *Psychology* (New York: Henry Holt, 1900), p. 1.

[86] William James, *Talks to Teachers on Psychology and to Students on Some of Life's Ideals* (New York: Henry Holt, 1916), p. 7.

[87] Francis W. Parker, "Work of the Illinois Society for Child Study," *Journal of Proceedings and Addresses, National Educational Association, 1896,* p. 845.

[88] Francis W. Parker, "Discussion of the Place of Art in General Education," p. 849.

[89] Francis W. Parker, *Talks on Pedagogics,* pp. 52, 146, 149, 373; Francis W. Parker, "The School of the Future," p. 83; John Dewey, "The Influence of Darwinism on Philosophy," *Popular Science Monthly,* **75** (July, 1909), 90–98.

[90] John S. Clark, "Discussion of the Aims of Art Education in General Education," pp. 851–854.

[91] Frank A. Fitzpatrick, "Francis Wayland Parker," *Educational Review,* **24** (June 1902), 24; Francis W. Parker, letter to The Trustees, dated July 31, 1899, Papers of Anita McCormick Blaine.

XI

The Politics of Educational Reform

Even when Parker was first formulating an education consistent with the democratic aims of the American Revolution, an economic revolution, was replacing the independent agrarian way of life with an interdependent industrial complex. Parker had always considered the problems of industrialization a far greater threat to democracy than the problems of slavery and states' rights which divided the nation at the time of the Civil War. He even believed that unless the people learned to fight with the weapons of intelligence—the knowledge of the science and art of education—the nation would be forced to use the "frightful weapons of devastation" once more in war.[1]

The great problem in the North was the capital–labor conflict. In the South the problem was centered on the Negro who had been given liberty, but, according to Parker, not true freedom. Parker believed industrial and racial injustice could be abolished only through the "new" education.[2] He actually charged that those who opposed this "new" education were really trying to destroy the common school as the "preeminent social factor" of democracy.[3]

Inasmuch as great social reforms were inherent in Parker's crusade against the forces of traditional education there were political as well as academic powers to overcome. Parker was convinced that the public schools, as social ladders by which the lower classes could climb, had won such support that they could no longer be abolished by direct political action. They could be destroyed, he believed, by "political chicanery" on the part of those secretly opposed to public education and the equal opportunity which it afforded. As long as boards of education kept public school teaching standards at a low level by not requiring professional training, the children of the upper classes would be driven into private schools and the lower class children would soon drop out for lack of interest.[4] Public education would thus be destroyed by default. Carrying the "new" education to the children of America, through the schools of professional teacher training, was therefore as much political in nature as pedagogical.

Just as Parker avoided identity with sectarian religions, he now sought to achieve political objectives outside the circle of partisan political parties. No longer associated with the Republican party, he was even attacked by boards of education dominated by the party of Lincoln.[5] His worst abuse, however, was at the hands of the Democrats. Not even the striking resemblance he was said to bear to President Grover Cleveland spared him from the opposition of the Democratic forces in Chicago.[6]

The destiny of Parker and the education of democracy which he was developing and sponsoring were in the hands of the Cook County Board of Education. This board was very much subject to politics. It was responsive to taxpayers who still did not believe in the education of other people's children, especially the public education of professional people, such as teachers. There was also the indifferent public that was satisfied with almost any kind of public school, so long as it was cheap. There were parents who opposed any educational methods which were different or new. There were those people from "the old world" who Parker said were impervious to the idea of the common school as a basis of democracy. School directors had to deal with all such groups, but party politics may have given Parker the greatest trouble. He found many school directors only held office for party purposes or for their own personal gain.[7]

It is certain that the Cook County Board of Education had influence to sell. It owned some of the most valuable lands in the county.[8] Temptation was especially strong in times of such rapid urban development and rising land values. Not many years earlier, for instance, Englewood had been a marsh where Chicago hunters went to shoot mud hens.[9] Now it was a center of land speculation. (It was annexed to Chicago, as mentioned earlier, in 1889.)

Chicago was growing so fast it could dispose of its sin and corruption no better than its garbage and sewage. The Chicago River was crusted over with refuse. In 1893, one observer found it was as easy to trace political swindles as to locate officially banned brothels.[10] A few years later Lincoln Steffens came to Chicago and reported on the "Hinky Dink" and "Bathhouse John" types of ward politicians that Jane Addams had been complaining about.[11] They ruled Chicago neighborhoods in the manner of medieval lords. The "hydra-headed" system of county, city, and town government made the electorate uncertain about the authority or responsibility of the men who represented them.[12]

Parker made enemies in Chicago by standing as a bulwark against political interference in the Normal School. Every other institution of the county was said to be the "prey of politicians." The hospitals, the poorhouses, the County Agent's office, and many other public agencies were claimed to be "parceled out" among politicians as their personal property.[13]

Parker offered no remedies for reform other than education, and the separation of education from politics. He was as obsessed with this single panacea as Henry George was with his single tax. Although Parker lectured on "Education into Democracy" at the Chicago Single Tax Club, he was not associated with the Henry George movement of social reform.[14] Parker did have to go into politics, however, outside the realm of the major parties. He became vice president of the Personal Rights League in Chicago. It sponsored "less police, prisons and gallows, but more education." It claimed to have "no party to serve, no persons to cater to," but it would "visit" all its wrath on any politician opposed to the Cook County Normal School.[15]

It was in 1887 that Parker had his first great clash with the politicians and was forced to take his case to the public. At that time the Cook County Board of Education cut his salary from $5,000 to $3,600. The county was in financial straits. As is generally true, the teachers were the first public servants to feel the effect of budget cutting. It was said that reducing their salaries had the least effect on men who "manipulate" caucuses and carry conventions.[16] The friends of Parker, however, were not without some political influence. They contended that the reduction of the Colonel's salary was part of a "prearranged movement" toward killing the Normal School. The matter of economy was simply a subterfuge.[17] A plot by a "gang" of politicians to get rid of Parker was discovered by the *Englewood Eye,* a local newspaper. The scheme was to reduce the Colonel's salary so as to force him to resign out of professional pride. Without Colonel Parker, the Normal School would be almost defenseless and at the mercy of the politicians. Rumors were even flying that the Normal School was to be destroyed so that certain interested parties could appropriate its real estate,[18] the terms of the original land donation being such that the property would revert to the original donors if it were not used for education.[19]

Whether the Cook County Board of Education had acted in good faith or not, a "Committee of Fifty" was formed in Englewood to investigate the rumors of plot and political corruption. Representatives of this committee were received by the board on June 23, 1887. They were informed by the board that there was no attempt to "squeeze" out Parker. The spokesman for the board said that $3,600 would command the services of a thousand good principals. When one board member was pressed for a statement, however, he blurted out that it was "time to get a man who had some business talent, and who would not override the orders of the Board of Education ...."[20]

The popular movement in support of Parker and his $5,000 actually took to the streets on the night of June 25, 1887. Several hundred citizens of Englewood massed at Arcade Hall and sang the praises of Colonel Parker. Their demonstration ended with a resolution that the profession of teaching should be of the greatest importance and dignity in the community, inferior to none of the learned professions.[21]

It is not certain to what extent Parker himself was behind this demonstration. He avoided direct responsibility at that time by being absent on a lecture engagement in Missouri.[22] Parker had made it clear, however, that he would get his $5,000 salary or resign.[23] In addition to personal financial reasons, Parker probably did not want to sacrifice himself in the manner of his predecessor, Daniel S. Wentworth, whose personal concessions had impoverished the school as well as himself. A stand had to be made, or the flood of protests against taxes in general would be allowed to wash away the whole commitment to public support for teacher training. Parker had to hold his ground, not so much for his own aggrandizement as for the professional dignity of his position. Businessmen and politicians who controlled the schools, he said, would only be impressed by an educator who could command a good salary.[24] At $5,000 per year, Parker was earning more than that of the County Superintendent of Schools, but even if his salary were high for an educator, it was not high in terms of the cost of living. It was also less than the wages of a hog buyer for one of the meat packers in the nearby Union Stockyards.[25]

The demonstration of June 25, 1887, would give any politician pause to reconsider the slash of Colonel Parker's salary. One member of the Board of Education said he did not find fault with the citizens of Englewood for wanting to improve their community, but he said they should not try to do it at the expense of the whole county. It was then revealed that the request for cutting expenses at the Normal School, especially the cut in the Colonel's salary, had come from the Cook County Board of Commissioners rather than from the Board of Education.[26] (The Board of Commissioners appropriated the funds for all county operations.)

A few days after the public demonstration, Parker's cause was joined by part of the German community in Cook County. Herman Raster, editor of the German-language newspaper, *Staats Zeitung,* gave ringing support to the Colonel. Raster editorialized that the crisis of 1776 only involved political autonomy; the crisis of 1861 only involved the emancipation of one race; but the crisis over the schools now involved the salvation of civilization.[27] It is not possible to measure the impact of the *Staats Zeitung,* but it is known that Raster had enough influence to wrest control of a seat on the Cook County Board of Education in the next election.[28] It is also known that, shortly after Raster's opinion was voiced, at least one member of the Board of Education agreed to change his vote.[29]

A rumor was circulating that the Colonel was being "bled" by a member of the Cook County Board of Education in exchange for his vote. A "crooked" commissioner was also said to be sharing Parker's salary for similar considerations. All such rumors were traced to enemies of the Normal School and exposed.[30]

When the Cook County Board of Education met to deliberate on the various resolutions received on behalf of Parker, some members even went so far as to propose successors for Colonel Parker's position. This attempt failed by a vote of five to three. By the same margin the board voted to reinstate Parker's full salary of $5,000 in order to retain his services.[31]

Parker thanked the whole school, both teachers and pupils, and the board for the "earnest, cordial manner" in which he and the "just claims" of the school had been supported. He observed that the history of all normal schools in the United States was full of opposition, even persecution. "The people are slow to learn the truth," he said, "that money cannot be expended to a better purpose than in the teaching and training of teachers for the common school."[32]

The money for the Normal School and Parker's salary had to be appropriated by the Cook County Board of Commissioners. There was enough money to meet expenses until the following September, according to the Superintendent of Schools, and thereafter, he argued, the educational department, like other charitable institutions, could not be closed up.[33]

The Board of Commissioners, with the power of the purse at its command, would not willingly leave off interfering in educational matters. Parker's victory in 1887 was by no means decisive. It was only an incident in his relentless struggle for survival in the political jungle of Cook County and Chicago.

When Charles S. Thornton was elected to the Cook County Board of Education in 1891, the Colonel was confronted by an antagonist who

who would carry the war out of the jungle and up to Olympian heights. The Parker-Thornton feud was ultimately portrayed in the newspaper as a battle between Achilles and Agamemnon. In a cartoon captioned, "A Chicagoized Scene from the Iliad of Homer," Thornton was dressed in the armor of Agamemnon and threatening to take away the Normal School from Parker. The Colonel, as the warrier Achilles, was reaching for his sword and defying the advances of the "most revengeful of men!"[34]

Not unlike the sturdy Agamemnon, Charles Thornton, almost fifteen years younger than Parker, was an imposing figure with dignified beard and mustache. A lawyer by profession, he specialized in real estate and was associated with the leading lawyers and law firms in Chicago. He was a prominent Democrat, having served the town of Lake as attorney and Auburn Park as school board president. It was said of him, however, that he was no politician in the usual sense and that he supported men of principle rather than party.[35]

When Thornton was an active candidate for a seat on the Cook County Board of Education, he appeared to be a friend of the Normal School. He professed sympathy, if not conversion, to the experiments Parker was working out. As soon as he was seated on the board in September of 1891 he was appointed to the school visiting committee for that month. He immediately began testing the academic proficiency of the children in the practice rooms of the Normal School. These examinations ended in a massive report which indicated "desultory work and careless inattention and idle habits." He found evidence of "intemperance" as well as "inaccuracy, and lack of power to think." That only three pupils in the eighth grade could tell how many pence were in a sixpence was an example of the "lack of power to think." Furthermore, Thornton said he had records for the year 1889 which showed that the Normal School had supplied 17 per cent of the pupils in the freshman class at Englewood High School and 31 per cent of the failures.[36]

Although Thornton said at that time he still had faith in the Colonel's theories, he indicated that the Colonel did not carry them out. Even later, when the Parker–Thornton conflict had degenerated into pure spleen, Thornton said he did not oppose Parker's "so-called system" or educational goals. "His theories," Thornton told a *Chicago Tribune* reporter, "are the same as those of the Chicago public schools, but his applications of them do not correspond. He does not practice what he preaches,"[37]

Parker stated, on the other hand, that his theory of education differed widely from that of Thornton. He said Thornton and other opponents of the new education were almost "wholly ignorant" of the work done at the Normal School.[38]

Thornton accused Parker of not knowing what was done at the Normal School. He said the Colonel was too often absent on lecturing tours for "pecuniary compensation." He introduced a resolution that Parker be required to furnish a monthly statement of his daily attendance. This resolution was never carried to a vote, but Thornton's charges that the Normal School produced inferior products led to an official investigation. Parker then refused to let Thornton back into the Normal School. He told the board he wanted a thorough examination of the school by experts. He said, "Go at it in the right way and if you find that Mr. Thornton's conclusions are right, I am ready to step out."[39]

The board suspended its decision until a full report from the new County Superintendent of Schools was received. Orville T. Bright made his own examination and submitted a formal and lengthy report on December 26, 1891. He acknowledged that there were "slow" children, to be sure, and that the Normal School was "far from perfect—a fact freely admitted by Colonel Parker." He did find, however, evidence to contradict Mr. Thornton's report. His own examinations determined that eighth-grade students at the Normal School were as good as the average ninth-grade students in the Chicago high schools.[40]

Superintendent Bright charged that Thornton's examination was more characteristic of a lawyer "bent on making out a case" than of a "disinterested and philosophic inquirer." He also insisted that the "dubious practice" of individual laymen going into schools and examining frightened children ought to be stopped. He said some children purposely did poorly on Mr. Thornton's tests because they did not like him. He also vouched for the fact that Mr. Thornton had been guilty of stealing reports from his office and misinterpreting as well as misrepresenting the data.[41]

While Bright had been preparing his report, endorsements of Parker and his methods flowed into the Cook County Board of Education from such educators as William T. Harris, G. Stanley Hall, and E. A. Sheldon. The director of the National German-American Teachers' Association, Herr Ernst Dapprich, examined the Normal School and commended its methods.[42]

In the end, the conclusion of Superintendent Bright prevailed with the board. In his bi-annual report to the board at the end of that year Bright wrote that 1891 had been a "somewhat eventful one, in that the sessions of the Board have been marked by sharp disagreements . . . ." He concluded, however, that the members of the board were impelled to controversy out of "true friendship" for the Normal School.[43]

Parker was by no means convinced that Thornton's actions were out of "true friendship." He said of Thornton that he was the kind of board member who used his influence to further political ends. Others said that Thornton was prejudiced against Parker from the first, when Parker had been brought to the Normal School by Dr. Champlin—Thornton's main rival in his alleged attempt to make himself "master of the Town of Lake politics."[44]

It was also believed that the Parker-Thornton feud grew out of their differences in politics. Thornton was a Democrat. It is more likely that Parker had first offended Thornton in 1883 when he asserted his right as principal to select and retain teachers. He apparently dismissed a teacher who was championed by Thornton. Parker said that the first time he had ever known of Thorton was when the "gentleman" had threatened to expell him if he did not rehire the teacher in question.[45]

Thornton may have opposed Parker, at least in the beginning, on higher ground. He may have learned his lessons too well in the traditional system of education and simply opposed Parker, as did so many academicians, on purely educational grounds. A graduate of the Boston Latin School and Harvard College, Thornton was a man who had been genuinely educated in the best traditions of academic excellence. Parker said that Thornton first opposed him because he did not teach "the old-fashioned word knowledge that he had learned.[46] As far as Thornton was concerned, Parker was "devoid of refinement, a man who possesses neither collegiate, academic nor high school education, and whose only stock in trade has been some theories of education which, like a sponge, he has absorbed."[47]

The fact that Parker had received an honorary Master of Arts degree from Dartmouth College in 1887 did not seem to impress Thornton.[48] The old guard of education weighed knowledge quantitatively in terms of words learned and degrees earned. An honorary degree did not represent the virtues of any mental discipline. One time, Thornton went so far as to tell Parker's pupils at an assembly in the Normal School that their principal was "an uneducated man." Thornton was hissed from the platform.[49]

Thornton went on to harass Parker on educational grounds. He ridiculed the "new education" because of its low regard for pure mathematics and the rules of grammar. He called the Normal School an "asylum for Colonel Parker and his friends." He opposed the field trips and excursions. He attacked the "show work" to please visitors, especially the time wasted on preparing birthday celebrations for board members. He suspected such celebrations were contrived to influence the votes of these members. He mocked the modesty of Colonel Parker who allowed himself to be greeted at assemblies with a chorus of "See, the Conquering Hero Comes; Sound the Trumpet, Beat the drum."[50]

Thornton believed there was too much fun going on at the Normal School for any education to be taking place. He complained that the school sessions were an unending "round of play."[51] In all this, Thornton was simply reflecting the views of tradition. He was probably sincerely interested in education. He once opposed the general slashing of teachers' salaries during a depression. He was more responsible than any other person in securing pensions for Chicago teachers. He made Latin an optional study in the Chicago schools. He was known for his persistent efforts to raise the sandards of scholarship for teachers and pupils.[52]

While Parker and Thornton were engaged in a battle of academic standards in Chicago, the same conflict was spreading across the nation. A journalist for *The Forum* magazine began conducting investigations of the academic standards in the public schools of thirty-six cities of the United States. Dr. Joseph Mayer Rice pursued his investigation in Chicago during June 1892. He pronounced the Chicago schools less progressive than those of New York or Philadelphia because there was a definite lack of teacher preparation. He found the Cook County Normal School, however, the most "progressive" and "suggestive" school he had ever visited. He explained to his readers that the Chicago school system ignored this source of teacher training.[53]

Rice exposed what he called the mechanical methods and the "unscientific" system of teaching in Chicago. In the lower grades he said that the pupils did little else but "read, write, and cipher all day long." The writing of the students on their slates might be mistaken for the "footmarks of flies with chalk legs." He charged the schools with providing only one reading-book which was read over and over again by the children. Geography was a drill of facts. Pupils "trembled" from head to foot when reciting.[54]

Rice's articles in *The Forum,* sounding so much like the polemics of Parker, impelled the *Chicago Post* to report, in the wake of political and educational consternation in Chicago, that the "unfair," "unjust," "unscientific," and "highly prejudicial" article on the Chicago schools was inspired by Colonel Parker. Having exposed Chicago teachers to national disgrace, Parker was said to be "cordially disliked by the teachers in the Chicago public schools."[55]

Parker blamed Thornton for spreading this rumor and said there was not a "shadow of truth" to the allegation.[56] It is unlikely that there was any collusion between Parker and Rice. They were simply both interested in "scientific" education. Rice could hardly have obtained all his criticism from Parker. He was especially critical of the Delsarte system which he found was a systematic method of teaching children to grimace and wag their tongues.[57]

The national interest and controversy Rice's articles stirred up about the schools was also a beginning of the journalistic effort to reform society in other respects as well. There was now a good market for what would come to be known as "muckraking."[58]

Gradually the Chicago press was beginning to fall in line behind Parker and the "new education." It was reported in New York by the *School Journal* that all the major Chicago papers except the *Chicago Tribune* had stopped their "flings" against the Normal School by 1896. It was said that the "power of the press" was beginning to exert itself in favor of a "progressive science in education."[59]

It was beginning to be dangerous for politicians to "meddle too openly with public interests," and "especially unsafe to meddle with the interests of the children."[60] Part of the support for Parker and the Normal School was derived from women's clubs and different institutions described as of the "amazonian type," such as the South Chicago Bicycle Association and the Englewood Bloomer Club.[61] Undoubtedly, women of the "amazon" spirit were important in pressing for municipal as well as educational reforms. In the days when teachers "boarded around," it was easy to interpret the schoolwork to the parents. In the growing urban complex, misunderstandings between parents and teachers were inevitable. To combat such misunderstandings, Parker had, early in his career at the Cook County Normal School, initiated a Parent–Teacher Association, one of the first organizations of that nature in the Middle West.[62] Through this organization Parker made known the methods and needs of the schools. The public was then aroused by the mothers. The concern of parents worried political bosses because these concerns would cut across party lines.

Mrs. Parker was a valuable aid in her husband's political struggles. She was a fighter who had been disciplined in the struggle for woman's emancipation. Susan B. Anthony was a personal friend. It was in freeing women from the bondage of clothing's "fashion" that Mrs. Parker added to the struggle for woman's equal rights. Active in the "Society for the Promotion of Correct Dress," she even had a display at the Chicago Columbian Exposition in 1893.[63]

Mrs. Parker was also active in the Fortnightly Club of Chicago and the Englewood's Women's Club. For some years she was chairman of the Committee on Topics and Papers for the Association for the Advancement of Women. She was chairman of the Educational Department of the Chicago Woman's Club in 1891. In 1894 she was elected president of the Chicago Political Equality League, which had just sprung from the Chicago Woman's Club.[64]

Out of the loose ends of dissatisfaction with the new and changing industrial society, many threads of protest were coming together into the common strand of thinking called Progressivism. Dissatisfactions with the inequality of the sexes and the inequality of wealth and opportunity stimulated this movement of reform. The movement was not characterized by any one social class. It has been interpreted as a "coalition of classes," with goals of restoring "economic individualism" and "political democracy." The moralizing sentiment that dominated the journalism of the times was to catch the conscience of all citizens, rich as well as poor.[65]

For Parker it was especially necessary to catch the conscience and the sympathy of the rich, who often represented the academic thinking of traditional education and dominated the school boards. One of the great concerns of the upper classes was whether Parker's education would prepare their children for college, the tradition-laden centers of higher learning. The charge that children made "mud pies" in the Normal School provoked a gasp of horror. It was necessary for Parker to make a public explanation of the mud pies. The children were shaping maps on level surfaces with sand in order to illustrate the topography of the earth's surface. A course in paper-folding was ridiculed as childish waste of time until Parker could properly explain the course as one in the teaching of geometric forms,[66]

Members of the new leaders in business were easily impressed by the standards of the old world. European values, often emulated by the new class of industrial entrepreneurs, had to be associated with the "new education." Parker began encouraging European evaluations of the Normal School. Complimentary letters from abroad began to find their way into Chicago newspapers. A most favorable view of the Normal School came from Jules Steeg in Paris. Steeg had visited Parker while representing France as an educational delegate to the 1893 Columbian Exposition in Chicago. Steeg's credentials were excellent. He edited the edition of Rousseau's *Emile* which was widely read in America. He was an inspector of schools in Paris, professor in the normal school at Fontenay-aux-Roses, director of the National Pedagogical Museum and Library, editor of the *Revue Pédagogique.* From the *Educational Times in London* came a report from the principal of the University Training College for Women. It mentioned Parker's name with reverence. From Denmark came word that the principal of the normal school in Copenhagen had translated Parker's work into a great influence among Danish teachers.[67]

Such views from the cultural centers of the Western World gave Parker's education a certain sparkle of cultural royalty. One Chicago newspaper editorialized that the Colonel would have been a "howling success in the promotion line" if he had not taken up pedagogics as a profession. Parker was no longer viewed as a tactless, antagonistic fighter. He was now described as a "smooth citizen."[68]

In his clashes with the political bosses, Parker was holding his own.

In his attempts to win over the support of the rich, Parker was making headway. He had definitely persuaded some of the leading commercial men of the city, such as Marshall Field and George M. Pullman, of the merits of manual training.[69] He was himself apparently won over by the "model" community that Pullman built for his workers. Parker included the "Pullman Car Works, at Pullman, a delightful suburb of Chicago" in his series of excursions for the students of the Normal School. He even planned for such an excursion, during that summer of 1894, when the workers in Pullman rose up in violence against low wages and high rents.[70]

While Parker rode the waves of popular social protest and the currents of scientific development which reached high tide in the last decade of the nineteenth century, he was not always consistent. He was definitely in the liberal stream, however, in his opposition to the Spencerian brand of sociology that preached the *status quo* and resignation to the laws of nature. In this regard he stood against William T. Harris, who found justification for using the schools as instruments of adjustment rather than reconstruction of society. The conservative philosophies of Hegel, Spencer, and the "conservative Darwinists," all provided Harris with continuity and supreme purpose in the struggles of a society that was otherwise caught up in a meaningless travail of industrial and urban development.[71] Parker was definitely in the liberal stream in his opposition to *Laissez-faire,* at least in the realm of education. He supported Federal intervention in the schools by way of financial relief. He favored a national normal school. He used his influence to support the various Blair bills in the 1880's which would have supplied Federal funds for education to the states on the basis of illiterate population.[72]

Parker argued that the schools, as they were, could not meet the needs of democracy. They could not deal with the problems of municipal reform. They could not overcome the "thirst for money, the desire to get something for nothing." They could not absorb the immigrants, the "vast number of people whose ancestors have been degraded through the ages of ignorance and oppression."[73]

"We must educate or perish," was the editorial sentiment of the *School Journal.* This weekly publication from New York brought Parker into its editorial circle in September of 1885. The editors could not understand at that time why the federal government had raised and paid for armies to put down a rebellion in the 1860's but was afraid to pay for an "army to conquer ignorance."[74]

Congress did not pass the Blair bills which would have led to massive federal aid to education. Powerful lobbies, however, succeeded in securing federal assistance for agricultural experiment stations in the

1880's, and by 1890 the Second Morrill Act conferred federal support for instruction in agriculture, mechanical arts, and various branches of physical, natural, and economic sciences in the land-grant colleges.[75]

Parker found powerful grass-roots support in his attack on academic traditions of education from the agrarian protests which were becoming articulate in the last quarter of the nineteenth century. It was such support which would help to overwhelm the brilliant logic of the academicians. The schools, after all, belonged to the people. The agrarian interests of the country were the first to organize resistance to the economic forces of concentration which were accused of mortgaging the people to Wall Street. The National Grange began working for legislation to regulate railroads, graneries, mills. It was such organization that had siphoned money out of the federal treasury for aid to the land-grant colleges.[76]

The educational philosophy of the agrarian protest was of the same seed as Parker's. Farm journals, such as *Wallace's Farmer,* argued for the "all-around development of children." It opposed the "cut-and-dried formula" of education which adhered to textbooks and knowledge of a by-gone era. The National Grange pushed for "practical knowledge."[77]

Parker, in turn, worked for a modernization of rural schools. Love of work and dignity of labor had to be cultivated even in rural schools. The farm and the city and the school had to be brought together. Parker was most enthusiastic about the way farm and school were becoming integrated. At one grange meeting in Michigan, he said it was one of the best meetings he had ever attended. Parents were vitally interested in what was going on in the school and what the school could do for the farm. The discussion was divided between the raising of potatoes and children.[78]

Parker was less enthusiastic about the protests of industrial labor. He was hostile to trade unionism and socialism. In this respect he was conservative but not out of line with the basic attitudes of the American public.[79]

Through the *School Journal* Parker poured satire on the flames of labor violence. The editors wrote that the children of a school in St. Louis "went out in a body," and that their pickets were watched with amusement by the railroad strikers who were glad to see their example spreading to the younger generation. In Philadelphia, the editors said, the "Knights of the Central High" struck for an increase of from fifteen to thirty minutes for recess. Admitting "real grievances" for the children, such as the "cramming process" of traditional education, the editors appealed for moderation, and they hinted seriously that the violence of the older generation would be imitated by the younger. Strikes and violence of any kind served as bad object lessons for the children.[80]

The editors of the *School Journal* were even opposed to the proposition of Terence Powderly of the Knights of Labor that unions should also be used for educational purposes. This was considered a trap in which workingmen would fall into the "bondage" of the "uneducated."[81]

Parker strenuously opposed collective bargaining by teachers. The peril of equal pay was that it did not reward the exceptional or artist teacher and it tended in the long run to keep all wages equally low.[82] It is even probable that he opposed pensions for teachers because such security only encouraged bad teachers to stay at their jobs. It was his great enemy, Charles S. Thornton, who acted as "counsel, friend, and co-worker" in the fight for the teachers' pension bill which became law for Chicago teachers in May of 1895.[83]

Later, when the women grade teachers of Chicago carried on a long legal and political fight for higher wages, Parker remained out of the battle, although it was generally supposed that he sympathized with the teachers.[84] It was this fiight which led to the organization of the Teachers Federation in Chicago. The teachers had been turned down by the legislature when they appealed for a higher tax levy out of which their wages could be increased. Then they appealed to the courts for a more realistic assessment of property values. Millionaires such as Marshall Field, for instance, had property assessed at only $20,000, and George M. Pullman, who owned the whole town of Pullman, was taxed on a property assessment of $12,000. Through the efforts of the Teachers Federation, the courts revised the corporation assessments and greatly added to the public treasury, but Parker had refrained from public endorsement of the Teachers Federation.[85]

As co-editor of the *School Journal,* Parker also let it be known that he was opposed to strikes. He allowed that no man with pick and shovel worked as hard or was as poorly paid as a teacher, but he said that if teachers wanted better wages they should teach better and make themselves more indispensable to the people.[86] This sentiment was fully consistent with the philosophy of big business, which had turned Spencer's theory of the "survival of the fittest" into a natural justification for *laissez-faire.*[87]

Parker was again on the conservative side when a demonstration by striking laborers and various socialist and anarchist sympathizers led to violence in Chicago's Haymarket on the night of May 4, 1886. The old market square at the corner of Randolph and Desplaines was about sixty-eight blocks north of the Normal School, but the bomb that went off that night was heard all over Chicago and had repercussions across the nation. The whole labor movement was discredited.[88]

Parker used the occasion for urging more attention to education before "bombs thunder in our streets, shaking society to its very foundations."[89] Society paid more attention to its police and courts. Four anarchists and socialist leaders were tried and hanged for murder, although there was no positive evidence that they had done more than agitate violence. Although, liberals, then and since, considered these executions "political murder,"[90] Parker and the other editors of the *School Journal* supported the ruling of the court, which held that advice to commit violence makes the advisor guilty of whatever bloodshed results. The editors even added that this principle should apply to school government as well as to criminal prosecution.[91]

It might also be significant that Parker received support among the Germans from the *Staats Zeitung,* a conservative publication. August Spies, editor of the *Arbieter Zeitung,* was one of those hanged for advocating violence at that fateful incident in the Haymarket of Chicago. The *Arbieter Zeitung* had long represented the radical elements of the German community in Cook County.[92]

A conservative in his views on collective bargaining and "socialist" reform, Parker was nevertheless radical in his support of a much more collective society. He stood for a society based on the social responsibility of all. He engendered this in his teaching. Before dismissing students from their morning exercises at the Normal School, he would always ask them for the one great word. The children would instantly shout back, "Responsibility!"[93]

Parker did not believe that the working classes should bear the responsibility for anarchism, nihilism, and socialism. He said the rulers who "fatten on the vitals of the people" are responsible for such "political insanity."[94]

Despite these overtones of the exploitation of the proletariat, Parker was so convinced that his brand of education would solve the problems of society that he refused to be moved by moderate reformers who granted that education would elevate the masses but insisted that the masses could not afford the time to attend public schools.

By 1890, less than 70 per cent of the children between ages five and seventeen were enrolled in the public schools of the nation, and daily attendance was much less. Not even 4 per cent graduated from high school. Statistics for the schools of Cook County, Illinois, in 1882, showed that 68 per cent of the pupils left school as soon as they completed a primary education, that 40 per cent withdrew by the third grade. Parker admitted in 1894 that three-fourths of the children in large cities left school before the fifth grade.[95] Parker, however, did not blame economic necessity for this "drop out." Children left, he argued, because "the street, the shop, and the manufactory are more attractive than the school. If children loved school work, most parents would work their fingers to the bone to keep them there."[96]

One of the techniques for reaching the interests and needs of the masses was manual training. Parker considered it the most important factor in primary education. It was central in motivation as well as in developing motor and mental coordination. He also believed that manual training had social significance, observing that the aristocracy always had looked down on manual labor. Contempt for labor was a symbol of all "ruling classes," and it was therefore dangerous for this attitude to exist in a democracy.[97]

It was organized labor, ironically, which opposed the introduction of manual training in the schools. Labor viewed this as a plot by big business to supply itself with skilled laborers at a time when unions were attempting to regulate and control such a supply. It is true that J. P. Morgan advanced half a million dollars in 1892 for the New York Trades Schools, that the National Association of Manufacturers advocated manual training.[98] It was Marshall Field, dry goods merchandiser of Chicago, who advanced privately the largest subscription for Parker's manual training project at the Normal School.[99] Parker gave public credit for financial assistance to the Commercial Club of Chicago. This was composed of the wealthy commercial families of the city. Among its board of trustees were Marshall Field and George M. Pullman.[100]

The impetus for manual training actually began at the college level. President John D. Runkle of the Massachusetts Institute of Technology had been impressed by a display from the Moscow Imperial Technical School at the Philadelphia Centennial Exhibition in 1876. The system of breaking each industrial skill and operation into separate, interchangeable parts, was as revolutionary in industrial education as the system of manufacturing separate, interchangeable parts was to the mass production methods of industrialism itself. Runkle initiated this system at Massachusetts Institute of Technology for the improved training of engineers.[101]

Calvin M. Woodward of Washington University in St. Louis, Missouri, brought the system down to the high school level. Like Parker, he railed against traditional education which concentrated only on the mind. He wanted an educational system for the industrial age which would meet the demand for skills other than clerical. It was his model which was followed by the Chicago Manual Training School. This school was founded in April of 1883 by the same forces which supported Parker's manual training at the elementary level.[102]

Woodward's work was advanced by Washington Gladden, the Congregational clergyman who sought social reform through religion. Gladden pointed out that Christ was a carpenter, that manual training would make better men and better citizens out of children. He believed manual training would be especially effective in the lower grades where children were especially restless and hard to manage.[103]

Parker was most responsible for bringing manual training to the elementary school level. The idea was much against the best judgments of the Cook County Board of Education, and he therefore had to do it with private funds, continually assuring the Board that his purposes were educational, not vocational.[104] The Board of Education was under the influence of either trade unions, who opposed the mass production of skilled workers, or the academicians, who opposed anything which did not fit the intellectual function of the school.

As Parker viewed education, not collective bargaining, as the means of integrating industrial wage slaves into the new industrial society, he also viewed education as the means of integrating the former Negro slave. In league with Booker T. Washington, who sought accommodation with the ruling order in the South, Parker supported vocational and technical training for the Negro. Armed with skills, the Negro could eventually command respect and gain a place in society. In league with Parker, Booker T. Washington also despaired of bookish, traditional education. This tended to reinforce the freedman's hostility toward manual labor which had been inherited from slavery.[105]

While still co-editor of the *School Journal,* Parker was associated with the editorial which claimed the "co-education of the races—not sexes—is a subject our nation more than any other is called upon to consider." It was argued that all races must go to school but the question was whether they should all go to school together. Parker and his co-editors sanctioned segregated schools for the different races, but only until the culture of the segregated race could approximate American customs and laws.[106]

Since Parker considered segregation and "stratified education" the "foundation of thrones and monarchs," he was ultimately opposed to segregation.[107] Just how he expected the Chinese—the race which was causing Americans the most alarm in the 1880's—or the Negro to approach American customs and laws without integration into those customs and laws is not clear. Parker's general hostility to segregation, however, may have been tempered at this time by his co-editors of the *School Journal.*

The worst segregation of all, as far as Parker was concerned, was caused by "rich people taking their children out of the public schools and putting them by themselves . . ." He criticized parents who did not want their children to mix with the "hoi polloi." He said they were as much opposed to democracy as to the common school.[108]

It was not for Parker or his generation to complete the work begun—the abolition of slavery and the integration of the Negro into American society. He and his generation were involved in the problem of integrating millions of alien immigrants. By 1890 there were not only hordes of unassimilated immigrants but an enormously increased generation of Americans to absorb. The population of the United States had doubled in the thirty years since the Civil War.[109] In a sense, all Americans of Parker's generation were immigrants, immigrants in a new world created by industrialization. A new education was needed for the new Americans.

Parker received vital support from the social settlement workers in the cities. The idea of social settlements had spread to the United States from England in the 1880's and was concerned with the cultural separation between the high and low levels of society as well as the cultural gap between the native Americans and the new immigrants. Jane Addams of Hull House, later a member of the Chicago Board of Education, was as impatient with traditional education as was Parker. She said there was too much stress on reading and writing. "Socialized" education was needed for the immigrant and practical education for the poor. Adjustment to present life, to American life, became the goals of education for the settlement workers, and they established their own schools with courses in cooking, child care, and health, as well as in recreation and vocational pursuits.[110]

In the 1890's with the rising tide of immigration, disunity on a cultural level was a severe problem. Parker fought for unity in the 1890's as he had in the 1860's. Now it was the children who were the shock troops and the common school that was the battleground. Parker challenged the "rampant, bigoted Americanism" which was rising to meet the flood of new immigrants. Parker said the common school must continue to be the agent that "fused, blended, melted" children from the Old World.[111] By the same token it occurred to Parker that the American common school could overcome the hates and cultural diffusion of the whole world. Caught up in the same social currents which produced progressive reforms at home and economic and moral imperialism abroad, Parker sought to Americanize the whole world through democracy. He believed "God made America the schoolhouse of the world." He believed true patriotism embraced the whole world, that it was as broad as Christianity. Progress in democratic living, through the common schools in America, would therefore bring "universal salvation."[112]

In the end, Parker's education transcended party lines and nationalism. His work was for the children of the world.

NOTES

[1] Francis W. Parker, "Application of Child Study in the School," *Journal of Proceedings and Addresses, National Educational Association, 1895,* p. 428; Francis W. Parker, "The Need of the Hour," newspaper clipping, Parker Scrapbooks, 1893, Archives, Harper Library, University of Chicago.

[2] Francis W. Parker, "Discussion of the South and Its Problems," *Journal of Proceedings and Addresses, National Educational Association, 1894,* p. 587.

[3] Francis W. Parker, "The School of the Future," *Journal of Proceedings and Addresses, National Educational Association, 1891,* p. 87.

[4] *Ibid.*

[5] The Cook County Board of Commissioners, which opposed Parker so violently in 1894, was acknowledged as Republican in "Spigot Economy and Bunghole Waste," *Chicago Evening Journal* (Chicago, Ill.), January 27, 1894.

[6] Parker's abuse at the hands of the Democratic administration of Carter H. Harrison, Jr., is discussed in the next chapter. "Col. Parker bears a striking resemblance to the portraits of President Cleveland, though he is a much finer looking man. . . ." Newspaper clipping [alleged to be a St. Cloud, Minnesota paper of June 1888], Parker Scrapbooks, 1888.

[7] Francis W. Parker (Ed.), "Englewood's Schools, Their Rise, Progress and Present Status Graphically Described," p. 3 (typed copy from *Daily Evening Call* (Englewood, Ill.), Special Number, Thursday, October 9, 1890), Historical Files, Chicago Teachers College South.

[8] Bessie Louise Pierce, *A History of Chicago,* Vol. III (New York: Alfred A. Knopf, 1957), pp. 324–325.

[9] "Parker and His Job," *Chicago Evening Post* (Chicago, Ill.), January 30, 1894.

[10] William T. Stead, *If Christ Came to Chicago, A Plea for the Union of All who Love in the Service of All who Suffer* (Chicago: Laird and Lee, Publishers, 1894), pp. 171–175, 460–472.

[11] Lincoln Steffens, *The Autobiography of Lincoln Steffens* (New York: Harcourt, Brace, 1958), pp. 423, 425–428; Jane Addams, *Twenty Years at Hull-House* (New York: New American Library, 1961), pp. 222, 224, 240, 241.

[12] Bessie Louise Pierce, *op. cit.,* pp. 40–44; 140; 339.

[13] "Sandbagging a Public School," *Chicago Herald* (Chicago, Ill.), January 29, 1894.

[14] Parker was scheduled to speak at the Chicago Single Tax Club on Friday evening, March 24, 1899 according to "Announcement," Parker Scrapbooks, 1899. No reviews of this address could be found in a search of Chicago newspapers. Parker did believe there was land enough for all, that the problem was the right distribution of labor and effort. Francis W. Parker, *Talks on Pedagogics: An Outline of the Theory of Concentration* (New York: E. L. Kellogg and Co., 1894), p. 416.

[15] "A Vice President of the Personal Rights League," newspaper clipping, Parker Scrapbooks, 1892.

[16] "Cutting the Normal School Salaries," *Goodalls Daily Sun* (Chicago, Ill.), June 22, 1887; "Prophet of the Public School; Englewooders up in Defense of Colonel Parker and the Normal," newspaper clipping dated Friday, June 24, 1887, Parker Scrapbooks, 1887; "Cause of Education Crippled," *Chicago Herald,* January 28, 1894.

[17] "Cutting the Normal School Salaries."

[18] "The Normal Outrage," newspaper clipping from *The Englewood Eye* (Englewood, Ill.), Parker Scrapbooks, 1887; "Call a Meeting," *Goodalls Daily Sun,* June 22, 1887.

[19] "Parker and His Job."

[20] "Prophet of the Public School; Englewooders Up in Defense of Colonel Parker and the Normal."

[21] "The Normal Meeting," *Goodalls Daily Sun,* June 27, 1887.

[22] "Save the Normal," *Goodalls Daily Sun,* June 23, 1887.

[23] "The Normal Outrage."

[24] The idea that salaries represented dignity was an important consideration at the mass rally for Parker on June 25, 1887, as reported in "The Normal Meeting." Parker once said that, in "this age of gold," he was forced to carry the case for public education down to the level of "dividends" that owners of local real estate would reap through an improvement of the schools. Francis W. Parker, "Englewood's Schools, Their Rise, Progress and Present Status Graphically Described."

[25] "Save the Normal"; *Official Proceedings of the Board of Commissioners for the Year 1895-1896, Being from December 2, 1895 to December 5, 1896* (Chicago: Cameron, Amberg and Co., 1896), p. 326. When John Dewey came to Chicago a few years later at $4,000 a year, he protested that such a sum was inadequate to meet the needs of his family in Chicago. Robert L. McCaul, "Dewey's Chicago," *The School Review* (Summer, 1959), 259–260.

[26] "Will Get His Salary," newspaper clipping, Parker Scrapbooks, 1887.

[27] "Letter of H. Raster" [Translated into English and submitted to a Chicago newspaper around the Fourth of July, 1887, on behalf of the *Illinois Staats Zeitung*], Parker Scrapbooks, 1887.

[28] *Biennial Report of the County Superintendent of Schools from July 1, 1886 to June 30, 1888* (Chicago: J. M. W. Jones Stationery and Printing Co., 1888), p. 42.

[29] Ex-Justice Summerfield said he changed his vote when he learned that Colonel Parker would not accept the cut in salary "Colonel Parker's Day," newspaper clipping dated July 6, 1887, Parker Scrapbooks, 1887.

[30] "The Normal Outrage."

[31] "Colonel Parker's Day"; "Will Get His Salary"; "The Normal Saved" and "The Normal School," newspaper clippings, Parker Scrapbook, 1887.

[32] *Biennial Report . . . 1886–1888,* p. 61.

[33] "County Attorney Bliss to County Superintendent Lane," *Goodalls Daily Sun,* July 7, 1887.

[34] "A Chicagoized Scene from the Iliad of Homer," cartoon, Parker Scrapbooks, 1898.

[35] "Charles S. Thornton, Lawyer and School Board Member," *Chicago Evening Post,* February 10, 1894.

[36] *Biennial Report of the County Superintendent of Schools from July 1, 1890 to June 30, 1892* (Chicago: J. M. W. Jones Stationery and Printing Co., 1892), p. 38; "C. S. Thornton Again Attacks Col. Parker," newspaper clipping attributed to the *Daily Globe* (Chicago), November 22, 1891, in Parker Scrapbooks, 1891; "His Hunt for Facts," *Chicago Tribune* (Chicago, Ill.), December 27, 1891.

[37] "C. S. Thornton Again Attacks Col. Parker"; "Col. Parker Keeps Cool, Makes No Particular Fuss Over the Normal School Deal," *Chicago Tribune,* January 31, 1896.

[38] *Ibid.*

[39] "C. S. Thornton Again Attacks Col. Parker."

[40] "His Hunt for Facts, O. T. Bright's Investigation of the Normal School," *Chicago Tribune,* December 27, 1891; "Bright's Long Report," *Chicago Herald,* December 27, 1891.

[41] "His Hunt for Facts, O. T. Bright's Investigation of the Normal School"; "The Normal School," *Chicago Herald,* December 28, 1891; "Thornton Makes Reply," newspaper clipping reputed to be from *Chicago Times* (Chicago, Ill.), December 29, 1891, Parker Scrapbooks, 1891.

[42] *Biennial Report . . . 1890-1892,* pp. 26–27; "Bright's Long Report."

[43] *Biennial Report . . . 1890–1892,* p. 46.

[44] "Thornton's Living Spite, Why the Lawyer Has Hounded Col. Parker of the Normal School for Years," *Chicago News* (Chicago, Ill.), November 1, 1898.

[45] *Ibid.;* "Will Thornton Now Subside?" *Chicago Evening Post,* July 1, 1898.

[46] "Charles S. Thornton, Lawyer and School Board Member"; "Thornton's Living Spite."

[47] "Hot Shot for Parker, C. S. Thornton Scores the Normal School and Its Principal," *Chicago Evening Post,* August 12, 1894.

[48] "Francis Wayland Parker (A. M.) 1887," *Dartmouth College Necrology, 1901–1902,* compiled by Ernest Martin Hopkins (New Hampshire Historical Society, Concord, N. H. n. d.), pp. 51–52. "Francis W. Parker, A. M., Dartmouth College," *Journal of Proceedings and Addresses, National Education Association,* 1895, p. 1040.

[49] "Col. Parker Keeps Cool."

[50] "Hot Shot for Parker"; "C. S. Thornton Again Attacks Col. Parker."

[51] "Hot Shot for Parker."

[52] "June 3, 1896," *Proceedings of the Board of Education of the City of Chicago. July 17, 1895–July 1, 1896* (Chicago: Press of John H. Higgins, n.d.), p. 427; Meta Wellers, "Chicago's Pension Law," *Journal of Education,* **44** (November 12, 1896), 331; "Rally for a School," *Chicago Evening Post,* January 29, 1896.

[53] J. M. Rice, "The Public Schools of Chicago and St. Paul," *The Forum,* **15** (March 1893), 200–205; *Biennial Report . . . 1890–1892,* p. 40.

[54] J. M. Rice, *op. cit.,* pp. 202–205.

[55] "Hot Shot for Parker."

[56] "Parker Strikes Back, Vigorously Repels the Charges of 'This Man Thornton,' " *Chicago Post* (Chicago, Ill.), September 7, 1894.

[57] J. M. Rice, *op. cit.,* pp. 205–206.

[58] Lawrence A. Cremin, *The Transformation of the School, Progressivism in American Education, 1876–1957* (New York: Alfred A. Knopf, 1961), pp. 3–8; Richard Hofstadter, *The Age of Reform, from Bryan to F. D. R.* (New York: Vintage Books, 1960), p. 186; *Years of Conscience. The Muckrakers,* edited and introduced by Harvey Swados (Cleveland: World Publishing Co., 1962), p. 10.

[59] "Sand-Bagging the C. C. N. S.," *School Journal,* **48** (Feb. 10, 1894), 153.

[60] M. F. W. [Marion Foster Washburne], "City and the Normal School," *Chicago Evening Post,* December 24, 1895.

[61] "May Take Normal School," clipping, presumably from a Chicago newspaper, dated January 29, 1896, Parker Scrapbooks, 1896.

[62] Helen M. Hefferan, "Col. Francis Wayland Parker," *Chicago Schools Journal,* **18** (September 1936), 7.

[63] Annie White Johnson, "Society for the Promotion of Correct Dress" and "Letters of Condolence," *Frances Stuart Parker, Reminiscences and Letters* (Chicago: C. L. Ricketts, 1907), pp. 59, 123. Mrs. Frank Stuart Parker also authored *Expression of Thought Through the Body* (Chicago: Physical Culture Extension Society, 1895).

[64] Helen E. Starrett, "Interest in Club Life," Julia Ward Howe, "Assocaition for the Advancement of Women," Alice D. Hoswell, "Englewood Woman's Club," Ada C. Sweet, "Chicago Woman's Club," and Ellen A. Martin, "The Chicago Political Equality League," *Frances Stuart Parker, Reminiscences and Letters,* pp. 53–55, 57–58, 60–61, 55–56, 61.

[65] Richard Hofstadter, *op. cit.,* pp. 5, 320.

[66] "Parker and His Job," *Chicago Evening Post,* January 30, 1894; "The Chicago Fads," *Journal of Education,* **37** (May 11, 1893), 292.

[67] "Once More in Peril," *Chicago Inter-Ocean* (Chicago, Ill.), January 29, 1894; Will S. Monroe, "M. Jules Steeg," *Journal of Education,* **48** (July 7, 1898), 48.

[68] "Parker and His Job."

[69] Dr. A. H. Champlin, "Memories of 'Normal'," *Dedication of the Chicago Normal School, April 20 and 21, 1906* (Chicago: The Chicago Normal School Press, n.d.), p. 108; Francis W. Parker, "An Account of the Work of the Cook County and Chicago Normal School from 1883 to 1899," *Education Report, 1901–1902* (U. S. Office of Education, Report of the Commissioner of Education for the Year 1902), p. 255; "Chicago Manual Training School," *Journal of Education,* **18** (December 20, 1883), 390.

[70] *Cook County Normal Summer School* [Bulletin] *Three Weeks Beginning July 9th, 1894,* p. 8, at Tolman Farm, Tolman Pond, Nelson, N. H.

[71] Lawrence A. Cremin, *op. cit.,* pp. 15–16; William T. Harris, "Discussion of the Report of the Subcommittee on the Correlation of Studies in Elementary Education," *Journal of Proceedings and Addresses, National Educational Association, 1895,* p. 350; William T. Harris, "Comment on Demands of Sociology upon Pedagogy," *Journal of Proceedings and Addresses, National Educational Association, 1896,* pp. 196–197.

[72] "National Aid to Education," *School Journal,* **31** (March 6, 1886), 147; Francis W. Parker, "Discussion of the German System of Normal Schools," *Journal of Proceedings and Addresses, National Educational Association, 1887,* p. 493.

[73] Francis W. Parker, "Application of Child Study in the School."

[74] "National Aid to Education." (The first notice of Parker as one of the editors appears in the *School Journal,* **30** (September 26, 1885) and the last in **32** (October 16, 1886).)

[75] R. Freeman Butts and Lawrence A. Cremin, *A History of Education in American Culture* (New York: Henry Holt, 1953), pp. 372–375, 427, 422.

[76] Richard Hofstadter, William Miller, and Daniel Aaron, *The United States, The History of a Republic* (Englewood Cliffs, N. J.: Prentice-Hall, 1957), pp. 495–501. Parker credited the "agricultural people" with the founding and supporting of state normal schools. Francis W. Parker, "The School of the Future," *Journal of Proceedings and Addresses, National Educational Association, 1891,* p. 88; Lawrence A. Cremin, *op. cit.,* pp. 42–43.

[77] *Ibid.,* pp. 43–44, 46.

[78] Francis W. Parker, "The Farm as the Center of Interest," *Journal of Proceedings and Addresses, National Educational Association, 1897,* p. 535.

[79] Francis W. Parker, "A Sketch of the Work in the Quincy Schools from 1875 to 1880, II, *School Journal,* **29** (June 13, 1885), 374; Francis W. Parker, "A Sketch of the Work in the Quincy Schools from 1875 to 1880," V, *School Journal,* **30** (August 1, 1885), 70. Henry Adams thought there was some "narrow trait of the New England nature" which seemed to "blight" socialism. Henry Adams, *The Education of Henry Adams* (New York: The Modern Library, Random House, 1946), p. 225. The role of public opinion is noted in Thomas A. Bailey, *The American Pageant, A History of the Republic* (Boston: D. C. Heath, 1956), p. 537.

[80] "Editorial," *School Journal,* **31** (May 15, 1886), 308.

[81] *Ibid.*

[82] Francis W. Parker, "A Sketch of the Work in the Quincy Schools from 1875 to 1800," V, p. 70.

[83] Parker's silence was significant in the era in which teachers were struggling for pensions. Parker's manager of the Normal School, Wilbur S. Jackman, however, was definitely in opposition. Wilbur S. Jackman, "Pensions for Teachers," *Journal of Education* **39** (February 15, 1894) 100. Thornton's efforts in support of the pension are described in Meta Wellers, *op. cit.,* p. 331.

[84] Jane Addams, *op. cit.,* p. 231.

[85] "The Chicago Salaries," *Journal of Education,* **47** (March 10, 1898), 152; "Mrs. Young and Mrs. Hull," *Journal of Education,* **47** (April 7, 1898), 219; Meta Wellers, "The Black Year," *Journal of Education,* **51** (May 24, 1900) 329; William T. Stead, *op. cit.,* p. 207; "Chicago Woman's Success," *Journal of Education,* **52** (November 8, 1900), 296; "Great Chicago Victory," *Journal of Education,* **53** (May 9, 1901), 300. There is no mention of Parker in any account of the struggle for higher wages. Mayor Harrison, who tried to drive Parker out of the Normal School, however, was one of the supporters of the teachers. "Chicago Salaries," *Journal of Education,* **49** (January 19, 1899), 40.

[86] "Editorial," *School Journal,* **32** (July 31, 1886), 67.

[87] Richard Hofstadter, *Social Darwinism in American Thought* (Boston: The Beacon Press, 1955), pp. 44–48, 54.

[88] *Chicago Herald,* May 5, 1886; Ray Ginger, *Altgeld's America, The Lincoln Ideal Versus Changing Realities* (New York: Funk and Wagnalls, 1958), p. 49. An excellent study of the labor scene and Haymarket trial of this time may be found in Henry David, *The History of the Haymarket Affair* (New York: Farrar and Rinehart, 1936).

[89] *Biennial Report of the County Superintendent of Schools from July 1, 1884 to June 30, 1886* (Chicago: J. M. W. Jones Stationery and Printing Co., 1886), p. 50.

[90] Ray Ginger, *op. cit.,* pp. 35–60, 79, 86.

[91] "Editorial," *School Journal,* **32** (September 4, 1886), 116.

[92] "Letter of H. Raster"; Bessie Louise Pierce, *op. cit.,* p. 24; Ray Ginger, *op. cit., p. 40.*

[93] Wilbur S. Jackman, "Francis Wayland Parker," *Education Report, 1901–1902* (U. S. Office of Education, Report of the Commissioner of Education for the Year 1902), p. 232-233.

[94] Francis W. Parker, *Talks on Pedagogics,* p. 418.

[95] *Biennial Report of the County Superintendent of Schools from July 1, 1882 to June 30, 1884* (Chicago: J. M. W. Jones Stationery and Printing Co., 1884), p. 37; "Elementary and Secondary Schools, Enrollment and Attendance, and High School Graduates: 1870–1956," U. S. Bureau of the Census, *Historical Statistics of the United States, Colonial Times to 1957,* Washington, D. C., 1960, p. 207; Francis W. Parker, "The Report of the Committee of Ten—Its Use for the Improvement of Teachers Now at Work in the Schools," *Journal of Proceedings and Addresses, National Educational Association, 1894,* p. 449.

[96] *Ibid.*

[97] Francis W. Parker, *Talks on Pedagogics,* pp. 254–255.

[98] Lawrence A. Cremin, *op. cit.,* pp. 33, 36–37.

[99] Dr. A. H. Champlin, *op. cit.,* p. 108.

[100] Francis W. Parker, "An Account of the Work of the Cook County and Chicago Normal School from 1883 to 1899," p. 255; "Chicago Manual Training School," p. 390.

[101] Lawrence A. Cremin, *op. cit.,* pp. 24–26.

[102] *Ibid.,* pp. 26–29, 32; "Chicago Manual Training School," p. 390.

[103] Washington Gladden, "Christianity and Popular Education," *The Century, Illustrated Monthly Magazine,* **31** (November 1885 to April 1886), 940–943.

[104] Parker acknowledged that manual training was in some high schools, and two private schools, but there was "scarcely a trace" of it at the elementary level until he introduced it. Francis W. Parker, "An Account of the Work of the Cook County and Chicago Normal School from 1883 to 1899," p. 254. Later he said his efforts were "probably the first." Francis W. Parker, "Discussion on Manual Training," *Journal of Proceedings and Addresses, National Educational Association, 1901,* p. 269; *Biennial Report . . . 1882–1884,* p. 64; Francis W. Parker, "Art in Everything," *Journal of Proceedings and Addresses, National Educational Association, 1900,* pp. 510, 512–513.

[105] Merle Curti, *The Social Ideas of American Educators* (Paterson, N. J.: Littlefield, Adams and Co., 1959),pp. 288–309. It is possible that Parker derived educational inspiration from the same source as Booker T. Washington. He was granted a two-week vacation for the purpose of visiting "Hampton, Virginia," in 1879. April 5, 1879, "Record of the General School Committee for the Town of Quincy," Board of Education, Quincy, Mass.

[106] "Editorial," *School Journal,* **31** (March 13, 1886), 163.

[107] Francis W. Parker, "The School of the Future," p. 85.

[108] "Worst segregation of all," newspaper clipping from Marion, Ind., dated April 4, 1896, Parker Scrapbooks, 1896; Francis W. Parker, "The School of the Future," p. 88.

[109] Estimated Population of the United States: 1790 to 1957," and "Immigrants, by Country: 1820 to 1957," U.S. Bureau of the Census, *Historical Statistics of the United States, Colonial Times to 1957,* Washington, D.C., 1960, pp. 7, 57.

[110] Lawrence A. Cremin, *op. cit.,* pp. 59–62.

[111] Francis W. Parker, "The School of the Future," pp. 86, 87.

[112] Francis W. Parker, *Talks on Pedagogics,* p. 448; Francis W. Parker, "Discussion of the South and Its Problems," p. 588; *Biennial Report . . . 1884–1886, op. cit.,* pp. 49–50.

XII

Wars of Succession at the Cook County and Chicago Normal School

Parker's position at the Normal School was continually subject to attacks from spoilsmen, or political and educational traditionalists, but the campaign to depose him broke into a full-scale war in 1894. The Cook County Board of Commissioners, who controlled the county finances, met on January 22, 1894, and proceeded to cut the budget for the Normal School almost in half. Not only did the commissioners slash appropriations for Parker's school, they also dictated to the Cook County Board of Education how to expend the funds. Parker's salary, for instance, was specifically tagged for a $2,000 cut.[1]

The Board of Commissioners had legitimate reasons for economizing. The national economic "convulsions of 1893" had wiped out fortunes among the rich, spreading unemployment and misery among the poor. The Columbian Exposition had just closed down in Chicago and cut off that source of employment and municipal income. These were days of grim depression for Chicago and the nation, as well as for the Normal School. The Board of Commissioners found that the depression was not the only cause for dwindling revenues. Within the last few years, the town of Lake—including the villages of Englewood, Hyde Park, Jefferson, Lake View, and part of Cicero—had been annexed by Chicago. Local school officers relinquished control of their schools to the Chicago Board of Education and turned over to the city all the books, papers, and money belonging to the township.[2] The Cook County Board of Education was thus stripped of many schools while the Cook County Board of Commissioners lost financial resources.

Furthermore, the Board of Commissioners did not like financing the Normal School, which was now within the city limits of Chicago.

It soon became perfectly clear that the Board of Commissioners had acted more maliciously than judiciously in regard to its economy measures. Parker's "public relations" people went into action. There was no "essential reduction" in appropriations for other departments of county government, they reported. If the commissioners were acting only out of economic necessity, it is difficult to explain why they economized only at the expense of the Normal School.[3]

There were hints in some quarters, possibly instigated by Parker or his friends, that this financial attack on the Normal School was inspired by Parker's adversary on the Board of Education, Charles Thornton. Thornton's name was actually linked to G. W. Kunstman, chairman of the Financial Committee, Cook County Board of Commissioners. Commissioner Kunstman denied any conspiracy with Mr. Thornton and even claimed he had never met or spoken with the man. He dismissed the charges that he was activated by anything other than economy as "rot—utter rot."[4]

Thornton himself denied that he had any knowledge of the commissioners' plan to cut appropriations until it was publicly announced.[5]

Although the Cook County Commissioners had sound financial reasons for trimming the Normal School budget, they had acted without consulting the Board of Education. They had even gone beyond their own legal jurisdiction by making educational decisions. Not only had they submitted a salary schedule for the whole staff but they had made a curricular decision when they eliminated the salary for the teacher of manual training.[6]

The Board of Education was always divided over the question of Parker, but it was not nearly so divided over the question of protecting its own legal prerogatives. Some members wanted to test the question in the courts, but the board agreed first of all, to petition the commissioners for a special hearing on the matter.[7]

Charles Thornton did not sign this petition, nor was he a member of the special committee granted a hearing before the commissioners late in January. He made himself present at the hearing, however, and got embroiled in the discussion. He said he found fault with the Normal School because of the "inefficiency of its principal," and he reviewed the findings of his academic examinations of the Normal School three years earlier. He insisted that the Normal School was not up to the standards of the city grade schools.[8]

One of the commissioners kept interrupting Thornton with laughter and "side remarks." He represented the second district, which formerly included Englewood, and he was apparently one of the few commissioners who supported Parker and the Normal School. He called Thornton a "windbag" and an "interloper." He said that Thornton had only come to vent spite on Colonel Parker. "It is simply your own hatred," the commissioner said. "You got into the board of education to work out that spite. You hate Parker above ground, and I suppose you will when he is dead."[9]

The commissioner was quickly called to order, and Thornton was allowed to continue. "I am prejudiced against Parker," Thornton admitted, "but when I got into the board of education I had not the slightest spite against him."[10]

"Everybody knows better than that," the hostile commissioner interrupted again. Nevertheless, the Board of Education received no satisfaction as a result of the hearing. The Board of Commissioners refused to allow Parker his $5,000 salary or to restore any appropriations for the Normal School. County Commissioner Kunstman argued that the right to hire teachers, a prerogative of the Board of Education, did not include the right to fix salaries. He said the commissioners would "recede from their position" only if advised to do so by legal counsel.[11]

The County Attorney subsequently reported in favor of the Board of Education. It was his opinion that the power to hire teachers involved the power to have charge of the "expenditures." He held that the teachers were not strictly employees of the county, nor were they county officers. He believed the Cook County Board of Education had the power to hire and fix the salaries of teachers so long as it kept the total of its expenses within the allotted appropriations.[12]

The Cook County Board of Education then defied the Commissioners by ignoring the schedule of salaries which had been foisted on them. The board even reinstated Parker's salary of $5,000. It was impossible, of course, for the Board of Education to increase the appropriations for the Normal School, but it could distribute the appropriations in any way desired. The intention of the board was to round out Parker's salary with funds received from student tuition and from profits of the boarding house.[13]

The Cook County Board of Commissioners took immediate steps to block this avenue of income. The commissioners ordered the County Superintendent of Schools to make a regular accounting of these special funds and to return them to the county treasury.[14]

Before the Board of Education could respond to this challenge, the Board of Commissioners was restrained by its own legal counsel. The County Attorney advised the commissioners that they could not rightly require the County Superintendent of Schools to account for funds which were under the control of the Board of Education. The County Attorney added, however, that it was not the purpose of a municipality to conduct a profit-making business. If profits did ensue from the exercise of proper functions, such as those from the boarding house of the Normal School, the profits properly belonged to the county treasury.[15]

Without the cooperation of the Cook County Board of Education, however, the commissioners could not get an accounting of these special revenues. One of the commissioners complained that his request for such information was continually turned down by the Board of Education.[16]

Charles Thornton charged that Parker was more interested in profits than education, that he had turned the boarding house into a "World's Fair Hotel." His evidence was the public advertisement from the previous summer which described the Normal School as only "ten minutes" from the fair grounds. Further allegations that Parker was guilty of "gross dishonesty" in regard to the profits of the boarding house led the Board of Education to institute a formal investigation. This resulted in complete repudiation of the charges by the county Superintendent of Schools and the investigating committee. "Not a leak the size of a pin hole can be found anywhere," reported the *Chicago Inter-Ocean*.[17]

It was further established that under Parker's efficient management the boarding house had been completely renovated. Whereas it had once been as poorly furnished as the county poorhouse, it was now "neatly papered throughout," and even had Brussels carpets on every floor. Efficient and honest handling of profits also contributed to the school library. Since the advent of Parker the library had grown from around three hundred volumes to over eleven thousand.[18]

One newspaper considered the profits due to the drawing power of Parker's name as well as to his efficient management. Tuition receipts from all nonresidents had increased since Parker's arrival from little over a hundred dollars a year to well over two thousand.[19]

Thorton's attempt to discredit Parker with such allegations of corruption backfired. It was even established that Parker had spent hundreds of dollars from his own pocket to supply books, apparatus, and manual training equipment.[20] Thornton continued, nevertheless, to stir up the press with criticisms of Parker's pedagogy. The curriculum of Parker's "Fad Factory" was called "pudding." It was "dainty and attractive, but extremely unsubstantial and unnourishing." Thornton charged that eleven out of every twelve graduates from the Normal School failed the examinations for teaching in the Chicago school system.[21]

Parker admitted that some poor teachers were graduated from the practice department of the Normal School. In addition, he admitted that some teachers were especially weak in subject matter. He expained that he admitted high school graduates and gave professional, not academic, training. If some of the teachers were found wanting in academic subject matter, then it was a reflection of the academic high schools, not the Normal School training. He also pointed out that the tests for certification in the Chicago schools were academic, not professional, instruments.[22]

Parker appealed for a fair and open test of the defamed Normal School by professional educators. The Cook County Board of Education agreed to this and proposed to work with the Board of Commissioners in selecting a competent body of educational experts. The County Commissioners, however, tabled the proposal that was submitted to them. The Board of Education then proceeded on its own and brought together such men as William T. Harris, G. Stanley Hall, and A. S. Draper. These men examined and praised the Normal School.[23] But the Board of Commissioners, through which appeals for more substantial support of the Normal School must pass, remained lined up against Parker by a count of twelve to three.[24]

During that summer of 1894 the same depression which had occasioned the cut in appropriations for the Normal School had reduced wages at the Pullman Palace Car Company to the level of desperation. The Cook County village of Pullman went out on strike against its chief employer and landlord. The strike spread to the railroad brotherhoods and across the nation. While Parker and his friends were up in arms over the reduced appropriations for the Normal School, the Pullman workers were taking to the streets. Rioting and pillaging accompanied the attempts of the railroad companies to break up the strike. Federal troops moved into Chicago and the strike was put down, but the events of that hot, desperate summer must have confirmed Parker's prophecy that the capital-labor strife must be settled by education or war.[25]

When the County Commissioners were investigating the need for relief in Pullman, Illinois, Commissioner Kunstman appeared more interested in the September elections for two openings on the Cook County Board of Education. One of the openings was provided by Charles Thornton. Commissioner Kunstman contacted Thornton as early as August 7, 1894. "Permit me to state," Kunstman wrote, "that should you desire to become a candidate for re-election to the board of education, I shall deem it a privilege to be allowed to present your name and use my best efforts to secure your election."[26]

Thornton, however, chose not to run. "During my three years' service," he replied to Kunstman's letter on August 17, "I have spent much time in investigating the condition of the Cook County Normal School and I think that I have filled the full measure of service which can be required justly of a member of the board."[27] Thornton had already become involved in a much broader educational field as a member of the Chicago Board of Education. He was at that time the chairman of the Committee on College Preparatory Schools.[28]

Although Thornton was withdrawing from the immediate battle against Parker in Cook County, he contributed to the support of anti-Parkerites in the fall elections.[29]

As the date of election approached, Commissioner Kunstman finally admitted that he had been the one responsible for the reduction of appropriations for the Normal School. He also let it slip to the press that he favored William T. Harris, United States Commissioner of Education, for Parker's successor. In spite of his responsibility for slashing Normal School appropriations, he was reported to have said he would be willing to pay Harris $6,000 a year, $1,000 more than Parker's controversial salary.[30] This tended to serve notice that if the Board of Education rid itself of Parker it could expect better financial support from the county commissioners. (It also seems apparent that Kunstman had not told the truth when he earlier claimed only economy as the reason for cutting Parker's salary.)

While Chicago was still buzzing with the prospect of drawing the United States Commissioner of Education, Parker got into print a personal letter he had received from William T. Harris. Harris made it clear that he did not seek such a place and that he would not accept even if it were offered.[31] Thus, the Harris boom was struck a fatal blow.

No favorite son on the local scene could match the Parker reputation; consequently, without a substantial alternative to Parker, the opposition fell apart. The two openings on the Board of Education ultimately went to "Parkerites," and the Parker faction even elected one of its own as president of the board.[32] Parker had also shaken off the thorn in his flesh, Thornton, but the Normal School was still crippled by the niggardly appropriations of the hostile Board of Commissioners. Moreover, Parker's school occupied an unnatural position in its relations with the city which housed it. The Chicago Board of Education failed to make any distinction between a graduate of the Cook County Normal School and teacher candidates with no special professional training at all. Parker complained that diplomas from the Cook County Normal School were recognized everywhere in the United States except Chicago.[33]

It had been the practice in Chicago to assign high school graduates, who passed the certification examination, as "cadets" in the various schools. When they were considered successful in discipline and ability to teach at the assigned grade level, they were given classes of their own.[34] In April of 1893 the Chicago Board of Education established a special training school for "cadets." Candidates for teaching positions were required "to cadet" during the forenoon in their assigned schools and receive special instruction in educational principles and methods in the afternoon. Only a corner of the Thomas Hoyne School, with two special teachers, was reserved for this afternoon training.[35] (This slight accommodation for teacher training might have been stimulated by the adverse publicity the Chicago schools received from the Joseph Rice articles in the 1892 issues of the *Forum.*)

Over three hundred "cadets" completed this course in the 1893–1894 academic year, more than four hundred in 1894–1895, while the Cook County Normal School, with all its facilities, graduated less than a hundred a year.[36] Charles Thornton, as member of the Chicago Board of Education, proudly boasted that Chicago could train its teachers at a cost of twelve dollars and ninety-three cents apiece. The Cook County Normal School produced inferior teachers, he said, at a cost of more than $500 each. He argued that the Cook County Normal School ought to come under the Chicago Board of Education, where it would be better and more economically managed.[37]

Chicago was in need of greater facilities for training its teachers, and at the same time the Normal School was in need of greater educational outlets. The mutual need of both appeared to be recognized on December 9, 1895, when the Cook County Board of Commissioners resolved to convey the Normal School properties to the Chicago Board of Education. When word leaked out to the press, the president of the Board of Commissioners pleaded financial inability on the part of the county as the sole reason for offering the Normal School to the city of Chicago.[38]

The Committee on Buildings and Grounds, which negotiated for the Chicago Board of Education, recommended that the board accept the gift, if the "various conditions contained" were legal. One important condition was that the Normal School should always be open to residents of Cook County without charge. Some argued that this would invalidate the entire tax levy of Chicago. People could not be required to pay taxes to educate students beyond the city limits.[39]

The Chicago Board of Education hesitated to accept the gift. Some members said they were "suspicious." They wondered if the county had any legal right to transfer the property. Such transfer, if illegal, would invalidate the original deed. This might be a plot by Dr. Beck, who had donated ten of the original twenty acres, to get his property back. In the midst of this rumor, the old doctor offered to waive any claims for a fee of $25,000. He said he would have no regrets about losing the name of benefactor. He thought he had been forgotten anyway. Even if he were remembered, he believed the Normal School had nothing in particular to recommend it.[40]

On December 20, 1895, the Chicago Board of Education reviewed the terms of transfer and the original deeds of the property. It was decided to continue negotiations with the County Commissioners and make no agreement before the expiration of the school year on June 30, 1896.[41]

The hesitation in accepting a gift worth $300,000 to $400,000 would seem absurd except for the fact that two hundred pounds of Parker went with it. One member of the Chicago Board of Education was reported to have said that Parker had "laid out" fifteen County Commissioners "stiff" and that the commissioners were now giving up the property for the chance of "unloading Colonel Parker and his feud upon us." Another member said it would be a pity to see "discord and contention" consume the Chicago Board of Education, as it had the Cook County Board. "Colonel Parker," he said, "is teaching a system concerning which there is a diversity of opinion, and which is totally irreconcilable with the system in use in our schools. To adopt him is to adopt his system."[42]

The president of the Cook County Board of Commissioners was not willing to keep up the Normal School until June. He said such delay was "impossible." As to the rumor that the commissioners wanted to "unload" Parker, the president said, "we are not dependent on the city to relieve us of him. We are going to get rid of him easily enough, whether the city takes him or not. We are not going to pay him another cent...."[43]

The commissioner railed out against the delaying tactics of the Chicago Board of Education and threatened to turn the property into a school for dependent children. In any event, the county was through with the support of the Normal School. The president of the Board of Commissioners was just as opposed to the Normal School in principle as he was to its principal. "It would be just as fair," he said, "to educate our doctors, lawyers, and preachers at public expense as our teachers."[44]

When bills for the Normal School were submitted to the Cook County Board of Commissioners in January of 1896, the bills were returned with the communication that the county appropriations for the year were all budgeted and no provision whatsoever had been made for the Normal School. There was no pay for any of the teachers that January.[45]

It was not hard to divine that Parker's enemies hoped to force him and his band of unpaid teachers to resign while the Chicago Board of Education delayed acceptance. Once Parker and his teachers resigned, the Chicago Board of Education could accept the school and staff it with teachers of its own choosing.[46]

Parker and his teachers refused to resign. This may have been one of the most unusual strikes in history. The teachers protested by working without pay. They carried their cause to the conscience of the city.

Mrs. Marion Foster Washburne, who Parker said reacted "like a tigress fighting for her young," was typical of the kind of female support the Normal School received. Mrs. Washburne was largely responsible for breaking into print with the stories of teachers going without pay and the political attempts to "sandbag" the Normal School. She became "school editor" of the *Chicago Evening Post* and the *Chicago Herald* through the office of their owner, a wholesale baker who had been a patient of Mrs. Washburne's father.[47]

"I had to make news," Mrs. Washburne remembered some years later, "for most readers of newspapers don't care much for school struggles to find better ways of educating children." She made human interest stories about the teachers at the Normal School who were carrying on their work without pay. She interviewed famous people all the way up to William James. She was authorized by such educators as Nicholas Murray Butler of Columbia University and William Harper of the University of Chicago to write any articles she wished and use their names. Jane Addams of Hull House also offered her name for any purpose which Mrs. Washburne thought necessary.[48]

The unpaid teachers at the Normal School were not the only educators in need of public attention. The city of Chicago had recently slashed the salaries of all its teachers by 25 per cent. This was lampooned by the editor of one educational journal as a case in which economy was necessary because it was found that more money was required to educate children than to hire policemen for the protection of saloons and brothels.[49]

The power of the press was beginning to roll. In September of 1895 the Chicago Woman's Club had been told that only professionals cared to read about the schools. Now, a few months later, with the crisis at the Normal School, whole columns were devoted to the educational scene. Mrs. Washburne's pen even pricked the conscience of the nation when her views came out in *The Arena,* a magazine of wide circulation. The "educational crisis in Chicago," she wrote, was a crisis for the nation. The conflict between the old and the new education was really a struggle between despotism and democracy.[50]

By the end of January 1896 Chicago was said to be at "white heat educationally."[51] The Chicago Woman's Club and similar organizations deluged the Chicago Board of Education with demands that the Normal

School be accepted at once; John Dewey of the University of Chicago made an appeal for its acceptance; principals and teachers in the Chicago schools endorsed Parker and his school; Chicago's Jewish community was said to be "rousing and preparing to take a hand." Rabbi Hirsch, whose influence was extensive, had always been a friend of the Normal School, as had Principal Bamberger of the Jewish Manual Training School.[52]

The German population of Chicago was also stirred up in favor of the Normal School with its methods of Pestalozzi, Froebel, and Herbart. Even labor organizations were calling for its early acceptance, as was the social settlement of Hull House. The Roman Catholic leaders of Chicago urged their faithful to support the Normal School. The State Teachers Association went on record in favor of the Normal School and its principal.[53]

Members of the Chicago Board of Education were kept busy receiving delegations which supported the Normal School and argued that it had no equal in "all the most civilized countries of the world." When a mother in one such delegation said her children so loved going to the Normal School that they "dreaded Saturday," one board member thought she "was putting it a little too strong," but other mothers confirmed it.[54]

"I have had two hundred women after me today," said one member of the Chicago Board of Education to a reporter. "I want the school, and I want it quick, and I'll do all I can to please 'em. Any man who wants to be popular with the ladies would better join the board of education these days."[55]

Just before the last meeting in January, at which time the Chicago Board of Education had promised to consider the transfer once more, Mrs. Washburne exposed the "land conspiracy" between Dr. Beck and Charles Thornton. The story that Beck and Thornton were plotting to destroy the Normal School so that the property would revert to Beck was old and had been used before to neutralize the impact of Thornton's attacks on Parker and the Normal School. The facts were well known. Dr. Beck had lost most of his property in the years since he generously donated ten acres to the Normal School. About all he retained now was a thirteen-foot strip of land south of the Normal School which he had originally set aside for a street. He sought to exploit that land to the best advantage by building on it a long, narrow tenement house, later known as the "sunlight flats," which he subsequently sold to one Dr. Teed, founder of a new religion, and became known as a "heaven" for Teed's "flock of angels." Dr. Teed eventually lost the property, and it reverted to Beck, who allowed it to deteriorate until it constituted a nuisance. Local citizens retained Mr. Thornton to institute proceedings against Dr. Beck. Nothing ever came of the case. "Parkerites" often winked and affected stage whispers in asking why Thornton had not quit the case or taken action.[56]

Now Mrs. Washburne said she had proof that Thornton was really working in the interests of Dr. Beck and that he would get half the value of the real estate if it were returned to Beck. Actually, Mrs. Washburne admitted privately that she had not "an atom of documentary evidence." She said, however, that Parker had actually seen a copy of the contract between Beck and Thornton, but the stenographer who had copied the document disappeared. Without exposing herself or the newspapers she represented to charges of libel, Mrs. Washburne simply interviewed people and asked if they had heard the rumor about Beck and Thornton. The replies were that they had no "first-hand knowledge," but the idea was planted and Thornton's motives in attacking Parker and delaying action on accepting the Normal School appeared selfish and base. Thornton then made such an extreme personal attack on Parker that it was "exceedingly regretted by everyone" on the board.

On January 29, 1896, under the head of "unfinished business," the Chicago Board of Education voted to adopt the Normal School immediately and retain its staff until July 1, 1896. Thornton added his voice to the resounding affirmative vote.[58]

The Cook County Board of Education then closed its books on the Normal School with the pronouncement that the school would no longer be retarded by its isolation from the public schools of Chicago. Parker announced the move "an epoch" in the history of the school.[59]

Parker was not really enthusiastic. He only expressed gratification for the way his friends had "denounced" Charles Thornton. He was now once more in the clutches of a board which included Charles Thornton. His tenure would hold only until July 1. Furthermore, most of his trained staff was not yet officially elected. Their salaries, suspended since December, were not yet ordered paid. At the same time, the Chicago Board of Education resolved to practice the "strictest economy" in light of the "present financial depression."[60]

Legal transfer of the Normal School was officially effected on April 22, 1896, when a voucher for one dollar was given to the Cook County treasury in "consideration of the several covenants and agreements contained in the deed of conveyance . . . ."[61] Old Dr. Beck was heard from once more when he claimed that his donation could not be sold. Since Cook County had never possessed "a title in fee," it had no power to convey the land to anyone else for a fee. Dr. Beck claimed that he would carry his case to the Supreme Court if necessary. If the case ever came to court it was not appealed, and Dr. Beck faded from the scene where his gift of former swampland had created a quagmire of educational controversy.[62]

Parker and Parkerism now went on trial. The Chicago Board of Education set committees to work at investigating its new acquisition and the system of education which the *Chicago Tribune* called "altogether original."[63]

That Parker was impressing the official visitors and gaining ground in his campaign to remain at the principalship of the school was indicated by the sudden resignation of Charles Thornton on May 20, 1896.[64]

Parker now had great plans for introducing new scientific methods of education into the public schools of Chicago. Early in June he wrote to a friend that if his plans passed the Board of Education at its next meeting there would be "the most effective Normal School in America, if not the world . . . ." A few days later he added that he was still "wrestling" with the Normal School Committee of the Board of Education, but that the real "tug of war" was only on the matter of salaries.[65]

On June 17, 1896, the chairman of the Committee on the Normal School reported to the board that his committee had given a patient hearing to those who were strongly opposed to Parker and to those strongly in his favor. "Your committee," he reported, "recommends that the present management of the Normal School be maintained, with such changes in the methods as it may be deemed wise to make, owing to the absorption of the school into the city system." The "cadets" and their small staff of professional teachers were ordered joined to the Normal School. It was further recommended that the school should hereafter be called "the Chicago Normal School." The report was unanimously adopted. On June 26, 1896, Parker and his staff were officially approved for another year in the school now known as the Chicago Normal School.[66]

Parker was at the height of his power just as public attention was turning to the proceedings of the Democratic National Convention which met in Chicago that summer of 1896. The convention was transformed into a Populist crusade by William Jennings Bryan's "Cross of Gold" speech.[67] The issue of sound education faded into the issue of sound currency, and the educational battles between Parker and Thornton gave way to the presidential contest between Bryan and William McKinley.

The Republican Party swept its candidate into the presidency, checking the rise of Bryan and free silver liberalism, but the Democratic Party came out on top in Chicago. Carter H. Harrison, Jr., gained the mayoralty on the Democratic ticket which was pledged to protect the public interest in regard to franchises for streetcar companies.[68] Harrison was apparently determined to extend the "public interest" to the public schools.

The *Chicago Inter-Ocean,* generally regarded as a conservative but reliable paper, would remember the Harrison administration for its "disorganization and corrupting work in many departments of the city government," but the administration was most criticized for its attempt at "incorporating" the Chicago Board of Education into its "political machine."[69]

It was rumored in October of 1897 that "Bob" Burke, "chief sachem of the democratic tribe," had demanded of Mayor Harrison that Parker's head must "be caressed by the executive axe with all due speed."[70] The mayor's recently appointed corporation counsel, Charles Thornton, was no less determined to rid the Chicago schools of Parker and Parkerism.[71]

When war with Spain broke out in the spring of 1898, the sixty-year-old Parker was again fighting for his life as principal of the Normal School. Mayor Harrison was primarily interested in replacing Albert G. Lane, Republican Superintendent of the Chicago schools, but he also let it be known that, if he had a voice in the matter, he would also favor Parker's retirement.[72]

Unlike Parker, Superintendent Lane had never been an extremist or bone of contention between factions. There never seemed to be any professional disagreements between Lane and the board, although the Superintendent had always been loyal to Parker.[73] Mayor Harrison, however, thought Lane had played more politics in school affairs than he himself had played in City Hall. He chose as Lane's successor an outstanding educator—Dr. Elisha Benjamin Andrews, president of Brown University and once mentioned as a presidential candidate for the University of Chicago.[74]

Andrews was now available for Mayor Harrison's political intrigue because of some political intrigues of his own. His stand in 1896 on international bimetalism had branded him a Bryan Democrat. The election of 1896 tended to divide the nation between the rights of people and the rights of property. Andrews was forced to resign as president of Brown University because his political views were on the wrong side of property rights and might jeopardize future endowments from wealthy alumni. Outrage at his dismissal so aroused professional educators and liberal alumni that the Corporation of Brown University was pressured into reinstating Andrews, but Andrews was in no mood to remain. These political difficulties at Brown, however, had served to make Andrews something of a hero with the Democratic forces in charge of Chicago.[75]

Mayor Harrison attempted to force members of the Board of Education to support Andrews on the basis of party discipline rather than educational principles, but the remarkable credentials of Andrews tended to split the board on educational as well as political lines. Parker threw his weight to Lane and indicated it would be hard to find a better man. Dr. William R. Harper, president of the University of Chicago as well as member of the Chicago Board of Education, had been a Parkerite but he came out for Mayor Harrison's choice. He had personal as well as professional reasons. Dr. Andrews had been president of Denison University in Ohio when Dr. Harper began his teaching career there. Harper remembered Andrews as "his intellectual father."[76] Now Harper worked actively behind the mayor's open attempt to replace Lane with Andrews. The friends of both Parker and Lane were being split and it was not certain whether they would split their ballots in regard to Parker's election.

In June of 1898, while the Cuban Expedition, including Theodore Roosevelt and the Rough Riders, was enroute to Cuba, the Chicago Board of Education was approaching the election of teachers and administrators for the following year.[77] Opponents of Parker sent out skirmishers before the balloting and sniped at Parker and discredited the Normal School. One member of the board let it be known that a student had been denied a diploma at the Normal School for personal rather than academic reasons. The same board member demanded an investigation of the "ill temper" and "bad judgment" which he said characterized the management of the Normal School.[78]

The investigation which followed brought forth a weeping Miss Pearl Baker and her mother. Miss Baker testified that she had been called insane by some of her teachers. Teachers testified that Miss Baker was told she had a wandering mind, that her work was uneven. It took only five minutes for a committee of board members to exonerate the Normal School, but the board held that a diploma could be withheld only if a student failed the written examination.[79]

Parker had another clash with board members when he submitted his recommendations for the appointment of new teachers. One board member shook the typewritten list in the Colonel's face and called the recommendations "criminal." This member repeated charges from some teachers in the Chicago schools that Parker was hiring graduates from the University of Chicago in preference to experienced teachers from the public school system.[80]

A group of teachers had indeed brought such charges before Mayor Harrison, but Jennie Goldman of the Teachers' Club denied that her organization was behind the complaints.[81] Some teachers were indeed hostile to the hiring policy of Parker, but testimonials from prominent educators kept reinforcing Parker's position. Nicholas Murray Butler of Columbia University wrote one member of the board that the work of the public schools in New York would be increased "in power and efficiency one hundred per cent" if Colonel Parker and his "incomparable faculty" were to train New York teachers for only five years.[82] Nevertheless, the Colonel had to face ridicule at the hands of the Chicago Board of Education. "How long must we stand this kind of thing?" Parker was heard to have said, in an aside to President Harper of the University of Chicago, when Parker's list of recommendations was shaken in his face.[83]

Parker's friends would not put up with such treatment. One petition with fifteen thousand names was forwarded to the board in support of Parker. Even millionaires, such as the McCormicks, petitioned the board . It was said that "Society" had taken up the fight for the Colonel, and it had ruined the social life of Mayor Harrison. Dinners, teas, and receptions became a "terror" for him, as everyhere he went among the higher classes of Chicago, he met with concern about Parker. Even the North American Turner-Bund, representing twenty-four associations, mobilized for Parker and petitioned the board.[84]

Ministers even advocated Parker's cause from the pulpit. The Reverend R. A. White, pastor of the Stewart Avenue Universalist Church, took Parker as his text when he preached on the "Ethical and Religious Tendencies of the New Education." At the end of the service all but one of the eight hundred members in congregation signed a pledge to write the mayor or see some member of the Board of Education in support of Parker and Lane.[85]

The Reverend B. F. Metraw, rector of St. Bartholomew's Episcopal Church in Englewood, wrote an open letter to the board in which he implored the members to assert their authority and not let "ward politicians come forward and attempt to place their unscrupulous hands" on the public schools and the little children.[86]

Mayor Harrison, however, continued to press for party discipline in the election of the school superintendent. Informal polls had it that the members of the board were almost evenly divided on the matter of retaining Parker. Lane's position was less certain. Mayor Harrison therefore began exerting delaying tactics in order to stall off the voting for Parker and Lane. If the board remained deadlocked until July, a new board would be convened. On this new board, there would be seven openings, to be filled by appointees of the mayor. Only one of the seven members whose terms expired at the end of June was said to be in line with Mayor Harrison. The new board, with one-third of its members newly appointed by Harrison, would therefore be able to endorse the mayor's every candidate and whim.[87] It was necessary for the Parker and Lane forces to break the deadlock before the end of June and the expiration of the present board.

One member, A. S. Trude, was believed to hold the balance. Trude was not opposed to Lane and he had supported Parker in the past, but he was a Democrat and wanted to accommodate Mayor Harrison. Parker appealed to his friend, Mrs. Emmons Blaine, the McCormick Reaper heiress, for help. In 1896, she had been asked to use her good offices with the publisher of the *Chicago Tribune* to call off one reporter who was particularly hostile to the Normal School. Now she was asked to "drop" Mayor Harrison a note. She was also asked to intercede with A. S. Trude. Parker said he was sorry to trouble her, but he noted how much influence she had with Trude in the past.[88]

It is not certain what influence Mrs. Blaine was able to bring to bear on Harrison or Trude. Trude actually avoided a decision in his conflict of interests by receiving an "urgent call to Indianapolis to attend to legal business." He was not on hand for the crucial vote in mid-June. The deadlock was confirmed. The board supporters of Parker and Lane could not muster a simple majority. There would be only one more meeting in June.[89]

Meanwhile, as a result of this impasse, no teachers or administrators in the city were elected to their jobs for the following year. It was said that many of them anxiously delayed their vacations, but Parker and his wife went ahead with their plans to lecture at the Summer School in Honolulu.[90] The Colonel actually left Chicago without much hope of re-election.[91] The Parkers were en route to Hawaii when a break occurred in the stalemate between the supporters of Mayor Harrison and Colonel Parker.

A few days before the last meeting of the board in June, Otto Gresham, a Democratic member of the board, suddenly submitted his resignation. This stirred up so much conjecture that he was besieged by reporters. He said that Mayor Harrison had a superb opportunity to improve the education of the city schools but that such reforms could only be brought about by men of the highest character and active interest in the proceedings of education. Gresham then admitted he had been asked how he would vote, and he resigned rather than to submit to pressure.[92]

Such a revelation was highly embarrassing to Mayor Harrison who had been building a public image as the people's guardian against the pressures of powerful vested interests. He immediately denied any effort to coerce votes, especially speaking to Gresham about how he would vote or authorizing anyone else to do so. He admitted that he favored the election of Dr. Andrews but insisted that he had not brought out this candidate until he had been "boomed" by Dr. Harper. He also insisted he had never opposed Colonel Parker officially, that he had only said unofficially that he would vote to retire Parker, were he to be in a position to do so.[93]

Otto Gresham later confirmed that the mayor himself had not broached the subject. It was Charles Thornton, the city corporation counsel, who had told him the mayor wanted Lane and Parker defeated.[94] Now that the mayor had been forced to withdraw any official disapproval of Parker and the dismissal of Parker would actually smack of bossism, the various forces which opposed Parker had to reconsider.

On June 30, 1898, Parker's name was placed in nomination at the very last meeting of the board. Dr. Harper seconded the nomination because he said he had not been able to find a better man. On the first ballot eighteen votes were cast and Parker picked up thirteen of them. There was not a vote cast against him, only five blank ballots.[95]

In the end, it appeared that Thornton was the major factor in contributing to his old opponent's victory. He had gone too far and forced men of conscience to speak out. One board member was reported to say, "I am sorry for poor Charlie," and a member of the Harrison faction declared that, "if Thornton had not put his oar in," Parker probably would have lost.[96]

Superintendent Lane, however, was not so fortunate. He failed by one vote to secure re-election and his candidacy was thrown over into the first session of the new board.[97]

When the Chicago Council approved of Mayor Harrison's seven new appointees to the board, it unanimously resolved that the Board of Education ought to confine its selection of a Superintendent of Schools to a resident of the state of Illinois. This was a direct mandate by the Chicago Council to re-elect Lane or some educator from the state and to drop the candidacy of Dr. Andrews from Brown University in Rhode Island. Many Democrats were beginning to fear that the obvious tampering with the schools would turn parents, whether Democrats or Republicans, against them in the next election. Furthermore, Lane was a popular local man who had given satisfaction for many years. Dr. Andrews knew nothing about the problems of Chicago and his educational experience was considered to be in "the university line, not the common-school . . . ."[98]

In spite of this obvious mandate by the Chicago Council, Dr. E. Benjamin Andrews was elected Superintendent of Schools at the first meeting of the newly constituted Board of Education in July. The board did create a new office, and nominated Albert G. Lane to fill it. This office—assistant superintendent of schools—would keep Lane at his old salary and most of his old duties. Lane reluctantaly accepted.[99]

Although Parker had apparently won a decisive victory and Lane had, at least, not been routed from the field, the political climate of the Harrison administration was harsh and unfriendly to the new education. Even before his enemies could plot their next attack, Parker was preparing a move which would take him and the new education out of their reach.

NOTES

[1] "Is Aimed at Parker, County Board's Attack on the Normal School," *Chicago Evening Journal* (Chicago, Ill.), January 29, 1894; "Fancy Salaries Cut, County Board Making Up for Extra Expenses," *Chicago Tribune* (Chicago, Ill.), January 30, 1894.

[2] Henry Adams, *The Education of Henry Adams* (New York: Random House, Modern Library, 1931), p. 346; Ray Ginger, *Altgeld's America, The Lincoln Ideal Versus Changing Realities* (New York: Funk and Wagnalls, 1958), p. 92; *Biennial Report of the County Superintendent of Schools from July 1, 1888 to June 30, 1890* (Chicago: J.M.W. Jones Stationery and Printing Co., 1890), p. 15.

[3] "Once More in Peril," *Chicago Inter-Ocean* (Chicago, Ill.), January 29, 1894; "Oppose the Reduction, Normal School Officials Perturbed Over a Cut in Expenses," *Chicago Times* (Chicago, Ill.), January 28, 1894.

[4] "Parker's Big Salary, Commissioner Kunstman Defends the Reduction Made," *Chicago Evening Post* (Chicago, Ill.), January 29, 1894; "Fancy Salaries Cut."

[5] "Is Aimed at Parker."

[6] "Cause of Education Crippled," *Chicago Herald* (Chicago, Ill.), January 28, 1894; "Is Aimed at Parker"; "Parker's Big Salary."

[7] "Cause of Education Crippled"; "Parker's Big Salary."

[8] *Ibid.;* "Calls Him a Windbag, Mr. Green Attacks Mr. Thornton," *Chicago Herald,* January 31, 1894.

[9] *Ibid.*

[10] *Ibid.*

[11] *Ibid.;* "School Board Objects, Strong Protest Against Reducing the Normal School Appropriation," *Chicago Evening Journal,* January 30, 1894; "Parker's Big Salary."

[12] *Official Proceedings of the Board of Commissioners for the Year 1893–1894, Being from December 4, 1893 to December 3, 1894 inclusive* (Chicago: J.M.W. Jones Stationery and Printing Co., 1895), pp. 214–215.

[13] "To Oust Col. Parker," *Chicago Evening Post,* August 29, 1894.

[14] *Official Proceedings of the Board of Commissioners . . . 1893–1894, op. cit.,* p. 251.

[15] *Ibid.*

[16] "Parker and His Job," *Chicago Evening Post,* January 30, 1894.

[17] "To Oust Col. Parker"; "Cook County Teachers Institute," advertise-

ment, Parker Scrapbooks, 1893, Archives, Harper Library, University of Chicago; "Sand-Bagging the C.C.N.S.," *School Journal,* 48 (February 10, 1894), 153; *Biennial Report of the County Superintendent of Schools from July 1, 1892 to June 30, 1894* (Chicago: J.M.W. Jones Stationery and Printing Co., 1894), p. 35; "Hot Shot for Parker, C. S. Thornton Scores the Normal School and its Principal," *Chicago Evening Post,* August 12, 1894.

[18] "Once More In Peril."

[19] "Cause of Education Crippled."

[20] *Biennial Report . . . 1892–1894,* p. 36; "Parker Strikes Back," *Chicago Evening Post,* September 7, 1894.

[21] "Colonel Parker's Pudding is Dainty and Attractive, but Extremely Unsubstantial and Unnourishing, Milk for Babes, Meat for Strong Men . . . ," newspaper clipping, Parker Scrapbooks, 1894; "Colonel Parker and His Fad Factory," *Chicago Tribune,* January 30, 1894; "Col. Parker's Fad Factory," *Chicago Evening Post,* January 30, 1894; "Charles S. Thornton, Lawyer and School Board Member," *Chicago Evening Post,* February 10, 1894.

[22] "Parker Strikes Back."

[23] *Ibid.; Official Proceedings of the Board of Commissioners . . . 1893–1894,* p. 297; *Biennial Report . . . 1892–1894,* p. 36.

[24] "To Oust Col. Parker."

[25] Francis W. Parker, "The Need of the Hour," newspaper clipping, Parker Scrapbooks, 1893; Waldo R. Browne, *Altgeld of Illinois* (New York: B. W. Heubsch, 1924), pp. 117–126, 154–156.

[26] *Official Proceedings of the Board of Commissioners . . . 1893–1894,* p. 85; "Hot Shot for Parker."

[27] *Ibid.*

[28] *School Report: Public Schools of the City of Chicago. Forty-second Annual Report of the Board of Education for the Year Ending June 26, 1896* (Chicago: J.M.W. Jones Stationery and Printing Co., 1896), n.p.

[29] "Hot Shot for Parker."

[30] "To Oust Col. Parker."

[31] "Parker Strikes Back"; *Biennial Report . . . 1892–1894,* p. 42.

[32] "To Oust Col. Parker"; *Biennial Report of the County Superintendent of Schools from July 1, 1894 to June 30, 1896* (Chicago: J.M.W. Jones Stationery and Printing Co., 1896), p. 83.

[33] *Ibid.,* p. 85; "Parker and His Job." (Out of the more than four thousand teachers in the Chicago schools in 1895, only two hundred were said to have received instruction at the Cook County Normal School. "Editorial: The Normal School," *Chicago Tribune,* March 9, 1896.)

[34] *School Report . . . 1896,* pp. 69–71.

[35] "April 26, 1893," *Proceedings of the Board of Education of The City of Chicago, July 6th, 1892, to July 5th, 1893* (Chicago: Press of John F. Higgins, n.d.), p. 423.

[36] *School Report . . . 1896,* p. 71; *Alumni of the Chicago Normal School* (published by the officers of the Alumni Association, 1908–1909), Historical Files, Chicago Teachers College South.

[37] "Hot Shot for Parker."

[38] The resolution of December 9, 1895, was not carried and read into the proceedings until December 16, 1895. *Official Proceedings of the Board of Commissioners for the Year 1895–1896, Being from December 2, 1895 to December 5, 1896* (Chicago: Cameron, Amberg and Co., 1896), p. 29;

"Healy Sends a Letter, Asks Conference with the Board of Education," *Chicago Tribune,* December 12, 1895.

[39] *Proceedings of the Board of Education of the City of Chicago, July 17, 1895 to July 1, 1896* (Chicago: Press of John F. Higgins, n.d.), p. 205; "Terms Are Illegal," *Chicago Herald,* December 24, 1895.

[40] "Beck Is in the Way, Threat as to Normal School," *Chicago Herald,* December 20, 1895.

[41] *Proceedings of the Board of Education . . . 1895–1896,* p. 220.

[42] "Healy Sends a Letter, Asks Conference with the Board of Education"; "Halle Afraid of Col. Parker," newspaper clipping, Parker Scrapbooks, 1895.

[43] *Ibid.;* "Test Vote Taken," newspaper clipping, Parker Scrapbooks, 1895.

[44] "The County Normal School," newspaper clipping, Parker Scrapbooks, 1895.

[45] "No Pay for Teachers, Normal School Faculty Has Had No Money Since Christmas," *Chicago Evening Post,* January 28, 1896.

[46] "Rally for a School," *Chicago Evening Post,* January 29, 1896.

[47] Carleton Washburne [Superintendent of Schools, Winnetka, Illinois], letter to Mr. Bartky [President of the Chicago Teachers College], September 18, 1940, in which was included the letter from his mother, Marion Foster Washburne, Historical Files, Chicago Teachers College South.

[48] *Ibid.*

[49] Albert E. Winship, "Skirmishing in the West," *Journal of Education,* **43** (February 27, 1896), 144.

[50] Marion Foster Washburne, "The Educational Crisis in Chicago," *The* Arena, **15** (March 1896), 611, 614.

[51] Albert E. Winship, *op. cit.,* p. 144.

[52] "Shirked Their Duty, School Board Members Postpone Accepting the Normal, Display of Sordid Suspicion, University Professors Disgusted with the Proceedings—Forcible Words from Two of Them," newspaper clipping, Parker Scrapbooks, 1895–1896; "Rally for a School."

[53] *Ibid.;* "For Those Who Teach, Springfield, Illinois, December 26, 42nd Annual Meeting of State Teachers Association," *Chicago Tribune,* December 27, 1895.

[54] "Rally for a School."

[55] *Ibid.*

[56] "Parker and His Job."

[57] Carleton Washburne, *op. cit.;* "May Take Normal School," newspaper clipping, Parker Scrapbooks, 1896.

[58] *Proceedings of the Board of Education . . . 1895–1896,* p. 262.

[59] *Biennial Report . .. 1894–1896,* pp. 52, 85, 94.

[60] "Col. Parker Keeps Cool, Makes No Particular Fuss over the Normal School Deal," *Chicago Tribune,* January 31, 1896; "Affairs Coming to a Crisis, Normal School Matters in a Decidedly Bad Way," *Chicago Tribune,* December 24, 1895; *Proceedings of the Board of Education . . . 1895–1896,* pp. 346, 358; *Official Proceedings of the Board of Commissioners . . . 1895–1896,* p. 342.

[61] *Proceedings of the Board of Education . . . 1895–1896,* p. 387.

[62] "Mr. Beck Takes an Inning," newspaper clipping, Parker Scrapbooks, 1896. Mention of the Beck case was not found in *Illinois Reports,* Vols. 159–

205, *American Digest,* 1897–1906, *Illinois Appellate Court Reports,* 1896–1901.

[63] *Proceedings of the Board of Education . . . 1895–1896,* p. 340; "Editorial, The Normal School," *Chicago Tribune,* March 9, 1896.

[64] *Proceedings of the Board of Education . . . 1895–1896,* p. 409.

[65] F. W. Parker, letter to Mrs. Blaine, June 6, 1896, Papers of Anita McCormick Blaine, McCormick Collection, Wisconsin State Historical Society, Madison, Wis.; F. W. Parker, letter to Mrs. Blaine, June 12, 1896, Papers of Anita McCormick Blaine.

[66] *Proceedings of the Board of Education . . . 1895–1896,* pp. 108, 480–481, 488–490.

[67] Margaret Leech, *In the Days of McKinley* (New York: Harper and Brothers, 1959), pp. 84–85.

[68] Ray Ginger, *op. cit.,* p. 180.

[69] "As Chicago Sees Herself," *Journal of Education,* **51** (May 17, 1900), 312.

[70] "Col. F. W. Parker Is to Go," *Chicago Daily News* (Chicago, Ill.), October 14, 1897.

[71] "Col. Parker and the Normal School," *Chicago Evening Post,* June 23, 1898; "Will Thornton Now Subside?" *Chicago Evening Post,* July 1, 1898.

[72] "Mayor Not for Col. Parker," *Chicago Daily News,* June 23, 1898; "Mayor Does Not Like Col. Parker," newspaper clipping, Parker Scrapbooks, 1898.

[73] "The Chicago Situation," *Journal of Education,* **47** (June 9, 1898), 360.

[74] "Gresham Quits the Board," newspaper clipping, dated June 30, 1898, Parker Scrapbooks, 1898; William Adams Slade, "Elisha Benjamin Andrews," in Allen Johnson (Ed.), *Dictionary of American Biography,* Vol. I (New York: Charles Scribner's Sons, 1943), pp. 286–289.

[75] *Ibid.;* "More Gall for Thornton," *Chicago Inter-Ocean,* July 12, 1898; "What Will Andrews Do?," newspaper clipping, Parker Scrapbooks, 1898.

[76] William Adams Slade, *op. cit.,* p. 287; "Last Hope for Lane," *Chicago Evening Post,* June 29, 1898; "Andrews in Town Today," *Chicago Tribune,* June 29, 1898; F. W. Parker, letter to Mrs. Blaine, June 4, 1898, Papers of Anita McCormick Blaine.

[77] Margaret Leech, *op. cit.,* pp. 226–227; "Mayor May Find Way to Win," newspaper clipping, dated June 16, 1898, Parker Scrapbooks, 1898.

[78] "The Board of Education Completes the Chain—Election of Teachers Put Off until June 29—Gresham Chosen Again—Other Action," newspaper clipping, dated June 16, 1898, Parker Scrapbooks, 1898.

[79] "Normal Test Is Good," *Chicago Times-Herald* (Chicago, Ill.), June 22, 1898; "Appeal to Mayor," *Chicago Times-Herald,* June 26, 1898; "To Look into Parker's Acts," *Chicago Daily News,* June 10, 1898.

[80] "Protest Against Harper and Parker, Common School Teachers Object to Their Favoring University Graduates," newspaper clipping, dated June 21, 1898, Parker Scrapbooks, 1898.

[81] *Ibid.*

[82] "Come to Parker's Aid," newspaper clipping, dated June 22, 1898, Parker Scrapbooks, 1898; Nicholas Murray Butler, letter to Hon. E. G. Halle, Acting President, February 3, 1898, Papers of Anita McCormick Blaine.

[83] "Protest Against Harper and Parker."

[84] "Cheers for Parker, Scene at a Sunday Service," newspaper clipping, dated July 27, 1898, Parker Scrapbooks, 1898; "Fight for Colonel Parker," *Chicago Times-Herald,* June 23, 1898; "Andrews in Town Today"; "Lane and Parker Up," *Chicago Times-Herald,* June 29, 1898; "Rally About Parker," *Chicago Record,* June 29, 1898; *Proceedings of the Board of Education of the City of Chicago, July 14, 1897–July 1, 1898* (Chicago: Press of John H. Higgins, n.d.), p. 534.

[85] "Cheers for Parker."

[86] "Appeal to Mayor," *Chicago Times-Herald,* June 26, 1898.

[87] "Vote Parker In," *Chicago Chronicle* (Chicago, Ill.), July 1, 1898; "More Gall for Thornton"; "A Canvass of The Board," *Chicago Times-Herald,* June 28, 1898; "Last Hope for Lane."

[88] *Ibid.;* F. W. Parker, letters to Mrs. Blaine, June 12, 1896, June 4, 1898, and June 5, 1898, Papers of Anita McCormick Blaine.

[89] "Last Hope for Lane."

[90] "Big Petition for Mrs. Hull," *Chicago Times-Herald,* June 28, 1898; F. W. Parker, letter to Mrs. Blaine, June 4, 1898.

[91] F. W. Parker letter to Mrs. Blaine, June 29, 1898, Papers of Anita McCormick Blaine.

[92] "Gresham Quits the Board"; "Vote Parker In"; "Need of a Reorganization," newspaper clipping, Parker Scrapbooks, 1898.

[93] *Ibid.* Although Mayor Harrison had been picked and supported by the former governor of Illinois, the liberal John Peter Altgeld, Harrison appointed people to office who were Altgeld's worst enemies. Ray Ginger, *op. cit.,* p. 180. Some years later, Lincoln Steffens described Harrison as a man "without ideals" who only did "what is demanded of him." Lincoln Steffens, *The Shame of the Cities* (New York: Sagamore Press, 1957), p. 192.

[94] "Vote Parker In," *op. cit.*

[95] *Proceedings of the Board of Education . . . 1897–1898,* p. 587; "No Candidate Against Parker," *Chicago Times-Herald,* July 1, 1898.

[96] "Need of a Reorganization"; "If Thornton had not put in his oar," newspaper clipping, Parker Scrapbooks, 1898.

[97] *Proceedings of the Board of Education . . . 1897–1898,* p. 587.

[98] "More Gall for Thornton."

[99] "Chicago's Superintendent," *Journal of Education,* **48** (July 21, 1898), 80; "Vote Parker In."

XIII

The Tactical Move from Public to Private Education

The common school was the one central means by which Parker believed the problems of human liberty could be solved. He had even gone so far as to suggest that no one could be educated for life in the Republic outside public schools. It was to such schools that he had pledged himself "now and forever" in 1882.[1] Sixteen years later, when war with Spain had broken out and the Democratic forces of Chicago were mobilizing against him, Parker was beginning to lose his resolve. He had fought too many battles with public boards of education. He now dreamed of an ideal school which could be realized through private patronage.

His dreams involved more than one private venture. He would have a "Slum" school to show what could be done for the lower classes. Modeled somewhat after Hull House, it would attempt to bridge home and school. It would have an assembly hall for parents as well as children. There would be a kindergarten to take the "little ones" off the streets and offer them "a little heaven." There would be a playground with green grass and flowers, a gymnasium, modern bathrooms, and a library with "sweet good literature." In addition to the "three R's" the curriculum would include manual training, art work, and housekeeping. He also dreamed of a private school on the fashionable North Shore where wealthy patrons could be enlisted. It was at this school that he would establish his "normal college." He even envisioned a "Woman's Class" to prepare nonteaching candidates for motherhood.[2]

These ideas were inspired by Mrs. Emmons Blaine. It would have been out of character for the Colonel to think of leaving the public schools, except from sheer desperation. As the century was drawing to a close, he was strongly convinced that his days as principal of the Normal School were going to be brought to an untimely end.[3] It was Anita McCormick Blaine who made Parker's "wishful thinking" financially realistic. Parker's dreams were hers, as well, according to Mrs. Blaine, and she needed only the consent of Parker to finally bring some of them into actuality.[4]

The McCormick Reaper would help the Colonel harvest a lifetime of work for the revolution of education. Daughter of Cyrus McCormick, Anita McCormick Blaine enjoyed the wealth arising from the invention of the reaping machine, a machine which had revolutionized agriculture. As daughter-in-law of Secretary of State James G. Blaine, she had the advantages of political as well as economic and social influence. In her personal life, however, Mrs. Blaine was less fortunate. She was left a widow in her middle twenties, after only a few years of marriage. Her young husband, Emmons Blaine, died suddenly of acute appendicitis in June of 1892, just after he almost succeeded in booming his father for the presidential nomination at the Republican National Convention. He was generally mourned. Even the Democratic National Convention, meeting later that summer in Chicago to nominate Grover Cleveland, extended sympathy to the Blaine family.[5]

Left with an infant son to raise and educate, and having been repelled since girlhood by traditional education, Anita McCormick Blaine came, quite naturally, under the influence of the work being done by Parker at the Cook County Normal School. In 1894, she went so far as to invite the Colonel to call on her some "Tuesday or Wednesday evening." Two years later she apparently offered to set Parker up in his own school when he was under the severe attack that came with the transfer of the Normal School from county to city control. At that time he would not consent to such an arrangement. According to contemporary opinion, Mrs. Blaine—in addition to wanting to provide the best education for her own son—had a deep concern for all children. Interest in Parker was probably furthered through her club activities which must have brought her into frequent association with Mrs. Parker.[6]

In 1897, Parker delivered a series of lectures at the Blaine mansion, and Mrs. Blaine even attended some of his classes at the Normal School. By June of 1898 their relationship had grown to the actual point of collaboration. (Mrs. Blaine already had used her social and political influence to help keep the Colonel in power.) In 1898 she was extending her economic influence. Parker was now "delighted," he said, to be receiving her checks. At that time she was helping set up as many as five "vacation schools" to give slum children a "glimpse of country life" for the summer. Parker was probably not hesitant to work openly with Mrs.

Blaine in this project, since the city had not adequately provided for summer schools in the past, even though police records showed a juvenile crime increase of 60 per cent during the summer vacation months.[7]

Parker's more ambitious plans, involving his permanent separation from the public schools, were being made that same summer of 1898 but kept in strict confidence. Parker must have been so hesitant about abandoning the public schools that he even hid the plans from his devoted teachers. Full collaboration with Mrs. Blaine was contingent on his dismissal from the Normal School. He counted on his teachers, however, to follow him into exile as soon as the Chicago Board of Education voted him out of the principalship.[8]

Even though Parker was negotiating for a business manager and actually preparing circulars for a late October opening, hardly a word of his actual plans leaked out to the press.[9] He was probably afraid that an exclusive school, privately supported, would appear incongruous with his purposes of democratic education. Actually, he was planning to improve the preparation of teachers for the city schools as well as to provide "models" which would demonstrate what could be done by the public if enough money were provided. In this respect he was not really abandoning his principles. He had long upheld the legitimacy of private schools, both sectarian and secular, if they contributed directly to the good of the common school.[10]

Rather than fight for the Chicago Normal School to the very last, however, Parker let fate decide his course between public and private education. He went ahead with his commitment to lecture at the summer school in Honolulu for the Hawaiian Department of Public Instruction. That would entail his leaving Chicago right after the June graduation of the Class of '98 and before the decisive meeting of the Chicago Board of Education.[11]

To some extent the fight was going out of Parker. It was his wife, he later said, who had been the real fighter.[12] Now she was failing. She had submitted to surgery for a malignancy early in May of 1898. During that first week in May, while Americans were waiting tensely for news of Admiral Dewey at Manila Bay, Parker was with his convalescing wife at a sanatorium in Battle Creek, Michigan. At this crucial time the Colonel was not able to marshall forces in defense of his position at the Normal School. He did keep in touch with his teachers and told them to "stand by" and keep "steady." He also informed them that Mrs. Parker was about the same—not sleeping or eating well. He said he would stay with her until recovery was assured.[13]

It seemed impossible for his wife to survive, but Parker rejoiced at how, miraculously, she began to grow stronger after the operation.[14] By

June Mrs. Parker's doctors believed she would be able to make the trip to Hawaii. Accompanied by a nurse and a Miss Allen, one of the kindergarten teachers at the Normal School, the Parker party left for their port of departure, Vancouver, British Columbia. They made railroad connections in Minneapolis. On their way to Minnesota they may have stopped off in Appleton, Wisconsin. Whether he was there in person or not, Parker was granted a doctor of laws honorary degree by Lawrence University.[15] The commencement speaker took the occasion to rail out against the ignorant and uncultured Spaniard who substituted the bullfight for the college and the "drill-master."[16] If Parker was there, he must have squirmed at the idea of an educational "drill-master," if not at the hateful remarks about the enemy.

After the arrival in Minneapolis on June 23, 1898, Mrs. Parker saw a medical specialist recommended by Mrs. Blaine. Parker wrote that night to Mrs. Blaine and reported that the "dreadful truth" he had suspected for so long was confirmed. His wife had cancer. He told Mrs. Blaine that he could still do his best to "prolong her precious life." He then scribbled in a postscript that he had been made a doctor by Lawrence University. He asked her "not to mention it." [17]

The uncertain future of his wife and career must have troubled Parker's thoughts as the train rattled over the Rocky Mountains, but he took time to study the landscape that rolled by. Looking through his field glasses, he continually consulted the aneroid barometer to determine the altitude. Mrs. Parker was more interested in the esthetics of the view.[18]

Although he was moving farther and farther away from the struggles in Chicago, Parker kept up a rearguard action. He advised Zonia Baber to fight to the last and to keep "cool" and "tell everybody." Apparently, he had some small hope that he would keep his position and carry on in the public school tradition. He assured Miss Baber, in a later letter, that he appreciated the "splendid battle" she and the other teachers had fought. With these words he embarked on June 30, 1898, and was underway for the Republic of Hawaii just as the Chicago Board of Education was to decide his fate.[19]

At sea, Parker was once under an opened porthole when water poured through and drenched him to the skin. Rough weather gave Miss Allen, the kindergarten teacher, some uneasiness and sickness, but the invalid Mrs. Parker only found the voyage "delightful." She often read Kipling to the Colonel on calmer seas, when they could lounge topside in their deck chairs. Once the Parkers quarreled with two English contemporaries of Kipling who shared the deck with the Parkers but not the idea of educating the masses.[20]

The first landfall was probably the island of Molokai, where they might have caught a glimpse of Makanalua Peninsula, site of the famous leper colony. On their approach to Oahu, they no doubt passed the two extinct volcanoes, Koko Head and Diamond Head, before sighting the deep green hills of Honolulu Harbor.[21]

While their steamer was being secured to the heavy piles along the docks, July 8, 1898, the Parkers saw a forest of masts and stacks bobbing over American troop transports, monitors, and other warships. One transport, crowded with American soldiers, steamed past on its way to the open sea. The Parkers hung over the rail and shouted, "Chicago!" Dozens of hats went up on the troop ship. Mrs. Parker actually cried. The war, she said, had come "home" to her for the first time.[22]

By the time the Parkers arrived in the Republic of Hawaii, the United States House of Representatives had approved the annexation of the Islands, but the decision of the Senate was not then known. The Republic was therefore in violation of all precedents of international law by receiving and supplying these American warships and transports which were bound for action in the Philippines.[23]

The Colonel would soon be involved in the politics of annexation as well as the techniques of the new education, but Mrs. Parker allowed herself to be simply captivated by the grandeur of the Islands. Except for the heat, she found Hawaii so "wonderful" that she never wanted to leave. She only missed her grandchildren. A local judge had put his house and two Chinese servants at the disposal of the Parkers for the duration of their stay. An arcade of royal palms led to their little house where they were happy as "larks." Even though Parker protested that he looked like a canvasback duck in his tropical suit, Mrs. Parker wrote to her daughters that he really thought he was so grand "no one in the place can touch him." She also revealed his misadventures on an expedition up the extinct crater behind Honolulu. He was thrown over a mule's head at least twice, and he even got lost. Mrs. Parker insisted he had a black-and-blue mark on his hip that measured ten by twelve inches. She said it was a "picture to see him sit down."[24]

Parker was down to business, however, when the summer school opened on July 11, 1898. Sanford B. Dole, the first (and only) President of the Republic of Hawaii, opened the initial session with the story of how New England missionaries brought the common school to Hawaii. Grateful for the common school, President Dole was, nevertheless, quite critical of the traditional curriculum that came with the missionaries. Such a curriculum, he said, was not adapted to local needs. Parker then followed President Dole to the platform and said he came with no principles to lay down. First he wanted to see what the local needs were. It was also important, he suggested, that every teacher should first find the needs of his students.[25]

It was soon apparent enough to Parker that the Hawaiians needed a "thorough-going education," but not one imported from New England. Such education had covered the Hawaiians with an alien and inappropriate culture, as poorly fitting as the "Mother Hubbards" which New England modesty had foisted to esthetic disadvantage on the Hawaiian women. Parker believed the people needed an education for citizenship which would be especially tailored to their environment and natural qualities. That education, he began insisting, should center around hand and mechanical arts. In this endeavor, he helped organize a society to promote industrial and agricultural education. Named for Samuel C. Armstrong, a native son of Hawaii, it took inspiration from Armstrong's monumental work for the freedmen after the Civil War—the Hampton Normal and Agricultural Institute.[26]

Although Parker went along with the common impression that the Hawaiians were indolent, he blamed this on a broken spirit rather than race. That spirit had been broken by an alien culture, but he believed it would revive under proper educational guidance.[27]

He had hardly begun his work in Honolulu when the next scheduled ship from the United States put into port. Hawaii was dependent on such ships for news of the outside world since neither radio nor telegraphic cable connected it to the Mainland. This steamer was decked with American flags to proclaim from a distance that annexation to the United States was now official. The ship also brought news that the Spanish fleet of Cervera had been destroyed more than a week earlier at Santiago de Cuba. Week-old newspapers and letters from Chicago also brought word to Parker that the Chicago Board of Education had voted to retain him.[28] All at once his life had the promise of continuity in the work for the common schools, but the life of Hawaii would be forever changed.

The annexation of the Hawaiian Islands had been delayed for years because it was generally believed that the revolutionaries who overthrew the monarchy and appealed for annexation represented the plantation owners and large trading interests and lacked real popular support. Parker was now asked to prepare a series of observations on this matter for use by the United States Commissioners. He reported that a majority of the population, white as well as Hawaiian, was against annexation. Annexation, he found, had been engineered by a small band of men, though they were among the most prominent and intelligent in the Islands. He contended that these men had acted out of the need for a perfectly stable government. Parker considered President Dole no politician in the ordinary sense of the word. Dole was a man who acted intelligently for the good of the people. In general, Parker believed the Hawaiians were against annexation because they had been misled by stories and slanders.[29]

The Parkers had places on the first balcony of the government building for the official ceremony of annexation. The Hawaiian national anthem was played while the Hawaiian flag came down, and Mrs. Parker remembered the tears as the Stars and Stripes went up.[30]

Parker's educational work in the Islands was said to have been "peculiarly opportune" because of the great change in the social and political climate of the times. His public addresses, given several nights a week, were as well attended as were his daily lectures at "Progress Hall," but Parker was not really bringing any new educational ideas to Hawaii. His popularity, as well as his theories, had preceded him, and some of his practices had been adopted in Hawaii as early as 1881. In some respects, education was actually more advanced on the Islands than on the Mainland. It was not only free but compulsory. Moreover, needs of the schools were said to be considered before any other public improvements.[31]

Parker may have learned more than he taught. He went to the Islands opposing annexation, but he came away believing that imperialism would benefit the Hawaiians. He also came away with evidence for his theory that people must be prepared for liberty. They must be educated into it.[32]

Parker therefore compromised democracy at home with imperialism abroad. Even before he had left for the Islands, he had convinced himself that the school system could also survive half free and half private. His views were probably conditioned by the belief that his theory of education was a liberating force for the mind of the child.

Parker would soon have the pleasure of learning that his former student and colleague, Alex E. Frye, was charged with the formation of a school system for the "reconstruction" of Cuba.[33] When Parker returned to take up his duties again at the Chicago Normal School that September, he may have been optimistic that the children of other parts of the world would soon be educated into democracy.[34]

Parker returned to find the Chicago Board of Education was "about as bad as it can be," but he soon came to appreciate the work of the new Superintendent. E. Benjamin Andrews had assumed the duties of his office in August, at the time Spain was suing for peace. One of his first public announcements was that Spanish ought to be taught in the common schools. He believed, as did Parker, that the annexation of Spanish possessions would be good because it would deliver people from oppression and give them an opportunity to prosper.[35]

Andrews made a token cut in some of the salaries at the Normal School, but only to appease the hostile board, which was now largely under the influence of Mayor Harrison. Mayor Harrison, however, had seriously miscalculated if he thought the new Superintendent would submit to political dictation. The former Superintendent, though a Republican, had never given the board so much trouble. It was soon acknowledged by educators throughout the country that never before in the history of America had any superintendent "called down" a city board of education so suddenly and completely as did Dr. Andrews in the first few months of service.[36]

In September, Andrews had demanded a seat, though no vote, on the Board of Education. He was turned down but the reasonableness of his demand received wide circulation. In December he argued that the Superintendent, rather than the board, should be responsible for appointing and re-appointing principals and teachers. He was again turned down but authorized to draw up plans for the guidance of the board on this proposal.[37] If Andrews could win the fight, Parker's position, as well as that of all the public employees of the Chicago Board of Education, would rest on the professional judgment of the superintendent rather than the whim or scheme of members of the board.

Political influence, favoritism, violation of salary schedules, were no secrets in the public schools, or in the administration of other public offices. At this time, reformers of the "Progressive" persuasion were attempting to clean up politics by making all public positions subject to ability rather than patronage. The Harrison administration, with the legal counsel of Charles Thornton, had fought the new Civil Service laws all the way to the Supreme Court, and had lost.[38] It was not likely that this administration would want to give up its last unrestricted hold on the public payroll and let the Superintendent of schools make all appointments. Strangely enough, however, the educational commission appointed by Mayor Harrison recommended that the Superintendent should appoint supervisors and teachers, fix all salaries, and dismiss or promote personnel connected with the schools. Andrews, more of a fighter than Superintendent Lane, carried on this fight until victory. Late in 1900, the Chicago Board of Education would finally abdicate its power of appointment.[39]

Parker appreciated these fighting qualities in Andrews. He had to admit that "Dr. Andrews is a *great* man—just the man to lead us to victory for the children." He also learned, about this time, that Andrews had lost one eye in the same trenches around Petersburg where Parker had been wounded in the throat. Now they were both engaged in an even more serious cause. "We must win or free government *will* fail," Parker said. He confided in Mrs. Blaine that he would give up if Andrews did not "stand so firmly and bravely for the right."[40]

While Andrews kept up the fight, the fight was going out of Parker. He was again dreaming of a way out of the continual frustrations of public control. In December of 1898 he even sent Mrs. Blaine a sketch of a proposed school and confided in her that he had lately allowed himself to dream of what great things they could do together. He had visions of a school which would develop the highest type of community life and demonstrate the awful waste of energy in the blind memorization and drill of traditional education. He was now ready to follow through with the tentative plans made during the previous spring.[41]

Mrs. Blaine later revealed that it was the Colonel's wife who had finally broken down his objections to private education. The editor of Boston's *Journal of Education* actually believed that Mrs. Blaine's financial backing of the Colonel's ideal school was to memorialize Mrs. Parker. It is true that the two women were friends, and Mrs. Parker may have had some influence with Mrs. Blaine. It was Mrs. Parker's influence with the Colonel, however, which was apparently the most vital.[42]

By November of 1898, Mrs. Parker had taken to her bed. She was in such pain that she began to think life "wasn't worth the candle." She wrote to Mrs. Blaine that she could now do nothing but think of *"his plan."*[43]

Mrs. Parker had begun to fade rapidly after she returned from Hawaii. The secret that she could never recover was no longer kept from her, but she remained cheerful and planned for herself and others as though she would one day rise and take up her work again.[44]

The Parkers moved from their large frame house on Honore Street to 6640 Parnell Avenue, possibly because this new residence was only a few blocks from the Normal School and the Colonel could more easily attend to both his wife and professional duties.[45] The health of Mrs. Parker had also become a matter of concern for educators generally. The editor of the *Journal of Education* worried about the impact her death would have on the Colonel. "There has been no instance in our American history," wrote the editor, "in which the wife of an educator has been so widely recognized as an essential factor in his progress . . . ."[46]

Mrs. Parker, known as "cool-headed and clear in her thinking," helped smooth out the Colonel's own rough and ready actions. She helped interpret his ideas and work as well as organize community forces in his behalf. Her death would rob him of her clarity of mind, her forceful personality that sustained him in times of trial. It would also leave his life empty. Their work-desks stood side by side. The Colonel could talk to his wife as to no one else. They took their vacations together and Mrs. Parker often edured the outdoor camping which the old soldier so loved.[47]

They both had a sense of humor and enjoyed playing jokes on each other. Parker would often wake his wife in the morning with impassioned oratory on the most trivial of subjects, or read with a serious voice some exaggeration he made out of an account in the morning newspaper. Mrs. Parker, in turn, loved to read the Finley Peter Dunne articles that appeared as "Mr. Dooley" in the *Chicago Evening Post.* She was known for her renditions of "Mr. Dooley" in a mock Irish brogue.[48]

For Mrs. Parker, death was not the end. Like her husband, she was not strictly sectarian in her religious beliefs, but she had a strong faith in God and immortality. Her idea of death was a passage into "the light beyond." At the end of life she had her daughters and husband with her. On April 1, 1899, the day before Easter Sunday, she repeated the words, "I am the Resurrection and the Life," but she could not go on. Looking at the Colonel who had remained at her side during the final crisis, she said, "Finish it." She turned her face to the wall and went to sleep for the last time.[49]

There was much for Parker to finish. He was deeply involved in both legal and educational arrangements with Mrs. Blaine. Shortly after his wife's death, he suggested that the new school be named The Emmons Blaine School for Teachers and Children.[50] It was not until May 29, 1899, that he got around to officially accepting the task of heading this proposed school. He offered at the same time a prayer that God would help him to do "this work for His children."[51]

The newspapers knew of the developments even before Parker had officially put his stamp of approval on them. Neither he nor Mrs. Blaine could be persuaded to discuss the matter when interviewed on May 28, 1899. Parker only expressed regret that any publicity should have been given the project at this time. Nevertheless, the *Chicago Times-Herald* had it on "good authority" that "at least $500,000 would be set aside by Mrs. Blaine, and that several other wealthy persons interested in educational matters would add a like amount." "The only institution approaching it in its full conception," editorialized the *Chicago Times-Herald,* "is the Teacher's College of New York . . . ."[52]

The next day—May 30, 1899—the *Chicago Times-Herald* was able to verify Parker's resignation from the Normal School. It was said to have been received by the Chicago Board of Education as a "thunderbolt." Even if board members had read their newspapers, they had not believed them or did not expect Parker to resign until the fall of 1899.

In his letter of resignation, Parker expressed "profound sorrow," but he said he acted with the conviction that he would be able to work more effectively for the common schools of Chicago and the country through the new position offered him.[53] Parker's resignation was read into the minutes of the Chicago Board of Education on May 31, 1899. It was accepted without opposition. A commendation was proposed which would express the board's gratitude to the Colonel for making the Normal School "the standard of pedagogical excellence." It was resolved and approved by "a rising vote" that the commendation be engrossed and forwarded to Colonel Parker.[54]

Although the board officially regretted the resignation of Parker, it is probable that he would not have been re-elected in June. Although Parker officially expressed regret at resigning, it is probable he felt relief. One newspaper went so far as to editorialize that it was a "cause for wonder" that any gentleman who had to feel for his scalp every morning for sixteen years could regret his resignation.[55]

Parker said he considered his resignation the "hardest pull" of his life. "No other step in my life has given me greater pain than to leave the school I love," he told his friends. He said nothing could induce him to break the bonds to the children he loved and the graduates of the Normal School unless he was sure he could do better work elsewhere. He asked his friends to continue the fight for "God's little ones."[56]

Strong feeling would endure in some quarters that Parker had been driven out of the public schools.[57] Parker insisted that he left of his own volition and not because he was tired of the long fight with the Chicago Board of Education. "Why, bless you," he told his friends, "my system of teaching has been opposed by some ever since I received my first school . . . ." At a parents' reception held in his honor at the Chicago Normal School on June 16, 1899, Parker asked the guests, "What could I do? Much more can be done for the schools there than here . . . ." He said that he left no enemies behind, "not one." "The opposition," he said, "has been honest, and honest opposition . . . is one of the greatest helps on earth.[58] There was not even a parting shot at Charles Thornton.

On June 28, 1899, fourteen of his teachers at the Normal School resigned and cast their lot with Parker and his new school venture.[59] It was said that many pupils at the Normal School also announced their intention of following their teachers to the new institution. Ironically, Parker was thus weakening the very school he had worked so hard to build. Even more ironic was his purpose in leaving—to "enhance the efficiency of the public schools, thus making private schools unnecessary."[60]

Bereaved of both wife and school he loved at about the same time, Parker would begin a new life for himself and for American education in the last year of the nineteenth century.

NOTES

[1] Francis W. Parker, "The School of the Future," *Journal of Proceedings and Addresses, National Educational Association, 1891,* pp. 86–87; F. W. Parker, letter to Dr. A. H. Champlin, October 5, 1882, as printed in "The History of Col. Parker's Normal Connection," *Chicago Sun* (Chicago, Ill.), July 5, 1887.

[2] F. W. Parker, letter to Mrs. Blaine, June 29, 1898, Papers of Anita McCormick Blaine, McCormick Collection, Wisconsin State Historical Society, Madison, Wisconsin.

[3] ***Ibid.***

[4] Anita McCormick Blaine, "The Founding of the School of Education," *The Elementary School Teacher,* **14** (September–October, 1913), 11.

[5] William Bruce White, "The Philanthropies of Anita McCormick Blaine" (unpublished Master of Science Thesis, University of Wisconsin, 1959), pp. 2, 13–14, 24; David Saville Muzzey, *James G. Blaine, A Political Idol of Other Days* (New York: Dodd, Mead, 1935), pp. 461, 478–479, 489.

[6] *Anita McCormick Blaine, 1866–1954,* as seen by Charlotte G. Kuh, Nancy Blaine Harrison, Katharine Taylor, (no publisher or date, except that speeches were part of a program in memory of Mrs. Blaine held at the Francis W. Parker School on the evening of April 22, 1955), pp. 1–2, 7 Topping Collection, 1325 Stony Brook Lane, Mountainside, N. J.; Anita McCormick, "A Dissertation on the Disadvantages of Being a School-girl," dated March 26, 1881, and Anita McCormick, "The Poorest Education Which Teaches Self-Control is Better than the Best Which Neglects It," dated October 30, 1882 [1881 Folder], Papers of Anita McCormick Blaine; F. W. Parker, letter to Mrs. Blaine (no date, but included with 1894 mail in 1890–1899 Folder), Papers of Anita McCormick Blaine; Anita Blaine, letter to Martha Fleming, October 23, 1903, Papers of Anita McCormick Blaine; "Normal School, Col. Parker Bids Farewell," newspaper clipping, probably from *School Weekly,* June 22, 1899, Parker Scrapbooks, 1899, Archives, Harper Library, University of Chicago.

[7] William Bruce White, *op. cit.,* pp. 29–30; F. W. Parker, letter to Zonia Baber, January 8, 1897, Topping Collection; F. W. Parker, letter to Mrs. Blaine, June 4, 1898, and "Report of Chicago Vacation Schools, August 12, 1898," Papers of Anita McCormick Blaine; "Vacation Schools," *Journal of Education,* **47** (April 14, 1898), 232; "Vacation Schools Opened," newspaper clipping, Parker Scrapbooks, 1898.

[8] F. W. Parker, letter to Mrs. Blaine, June 29, 1898.

[9] *Ibid.* Some knowledge of Parker's plans must have been circulating. One newspaper indicated that some of Parker's friends were preparing to establish a school for him "north of the river." There was a rumor that one woman had offered $10,000 and that others were willing to advance

funds. "Salaries Are Raised," newspaper clipping, dated June 28, 1898, in Parker Scrapbooks, 1898.

[10] F. W. Parker letter to Mrs. Blaine, June 29, 1898; Francis W. Parker, "The School of the Future," pp. 87–88.

[11] "Get Diplomas of Graduation," newspaper clipping, dated June 18, 1898, and "Normal School's Year Ends," newspaper clipping, dated June 17, 1898, Parker Scrapbooks, 1898.

[12] Martha Fleming, "Family and Home Life, Chicago," *Frances Stuart Parker, Reminiscences and Letters* (Chicago: C. L. Ricketts, 1907), p. 22.

[13] F. W. Parker, letter to Mrs. Blaine, June 4, 1898, Francis W. Parker, letter to Zony [Zonia Baber], dated 15 [nearly illegible and may be 10 or 16] May, 1898, Topping Collection; Burton Holmes, *Travelogues,* Vol. 5 (New York: The McClure Co., 1910), p. 142; Mark Sullivan, *Our Times, The United States 1900–1925,* Vol. I (New York: Charles Scribner's Sons, 1926), pp. 318–321; "The Week in Review," *Journal of Education,* **47** (May 5, 1898), 280; "The Week in Review," *Journal of Education,* **47** (May 12, 18,98), 297.

[14] F. W. Parker, letter to Mrs. Blaine, June 4, 1898.

[15] *Ibid.;* "At Lawrence," *Appleton Crescent* (Appleton, Wis.), June 25, 1898; "Commencement," *Appleton Weekly Post* (Appleton, Wis.), June 30, 1898. (There is some doubt as to the date of commencement. Both Appleton papers carry "Thursday, June 23, 1898" datelines for their articles. If this is a report of commencement on June 22, the Parkers could have been there. It can be established that they arrived in Minneapolis, less than a day away from Appleton, on June 23. F. W. Parker, letter to Mrs. Blaine, June 23, 1898, Papers of Anita McCormick Blaine.)

[16] "Commencement," *Appleton Weekly Post,* June 30, 1898.

[17] F. W. Parker letter to Mrs. Blaine, June 23, 1898. The undertaker's report gave cause of death as Carcinoma Uterus, "two years' duration," on her death in 1899. Undertaker's Report of Death of Frances Stuart Parker, Department of Health: City of Chicago: Bureau of Vital Statistics, 130 North Wells Street, Chicago 6, Illinois.

[18] "Extracts from Mrs. Parker's letters, June 1898," *Frances Stuart Parker, Reminiscences and Letters,* p. 63; F. W. Parker, letter to Zonia Baber, June 30, 1898, Topping Collection.

[19] F. W. Parker letters to Zonia Baber, June 23, June 30, 1898, Topping Collection.

[20] "Extracts from Mrs. Parker's letters," p. 64.

[21] This was observed by the famous traveler, Burton Holmes, who was in Hawaii at the same time as the Parkers. Burton Holmes, *op. cit.,* p. 7.

[22] F. W. Parker, letter to Zonia Baber, July 8, 1898, Topping Collection; "Extracts from Mrs. Parker's letters," p. 64.

[23] Burton Holmes, *op. cit.,* pp. 9, 39.

[24] "Extracts from Mrs. Parker's Letters," pp. 65, 105.

[25] *Ibid.;* "Col. and Mrs. Parker in Honolulu," newspaper clipping dated July 1898, "Honolulu," dated July 12, 1898, *The Pacific Commercial Advertiser,* and "Three Educators" and "Opening of Summer School," all in Parker Scrapbooks, 1898.

[26] "Needs of Hawaii, Education, With Manual Training," *Chicago Times-Herald* (Chicago, Ill.), September 18, 1898; "Extracts from Mrs. Parker's letters," pp. 64, 76; Merle Curti, *The Social Ideas of American Educators* (Paterson, N. J.: Littlefield, Adams and Co., 1959), pp. 289–290.

[27] "Needs of Hawaii, Education, With Manual Training."

[28] Burton Holmes, *op. cit.,* p. 10; "Extracts from Mrs. Parker's letters," pp. 69, 93.

[29] Margaret Leech, *In the Days of McKinley* (New York: Harper and Brothers, 1959), pp. 145–147, 212–214; "Colonel Parker Is Home," *Chicago Evening Post* (Chicago, Ill.), September 14, 1898; "Needs of Hawaii, Education, With Manual Training."

[30] "Extracts from Mrs. Parker's letters," p. 96; "The Week," *The Nation,* **67** (August 25, 1898), 139.

[31] Henry Townsend, "Extends to Hawaii, A Kind of Quincy Teacher Discovered There as Early as 1881, Republic of Hawaii, Department of Public Instruction, Honolulu, Hawaiian Islands, March 1, 1900," *Quincy Patriot* (Quincy, Mass.), April 21, 1900; "Needs of Hawaii, Education, With Manual Training"; "Schools in Hawaii," *Journal of Education,* **49** (February 23, 1899), 117.

[32] "Needs of Hawaii, Education, With Manual Training"; Francis W. Parker, "The Plan and Purpose of the Chicago Institute," *The Course of Study,* **1** (July 1, 1900–June 1, 1901), 21; "Colonel Parker on the School," *School Journal,* **58** (March 25, 1899), 340.

[33] Isaac Freeman Hall, *In School from Three to Eighty* (Pittsfield, Mass.: The Eagle Printing and Binding Co., 1927), pp. 227–230; "Harvard and the Cuban Teacher," *Journal of Education,* **51** (April 12, 1900), 237; "Cubans at Cambridge," *Journal of Education,* **52** (June 28, 1900), 10; Clarence Ross Gale, "The Reconstruction of Cuba," *Journal of Education,* **50** (December 21, 1899), 416.

[34] "Colonel Parker is Home."

[35] "Superintendent Andrews of Chicago," *Journal of Education,* **48** (September 8, 1898), 160; F. W. Parker, letter to Mrs. Blaine, October 30, 1898, Papers of Anita McCormick Blaine.

[36] *Ibid.;* "Normal Salaries Cut," *Chicago Record* (Chicago, Ill.), August 31, 1898; "Dr. Andrews' Leadership," *Journal of Education,* **49** (January 12, 1899), 24.

[37] "Superintendent Andrews is Right," *Journal of Education,* **48** (September 22, 1898), 192; "Dr. Andrews' Leadership," p. 24; "Superintendent Andrews' Victory," *Journal of Education,* **48** (December 15, 1898), 388.

[38] "As Chicago Sees Herself," *Journal of Education,* **51** (May 17, 1900), 312; "Will Thornton Now Subside?" *Chicago Evening Post,* July 1, 1898.

[39] "Chicago Ideals," *Journal of Education,* **49** (January 5, 1899), 9; "Chicago's Latest," *Journal of Education,* **52** (October 25, 1900), 264.

[40] F. W. Parker, letter to Mrs. Blaine, October 30, 1898.

[41] F. W. Parker, letter to Mrs. Blaine, December 15, 1898, Papers of Anita McCormick Blaine.

[42] Anita McCormick Blaine, "The Chicago Institute," *Frances Stuart Parker, Reminiscences and Letters,* p. 38; A. E. Winship [editor], "Colonel Parker's Great Opportunity," *Journal of Education,* **51** (April 12, 1900), 232; "Colonel Parker's Change," *Journal of Education,* **49** (June 8, 1899), 360. Although Mrs. Blaine sent flowers to the ailing Mrs. Parker at one time, it is doubtful if Mrs. Parker would have returned thanks as "Frances Stuart Parker" if they were as close in friendship as suggested by the previously cited articles. Mrs. Frances Stuart Parker, letter to Mrs. Blaine, November 25, 1898, Papers of Anita McCormick Blaine.

[43] *Ibid.*

[44] "Mrs. Frank Stuart Parker," *Journal of Education,* **49** (April 6, 1899), 216.

[45] The change of address from 6640 Honore Street to 6640 Parnell Avenue is first noted on the date line of a letter to Mrs. Blaine in December of 1898. F. W. Parker, letter Mrs. Blaine, December 15, 1898. It is at this address that Mrs. Parker died. Undertaker's Report of Death of Mrs. Frances Stuart Parker.

[46] "Colonel Parker's Change."

[47] Martha Fleming, *op. cit.,* pp. 22, 24; Frank Stuart Parker, letter to Zonia Baber, September 1, 1883 [handwriting nearly illegible; date might be 1898], Topping Collection. (There are several photographs in the Topping Collection which show the Parkers in camping attire. The Colonel is invariably lying down and Mrs. Parker, dressed to the ankles, is standing about.)

[48] Martha Fleming, *op. cit.,* p. 24; Flora J. Cooke, "Sunday Evenings," *Frances Stuart Parker, Reminiscences and Letters,* p. 33.

[49] *Ibid.;* Martha Fleming, *op. cit.,* pp. 29–30; "Mrs. Frank Stuart Parker," p. 216; Undertaker's Report of Death of Mrs. Frances Stuart Parker.

[50] F. W. Parker, letter to Mrs. Blaine, May 2, 1899, Papers of Anita McCormick Blaine. The name Parker suggested was caught by newspapers. "Harper Gets Parker," *Chicago Record,* May 31, 1899.

[51] F. W. Parker, letter to Mrs. Blaine, May 29, 1899, Papers of Anita McCormick Blaine.

[52] "To Aid Teachers," *Chicago Times-Herald,* May 29, 1899.

[53] "Col. Parker Resigns," *Chicago Times-Herald,* May 30, 1899.

[54] *Proceedings of the Board of Education of the City of Chicago, July 13, 1898–June 28, 1899* (Chicago: Press of John H. Higgins, n.d.), p. 649.

[55] "Col. Parker Resigns." Another newspaper predicted also that "the present school board would accomplish what its predecessors failed to do—the deposing of the normal-school chief . . . ." "Col Parker Resigns," *Chicago Record,* May 30, 1899.

[56] "In a husky voice, as he looked out the broad school grounds where scores of children still lingered to play or sit in the shade despite the fact that school had been 'out' for nearly an hour," newspaper clipping, Parker Scrapbooks, 1899; Francis W. Parker, "The Normal School," *Elementary School Teacher and Course of Study,* **2** (July 1, 1901–June 1902), 780.

[57] Margaret A. Haley, "From the Funeral," *Journal of Education,* **55** (March 27, 1902), 204.

[58] "Normal School, Col. Parker Bids Farewell," newspaper clipping, dated June 22, 1899, Parker Scrapbooks, 1899.

[59] *Proceedings of the Board . . . 1898–1899, op. cit.,* p. 735.

[60] "Blaine Faculty Is Chosen by Trustees," *Chicago Evening Journal* (Chicago, Ill.), June 19, 1899; "Plans of Pedagogical School," *Chicago News,* (Chicago, Ill.), May 31, 1899; "Col. Parker's Good-By," *Chicago Inter-Ocean,* (Chicago, Ill.), June 11, 1899; "Will Take Up a New Work," newspaper clipping, dated June 1, 1899, Parker Scrapbooks, 1899.

XIV

Retreat from the Chicago Institute to the University of Chicago

Once conceived and announced to the public, the plans for the privately endowed educational experiment matured rapidly. Mrs. Blaine associated herself with Owen F. Aldis, Henry B. Favill, Cyrus Bentley, and Stanley McCormick in order to form a board of trustees. They applied for incorporation in July of 1899 and were empowered to establish and maintain one or more schools in Chicago.[1]

It was not planned to open the doors of the school for a full year.[2] In fact, there was not a door to open, not a single classroom, not even a suitable site for building a school. The Board of Trustees had begun to erect a great school by starting with a faculty rather than with bricks and mortar. They started with Colonel Parker. Parker was joined by those fourteen teachers who had resigned all in a body from the Normal School on June 28, 1899. Rumor had it that as many as thirty of the thirty-six teachers comprising Colonel Parker's former staff would eventually "secede" from the Chicago Normal School as soon as the "Blaine School" was expected to open in July of 1900. All who did resign were immediately engaged by the Board of Trustees at full salary, even though there would be no students to teach for a year. Parker also recommended large salary increases for his following, including a $3,000 jump in his own compensation. He even put through a proposal for financing the advanced training of these teachers. And although he entertained the notion himself of studying abroad, possibly in England, he finally settled for working on the more immediate needs of the new school.[3]

Parker's select "corps" of teachers then scattered to the end of the earth in search of truth and the means of teaching it. One studied children's literature in Norway. One went to Paris for training in the Delsarte system. Some chose to study science and physical education in Germany. Others studied at the Metropolitan Museum in New York and the Smithsonian Institution in Washington. Many sought degrees in such colleges as Columbia, Harvard, Clark, and the University of Chicago, while some broadened themselves by touring the world.[4]

Meanwhile Parker kept himself busy with budgets, selecting new teachers, writing preliminary announcements, and sketching a short history of his work at the Cook County and Chicago Normal School. He was also involved in the plans for building and equipping a physical plant. Such plans were soon let out to architects. In the meantime, three rooms on the sixth floor of the Marquette Building in downtown Chicago had been rented for offices. The press kept referring to this educational project as "the Emmons Blaine School for Teachers and Children," or simply as "the Blaine School." In October the Trustees officially established the school as the Chicago Institute, Academic and Pedagogic. Later in October, they gave Parker the title of "president."[5]

The "president" was determined to make this school a perfect exposition of the new education, a model for other schools to follow. Free government, he told the trustees, depended on the success of their experiment. He also tried to prepare his new directors for the opposition and ridicule that could be expected. He told them his brand of education was still "absolutely different" from the "prevailing point of view as to education in general." There was even misunderstanding, he said, among those who opposed traditional education. He may have had reference to the controversy which still raged over the meaning of concentration and correlation and coordination of studies, but he advised the trustees that a "new nomenclature" was actually needed for his new doctrines of education.[6]

Parker was not really so pessimistic. Twenty-five years earlier, he noted that the work of Mann and Barnard was hardly known, the kindergarten was only a fad, and the "ABC method" and flogging were universal. Looking back over the last quarter of a century, Parker was encouraged by the coming of physiological psychology, the Child Study Movement, manual training in the elementary schools, and especially by the development of departments of education in some of the colleges and universities.[7]

It was just twenty-five years since Parker began his much publicized work in Quincy. Since then he had waged a campaign against "mechanical methods" which some of his contemporaries considered as forceful as the efforts of Horace Mann. By 1900 it was said that Parker had triumphed, that he no longer had any real opponents among educational leaders. At the same time it was pointed out that Parker was not the radical he had seemed to be twenty-five years earlier. The issues he had raised then would not hold an audience any more. His ideas had either been adopted and were now taken for granted or they had been "laughed out of court." As the century neared the end, it was even said that the Colonel was more often conservative than liberal. In fact, many of his "utterances of late" were called antagonistic and hostile to newness.[8] Perhaps success had made a conservative out of the Colonel. He had certainly succeeded, some said, in making children the center of the universe.[9]

Successful as he was, his appointment to the presidency of the Chicago Institute greatly contributed to his prestige and reputation. It was said that in his new position he was destined to make for himself a great place in professional leadership.[10] That great place was soon recognized in the celebration of the Silver Anniversary of Parker's coming to Quincy. Notice of the "Parker-Quincy Celebration" went out in the *Journal of Education* on March 15, 1900. Superintendent H. W. Lull of the Quincy schools addressed letters of invitation to old board members, teachers, and students who could revive memories of April 20, 1875.[11]

Two hundred people were reported at the Vendome Hotel on April 20, 1900, for the banquet in honor of the Colonel. Charles Francis Adams, Jr., although detained by business on the West Coast, wrote that he could see no reason for changing his opinion of the Colonel after a quarter of a century. He insisted that the "educational new departure" at Quincy had been a special "creation." William T. Harris, in attendance at the banquet, observed that "It is not often that a hero, at least in education, hears his praises sung . . . ."[12]

The hero of the Quincy Celebration, however, was facing heroic problems with the Chicago Institute. Unable to convince the Board of Trustees that they should establish a junior college, he was also thwarted in an attempt to develop a curriculum with phonetic spellings. Mrs. Blaine had to inform him in September of 1899 that the trustees thought it unwise to announce the use of phonetic spelling in the new school. They felt the public would distrust it and misjudge the purpose of the new institution.[13]

Parker was used to such frustration but he might have expected the trustees would be less subject to public pressure than the Chicago Board of Education. He then carried his battle for simplified, phonetic spelling to the National Educational Association. He argued that the manner of spelling words is simply a fashion and should change with fashion. He argued that thousands of dollars were spent needlessly in teaching children how to spell anomalous words. It was a waste of time, a waste of effort by the children. He even argued that simplified spelling would hasten the Americanization of the millions of people in the new possessions. The National Educational Association would have no more of Parker's proposals than his own Board of Trustees. William T. Harris argued that teachers had no authority to introduce spelling reforms without the permission of school committees or without the support of the "entire English-speaking people."[14]

Parker was also restrained in his attempt to establish a "slum" school as a branch of the Chicago Institute. (Such a school had been contemplated by Parker and Mrs. Blaine in their first private negotiations.) The location of the slum school had become the greatest obstacle. Ideally, Parker wanted slum children to mix with children of all classes, but transportation was slow by cable car and the city was segregated into widely separated areas of rich and poor. Parker had at first planned to locate the school next to Hull House and emulate the "socialized" education of Jane Addams. Later he wrote Mrs. Blaine to resist any affiliation with Hull House or other social settlement.[15]

Mrs. Blaine may have been following the advice of Parker when she argued at the board meeting on July 23, 1899, that the social side of the new education should be pursued in a different way than that of the social settlement. Jane Addams had been invited to the same meeting because the advisability of the slum school, as well as its location, was on the agenda. Miss Addams made a plea for educational aid to the foreign-born child. She said the "southern European element" was the "hardest nut" to crack and that the only connection with the parents was through the children. When members of the Board of Trustees talked about the location of the "free" school, Jane Addams cited her own ward—the nineteenth—as the most needy.[16]

Colonel Parker talked against locating the school in what he called the "vicious ward." There was no permanency of residence there. An experiment could not be fairly tested over the years in such a migratory section of town. When the trustees asked Miss Addams how the Catholic Church in her ward would receive the school, she had to admit that the attitude of the Church was "not friendly."[17]

The trustees decided that the most difficult problems were the most attractive but the most important thing for the model school was to succeed. The Nineteenth Ward was abandoned and the trustees sought the "most promising ward" rather than the most challenging. They met on various occasions in August to consider the "free" school and various proposed sites. By August 23, the trustees had decided that the undertaking of two schools at the same time was too difficult. Plans for the "free" school were then tabled.[18]

All efforts were then concentrated on the main concern—the institute for the training of teachers. There had never been any controversy over the location of *this* institute. It would be somewhere in the residential vicinity of its patrons. On July 29, 1899, Mrs. Blaine had purchased a tract of land on the North Shore which was larger than two city blocks. Besides being convenient to the "best residential districts of Chicago," the property was near Lincoln Park, an academy of science, a botanical garden, and a zoo.[19]

Parker's great plans, however, were beginning to make millionaires stop to count the cost. Only $250,000 to $300,000 had been budgeted for the land, which finally cost $425,000. The building was expected to cost around $282,000, but by April of 1900 the bids from three contractors were all over half a million dollars.[20] To make matters worse, Emanuel R. Boyer, Director of the Chicago Institute, had died suddenly in February of 1900. He had charge of the "physical part of the school," and Parker had only recently congratulated himself on being able to get a man who would "manage everything up to the mark."[21]

The trustees were now balking. New plans for the building were being considered, including reductions in space. One suggestion for cutting costs was to eliminate the gymnasium and the "west building."[22] Parker was in Des Moines, Iowa, at a Mothers' Congress in May of 1900 when he heard about the plans to cut space. He telegraphed Cyrus Bentley to fight for a "perfect building" no matter how long it would take. He suggested that temporary quarters could be found.[23]

On May 24, 1900, the trustees argued that it was a bad principle to start the habit of going beyond their financial limits. Wilbur Jackman pleaded at the meeting that time was secondary to efficiency. The trustees then put off any decision on the permanent building and concentrated on finding temporary quarters for the summer opening of the school. Even while the trustees argued over the expense of building, widespread labor difficulties in Chicago had led to strikes which, the trustees believed, would raise costs even higher.[24]

The Turngemeinde Building on the near North Side was then rented, as well as an adjoining store which had been occupied by a piano company. Alterations were quickly made and summer school began in July of 1900, as planned, but in a German gymnasium and a piano store, amid the hammering of carpenters and plumbers.[25]

During that summer session Parker was given the revised plans of the architect. He went over them and complained that the new assembly hall was not large enough. He wanted it to seat at least one thousand people and have level floors and movable chairs so that it could also be used for lessons. He insisted it should have a small stage for "entertainments."[26]

The assembly was the heart of Parker's system. Morning exercises brought together the "tots of the kindergarten" and all the pupils, teachers, and practice teachers. Parker said "togetherness" was the motto of the new century. The assembly hall was therefore the crucible out of which community life was fused.[27]

Parker found the revised plans not only reduced the size of the library but put it in the wrong place.[28] He criticized economizing at the expense of ornament and architectural beauty. The beauty, he said, would have a "profound moral effect upon every one."[29] He found fault with the corridors that were not open to light. He suggested that space on the roof be finished off as a promenade and provided with "settees for the purpose of sketching and other studies."[30]

All in all, he could not reconcile himself to modifying his plans. All the margins in the "Revised Plan of the New Building" were filled with Parker's suggestions and disappointments. Ideals could not be compromised, but the revised plans had to be accepted and the school space shrank from almost fifty thousand square feet to little more than thirty thousand.[31]

Dissatisfied as Parker was with the revised building plans, he was even more unhappy with the temporary quarters in the Turngemeinde Building. After a hectic summer school he informed the trustees that there were only four weeks left in which to prepare the improvised summer quarters for the opening of the fall term. He complained first of all that he needed more space. He called for funds to establish laboratories, to fit the building for electricity, and for filtered drinking water facilities. He called for funds to establish a school periodical known as *The Course of Study*. He called for appropriations for advertisement.[32]

The trustees finally called on Parker to cut current expenses and absolutely hold the budget at $95,000. Parker complied, but he did not cut the salaries of teachers. Clerks, stenographers, and janitors felt the slash. He omitted plans for a "carette" service to transport children to school. He cut fuel and gas expenses. He cut appropriations for stationery, printing, library, and museum supplies. He even cut down on the use of the telephone.[33]

It was reported that Parker's own personal library of some twelve thousand volumes was turned over to the school.[34] Fifteen thousand dollars went to equipment that was stored at the McCormick Theological Seminary until alterations were finished at the Turngemeinde Building.[35]

When the school opened in October of 1900 there was room for six hundred students but only 195 actually enrolled. This included students in kindergarten through twelfth grade, as well as two divisions of student teachers. The largest single class enrollment was twenty-two in ninth grade. The smallest enrollment was two students in grade eleven. Each of the divisions of student teachers, however, included thirty-four candidates.[36]

One of the ten members of seventh grade was Perry Dunlap Smith, son of Dunlap Smith who had been the real estate agent in acquiring the property. Mr. Smith presently admits to having been, up until that time, a "difficult" student in school. A school was a place to cause "riots" or shoot a bean or two when the teacher was not looking. He was surprised on his first day at the Chicago Institute when the teacher asked him to select his own desk. He was even more surprised when the teacher asked him how the desks should be arranged. When he went to the morning assembly he was astounded to find that the students of all ages sat together without teacher supervision. He thought this school was going to be a "push-over." Then he saw the Colonel. He was a "Santa Claus except for the white beard." When the Colonel sat down on the front platform he had no lap, only knees, but the kindergarten children who sat in front were soon climbing up on those knees. He had to brush them off the stage when it was time to start the program.[37]

Big, fat, with a "jolly laugh," the Colonel nevertheless had a way of appearing to look each student in the eye. No one could escape his glance. He explained the purpose of the school to the children, telling them they were part of a great experiment in education and must all work together to prove that boys and girls could learn in school without force. Perry Smith remembered that the Colonel had all the children on his side in ten minutes. That was the end of Perry Smith's career as a "difficult" student.[38]

That was the beginning of the Chicago Institute. Even though it was designed as a model to proclaim the superiority of the new education, there was no blueprint for the remodeling of the American school system. Parker granted that the "prevailing ideal" of education was for a ready-made course of study from which a teacher could mechanically work out the same lessons year after year. The new ideal, Parker explained to Mrs. Blaine, is based on the fact that the demands of society are constantly changing and that the nature of the child is subject to perpetual study. Under such an ideal there could never be a fixed course of study.[39]

The course of study for the Chicago Institute was therefore in the shape of a periodical rather than a table of laws. Under the managing editorship of Marion Foster Washburne, *The Course of Study* was published monthly as an exposition of the curriculum developments at the

Institute. It was intended as a basis for further curriculum development, a guide for methodology, and as a textbook for students in pedagogical courses. Since it consisted of the monthly plans and activities of all teachers, *The Course of Study* also served to keep the faculty continually in touch with everything being done in the school.[40]

While the course of study developed from day to day, the physical facilities for the proposed building did not get beyond the drawing board. The school survived the first winter in its temporary quarters, but such makeshift arrangements gave everything a sense of probation. One student remembered studying French in a room that had been a tavern. The smell of malt persisted. The feeling of impermanence persisted.[41]

All the while, financial problems kept interrupting the Colonel, disturbing his work and dreams. He was guilty of at least one mistake in budget calculations, but he was probably mostly criticized for his generosity in paying teachers and granting scholarships.[42]

It is not certain if financial and administrative desperation finally drove the Board of Trustees into an alliance with the University of Chicago. The board had discussed such a possibility as early as June of 1899 but then decided not "to affiliate at present."[43] It is possible that the negotiations which led to a merger with the University of Chicago were initiated by President William R. Harper. He was said to have been after Parker's services even before the Colonel carried the Blaine endowment.[44] Such a merger had long been anticipated by the Chicago press, because Mrs. Blaine was already a patron of the University of Chicago and associated with its causes. After her secret arrangements with Parker had been shelved in the summer of 1898, she contributed money to the University. Her endowment was turned into the "University of Chicago College for Teachers," with Harper and Dewey on its staff.[45]

Whether negotiations were initiated by representatives of the Chicago Institute or the University of Chicago, there would be mutual advantages to be gained in the sharing of faculty and financial resources. Regardless of motivation, the Board of Trustees had reached a definite understanding with the authorities of the University of Chicago by the first of February 1901. At that time Parker and Wilbur S. Jackman put their names to an agreement with Harper and Professor John Dewey. They agreed that, in case of union, a general plan acceptable to all parties would have to be adopted. This agreement also stipulated that the Institute and the University Department of Education would be considered "two distinct and coordinate factors" for administrative purposes. It was agreed that the Institute would continue under the direction of Parker, have its own faculty, and conduct the elementary school. The Department of Education at the University would continue under the direction of John

Dewey. Dewey would also be responsible for establishing a secondary school.[46]

A little more than a week after this agreement of cooperation was signed, Parker sent a sketch of plans to John Dewey. Concerned about the organization and administration of the merger, he confided in Dewey that even though the proposed plans promised a great opportunity to enhance the progress of education, he could not consent to the arrangement without an absolute assurance of "all-around efficiency." Parker made it clear that he did not want to invade "Dr. Dewey's zone of authority, but, for the sake of efficiency, he hoped for some interplay between the elementary and secondary schools. He anticipated scheduling situations in which economies could be effected by employing one teacher at both levels. He also believed some of his teachers could work at the secondary as well as the elementary level. He said he had spent years on the selection of his "corps" and thought the best thing about them was their willingness to learn. Finally, he indicated he would rather teach in a country school where all conditions were right than have charge of the largest city institution with restrictions that could not be overcome. Although he thought he might be putting too much value on his own life, he insisted on long and thoughtful consideration before entering these new arrangements.[47]

There was probably no fear on Parker's part that the philosophy of Dewey would conflict with his own. He had already told the Board of Trustees that he considered Dewey the real philosopher of the new education, and more recently he had requisitioned twenty copies of Dewey's *The School and Society* for use at the Chicago Institute.[48] Parker must also have felt assured that he had the confidence of Dewey, whose own children had been entrusted to the Normal School when their father first came to Chicago.[49] There was probably no fear on Parker's part that the University would dominate the elementary school. For years he had recognized the suzerainty of the higher levels of education. In Dewey's *The School and Society,* he had the professor's own word for it that great waste in education resulted from the isolation and separation of the various school levels.[50]

There were disadvantages, however, inherent in a union with the University of Chicago, and these must have given Parker some reason to hesitate. The Chicago Institute had been founded for a single purpose—to dramatize the ideals of the new education. Such a purpose required a tight organization. The University could not guarantee such unity.[51] In addition, the dramatic impact of the new school on community living might be lost amid the numerous undertakings of the University.

Ties with the University could further the danger of alienation between Parker's work and the public schools. President Harper of the University of Chicago was not popular with either the Chicago Board of Education or the teacher organizations in the city. Dr. E. Benjamin Andrews, the Superintendent of schools, had learned early that his association with the name of Harper was probably "fatal" to the success of many of his plans.[52]

In the municipal elections of 1898 and 1899 there were charges that President Harper and Mayor Harrison were plotting to make the public schools mere tributaries of the University of Chicago, and, even worse, to deliver the whole school system over to Standard Oil. These rumors could be traced to the Republican opponents and the Independent forces of former Democratic Governor John P. Altgeld, but there was fear on the part of Mayor Harrison that such rumors were widely believed.[53] There was real evidence, however, that President Harper was consolidating educational enterprises with the same energy and dispatch which characterized the propensity for monopoly among his contemporaries in the world of big business. Since 1896 the University had absorbed eighteen different schools, including the Chicago Manual Training School, and it was about to absorb the Chicago Institute.[54] When the unfair competition of large department stores was being attacked in Chicago, somewhat earlier, one newspaper editor thought the reformers ought also to "take a crack at Chicago University." He said the University had become a department store for all kinds of "cranial merchandise," the latest of which was pedagogy.[55]

There is no doubt that the Colonel was beginning to cool in matters of affiliation, especially after he learned that the University of Chicago would not match the funds which Mrs. Blaine had set up for the Institute. He was probably disappointed in the salary, which—while reported to be $8,000 for the school year 1901–1902—was apparently established at between $5,000 and $6,000 by the University of Chicago.[56]

By February 13, 1901, Parker reached the conclusion that negotiations with the University of Chicago should be terminated and that the Chicago Institute ought to carry on under its present plans, using the funds it had available. He told Mrs. Blaine at this time that he regretted to come to such a conclusion, especially after he once had entertained such "strong hopes for the union on a broad, effective basis."[57]

Parker had not reckoned with his teachers. At a special session shortly thereafter, thirteen out of the fourteen teachers present voted for affiliation with the University of Chicago. Parker then wrote to Mrs. Blaine on February 15th that he felt constrained to change his opinion and to recommend merger. "I do this," he said, "in decided opposition to my personal feelings . . ."[58] On another occasion, he wrote to someone else that his heart was for maintaining an independent course but his reason favored union.[59]

Mrs. Blaine went ahead with plans for union. The arrangements were apparently reviewed by John D. Rockefeller, Jr., early in March and found satisfactory. The New York trustees concurred, and merger of the two schools was common knowledge later that month.[60] The actual contract between the separate boards of trustees was notarized on April 16, 1901, at which time the University of Chicago agreed to establish on or before July 1, 1901, "The University of Chicago School of Education." In return, the Chicago Institute gave up its property holdings to the University. Francis W. Parker was scheduled to administer this School of Education as long as he "competently" discharged his duties. (There would be no annual struggles over tenure.) John Dewey was to remain as head of the Department of Philosophy, Psychology, and Pedagogy. He would also take charge of a proposed secondary school for the use of practice teachers. Neither the "Pedagogy" aspect of Dewey's department nor the proposed secondary school could be merged with the new School of Education until Dewey should choose to terminate his association with the university.[61]

Exercises connected with the official opening of the School of Education were in June of 1901 as the University of Chicago celebrated its tenth anniversary. In an impressive ceremony Colonel Parker broke ground for the permanent building which would one day house his theories and practices. Mrs. Blaine shared a carriage with President Harper and Mr. and Mrs. John D. Rockefeller.[62]

Parker's sphere of influence, well separated from Dewey's, was still largely on paper. It was to consist of a Pedagogic School for the training of teachers, a kindergarten, and an elementary school. It was soon to include another school on the North Shore. The Francis W. Parker School, with a kindergarten and eight grades, was designed by the Trustees of the Chicago Institute to meet the needs of its North Shore patrons who lived nearly two hours by cable car from the campus of the University of Chicago.[63] President Harper agreed to share the Colonel and the faculty of the School of Education with this extension as long as the new school would be open to the pedagogical department of the University. The agreement was tentative and could be terminated at any time.[64]

Friends of the Francis W. Parker School subscribed a guaranteed fund of $10,000 per annum for five years, and more than 150 children were conditionally registered even before the official announcement was made on June 1, 1901.[65] Such a response bore witness to the success of the Chicago Institute among the people who could afford to pay for their children's education.

Besides having Colonel Parker as its director and Miss Flora J. Cooke as its principal, the Francis W. Parker School was to be handsomely housed in the "English style," with huge fireplaces and wide hallways. Being built on the site originally bought for the Chicago Institute, the Francis W. Parker School was now on property belonging to the University of Chicago. The new school was granted the use of this land for six years, with an option to purchase.[66]

While the North Shore friends of Parker's Chicago Institute had insured the kind of education they wanted for their children, the South Side clientele of Dewey's Laboratory School fought to preserve the independence of their school. A branch of the University of Chicago and officially known as the University Elementary School, it nevertheless had to support itself on tuition and private subscriptions. It had grown from a few students in 1896 to nearly a hundred by 1898, but it was always under such financial stress that, even in 1899, Dewey despaired of keeping it going.[67]

Now the parents association of the University Elementary School appealed to President Harper to let the school continue on its former basis. Harper said it would appear to be an act of "bad faith" with Parker and the Trustees of the Chicago Institute to allow the independence of the Dewey school. He also argued that this would put too much strain on Dewey. He even indicated that the neighborhood population was too small for the support of two elementary schools. Nevertheless, he submitted to the demands. Dewey assured him he could supervise the laboratory school with ease. Mrs. Blaine said she had no desire to interfere in any way. Harper was probably most influenced by the bond of the parents to underwrite any financial deficits.[68]

Parker himself seemed to have no objection. When informed that the parents had raised money to continue the school on an independent basis, he said this was "striking proof" of the good work accomplished by the school, proof that intelligent people could appreciate the new education, no matter how radical it was in nature. His subsequent visit to the school convinced him that it was indeed a "marked success" and deserved to be continued as long as the "proper financial arrangements" could be made.[69]

If the educational practices of Parker and Dewey were similar, it is strange that the parent association of the University Elementary School were so fearful of merger with the Chicago Institute. It is probable that the parents were more concerned about losing the small classes and "near-tutorial instruction" that had been offered by Dewey while he was using the school as a laboratory for working out and testing principles and theories of education. Nevertheless, in curricular matters, the two elementary schools were to divide. Parker's would center subject matter around a child in nature. Dewey's would concentrate on a child in society.[70] The direction and style of the new education would depend on the energy and administrative zeal of Parker, but the energy was already running out of him.

NOTES

[1] Application was dated 10 July 1899 and official recording was dated 20 October 1899. This instrument is filed in the Recorder of Deeds of Cook County, Illinois, as document number 2,883,081, on page 374 of Book 6764 of *Records*.

[2] "Trustees Name Faculty," *Chicago Tribune* (Chicago, Ill.), June 19, 1899; "Blaine Faculty Is Chosen by Trustees," *Chicago Evening Journal* (Chicago, Ill.), June 19, 1899; F. W. Parker, letter to Board of Trustees, July 12, 1899. Papers of Anita McCormick Blaine, McCormick Collection, Wisconsin State Historical Society, Madison, Wis.

[3] F. W. Parker, letter to Mrs. Blaine, June 16, 1899, Papers of Anita McCormick Blaine; F. W. Parker, letter to Board of Trustees, July 12, 1899; "Teachers Will Not Desert," *Chicago Tribune,* June 18, 1899; "Will Secede from the Normal School," *Chicago Evening Journal,* June 17, 1899.

[4] "Trustees Name Faculty"; "Blaine Faculty is Chosen by Trustees."

[5] "August 16, 1899," "October 4, 1899," "October 18, 1899," Minutes of the Board of Trustees [Chicago Institute Proceedings, recorded by hand in a ledger by Mrs. Blaine, Secretary of the Board], Papers of Anita McCormick Blaine; F. W. Parker, letter to Mrs. Blaine, September 14, 1899, Papers of Anita McCormick Blaine. The name of Emmons Blaine School for Teachers and Children had been used in such accounts as "Harper Gets Parker," *Chicago Record* (Chicago, Ill.), May 31, 1899, and "Plans of Pedagogical School," *Chicago News* (Chicago, Ill.), May 31, 1899. Blaine School was more current later, as in "Blaine School Site," *Chicago Record,* August 3, 1899, "Site for Blaine School," *Chicago Evening Post* (Chicago, Ill.), August 3, 1899, and "Site for Blaine School," *Chicago Tribune,* August 3, 1899. The idea of naming the school Chicago Institute may have existed in Parker's mind for some time. He was reported, in the summer of 1898 before anyone knew he was planning to leave the public schools, to have said he wanted to take back from Hawaii many exhibits for the "Chicago Institute." Newspaper clipping, possibly from *The Pacific Commercial Advertiser,* dated July 18, 1898, Parker Scrapbooks, 1898, Archives, Harper Library, University of Chicago.

[6] Francis W. Parker, letter to the Board of Trustees, July 31, 1899, Papers of Anita McCormick Blaine; Charles De Garmo, "The Principles Upon Which the Coordination of Studies Should Proceed," *Journal of Proceedings and Addresses, National Educational Association, 1895,* p. 87.

[7] F. W. Parker, "Looking Backward," *School Journal,* **59** (August 12, 1899), 118.

[8] "The Chicago Situation," *Journal of Education,* **47** (June 9, 1898), 360.

[9] Eva D. Kellogg, "Progress in Primary Education," *Journal of Proceedings and Addresses, National Educational Association, 1895,* p. 1004.

[10] "Colonel Parker's Great Opportunity," *Journal of Education,* **51** (April 12, 1900), 232.

[11] "Anniversary Number of the Revival of Education in Quincy and the United States," *Quincy Patriot* (Quincy, Mass.), April 21, 1900; "The Parker-Quincy Celebration," *Journal of Education,* **51** (March 15, 1900), 168.

[12] Charles Francis Adams [Jr.], letter to H. W. Lull, Esq., Superintendent, March 24, 1900, as printed in *Quincy Patriot,* April 21, 1900; "The Vendome Banquet," *Journal of Education,* **51** (April 26, 1900), 260; William T. Harris, "Colonel Parker and the Quincy School," *Journal of Education,* **51** (June 7, 1900), 355.

[13] Anita McCormick Blaine, letter to Francis W. Parker [probably September 5, 1899], Papers of Anita McCormick Blaine.

[14] Francis W. Parker, "Discussion on the subject of simplified spelling," *Journal of Proceedings and Addresses, National Educational Association, 1901,* p. 216; William T. Harris, "Discussion on the subject of simplified spelling," *Journal of Proceedings and Addresses, National Educational Association, 1901,* p. 224; "Minutes of the Meeting of the Board of Directors for 1900-1901," *Journal of Proceedings and Addresses, National Educational Association, 1901,* p. 36.

[15] F. W. Parker, letters to Mrs. Blaine, June 29, 1898, and June 27, 1899, Papers of Anita McCormick Blaine; "Teachers Will Not Desert."

[16] "July 23, 1899," Minutes of the Board of Trustees.

[17] *Ibid.*

[18] *Ibid.;* "August 9, 1899," and "August 23, 1899," Minutes of the Board of Trustees.

[19] Real Estate Sale Contract between Clara F. Bass and Anita McCormick Blaine, signed by their agents, P. B. Bass and Dunlap Smith, July 29, 1899, Papers of Anita McCormick Blaine; "Blaine School Site"; "Site for Blaine School." Parker had actually mentioned a North Side location for the school as early as June of 1898. F. W. Parker, letter to Mrs. Blaine, June 29, 1898.

[20] Anita McCormick Blaine, letter to Dunlap Smith, July 13, 1899, Papers of Anita McCormick Blaine; Real Estate Sale Contract; "August 23, 1899" and "April 21, 1900," Minutes of the Board of Trustees.

[21] "February 26, 1900," Minutes of the Board of Trustees"; F. W. Parker, letter to Zonia Baber, January 3, 1900, Topping Collection.

[22] "April 29, 1900" and "May 4, 1900," Minutes of the Board of Trustees.

[23] F. W. Parker, telegram to Cyrus Bentley [from Des Moines, Iowa], May 24, 1900, Papers of Anita McCormick Blaine. Parker's attendance at a "Mothers' Congress" in Des Moines is established in his letter to Flora Cooke, May 26, 1900, Tolman Collection, Tolman Pond, Nelson, N. H.

[24] "May 24, 1900," and "May 28, 1900," Minutes of the Board of Trustees.

[25] "May 28, 1900," "June 28, 1900," and "July 2, 1900," Minutes of the Board of Trustees.

[26] F. W. Parker, "Suggestions on the Revised Plan of the New Building" [Chicago Institute Folder], Papers of Anita McCormick Blaine.

[27] Francis W. Parker, "Morning Exercises," *The Course of Study,* **1** (July 1, 1900–June 1, 1901), 599; Perry Dunlap Smith, interview, April 26, 1962, Winnetka, Ill.

[28] F. W. Parker, letter to Mrs. Blaine, July 28, 1900, Papers of Anita McCormick Blaine.

[29] F. W. Parker, letter to Mrs. Blaine, July 26, 1900, Papers of Anita McCormick Blaine.

[30] F. W. Parker, "Suggestions on the Revised Plan of the New Building."

[31] *Ibid.;* "Chicago Institute, Comparison of Old Plan with New Sketch, Number 3, July 22, 1900," Papers of Anita McCormick Blaine.

[32] F. W. Parker, letter to the Board of Trustees, August 27, 1900, Papers of Anita McCormick Blaine.

[33] F. W. Parker and W. S. Jackman, letter to Mrs. Blaine, December 15, 1900, Papers of Anita McCormick Blaine.

[34] "Trustees Name Faculty." The size of this library sounds reasonable because by all accounts he had an enormous personal collection when he lived in Englewood. See Amalie Hoffer, "The Chicago Normal Training School—A Dream Come True," *Kindergarten Magazine,* **4** (November 1896), 174–175; and Flora J. Cooke, "Colonel Francis W. Parker, His Influence on Education," *Chicago Schools Journal,* **29** (March 1938), 148. When Parker died he left only forty-five books. "A bill of appraisement of the estate of Francis W. Parker, late of the County of Cook and State of Illinois, deceased," Francis W. Parker, File 17/73/79, Docket 65, p. 297, Probate Court of Cook County, Chicago, Ill.

[35] "Comparison of Financial Features of Tripartite Agreement with what has been done, September 30, 1900," and "Directive authorizing movement of all the furniture, equipment, tools, etc. belonging to the Chicago Institute, and now in several buildings of McCormick Theological Seminary to Turngemeinde Building, 684 to 690 Wells Street, August 13, 1900," Papers of Anita McCormick Blaine.

[36] "Chicago Institute: Number of Pupils in School at present and possible, December 14, 1900," Papers of Anita McCormick Blaine.

[37] Perry Dunlap Smith, *op. cit.*

[38] *Ibid.*

[39] F. W. Parker, letter to Mrs. Blaine, March 28, 1901, The Papers of Anita McCormick Blaine.

[40] *Ibid.;* "The Course of Study," *The Course of Study,* **1** (July 1, 1900–June 1, 1901), 198.

[41] Perry Dunlap Smith, *op. cit.*

[42] F. W. Parker, letter to Mrs. Blaine, September 14, 1899, and a number of requests from Parker to the Board of Trustees for scholarships, the 1899 Folder, Papers of Anita McCormick Blaine.

[43] "June 9, 1899," and "June 10, 1899," Minutes of the Board of Trustees.

[44] "Dr. Harper," newspaper clipping, Parker Scrapbook, 1899. It was said that Parker came to the University of Chicago at the invitation of President Harper. Arthur G. Wirth, *John Dewey As Educator. His Design for Work in Education (1894–1904)* (New York: John Wiley and Sons, 1966), p. 216.

[45] "Harper Gets Parker"; "To Aid Teachers," *Chicago Times-Herald* (Chicago, Ill.), May 29, 1899; "University of Chicago College for Teachers," *Journal of Education,* **48** (September 8, 1898), 157.

[46] "Agreement, February 1, 1901," Papers of Anita McCormick Blaine.

[47] F. W. Parker, letter to John Dewey, February 9, 1901, Papers of Anita McCormick Blaine.

[48] F. W. Parker, letter to the Board of Trustees, July 31, 1899, and "Requisition, November 22, 1900," Papers of Anita McCormick Blaine.

[49] Arthur Gordon Melvin, *Education, A History* (New York: John Day, 1946), p. 323; Edna Parker Shepard, interview, October 14, 1962, Brookline, Mass.

[50] Parker once said, "in common with all teachers of Illinois I look to our State University as the true head of our common school system." Newspaper clipping, Parker Scrapbooks, 1894; John Dewey, "The School and Society," *Dewey On Education,* with an introduction and notes by Martin S. Dworkin (New York: Teachers College Press, 1959), p. 76.

[51] F. W. Parker, letter to Mrs. Blaine, February 13, 1901, Papers of Anita McCormick Blaine.

[52] "Hard on Dr. Harper," *Journal of Education,* **48** (December 15, 1898), 388.

[53] "Chicago: Supt. Lane Re-elected," *School Journal,* **59** (July 15, 1899), 70.

[54] "Chicago University," *Journal of Education,* **53** (April 11, 1901), 236.

[55] "Grabbing for the Earth," newspaper clipping, Parker Scrapbooks, 1895.

[56] F. W. Parker, letters to Mrs. Blaine, February 13 and 18, 1901, Papers of Anita McCormick Blaine; Ida B. DePencier, *The History of the Laboratory Schools, The University of Chicago, 1896–1957* (Chicago: University of Chicago, 1960), p. 20; "Budget, Salaries of Faculty, 1901–1902" [Chicago Institute Folder], Papers of Anita McCormick Blaine. Parker's salary at the University of Chicago may be inferred from an uncashed check of $500 from that institution that was found at the time of his death. On the basis of $500 a month, Parker's salary would have been $5,000 for a ten-month year or $6,000 for a twelve-month year. "Personal Estate," Francis W. Parker, File 17/73/79, Docket 65, Probate Court of Cook County, Chicago, Ill.

[57] F. W. Parker, letter to Mrs. Blaine, February 13, 1901.

[58] F. W. Parker, letter to Mrs. Blaine, February 15, 1901, Papers of Anita McCormick Blaine.

[59] F. W. Parker, letter to The Rev. R. A. Torrey, March 2, 1900, Papers of Anita McCormick Blaine.

[60] Thomas Wakefield Goodspeed, *A History of the University of Chicago, The First Quarter-Century* (Chicago: University of Chicago Press, 1916), p. 328; "Chicago's Institute and University," *Journal of Education,* **53** (March 28, 1901) 204.

[61] "Contract with Exhibits, 16 April 1901," [Chicago Institute Folder], Papers of Anita McCormick Blaine.

[62] William R. Harper, letter to Mrs. Blaine, June 13, 1901, Papers of Anita McCormick Blaine; Thomas Wakefield Goodspeed, *op. cit.,* p. 353.

[63] *To The Patrons and Friends of the Chicago Institute, Chicago, 1 June 1901* (three-page announcement published by the Chicago Institute), Topping Collection. The transportation problem was noted by Perry Dunlap Smith, *op. cit.*

[64] William R. Harper, letter to Mrs. Blaine, May 21, 1901, The Papers of Anita McCormick Blaine; "Articles of Affiliation, Memorandum" (a photostatic copy of three pages), Topping Collection.

[65] *To the Patrons and Friends of the Chicago Institute, Chicago, 1 June 1901.*

[66] *Ibid.*

[67] Ida B. DePencier, *op. cit.*, pp. 1, 8; Arthur G. Wirth, *op. cit.*, p. 216; Harriet A. Farrand, "Dr. Dewey's University Elementary School," *Journal of Education,* **48** (September 15, 1898), 172.

[68] Robert L. McCaul, "Dewey and the University of Chicago, July 1894–March 1902," *School and Society,* **89** (March 25, 1961), 153–154.

[69] F. W. Parker, letter to Mrs. Blaine, May 1, 1901, Papers of Anita McCormick Blaine.

[70] Robert L. McCaul, *op. cit.*, pp. 153–154; Robert L. McCaul, "Dewey's Chicago," *The School Review* (Summer 1959), 276. In a letter to Harper on June 23, 1898, Dewey insisted on keeping the classes small in size. Arthur G. Wirth, *op. cit.*, p. 70.

XV

The Parker Burial

Parker's physical and mental vitality had begun to decline when he left the public schools in 1899 to take up the burden of founding the Chicago Institute. He greeted the twentieth century at a sanitorium in Alma, Michigan. Just before Christmas he told Mrs. Blaine he was going there for a little rest. He assured his patron that he was not sick, only "a bit worn." He had probably convinced himself that this was the extent of his miseries because he confided in a friend that his health was really "first class" and he only needed "building up" and a "good brain rest."[1]

No one knows the effort it cost the Colonel to resume work that winter of 1900. No one knows how tired he was when he accepted the honors of his profession at the "Quincy Celebration" that April. Twenty-five years of relentless effort since he began his experiments at Quincy had finally worn him down, even as he had reached the height of his career. He was now president of the Chicago Institute and associated with the dignity of the Blaine name and fortune. He had finally become an officer of the National Educational Association, after twenty years of harassing and overcoming its conservative membership. He had even found admittance to the select National Council for Education.[2]

It was at this time, nevertheless, that Parker planned for retirement rather than greater challenges and successes. His mind was wandering back to the land of his childhood as much as to the educational interests of children. The Colonel had decided to go out to pasture on a farm of his own in New Hampshire.[3]

Parker had always returned to New Hampshire whenever time permitted. He especially enjoyed visits with the family of his younger sister, Emily, on the Tolman farm in the rugged Mount Monadnock country of New Hampshire. Emily said of her brother that he liked to put on blue overalls and pretend he was a farmer. He had started out on a farm and had run away from it, but Parker had always said that he wanted to teach school because he liked to see things grow. Now, it would seem, he probably wanted to run back to the farm. He must have had an early retirement in mind, as well as the idea of a vacation retreat, when he sent his carriage and the family horses—Dandy and Ned—to the Tolman farm. He then planned to buy adjoining acreage and go into partnership with his relatives.[4]

These plans required money, and the work of a lifetime had not earned the Colonel enough substance to retire gracefully, even though he had enjoyed unusually high salaries for an educator and was used to large fees for lecturing. He wrote to Zonia Baber in 1897 that he was always "low in the purse," but especially so since losing all his money in a bank failure.[5] Therefore, even as he struggled with financial troubles at the Chicago Institute, he negotiated with Mrs. Blaine for a loan of $15,000, presumedly for his farm. It is not known whether he ever received this particular loan, but in August of 1900 he placed his house on Honore Street in the hands of a trustee as security for a $5,000 loan.[6] The next month, he proudly wrote Mrs. Blaine that he was on his own "farm," and inquired if she would like some potatoes or cider.[7]

Having established roots again in New Hampshire, Parker's life in Chicago became a purely professional matter. He changed residence several times and kept a housekeeper, but there was no family life left. He always lived close to some of his teachers, however, and hung a white handkerchief in his window when he wanted company for talk or cards.[8]

It was under such circumstances that Parker struggled to make the Chicago Institute a landmark in educational development and under such strain that he agreed to a merger with the University of Chicago. The merger left him once more without the physical facilities he needed to further his work, and time was running out. It was not until June of 1901 that ground was broken for the building which would house his work and life. At a simple ceremony, Parker ended his address with Froebel's "Come let us live with the children." He himself would never live with the children in this building which was to rise out of the ground where he pushed the first shovel.

The following month, Parker opened a summer session in a public school near the University. A temporary one-story brick building was being quickly erected, but it was unfinished when Parker began his school in October of 1901. One of the teachers remembered trying to teach to the "accompaniment of hammering, sawing, and planing."[9]

When the Department of Superintendence of the National Educational Association met in Chicago that winter, Parker's absence was excused on account of "impaired health." Although it was whispered that his case was serious, no one at the meeting was prepared for the sudden turn of events.[10]

Early in February of 1902, Parker placed himself under the care of Dr. Bayard Holmes. Complaining vaguely that he was sick, he told Holmes to do with him what he pleased. Strangely, Parker refused to allow Dr. Holmes to consult with his regular doctor. After a two hour examination, Dr. Holmes prescribed the milder and moister climate of Pass Christian, Mississippi, on the Gulf of Mexico.[11] Mrs. Blaine was informed that the Colonel was going south to recuperate from his winter difficulties with "grippe and complications."[12]

The nature of Parker's final illness is not clear. "Grippe" he may have had, but it was the matter of complications that surely proved fatal. It is likely that he was suffering from some form of neuritis.[13] Diabetes, which was said to run in the family, may have been a complication. Urinalysis, however, on various occasions showed no sugar.[14] Symptoms, nevertheless, were weakness, loss of balance, headaches, little appetite, and fever. Treatment included rest, hydrotherapy, and cathartics.[15]

Accompanied by a male nurse, Mr. Alfred C. Olson, Colonel Parker set out on his last journey. The train was involved in a wreck and delayed for a few hours near Jackson, Mississippi. After a brief stop in New Orleans, Parker and his companion arrived in Pass Christian, Mississippi. They registered at the Mexican Gulf Hotel about the middle of February. Parker approved of the country and climate.[16]

Shortly after his arrival, Parker took the air in a carriage, but lost his balance when he tried to walk. After that he continually suffered from dizziness, which Olson attributed to weakness. Olson wrote to Dr. Holmes in Chicago and reported that Parker ate almost nothing, except a little oatmeal and a few oysters. He said the cathartic medicine was very hard for him to take. Olson sincerely hoped, he said, that all would be well with Parker. The Colonel was very "kind and considerate," he wrote.[17]

Near the end of February, Parker told his nurse that his mind was clearer than it had been for months. He said he could control it better. Only a few days earlier, however, Olson had been alarmed because the Colonel seemed "so weak and stupid." In lucid moments, Parker must have worried about what would come of his work at the University of Chicago. He managed to dictate a letter to Dr. Holmes on February 24 in which he complained of weakness and a "copperic" taste in his mouth, but he could not tell whether he was better or not. "The question," he said, "whether I am better or not is one of importance to me . . . ."[18]

The question was of importance to the development of American education. The answer was not good for Parker. He had left his work behind forever. By the first of March, a specialist from New Orleans had to be called in for a consultation with the local doctor. Parker was then feverish and in a semi-comatose condition. He was not expected to survive the night. Olson dispatched telegrams frantically. To Parker's stepdaughter in the East he wired that "Col. Parker is dying."[19]

Dr. Holmes left Chicago immediately when Mrs. Blaine told him she would spare no expense. Wilbur Jackman, Dean of the Institute, was also speeding to his old friend's side. Edna, Parker's stepdaughter, and her husband, T. H. Shepard, were hurrying their departure from New York, but Parker died at 6:43, Sunday night, March 2, 1902, before any of his family or friends could reach him.[20]

Mrs. Blaine believed his "dying off alone was pathetic." Others believed his death was caused by a broken heart. Some said he had never recovered from the death of his wife. Others said he never recovered from the shock of moving into private education. His "boy" from Quincy, Isaac Freeman Hall, believed overwork had killed the Colonel.[21]

Mourners were told that they would not have recognized their Colonel at the end. All the belligerency was gone. His hand, in death, "stretched out helplessly, as if seeking the children," according to one reporter, and it was consoling to many when they learned the Colonel had spent his last conscious hours in the company of two little children at the hotel. That night he told his nurse he had "such a happy day."[22]

Parker's death in 1902 may be said to mark the end of an era. Queen Victoria, having given her name to an age, had passed away only a year earlier, after a reign that began in 1837, the year of Parker's birth. Parker's death followed the assassination of President William McKinley by only a few months and came at the time a new political era was inaugurated by Theodore Roosevelt, just as a new educational era was beginning under John Dewey.

Parker's death was not a national disaster. In fact, it was reported that, outside Chicago and vicinity, the newspapers either failed to mention his passing or gave only scanty and inaccurate accounts. Even in New York City, only one of the prominent dailies devoted more than a few lines to his memory. According to the *School Journal,* which Parker once edited, the controversy which had wrapped him in life was not undone even at the end. There still remained hostility and even a tendency to belittle him and his work.[23]

In Chicago, however, there were as many as five funerals for Parker's remains which had been carefully embalmed and shipped up from Pass Christian. A "Companion" of the State of Illinois Military Order of the Loyal Legion of the United States, Parker had military honors at the General Meade Post. There were services at the Chicago Normal School and possibly at the Universalist Church in Englewood. His body, still heavy and fleshy in spite of the last illness, lay in state at the Haskell Oriental Museum of the University of Chicago on March 6, 1902. Final tributes were made, amid the solemnity of cap and gown, at the chapel of Cobb Hall. There were addresses by such men as Harper and Dewey, but the greatest homage paid the Colonel was probably from the little children who filed past and dropped flowers in his coffin.[24]

More intimate services were held at his home. Some thought that Froebel's spirit was there. After the benediction, the close friends of Parker saw their Colonel for the last time, and he seemed "absolutely at rest."[25]

Letters and telegrams began to develop into a whole literature of tribute. John Dewey remembered Parker for three things—his education for citizenship, his faith in the professional training of teachers, and his love of children. Dewey credited Parker with pioneering the new education. He said Parker was inspired by Plato and Christ. William T. Harris mourned Parker as a friend, even though they often differed on educational matters. Harris said that Parker's work would live and "bless the generations yet to come." G. Stanley Hall compared Parker to Socrates as a man who stirred things up. Even Alexander Graham Bell added his voice to the testimony of educators when he said that the children of America had lost a great friend.[26]

In April of 1902 the public school teachers of Chicago and Cook County sponsored "Memorial Exercises" for Parker at the great Chicago Auditorium.[27] But even as he was honored, his estate was coveted. He had a few hundred dollars in cash, some copyrights worth a few hundred dollars more. There were uncashed checks from the University of Chicago and the United States Pension Commissioner amounting to little more than $500. His life was insured for approximately $6,000; his furniture of massive mahogany and oak, all his remaining books, pictures, and bric-a-brac, added up to about $500 more. After debts were paid, his total estate came to only around $5,000, but this was enough to make creditors and friends uncomfortable. The estate was tied up in litigation until July of 1906.[28]

The undertaker in Chicago complained to the undertaker in Pass Christian that the bad feature about their business was waiting so long for their money. Their job, however, was not finished. Early in April, after a month in the grave, Parker was removed to a crematory and reduced to ashes. He then began the descent from the minds of educational leaders to the earth from which he had sprung. The long journey was completed on May 8, 1902, when Parker's ashes were mixed with those of his wife and a huge boulder was rolled over their grave in the Parker plot at the Piscataquog Cemetery in Manchester, New Hampshire.[29]

Parker had made the full circle, back to the land where he had grown up. From Manchester he had gone off to war. Now the Civil War generation was passing away. Even the "Gibson Girl" and the Cigar Store Indian were buried with Parker, along with the horse and carriage.[30] It was a new world, for a new generation, and Parker was buried with praise but quickly forgotten. Perhaps the most fitting tribute for the man who had fought so hard for the children came from A. E. Winship, editor of the *Journal of Education.* He called Parker an abolitionist of educational slavery. He asked the living to be dedicated to the unfinished work which he said was thus far so nobly advanced, in order that "the American public school shall, under God, have a new birth of freedom; and that the schools of the people, by the people, and for the child shall not perish from our land."[31]

Mrs. Blaine had been deeply concerned when "the leader" was taken away, and she expressed the hope that his work would go on. It remained to be seen who could fill Parker's place. Parker probably had more disciples than any other American educator since Horace Mann, but he left no real memorial or institution "embodying his spirit or his purpose."[32] The Cook County Normal School had been left to go its own way. The Chicago Institute had died. The School of Education at the University of Chicago had not yet been brought to life.

According to the contract of affiliation with the University of Chicago, the Trustees of the Chicago Institute had the right to appoint a successor to the School of Education if Parker died before 1907. They turned to John Dewey.[33] President Harper then pledged the University to "go forward" with the work already started and to hold the course to Parker's purpose and spirit. At the same time he remarked that the greatness of Parker was not fully apparent until he was "taken away."[34]

Without Parker, the educational enterprise of the University of Chicago was having trouble. The School of Education and Dewey's own Department of Philosophy, Psychology, and Pedagogy had been merged. Dewey now held sway over a high school, two elementary schools, various manual training centers, as well as undergraduate and graduate faculties in teacher training, philosophy, and psychology. A powerful personality such as Parker's might have mobilized these separate forces into a common crusade for better education, but Dewey seemed to lack the temperament for such leadership.[35]

When Dewey tried to link the University Elementary School, staffed by Parkerites, with his own Laboratory School and place his wife in charge, he had a revolt on his hands. The whole School of Education was threatened.[36] Mrs. Blaine held an informal session of the old Chicago Institute's trustees to entertain some of the complaints. Miss Emily Rice, who had been associated with Parker at the Normal School since 1883, strongly opposed Mrs. Dewey as principal. She talked of "troublous" conversations with John Dewey and complained that she was being "pushed into a corner."[37]

Dewey found relief from the administrative nightmare by resigning after the school year of 1904. When he moved East to Columbia University, he left the Parker disciples without a great leader. Wilbur S. Jackman carried on in the Parker fashion as best he could until his sudden death in 1907. No director of the School of Education was appointed until 1909, when Charles Hubbard Judd succeeded to the position. A great educator in his own right, Judd brought national recognition to the University School of Education with his program of measuring and testing, but he was not really in the Parker line of thought.[38]

Judd honored Parker, but according to one of Parker's disciples, Judd really "buried" the Colonel.[39] The new director of the School of Education believed that it required a genius to teach Parker's way. Judd wanted a "model T" plan that could be mass-produced for the average teacher's use. The Parkerites argued, in vain, that only idiots would go into teaching if lesson plans were developed for idiots to follow.[40]

Even where Parker was remembered, his vital touch was buried with him. Parker left no system for teachers to follow. This was the bane of his followers. Flora Cooke of the Francis W. Parker School was hard pressed by parent to explain why there was no "Parker method."[41] Parker had accepted no creed from the past and he refused to impose one on the future. He did not even suggest a watchword under which his disciples might rally. He left few books, and Jackman believed that those who knew Parker would not read them except as they represented history, "so far do they fall below the level of what he actually was in his work . . . ." This view was shared by several others who had worked with Parker.[42]

Wilbur Jackman recalled Parker's great flexibility of mind, but he he found this thinking was often "absurdly inconsistent." He said the rapid "shifting from point to point in the course of his thinking and exposition was often the despair of his students and faculty . . . ."[43] If

Parker's thinking was hard to follow in life, it would be impossible to follow in death. Nevertheless, John Dewey called Parker the father of Progressive Education, and the Progressive Education Association paid its respects to Parker when it was founded in 1919 and again in 1937 during the centennial celebration of Parker's birth.[44]

What had come to be called Progressive Education, however, was probably Parker's inspiration only to the extent that he made the whole nation aware of its new educational needs. The theories and methods were already practiced in various isolated places. Parker appropriated and tested them, but it was his dramatic conflicts with traditional educators and conservative boards of education that brought his work to the attention of the public. He could make "headlines" and "news" out of the new education at a time when newspapers, with their "muckraking" and "yellow journalism," were shaping public opinion.

Parker lectured extensively and was famed as a "lecturer for the masses." He even toured theaters with troupes of children and gave demonstration lessons which illustrated the magic of his methods. He was close to the people. He would "bubble" forth in "funny stories" and even engage in mimicry. He could lose his temper and fly off in wild passions.[45] Parker lacked the "education" and polish to speak effectively to the highly educated, even to those who supported him.[46] He could, however, reach the people. Since the people actually controlled the schools, Parker made it easier for intellectuals such as John Dewey to gain a public hearing later on.

Parker's enormous impact on the education of his time was therefore largely personal. Even in 1883, when he was introduced to the teachers of Illinois, Parker was called the "Quincy Method" in person.[47] He was a familiar figure, smiling and bowing his acknowledgments, as he came down the aisles of educational meetings and institutes throughout the country. His trademarks were personal—the big man with a round, bald head, a "walrus" mustache, squinting eyes, erect-military bearing, a bullet scar on his neck, a hoarse and wheezy voice, a shortness of breath.[48]

After his death there was no hard-hitting educator with a sense of showmanship and a common touch. Just six years after he was gone, it was observed that Parker's name was hardly used in the faculty meetings of the Francis W. Parker School in Chicago. His personality had been so dominant that teachers followed his commands, but, without his personal leadership, they were unable to know what Parker really wanted. Willard S. Bass, one of the first teachers Parker had hired when he went into private education, told the Francis W. Parker School faculty, mostly strangers to the Parker personality by 1908, that Parker did not want teachers to think the way he did. He wanted teachers to think for themselves.[49]

Parker was a dominant influence only in life. There was an attempt in 1941 to revive Parker's thinking, but his ideas without his life were doomed to failure. The "Francis W. Parker Society" was founded in New York by Professor A. Gordon Melvin of City College. Melvin had become disillusioned with Progressive Education until he found the "springs of Parkerism and Deweyism" were different. Parker, he believed, was much more sensitive of the "miraculous potential of human beings." Parker's pedagogy was not "soft" or lacking in fundamental direction. This Society, which tried to untangle the strands of Parker from the Gordian knot of Progressive Education, consisted mainly of a small group of friends who met informally for dinner. No records were kept and no meetings were called after 1943. Professor Melvin blamed the failure on the lack of a direct or living connection between any of the members and Parker. He also blamed the failure on the "cultural milieu" of New York in which most educators looked to Dewey. It was generally believed that Dewey had superseded Parker and any differences which Parker represented were old-fashioned or naive.[50]

The differences which Parker represented survived only in a few private schools.[51] The best application of his methods in public schools was probably worked out in Winnetka, Illinois. The "Winnetka" educational experiment was led by Carleton Washburne, son of Parker's public relations woman. He was a student of the Colonel as well as of Miss Cooke. Perry Dunlap Smith, another student of Parker's, established the private North Shore Country Day School in Winnetka. These schools, both public and private, formed a model which exerted the kind of concrete influence which Parker himself represented in life. The schools merged their facilities for the establishment of the "Graduate Teachers College of Winnetka," and the advisory board of illustrious educators included such names as William H. Kilpatrick and Harold Rugg.[52]

In 1957 the Parker Society was reincarnated in the form of the Parker Foundation, incorporated in Oklahoma. Helen F. Topping, a former student of Parker's, has supplied the initiative, and apparently much of the support herself. Her purpose is to promote world peace and democracy through the proletarian Christianity of the Japanese writer, Toyohiko Kagawa, as well as through the teachings of Parker.[53] Such a merger of East and West was not inconsistent with Parker's ideals of unity, brotherhood, and love.

Parker is survived by the science of education, which he strenuously promoted. It has been established in almost every institution of higher learning. The questions of educational purpose, content, and method, however, are as controversial as ever. Parker's work remains unfinished, but this must be as the Colonel would have wanted it.

NOTES

[1] F. W. Parker, letter to Mrs. Blaine, December 19, 1899, Papers of Anita McCormick Blaine, McCormick Collection, Wisconsin State Historical Society, Madison, Wis.; F. W. Parker, letter to Zonia Baber, January 3, 1900, Topping Collection, 1325 Stony Brook Lane, Mountainside, N. J.

[2] Report of the Committee on Nominations, July 12, 1900," and "National Council of Education," *Journal of Proceedings and Addresses, National Educational Association, 1900,* pp. 25, 300.

[3] Sadie French Tolman and Newton F. Tolman, personal interviews, October 13, 1962, Tolman Farm, Nelson, N. H. [Mrs. Sadie Tolman, Parker's niece by marriage, remembered these events clearly although she is in her nineties. Her son, Newton F. Tolman, was brought up on Parker anecdotes, and corroborated his mother's accounts.]

[4] Francis W. Parker, "Autobiographical Sketch," appendix in William M. Giffin, *School Days in the Fifties* (Chicago: A. Flanagan Co., 1906), p. 133; Sadie French Tolman and Newton F. Tolman, *op cit.*

[5] F. W. Parker, letter to Zonia Baber, May 5, 1897, Topping Collection. Corroborated by Edna Parker Shepard, personal interview, October 14, 1962, Brookline, Mass.

[6] F. W. Parker, letter to Mrs. Blaine, June 16, 1900, Papers of Anita McCormick Blaine; "Real Estate Inventory," Estate of Francis W. Parker, File 17/7379, Docket 65, Probate Court of Cook County, Chicago, Ill. Newton F. Tolman said Parker acquired half his parents' property at Tolman Pond, but left the property in such a way that it would revert back to the Tolmans when he died. Newton F. Tolman, letter to the present author, September 11, 1962.

[7] F. W. Parker, letter to Mrs. Blaine, September 14, 1900, Papers of Anita McCormick Blaine.

[8] Sadie French Tolman, *op. cit.* In 1900 his address was reported as 1931 Deming Place, within a few blocks of Lincoln Park and the proposed site of the Chicago Institute. *Journal of Proceedings and Addresses, National Educational Association, 1900,* p. 739. His last address was 5801 Washington, where his final services were held. Faculty of School of Education, letter to Mrs. Blaine, March 4, 1902, Papers of Anita McCormick Blaine.

[9] William R. Harper, "Address Delivered at the Services Held in Memory of Colonel Parker at the University of Chicago, March 6, 1902," *Education Report, 1901–1902* (U.S. Office of Education, Report of the Commissioner of Education for the year 1902), p. 265; Ida B. DePencier, *The History of the Laboratory Schools, The University of Chicago, 1896–1957* (Chicago: University of Chicago, 1960), pp. 21-23.

[10] "Department of Superintendence, Chicago Meeting, 1902, Third Day," *Journal of Proceedings and Addresses, National Educational Association,*

1902, p. 155; "The Late Colonel F. W. Parker," *Journal of Education,* **55** (March 6, 1902), 156.

[11] Dr. Bayard Holmes letter to Mrs. Shepard, April 8, 1902, Francis W. Parker, 1837–1902, Telegrams and Memoranda, Collections, Chicago Historical Society, Chicago, Ill.

[12] Anita McCormick Blaine, letter to "Darling Missy," March [?], 1902, Papers of Anita McCormick Blaine.

[13] No death certificate is available because the State of Mississippi did not begin to keep birth and death records until November 1, 1912. The Lang Funeral Home, where Parker was embalmed, is still in operation. According to its records, Parker died of "Nemitis." The word could not be clearly made out. Arthur W. Lang, Jr., letter to the present author, March 7, 1964. A survey of various medical dictionaries did not reveal any reference to nemitis. "Neuritis," however, might have been the word.

[14] Sadie French Tolman, *op. cit.* Urinalysis is mentioned in Alfred C. Olson letters to Dr. Holmes, February 15, 18, 21, and March 1, 1902, and Dr. A. R. Robertson, Urinalysis Report, Feb. 20, 1902, Telegrams and Memoranda.

[15] Numerous letters from Alfred C. Olson to Dr. Holmes, Telegrams and Memoranda.

[16] Alfred C. Olson, letter to Dr. Bayard Holmes, February 15, 1902, Telegrams and Memoranda.

[17] Alfred C. Olson, letters to Dr. Bayard Holmes, February 23 and 26, 1902, Telegrams and Memoranda.

[18] Alfred C. Olson, letter to Dr. Bayard Holmes, February 26, 1902; F. W. Parker, letter [dictated] to Dr. Bayard Holmes, February 24, 1902, Telegrams and Memoranda.

[19] Alfred C. Olson, telegrams to Dr. Bayard Holmes, March 1, 1902, 6:40 p.m. and 9:45 p.m., and telegrams to T. H. Shepard, March 2, 1902, 11:10 a.m. and 4.45 p.m., Telegrams and Memoranda.

[20] Dr. Bayard Holmes, letter to Mrs. Blaine, August 8, 1902, and letter to Mrs. Shepard, April 8, 1902; Anita McCormack Blaine, letter to Dr. Bayard Holmes, August 27, 1902; W. S. Jackman, telegram to Anna A. Chisholm, March 2, 1902, 8:22 p.m.; and Alfred C. Olson telegram to *Chicago Record Herald,* March 2, 1902, 8:50 p.m., all in Telegrams and Memoranda.

[21] Anita McCormick Blaine, letter to "Darling Missy," March [?] 1902; A. E. Winship, "Colonel Parker as a Leader," *Journal of Education,* **55** (May 15, 1902) 314; Margaret A. Haley, "From the Funeral," *Journal of Education,* **55** (March 27, 1902), 205; Isaac Freeman Hall, *In School from Three to Eighty* (Pittsfield, Mass.: The Eagle Printing and Binding Co., 1927), p. 186.

[22] Margaret A. Haley, *op. cit.,* p. 205; Alice H. Putnam, "A Memorial letter from Alice H. Putnam," *Kindergarten Review,* **12** (April 1902), 502–503.

[23] "Francis Wayland Parker Died March 2," *School Journal,* **64** (March 8, 1902), 284.

[24] Margaret A. Haley, *op cit.,* p. 205; "Last Rites for Col. Parker," newspaper clipping, Topping Collection; *Memorials of Deceased Companions of the Commandery of the State of Illinois Military Order of the Loyal Legion of the United States, From July 1, 1901, to December 31, 1911,* Vol. 2 (Chicago: 320 Ashland Block, 1912), p. 41; W. A. Cunningham, letter to

John H. Lang, March 12, 1902; John Lang, letter to George Hall, May 15, 1902; and A. Chrisholm telegram to Mrs. T. H. Shepard, March 3, 1902, all in Telegrams and Memoranda.

[25] Alice H. Putnam, *op. cit.*, pp. 502–503.

[26] "Addresses, Letters and Telegrams," *Education Report, 1901–1902* (U.S. Office of Education, Report of the Commissioner of Education for the year 1902), pp. 267–268, 271–273; "Dr. W. T. Harris," *Journal of Education,* **55** (March 27, 1902), 200.

[27] *In Memoriam: Colonel Francis Wayland Parker, October 9, 1837–March 2, 1902, Memorial Exercises Given by the Public School Teachers of Chicago and Cook County, Auditorium, April 19, 1902* [pamphlet form] (Chicago: Thos. P. Halpin and Company, Printers, n.d.).

[28] The sole heir was Edna Parker Shepard, but she herself showed no interest in the estate other than using the money for some kind of memorial for the Colonel. Estate of Francis W. Parker, File 17/7379, Docket 65, Probate Court of Cook County, Chicago, Ill.; Dr. Bayard Holmes, letter to Mrs. Shepard, April 8, 1902, Telegrams and Memoranda.

[29] W. A. Cunningham letters to John H. Lang, March 12 and April 19, 1902, Francis W. Parker, 1837–1902, Telegrams and memoranda, Collections, Chicago Historical Society; "Last Rites for Col. Parker," "Many Gaze on Noted Educator's Calm Face," and "Last Tribute to Col. Parker," newspaper clippings in Death Notices of Topping Collection; photograph of the stone taken by the author in cemetery, Manchester, N. H., on October 14, 1962.

[30] Suggested by Mark Sullivan, *Our Times, The United States, 1900–1925,* Vol. I (New York: Charles Scribner's Sons, 1926), pp. 194, 213, 230, 259, 268, 283, 475–504.

[31] A. E. Winship, *op. cit.*, p. 314.

[32] Anita McCormick Blaine letter to "Darling Missy," March [?] 1902; "The Late Colonel F. W. Parker," *Journal of Education,* **55** (March 6, 1902), 156; "Educational Monument," *Journal of Education,* **55** (March 27, 1902), 204.

[33] "Contract, Exhibit C" [Chicago Institute Folder], Papers of Anita McCormick Blaine; Robert L. McCaul, "Dewey and the University of Chicago, April 1902–May 1903," *School and Society,* **89** (April 8, 1961), 179; Ida B. DePencier, *op. cit.*, p. 24.

[34] William R. Harper, "The Educational Progress of the Year 1901–1902," *Journal of Proceedings and Addresses, National Educational Association, 1902,* pp. 349–350.

[35] Robert L. McCaul, *op. cit.*, p. 180.

[36] *Ibid.*

[37] "April 25, 1902," Minutes of the Board of Trustees [Chicago Institute Proceedings, recorded by hand in a ledger by Mrs. Blaine, Secretary of the Board], Papers of Anita McCormick Blaine.

[38] Robert L. McCaul, *op. cit.*, pp. 181–182; Robert L. McCaul, "Dewey and the University of Chicago, September 1903–June 1904," *School and Society,* **89** (April 22, 1961), 202; Ida DePencier, *op. cit.*, pp. 29, 37–38, 58, 61; Lawrence A. Cremin, *The Transformation of the School, Progressivism in American Education, 1876–1957* (New York: Alfred A. Knopf, 1961), pp. 186–187.

[39] Judd honored Parker with a biographical sketch, Charles H. Judd,

"Francis Wayland Parker," *Dictionary of American Biography,* **14** (New York: Charles Scribner's Sons, 1934), p. 221. It was the opinion of Gudrun Thompsen, a member of Parker's faculty at the Chicago Institute and University of Chicago, that Judd was a good one to "bury" the Colonel. Leif Thorne Thompsen, personal interview by telephone, April 25, 1962, Chicago, Ill. [Mr. Thompsen is the son of Gudrun Thompsen.]

[40] Perry Dunlap Smith, personal interview, April 26, 1962, Winnetka, Ill. [Mr. Smith participated in these discussions which involved Charles H. Judd and Flora Cooke.]

[41] Flora J. Cooke, "Colonel Francis W. Parker, His Influence on Education," *Chicago Schools Journal,* **19** (March 1938), 153.

[42] *Ibid.;* John W. Cook, "Remarks," *Journal of Proceedings and Addresses, National Educational Association, 1902,* p. 407; Wilbur S. Jackman, "Colonel Francis Wayland Parker," *Journal of Proceedings and Addresses, National Educational Association, 1902,* p. 401.

[43] *Ibid.*

[44] Lawrence A. Cremin, *op. cit.,* pp. 21, 129, 247; *Progressive Education,* **14** (December 1937), was devoted to centennial celebration of Parker's birth.

[45] Parker's face was said to "light up as from an intensely inward fire," but blaze into a volcano when he was attacked. Untitled newspaper clipping, December 27, 1883, Parker Scrapbooks, 1883, Archives, Harper Library, University of Chicago. Parker's humorous manner was described in "Pedantry Assailed," newspaper clipping in Parker Scrapbooks, 1896. Parker was advertised as the "lecturer for the Masses" when he delivered his "Great Popular Lecture 'Education by Doing'." Printed poster, Parker Scrapbooks, 1887. Parker claimed he had visited 21 states to speak at teachers' conventions and institutes by 1893. "The Need of the Hour," newspaper clipping, Parker Scrapbooks, 1893. Parker's demonstration class was seen at McVickers Theatre in Chicago. Perry Dunlap Smith, *op. cit.*

[46] Mrs. Emmons Blaine, "Francis Wayland Parker," *Dedication of the Chicago Normal School, April 20, 21, 1906* (Chicago: The Chicago Normal School Press, n.d.), p. 76.

[47] John Williston Cook, *Educational History of Illinois* (Chicago: The Henry O. Shepard Co., 1912), p. 274.

[48] M. S. Fenner and J. C. Soule, "Francis W. Parker—Liberator of the Classroom," *National Education Association Journal,* **35** (October 1946), 395; Flora J. Cooke, "Colonel Francis W. Parker as I Knew Him," *Illinois Teacher,* **24** (June 1936), 325; Florence C. Fox, "A Personal Glimpse of Colonel Parker," *Progressive Education,* **9** (January 1932), 59.

[49] Willard S. Bass, "Colonel Parker's Influence in the Parker School" (typewritten manuscript of address given at a faculty dinner on June 16, 1908), Topping Collection.

[50] "The Francis W. Parker Society," *"School and Society,* **54** (November 22, 1941), 474; A. Gordon Melvin, letter to the present author, October 29, 1962.

[51] Such schools were the Francis W. Parker schools of Chicago, San Diego, and Los Angeles; the Shady Hill School of Cambridge, Mass; the Hessian Hills School at Croton-on-Hudson, N. Y.; Edgewood School at Greenwich, Conn.; Sunset Hill School at Kansas City; the Ojai Valley School in California. Edward Dangler, "Francis Wayland Parker's Educational

Philosophy: Its Origins, Contents, and Consequences," *Abstracts of Theses October 1939–June 1939, New York University* (New York: New York University, 1940), pp. 15–17. [The complete dissertation has, unfortunately, been lost.]

[52] Carleton W. Washburne and Sidney P. Marland, Jr., *Winnetka: The History and Significance of an Educational Experiment* (Englewood Cliffs, N. J.: Prentice Hall, 1963), pp. 11, 19, 154–158, 125; *The Graduate Teachers College of Winnetka* (Bulletin, 1941–1943), Topping Collection; Perry Dunlap Smith, *op. cit.*

[53] Helen F. Topping, personal interviews, summer 1962, Downers Grove and Naperville, Ill.; State of Oklahoma, Department of State, Certificate of Incorporation, Topping Collection.

Bibliography

I. Books and Pamphlets

Abbott, Rev. Stephen G. *The First Regiment New Hampshire Volunteers in the Great Rebellion.* Keene, N.H.: Sentinel Printing Co., 1890.

Adams, Charles Francis, Jr. *An Autobiography.* Boston: Houghton Mifflin, 1916.

———. *History of Braintree, Massachusetts, 1693–1708; The North Precinct of Braintree (1708–1792), and The Town of Quincy (1792–1889).* Cambridge, Mass. Riverside Press, 1891.

———. *The Public Library and the Public Schools.* Boston: Estes and Lauriat, 1879.

Adams, Henry. *The Education of Henry Adams.* New York: Random House, 1931.

Addams, Jane. *Twenty Years at Hull House.* New York: New American Library, A Signet Classic, 1961.

Aiken, Henry D. *The Age of Ideology, The Nineteenth Century Philosophers.* New York: Mentor Books, The New American Library, 1961.

Andreas, Alfred T. *History of Cook County from Earliest Period to Present Times.* Vol. III. Chicago: A. T. Andreas Co. Publishers, 1886.

Bailey, Thomas A. *The American Pageant, A History of the Republic.* Boston: D. C. Heath, 1956.

Bartlett, Capt. A. W. *History of the Twelfth Regiment New Hampshire Volunteers in the War of Rebellion.* Concord, N.H.: Ira C. Evans, Printer, 1897.

Bestor, Arthur E., Jr. *Backwoods Utopias, The Secretarian and Owenite Phases of Communitarian Socialism in America: 1663–1829.* Philadelphia: University of Pennsylvania Press, 1950.

Bowman, Col. S. M., and Lt. Col. R. B. Irwin. *Sherman and His Campaigns: A Military Biography.* New York: Charles B. Richardson, 1865.

Browne, Waldo R. *Altgeld of Illinois.* New York: B. W. Heubsch, 1924.

Butterfield, Roger. *The American Past.* New York: Simon and Schuster, 1957.

Butts, R. Freeman. *A Cultural History of Education.* New York: McGraw-Hill, 1947.

Catton, Bruce. *Terrible Swift Sword.* Garden City, New York: Doubleday, 1963.

Commager, Henry Steel. *Theodore Parker.* Boston: Beacon Press, 1960.

________. *The American Mind, An Interpretation of American Thought and Character Since the 1880's* New Haven, Conn.: Yale University Press, 1959.

________ (Ed.). *Documents of American History.* New York: F. S. Crofts, 1947.

Conover, Charlotte Reeve (Ed.). *Dayton and Montgomery County, Resources and People.* New York: Lewis Historical Publishing Co., 1932.

Cook, John Williston. *Educational History of Illinois.* Chicago: Henry O. Shepard Company, 1912.

Cremin, Lawrence A. *The Transformation of the School, Progressivism in American Education, 1876–1957.* New York: Alfred A. Knopf, 1961.

________ (Ed.). *The Republic and the School, Horace Mann on the Education of Free Men.* New York: Teachers College Press, Teachers College, Columbia University, 1957.

________, David A. Shannon, and Mary Evelyn Townsend. *A History of Teachers College, Columbia University.* New York: Columbia University Press, 1954.

Curti, Merle. *The Social Ideas of American Educators* (new ed.). Paterson, N.J.: Littlefield, Adams, 1959.

David, Henry. *The History of the Haymarket Affair.* New York: Farrar and Rinehart, 1936.

Dedication of the Chicago Normal School, April 20 and 21, 1906. Chicago: Normal School Press, n.d.

DePencier, Ida B. *The History of the Laboratory Schools, The University of Chicago, 1896–1957.* Chicago: The University of Chicago, 1960.

Dewey, John. *The Child and the Curriculum: The School and Society.* Chicago: University of Chicago Press, 1956.

________. *Democracy and Education, An Introduction to the Philosophy of Education.* New York: Macmillan, 1950.

________. *German Philosophy and Politics.* New York: Henry Holt, 1915.

Drury, Rev. A. W. *History of the City of Dayton and Montgomery County, Ohio.* Vol I. Chicago: S. J. Clarke Publishing Co., 1909.

Dworkin, Martin S. (Ed.). *Dewey On Education, Selections with an Introduction and Notes.* New York: Teachers College Press, Teachers College, Columbia University, 1959.

Dyer, Frederick H. (Ed.). *A Compendium of the War of the Rebellion.* Des Moines, Iowa: Dyer Publishing Co., 1908.

Eisenschiml, Otto, and Ralph Newman (Ed.). *The Civil War, The American Iliad as Told by Those Who Lived It.* Vol. I. Introduction by Bruce Catton. New York: Grosset and Dunlap, 1956.

Fogg, A. J. (Compiler). *The Statistics and Gazetteer of New Hampshire.* Concord, N.H.: D. L. Guernsey, Bookseller and Publisher, 1874.

Frances Stuart Parker, Reminiscences and Letters. Chicago: C. L. Ricketts, 1907.

Francis Wayland Parker: His Life and Educational Reform Work, Souvenir Issued in Honor of the Silver Anniversary of the Quincy Movement. New York: E. L. Kellogg and Co., April 1900.

Fuess, Claude M., and Emory S. Basford (Eds.). *Unseen Harvests, A Treasury of Teaching.* New York: Macmillan, 1947.

Giffin, William M. *School Days in the Fifties.* Chicago: A. Flanagan Co., 1906.

Ginger, Ray. *Altgeld's America, The Lincoln Ideal Versus Changing Realities.* New York: Funk and Wagnalls, 1958.

Goodspeed, Thomas Wakefield. *A History of the University of Chicago, The First Quarter-Century.* Chicago: University of Chicago Press, 1916.

Grierson, Francis. *The Valley of Shadows.* Boston: Houghton Mifflin, 1948.

Guide to the Central National Soldiers' Home for Visitors and Citizens with Sketches of Dayton. Dayton, Ohio: The Guide Publishing Co., 1891.

Hall, Isaac Freeman. *In School from Three to Eighty.* Pittsfield, Mass.: The Eagle Printing and Binding Co., 1927.

Hamilton, Robert R., and Paul R. Mort. *The Law and Public Education.* Brooklyn, New York: The Foundation Press, 1959.

Heffran, Ida Cassa. *Francis Wayland Parker, An Interpretive Biography.* Los Angeles: Ivan Deach, Jr., 1934.

Higginson, Thomas Wentworth. *Army Life in a Black Regiment.* Boston: Beacon Press, 1962.

Historical Sketch of the Young Men's Christian Association of Chicago, 1858–1898. Chicago: R. R. Donnelly and Sons, 1898.

Historical Statistics of the United States, Colonial Times to 1957. Washington, D.C.: U.S. Bureau of the Census, 1960.

History of Bedford, New Hampshire Being Statistics, compiled on the Occasion of the One Hundredth Anniversary of the Incorporation of the Town, May 19, 1850. Boston: Printed by Alfred Mudge, No. 21 School Street, 1851.

History of Bedford, New Hampshire, Being Statistics, compiled on the Occasion of the One Hundredth and Fiftieth Anniversary of the Incorporation of the Town, May 15, 1900. Concord, N.H.: Rumford Printing Co., 1903.

History of Dayton, Ohio, With Portraits and Biographical Sketches of Some of Its Pioneer and Prominent Citizens. Dayton, Ohio: United Brethren Publishing House, 1889.

History of Greene and Jersey Counties, Illinois. Springfield, Ill.: Continental Historical Co., 1885.

History of Greene County, Illinois: Its Past and Present, Illustrated. Chicago: Donnelly, Gassette and Loyd, 1879.

Hoffding, Harold. *A History of Modern Philosophy, A Sketch of the History of Philosophy from the Close of the Renaissance to Our Own Day.* B. E. Meyer (Trans.). Vol. II. London: Macmillan, 1935.

Hofstadter, Richard. William Miller, and Daniel Aaron. *The United States, The History of a Republic.* Englewood Cliffs, N.J.: Prentice-Hall, 1957.

________. *The Age of Reform, From Bryan to F.D.R.* New York: Vintage Books, 1955.

________. *Social Darwinism in American Thought.* Boston: The Beacon Press, Inc., 1955.

Holmes, Burton. *Hawaiian Islands, Edge of China, Manila, Burton Holmes Travelogues.* Vol. 5. New York: McClure Co., 1910.

Hutchinson, John G. *Roster: Fourth Regiment New Hampshire Volunteers.* Manchester, N.H.: John B. Clark Co., 1896.

In Memoriam (Colonel Francis Wayland Parker, October 9, 1937–March 2,

1902. Memorial Exercises Given by the Public School Teachers of Chicago and Cook County. Auditorium, April 19, 1902). Chicago: Thomas P. Halpin and Co., Printers, n.d.

James, William. *Talks to Teachers on Psychology: And to Students on Some of Life's Ideals.* New York: Henry Holt and Company, 1916.

________. *Psychology.* New York: Henry Holt, 1900.

Kirkland, Edward Chase. *Charles Francis Adams, Jr., 1835–1915, The Patrician at Bay* (Cambridge, Mass.: Harvard University Press, 1965).

Kolesnik, Walter B. *Mental Discipline in Modern Education.* Madison, Wis.: The University of Wisconsin Press, 1962.

Krug, Edward A. (Ed.). *Charles W. Eliot and Popular Education.* New York: Teachers College Press, Teachers College, Columbia University, 1961.

Leech, Margaret. *In the Days of McKinley.* New York: Harper and Brothers, 1959.

________. *Reveille in Washington.* New York: Harper and Brothers, 1941.

Leidecker, Kurt F. *Yankee Teacher, The Life of William Torrey Harris.* New York: Philosophical Library, 1946.

Loewenberg, J. (Ed.). *Hegel Selections.* New York: Charles Scribner's Sons, 1929.

McPherson, Rosamond. *History of the Young Men's Christian Association of Dayton, Ohio, 1858–1953.* New York: Association Press, 1953.

Melvin, Arthur Gordon. *Education, A History.* New York: John Day Co., 1946.

Memorials of Deceased Companions of the Commandery of the State of Illinois Military Order of the Loyal Legion of the United States from July 1, 1901 to December 31, 1911. Vol. 2. Chicago: 320 Ashland Block, Chicago, Ill., 1912.

Miel, Alice. *Changing the Curriculum, A Social Process.* New York: Appleton-Century, 1946.

Miers, Earl Schenck (Ed.). *Wash Roebling's War, Being a Selection from the unpublished Civil War Letters of Washington Augustus Roebling.* Newark, Delaware: Printed at the Spiral Press and published in June 1961 for the friends of The Curtis Paper Company.

Muzzey, David Saville. *James G. Blaine, A Political Idol of Other Days.* New York: Dodd, Mead, 1935.

Nevins, Allan. *The War for the Union.* Vol. II. New York: Charles Scribner's Sons, 1960.

Parker, Augustus C. (Compiler). *Parker in America, 1630–1910.* Buffalo, New York: Niagara Frontier Publishing Co., n.d.

Parker, Francis Wayland. *Talks on Pedagogics, an Outline of the Theory of Concentration.* (Edited by Elsie A. Wygant and Flora J. Cooke.) New York: John Day Co., 1937.

________. *Talks on Teaching.* (Fifteenth Edition of *Notes of Talks on Teaching,* from New Plates.) New York: E. L. Kellogg and Co., 1903.

________. *The University of Chicago, The University Extension, The Lecture-Study Department No. 77, Science and Art of Teaching, Syllabus of a Course of Twelve Lecture Studies.* Chicago: The University of Chicago Press, 1895.

________. *Talks on Pedagogics, an Outline of the Theory of Concentration.* New York: E. L. Kellogg and Co., 1894.

________. *Outlines of How to Study Geography.* New York: D. Appleton, 1893.

———. *How to Study Geography*. New York: D. Appleton, 1890. (Reissued in 1892.)

———. *Arithmetical Charts*. Philadelphia: Cowperthwait and Co., 1887.

———. *Notes of Talks on Teaching*. (Reported by Lelia E. Patridge from Martha's Vineyard, Summer Institute, July 17 to August 19, 1882.) New York: E. L. Kellogg and Company, 1885. (Reissued as twelfth edition in 1891.)

———. *Tracts for Teachers. Spelling*. Boston: W. Small, 1882.

———. *Syllabus Arranged for How to Study Geography*. New York: D. Appleton, n.d.

———, and Nellie Lathrop Helm. *Uncle Robert's Geography. Play Time and Seedtime*. New York: D. Appleton, 1899.

———. *Uncle Robert's Geography. Uncle Robert's Visit*. New York: D. Appleton, 1897.

———. *Uncle Robert's Geography. On the Farm*. New York: D. Appleton, 1896.

———. *Uncle Robert's Geography. A River Journey*. New York: D. Appleton, 1904.

Parker, Francis Wayland, and Louis H. Marvel. *Supplementary Reading for Primary School*. Boston: R. S. Davis and Co., 1880.

Parker, Mrs. Frank Stuart. *Expression of Thought Through the Body*. Chicago: Physical Culture Extension Society, 1895.

Patridge, Lelia E. *The Quincy Methods*. New York: E. L. Kellogg and Co., 1885.

Patriot Souvenir Edition. Carrollton, Ill.: *Carrollton Patriot*, September 1896.

Paulsen, Friedrich. *An Autobiography*. New York: Columbia University Press, 1938. (Translated and edited by Theodore Lorenz, with a forward by Nicholas Murray Butler.)

———. *The German Universities, Their Character and Historical Development*. New York: Macmillan, 1895. (Authorized translation by Edward D. Perry, with an Introduction by Nicholas Murray Butler.)

Pettengill, Samuel B. *The College Cavaliers*. Chicago: H. McAllaster and Co., Printers, 1883.

Pierce, Bessie Louise. *A History of Chicago, The Rise of a Modern City, 1871–1893*. Vol. III. New York: Alfred A. Knopf, 1957.

Revised Register of the Soldiers and Sailors of New Hampshire in the War of the Rebellion, 1861–1866. Concord, N.H.: Ira C. Evans, Public Printer, 1895.

Roebling, Washington Augustus. *Wash Roebling's War, Being a Selection from the Unpublished Civil War Letters of Washington Augustus Roebling*. Earl Schenck Miers (Ed.). Newark, N.J.: The Curtis Paper Company, 1961.

Rogers, Dorothy. *Oswego: Fountainhead of Teacher Education, A Century in the Sheldon Tradition*. New York: Appleton-Century-Crofts, 1961.

Sanborn, Frank B. *New Hampshire, An Epitome of Popular Government*. Boston: Houghton Mifflin, 1904.

Sherman, John. *Recollections of Forty Years in the House, Senate and Cabinet, An Autobiography*. Vol I. Chicago: The Werner Co., 1895.

Spencer, Herbert. *Social Statics*. New York: Appleton, 1878.

———. *Essays on Education and Kindred Subjects*. (Introduction by Charles W. Eliot.) London: Everyman's Library, J. M. Dent and Sons, 1963.

Stead, William T. *If Christ Came to Chicago, A Plea for the Union of All Who Love in the Service of All Who Suffer.* Chicago: Laird and Lee, Publishers, 1894.

Stearns, Ezra S. (Compiler). *Genealogical and Family History of the State of New Hampshire.* Vol. I. Chicago: Lewis Publishing Co., 1908.

Steffens, Lincoln. *The Shame of the Cities.* New York: Sagamore Press, 1957.

________. *An Autobiography of Lincoln Steffens.* New York: Harcourt, Brace, 1931.

Sullivan, Gerald E. (Ed.). *The Story of Englewood, 1835–1923.* (Written and compiled under Englewood Businessmen's Association.) Chicago: Foster and McDonnell, 1924.

Sullivan, Mark. *The Turn of the Century, Our Times, The United States, 1900–1925.* New York: Charles Scribner's Sons, 1925.

Tate, Thomas T. *The Philosophy of Education, or The Principles and Practices of Teaching.* New York: E. L. Kellogg and Co., 1885.

Tharp, Louise Hall. *The Peabody Sisters of Salem.* Boston: Little Brown, 1950.

Tolman, Newton F. *North of Monadnock.* Boston: Little, Brown, 1961.

Washburne, Carleton W., and Sidney P. Marland, Jr. *Winnetka: The History and Significance of an Educational Experiment.* Englewood Cliffs, N.J.: Prentice Hall, 1963.

Wesley, Edgar B. *NEA: The First Hundred Years, The Building of the Teaching Profession.* New York: Harper and Brothers, 1957.

White, Morton. *Social Thought in America, The Revolt Against Formalism.* Boston: Beacon Press, 1959.

________. *The Age of Analysis, 20th Century Philosophers.* New York: Mentor Books, The New American Library of World Literature, Inc., 1955.

Wilson, Daniel Munro. *Three Hundred Years of Quincy, 1625–1925.* Quincy, Mass.: Published by authority of the City Government of Quincy, 1926.

Wilson, Ella C. *Pedagogues and Parents.* New York: Henry Holt, 1904.

Winch, George. *Outline History of State Work of the Young Men's Christian Associations of New Hampshire, 1852–1908.* Manchester, N.H.: Stratton, 1908.

Wirth, Arthur G. *John Dewey As Educator. His Design for Work in Education (1894–1904).* New York: John Wiley and Sons, 1966.

II. Encyclopedia Articles

Bates, Ernest Sutherland. "William Torrey Harris." *Dictionary of American Biography,* VIII. New York: Charles Scribner's Sons, 1943, pp. 328–330.

Eliot, Samuel A. "Samuel Chapman Armstrong." *Dictionary of American Biography,* VIII. New York: Charles Scribner's Sons, 1943, pp. 359–360.

Ford, Worthington Chauncey. "Charles Francis Adams, Jr." *Dictionary of American Biography,* I. New York: Charles Scribner's Sons, 1943, pp. 48–50.

Genzmer, George Harvey. "William J. Rolfe." *Dictionary of American Biography,* XVI. New York: Charles Scribner's Sons, 1943, pp. 118–119.

Johnson, Claudius O. "Carter Henry Harrison." *Dictionary of American Biography,* VIII. New York: Charles Scribner's Sons, 1943, pp. 335–356.

Judd, Charles H. "Francis Wayland Parker." *Dictionary of American Biography,* XIV. New York: Charles Scribner's Sons, 1934, p. 221.

Langer, William L. (Compiler and ed.). *Encyclopedia of World History*. Boston: Houghton Mifflin, 1956.

Morris, Richard B. (Ed.). *Encyclopedia of American History*. New York: Harper and Brothers, 1953.

"Parker, Francis W." *Encyclopedia of Biography of Illinois,* III. Chicago: The Century Publishing and Engraving Company, 1902, p. 407.

Shorey, Paul. "William Rainey Harper." *Dictionary of American Biography,* Allen Johnson (Ed.), VIII. New York: Charles Scribner's Sons, 1943, pp. 287–290.

Slade, William Adams. "Elisha Benjamin Andrews." *Dictionary of American Biography,* Allen Johnson (Ed.), I, pp. 286–290.

Tabor, Clarence Wilbur. *Taber's Cyclopedic Medical Dictionary*. Philadelphia: F. A. Davis Company, 1958.

III. Essays and Articles in Collections

Adams, Charles Francis, Jr. "The Development of the Superintendency." *Journal of Proceedings and Addresses, National Educational Association, 1880,* pp. 61–76.

Anthony, Susan B. "Letters of Condolence." *Frances Stuart Parker, Reminiscences and Letters.* Chicago: C. L. Ricketts, 1907, p. 123.

Barnes, Earl. "Punishment as Seen by Children." *Journal of Proceedings and Addresses, National Educational Association, 1895,* pp. 914–924.

Bell, Alexander Graham. "Letters and Telegrams from Friends." *Education Report, 1901–1902.* U.S. Office of Education, Report of the Commissioner of Education for the Year 1902, p. 272.

Blaine, Anita McCormick. "The Chicago Institute." *Frances Stuart Parker, Reminiscences and Letters.* Chicago: C. L. Ricketts, 1907, p. 38.

Blaine, Mrs. Emmons. "Francis Wayland Parker." *Dedication of the Chicago Normal School, April 20, 21, 1906.* Chicago: The Chicago Normal School Press, n.d., pp. 66–88.

Bright, Orville T. "Addresses at the Memorial Exercises Given by the Public School Teachers of Chicago and Cook County, Auditorium, April 19, 1902." *Education Report, 1901–1902.* U.S. Office of Education, Report of the Commissioner of Education for the Year 1902, pp. 273–276.

Butler, Nicholas Murray. "Forward." Friedrich Paulsen, *An Autobiography.* New York: Columbia University Press, 1938, pp. i–vii.

________. "Letters and Telegrams from Friends." *Education Report, 1901–1902.* U.S. Office of Education, Report of the Commissioner of Education for the Year 1902, p. 272.

________. "The Quincy Movement." *Education Report, 1901–1902.* U.S. Office of Education, Report of the Commission of Education for the Year 1902, pp. 242–244.

________. "Discussion of the Report of the Sub-committee on the Correlation of Studies in Elementary Education." *Journal of Proceedings and Addresses, National Educational Association, 1895,* pp. 347–348.

Champlin, Dr. A. H. "Memories of Normal." *Dedication of the Chicago Normal School, April 20, 21, 1906.* Chicago: Chicago Normal School Press, n.d., pp. 104–111.

Clark, John S. "The Aims of Art Education in General Education." *Journal of Proceedings and Addresses, National Educational Association, 1895,* pp. 808–834, 851–856.

Cook, John W. "Remarks." *Journal of Proceedings and Addresses, National Educational Association, 1902,* pp. 407–408.

Cooke, Flora J. "Sunday Evenings." *Frances Stuart Parker, Reminiscences and Letters.* Chicago: C. L. Ricketts, 1907, pp. 31–33.

Cooley, Edwin G. "The Chicago Teachers College." *Dedication of the Chicago Normal School, April 20, 21, 1906.* Chicago: The Chicago Normal School Press, n.d., pp. 39–65.

De Garmo, Charles. "The German System of Normal Schools." *Journal of Proceedings and Addresses, National Educational Association, 1887,* pp. 484–489.

———. "The Principles upon Which the Co-ordination of Studies Should Proceed." *Journal of Proceedings and Addresses, National Educational Association, 1895,* p. 96.

Dewey, John. "Letters of Condolence." *Frances Stuart Parker, Reminiscences and Letters.* Chicago: C. L. Ricketts, 1907, p. 121.

———. "Address . . . March 6, 1902." *Education Report, 1901–1902,* U.S. Office of Education, Report of the Commissioner of Education for the Year 1902, pp. 267–269.

Draper, A. S. "Letters and Telegrams from Friends." *Education Reports, 1901–1902.* U.S. Office of Education, Report of the Commissioner for the Year 1902, p. 271.

Fitzpatrick, Frank A. "Francis Wayland Parker." *Education Report, 1901–1902.* U.S. Office of Education, Report of the Commissioner of Education for the Year 1902, pp. 280–284.

Fleming, Martha. "Family and Home Life, Chicago." *Frances Stuart Parker, Reminiscences and Letters.* Chicago: C. L. Ricketts, 1907, pp 22–30.

Gilbert, C. B. "What Correlations of Studies Seem Advisable and Possible in the Present State of Advancement in Teaching?" *Journal of Proceedings and Addresses, National Educational Association, 1896,* pp. 299–308.

Gove, Aaron. "The Trial of the City Superintendent." *Journal of Proceedings and Addresses, National Educational Association, 1900,* pp. 217–218.

Greenwood, J. M. "Discussion of Parker's 'The Report of the Committee of Ten' . . ." *Journal of Proceedings and Addresses, National Educational Association, 1894,* p. 454.

Hall, G. Stanley. "The Content of Children's Minds." *Readings in Educational Psychology.* Charles Edward Skinner, Ira M. Gast, and Harley C. Skinner (Eds.). New York: D. Appleton, 1926, pp. 484–486.

———. "Discussion of William T. Harris' Paper on 'The Danger of Using Biological Analogies in Reasoning on Educational Subjects'." *Journal of Proceedings and Addresses, National Educational Association, 1902,* p. 221.

———. "Letters and Telegrams from Friends." *Education Reports, 1901–1902.* U.S. Office of Education, Report of the Commissioner of Education for the Year 1902, p. 273.

———. "Child Study." *Journal of Proceedings and Addresses, National Educational Association, 1894,* p. 174.

Harper, William R. "Address . . . March 6, 1902." *Education Report, 1901–1902.* U.S. Office of Education, Report of the Commissioner of Education for the Year 1902, pp. 279–280.

________. "The Educational Progress of the Year 1901–1902." *Journal of Proceedings and Addresses, National Educational Association, 1902,* pp. 349–353.

Harris, William T. "The Danger of Using Biological Aaalogies in Reasoning on Educational Subjects." *Journal of Proceedings and Addresses, National Educational Association, 1902,* p. 215.

________. "Colonel Parker and the Quincy School." *Education Report, 1901–1902.* U.S. Office of Education, Report of the Commissioner of Education for the Year 1902, pp. 245–248.

________. "Letters and Telegrams from Friends." *Education Report, 1901–1902.* U.S. Office of Education, Report of the Commissioner of Education for the Year 1902, p. 271.

________. "Discussion on the Subject of Simplified Spelling." *Journal of Proceedings and Addresses, National Educational Association, 1901,* p. 224.

________. "Comment on Demands of Sociology upon Pedagogy by Albion W. Small." *Journal of Proceedings and Addresses, National Educational Association, 1896,* pp. 196–198.

________. "The Necessity for Five Co-ordinate Groups of Studies in the Schools." *Journal of Proceedings and Addresses, National Educational Association, 1896,* p. 287.

________. "Discussion of the Report of the Sub-committee on the Correlation of Studies in Elementary Education." *Journal of Proceedings and Addresses, National Educational Association, 1895,* pp. 349–350.

Hirsch, Emil G. "Address . . . March 6, 1902." *Education Report, 1901–1902.* U.S. Office of Education, Report of the Commissioner of Education for the Year 1902, pp. 269–271.

Hoffer, Amalie. "The Social Settlement and the Kindergarten." *Journal of Proceedings and Addresses, National Educational Association, 1895,* pp. 518–520.

Howe, Julia Ward. "Association for the Advancement of Women." *Frances Stuart Parker, Reminiscences and Letters.* Chicago: C. L. Ricketts, 1907, p. ???

Jackman, Wilbur S. "Colonel Francis Wayland Parker." *Journal of Proceedings and Addresses, National Educational Association, 1902,* pp. 399–405.

________. "Francis Wayland Parker." *Education Report, 1901–1902.* U.S. Office of Education, Report of Commissioner of Education, 1902, pp. 231–237.

Johnson, Annie White. "Society for the Promotion of Correct Dress." *Frances Stuart Parker, Reminiscences and Letters.* Chicago: C. L. Ricketts, 1907, p. 59.

Journal of Proceedings and Addresses, National Educational Association, 1879–1902. (This annual publication appears under various titles and is published in various cities.)

Kellogg, A. M. "Col. Parker at Quincy and Chicago." *Francis Wayland Parker: His Life and Educational Reform Work. Souvenir Issued in Honor of the Silver Anniversary of the Quincy Movement.* New York: E. L. Kellogg and Co., 1900, pp. 42–45.

Kellogg, Eva D. "Progress in Primary Education." *Journal of Proceedings and Addresses, National Educational Association, 1895,* p. 1004.

Lewis, Cora E. "D. S. Wentworth." *Dedication of the Chicago Normal School, April 20, 21, 1906*. Chicago: Chicago Normal School Press, n.d., pp. 31–38.

Marble, A. P. "Discussion of Parker's 'The School of the Future'." *Journal of Proceedings and Addresses, National Educational Association, 1891*, p. 92.

Martin, Ellen A. "The Chicago Political Equality League." *Frances Stuart Parker, Reminiscences and Letters*. Chicago: C. L. Ricketts, 1907, p. 61.

Maxwell, W. H. "Discussion of William T. Harris's 'Curriculum in Secondary Schools'." *Journal of Proceedings and Addresses, National Educational Association, 1894*, pp. 508–509.

Mayo, Rev. A. D. "The New Teacher in the New America." *Journal of Proceedings and Addresses, National Educational Association, 1879*, pp. 57–69.

McMurry, Frank M. "Some Applications of Correlation." *Journal of Proceedings and Addresses, National Educational Association, 1896*, p. 529.

________. "Discussion of paper by Rev. James C. Mackenzie on 'The Feasibility of Modifying the Programs of the Elementary and Secondary Schools to Meet the Suggestions in the Report of the Committee of Ten'." *Journal of Proceedings and Addresses, National Educational Association, 1894*, p. 160.

"Mrs. Frank Stuart Parker." *Journal of Proceedings and Addresses, National Educational Association, 1899*, p. 246.

Parker, Francis Wayland. "Autobiographical Sketch." William M. Giffin. *School Days in the Fifties*. Chicago: A. Flanagan Company, 1906, pp. 109–137.

________. "An Account of the Work of the Cook Country and Chicago Normal School from 1883 to 1899." *Education Report, 1901–1902*. U.S. Office of Education, Report of the Commissioner of Education for the year 1902, pp. 248–264.

________. "The Quincy Method." *Education Report, 1901–1902*. U.S. Office of Education, Report of the Commissioner of Education for the Year 1902, pp. 237–242.

________. "Discussion of Domestic Science Conference." *Journal of Proceedings and Addresses, National Educational Association, 1901*, pp. 587–588.

________. "Henry Barnard as an Educational Critic." *Journal of Proceedings and Addresses, National Educational Association, 1901*, pp. 406–408.

________. "Discussion on Manual Training in Menomonite Schools." *Journal of Proceedings and Addresses, National Educational Association, 1901*, pp. 269, 646.

________. "Discussion on the Subject of Simplified Spelling." *Journal of Proceedings and Addresses, National Educational Association, 1901*, p. 216.

________. "Art in Everything." *Journal of Proceedings and Addresses, National Educational Association, 1900*, pp. 509–514.

________. "Discussion of W. T. Harris's 'Class Intervals in Graded Schools.' " *Journal of Proceedings and Addresses, National Educational Association, 1900*, p. 340.

________. "Discussion on What to Teach About Alkohol [alcohol]." *Journal of Proceedings and Addresses, National Educational Association, 1900* p. 255.

________. "The Farm as the Center of Interest." *Journal of Proceedings and Addresses, National Educational Association, 1897*, pp. 527–536.

———. "Work of the Illinois Society for Child Study." *Journal of Proceedings and Addresses, National Educational Association, 1896,* pp. 844–846.

———. "Address of Welcome." *Journal of Proceedings and Addresses, National Educational Association, 1895,* p. 61.

———. "Application of Child Study in the School." *Journal of Proceedings and Addresses, National Educational Association, 1895,* pp. 418–429.

———. "Discussion of John S. Clark's 'The Place of Art in General Education.'" *Journal of Proceedings and Addresses, National Educational Association, 1895,* pp. 846-851.

———. "Discussion of James L. Hughes's 'Comparison of the Educational Theories of Froebel and Herbart.'" *Journal of Proceedings and Addresses, National Educational Association, 1895,* p. 549.

———. "Discussion of the Report of the Sub-committee on the Correlation of Studies in Elementary Education, by William T. Harris." *Journal of Proceedings and Addresses, National Educational Association, 1895,* p. 344.

———. "Discussion of W. P. Search's 'Individualism in Mass Education.'" *Journal of Proceedings and Addresses, National Educational Association, 1895,* p. 408.

———. "Fourth Regiment, New Hampshire Volunteer Infantry." *Revised Register of the Soldiers and Sailors of New Hampshire in the War of the Rebellion, 1861–1866.* Concord, N.H.: Ira C. Evans, Public Printer, 1895, pp. 153–157, 189.

———. "The New Department." *Journal of Proceedings and Addresses, National Educational Association, 1895,* p. 949.

———. "The Training of Teachers." *Journal of Proceedings and Addresses, National Educational Association, 1895,* pp. 969–972.

———. "Discussion of Prof. Richard Jones's 'German Methods of Using the Mother Tongue.'" *Journal of Proceedings and Addresses, National Educational Association, 1894,* p. 483.

———. "Discussion on the South and Its Problems." *Journal of Proceedings and Addresses, National Educational Association, 1894,* pp. 586–590.

———. "The Report of the Committee of Ten—Its Use for the Improvement of Teachers Now at Work in the Schools." *Journal of Proceedings and Addresses, National Educational Association, 1894,* pp. 442–451.

———. "The School of the Future." *Journal of Proceedings and Addresses, National Educational Association, 1891,* pp. 82–89.

———. "The Child." *Journal of Proceedings and Addresses, National Educational Association, 1889,* pp. 479–482.

———. "Discussion, after Prof. Charles De Garmo's Paper on 'The German System of Normal Schools.'" *Journal of Proceedings and Addresses, National Educational Association, 1887,* p. 493.

———. "Discussion of Nathan C. Schaeffer's 'The Meaning and Limitations of the Maxim We Learn to Do By Doing.'" *Journal of Proceedings and Addresses, National Educational Association, 1887,* pp. 381–382.

———. "Discussion." *Journal of Proceedings and Addresses, National Educational Association, 1880,* pp. 49–50.

Putnam, Alice H. "A Reminiscence." *Frances Stuart Parker, Reminiscences and Letters.* Chicago: C. L. Ricketts, 1907, pp. 34–36.

Russell, James E. "The Training of Teachers for Secondary Schools." *Journal of Proceedings and Addresses, National Educational Association, 1901,* pp. 641–641.

Small, Albion W. "Demands of Sociology upon Pedagogy." *Journal of Proceedings and Addresses, National Educational Association, 1896,* p. 174.

Soldan, F. Louis. "Discussion of Charles A. McMurry's 'What Has Been Accomplished in Co-ordination in the Field of History and Literature'." *Journal of Proceedings and Addresses, National Educational Association, 1895,* pp. 113–114.

Spalding, John Lancaster. "Address Delivered at the Memorial Exercises Given by the Public School Teachers of Chicago and Cook County, Auditorium, April 19, 1902." *Education Report, 1901–1902.* U.S. Office of Education, Report of the Commissioner of Education for the Year 1902, pp. 276–279.

Starrett, Helen C. "The Fortnightly Club of Chicago." *Frances Stuart Parker, Reminiscences and Letters,* Chicago: C. L. Ricketts, 1907, pp. 53–55.

Sweet, Ada C. "Chicago Woman's Club." *Frances Stuart Parker, Reminiscences and Letters.* Chicago: C. L. Ricketts, 1907, pp. 55–56.

Washburne, Marion Foster. "Col. Francis W. Parker: The Man and Educational Reformer." *Francis Wayland Parker: His Life and Educational Reform Work, Souvenir Issued in Honor of the Silver Anniversary of the Quincy Movement.* New York: E. L. Kellogg and Company, April 1900, pp. 9–33.

Wheeler, Cora. "Early Life, Boston." *Frances Stuart Parker, Reminiscences and Letters.* Chicago: C. L. Ricketts, pp. 11–14.

IV. Interviews

Bailey, Mr. and Mrs. Parker. Bedford, N.H. October 13, 1962. (Mr. Bailey is a direct descendant of Charles Irving Parker. His wife recalled the Parker funeral in Manchester.)

Greenebaum, Miss Sarah. Francis Parker School, 330 West Webster, Chicago, Ill. April 25, 1962. (Student of Parker's and a teacher in the Francis Parker School since its beginning. She knew little of Parker directly but was full of information about Miss Flora Cooke of the Francis Parker School.)

Hall, Miss Katherine M. 5715 Kenwood Avenue, Chicago 27, Ill. July 12, 1962. (Daughter of Isaac Freeman Hall—one of "Parker's Boys." She did not know Parker directly but heard much about him from her father.)

* Shepard, Edna Parker (Mrs. Thomas H.). 89 Rawson Road, Brookline, Mass. October 14, 1962. (Stepdaughter of Parker's. Although in her 90's she is as keen and alert as a woman half her age. To her, Parker's personality was "overwhelming." She regretted that she was "so terribly young" when she knew Parker. She was twelve years old when her mother married the Colonel and in her thirties when he died. For someone in her 90's, age 12 is "terribly young.")

* Smith, Perry D. 455 Linden Avenue, Winnetka, Ill. April 26, 1962. (Student and advocate of Parker's. Founder of the North Shore Country Day School and now a professor at Roosevelt College, Chicago, he could recall the whole sweep of his educational life with great facility and accuracy.)

Thompsen, Leif Thorne. 80 East Westminister Road, Lake Forest, Ill. April 25, 1962. (Son of Gudrun Thompsen, member of Parker's faculty. He did not know Parker directly but was thoroughly familiar and in sympathy with his work.)

* Recently deceased.

Tolman, Francis Wayland Parker. Tolman Farm, Tolman Pond, Nelson, N.H. October 12–13, 1962. (Grandnephew of Parker's. He did not know Parker personally, but was aware of anecdotes about him.)

Tolman, Newton. Tolman Farm, Tolman Pond, Nelson, N.H. October 12–13, 1962. (Grandnephew of Parker's. He did not know Parker personally but he had always had a keen interest in the Colonel.)

* Tolman, Sadie (Mrs. Wayland). Tolman Farm, Tolman Pond, Nelson, N.H. October 13, 1962. (Niece of Parker's through marriage. Her husband was the son of Parker's younger sister, Emily. She is in her nineties but extremely alert. She recalled Parker very vividly from his visits to the farm and her visits to Chicago.)

Topping, Miss Helen F. 5151 Grand Avenue, Downers Grove, Ill. July 8, 23, 1962; August 12, 1962. (Miss Topping, as a child, was at the Chicago Institute in 1901 but did not remember Parker personally. She has crusaded for Parker's memory during the last half century in Japan, the Philippines, and the United States. She provided the author with her collection of sources which she had acquired from Flora J. Cooke and Mrs. Edna Shepard.)

V. Newspapers

"Anniversary Number of the Revival of Education in Quincy and the United States." *The Quincy* [*Massachusetts*] *Patriot.* April 21, 1900.

Appleton [*Wis.*] *Crescent.* June 25, 1898.

Appleton [*Wis.*] *Weekly Post.* June 30, 1898.

Carrollton [*Ill.*] *Gazette.* January 1858–October 1861.

Carrollton [*Ill.*] *Press.* March 1, 1861.

Chicago Chronicle. A spot check, 1898–1899.

Chicago Daily News. A spot check, 1898–1899.

Chicago Evening Journal. A spot check, 1894, 1898, 1899.

Chicago Evening Post. A spot check, 1894, 1896, 1898, 1899.

Chicago Herald. A spot check, 1886, 1887, 1891, 1894, 1895.

Chicago Inter-Ocean [Sometimes called *Daily*]. A spot check, 1883, 1886, 1887, 1890, 1894, 1896, 1898, 1899.

Chicago Record. A spot check, 1894, 1896, 1898, 1899.

Chicago Times. A spot check, 1894, 1896.

Chicago Times-Herald. A spot check, 1898, 1899, 1900.

Chicago Tribune. A spot check, 1883, 1887, 1890, 1891, 1892, 1894, 1895, 1896, 1898, 1899, 1900, 1902.

Daily Mirror and American [Manchester, N.H.]. September 1864–September 1865. September 1871–November 1871.

Daily Sun [Chicago Illinois]. (Sometimes called *Goodalls).* A spot check, June 1887–August 1887; 1891.

Dayton [*Ohio*]*Daily Ledger.* July 1868–April 1870.

Dayton [*Ohio*] *Journal.* January 1868–December 1873; March 1902–April 1902.

Herald [Dayton, Ohio]. (Sometimes called *Daily* or *Evening.)* April 1870–June 1872.

"The History of Col. Parker's Normal Connections," *Chicago Sun,* July 5, 1887. [Correspondence between Parker, A. H. Champlin and A. M. Kellogg.]

* Recently deceased.

"History of the Fourth New Hampshire Volunteers," *Mirror and Farmer,* November 11, 1865.
Manchester [*N.H.*] *American.* August 1844–November 1844.
Mirror and Farmer [Manchester, N.H.]. January 1865–July 1866; September 1871–November 1871; November 1885–December 1885.
New York Herald. April 15, 1865.
Quincy [*Mass.*] *Patriot.* January 1875–December 1880; March 1902; April 1916–May 1916; August 1937–July 1938.
Union [Manchester, N.H.] (Weekly until 1864 when it became *Daily.*) *July* 1861–November 1864.

VI. Periodicals

Adams, Charles Francis, Jr. "The New Departure in the Common Schools of Quincy (Colonel Parker's Experiment in the Common Schools of Quincy, Massachusetts)," *Elementary School Journal,* **35** (March 1935), 495–504.
————. "Scientific Common-School Education," *Harper's New Monthly Magazine,* **61** (October 1880), 934–942.
"An American Experiment," *The Journal of Education, A Monthly Record and Review.* London. No.164–No. 61, New Series (March 1, 1883), 91–92.
Blaine, Anita McCormick. "The Ideals Which Led to the Founding of the School of Education," *The Elementary School Teacher,* **24** (September 1913), 11–19; (October 1913), 73–81.
Camenisch, Sophia Catherine and Mabel Thorn Lulu. "Francis W. Parker Memorial," *Chicago Schools Journal,* **21** (November 1939), 71–77.
"Conference Commemorating the 100th Anniversary of the Birth of Francis W. Parker," *Progressive Education,* **14** (December 1937), 580–654; 583–588.
Cooke, Flora J. "Colonel F. W. Parker as I Knew Him," *Illinois Teacher,* **24** (June 1936), 325–326.
————. "Colonel Francis W. Parker, His Influence on Education," *Chicago Schools Journal,* **19** (March 1938), 145–153.
Course of Study. A Monthly Publication for Teachers and Parents Devoted to the Work of the Chicago Institute, Academic and Pedagogic, I (July 1, 1900, June 1, 1901). Chicago: The Lakeside Press, 1901. Parker was editor.
Dangler, Edward. "Philosophy of a Great American Educator, Col. Francis W. Parker (1837–1902)," *Education,* **69** (June 1949), 616–621.
————. "Francis W. Parker and Democracy in Education," *School and Society,* **67** (May 8, 1948), 354–356.
————. "From Quincy to Chicago—The American Comenius," *Harvard Educational Review,* **13** (January 1943), 12–24.
————. "Francis W. Parker, Father of the Activity Program," *School and Society,* **56** (October 24, 1942), 370–374.
————. "Consequences of Col. Parker's Educational Philosophy," *Education,* **62** (June 1942), 611–614.
Dearborn, Mary E. "A District Schoolmaster," *Journal of Education,* **51** (April 26, 1900), 259.
Dewey, John. "The Influence of Darwinism on Philosophy," *Popular Science Monthly,* **75** (July 1909), 90–98.
Eberhart, John F. "An Historical Sketch of the Cook County Normal School," *Chicago Schools Journal,* **17** (January–June 1936), 119–130.

Elementary School Teacher and Course of Study, II (July 1, 1901–June 1902). Chicago: University of Chicago Press, 1902. Parker was editor until his death. The June 1902 issue, 699–751, is devoted to Memorial Addresses.

Farrand, Harriet A. "Dr. Dewey's University Elementary School," *Journal of Education,* **48** (September 15, 1898), 172.

Fenner, M. S. and J. C. Soule. "Francis W. Parker—Liberator of the Classroom," *National Education Association Journal,* **35** (October 1946), 394–395.

Fitzpatrick, F. A. "Francis Wayland Parker," *Educational Review,* **24** (June 1902), 23–30.

Foote, Shelby. "Du Pont Storms Charleston," *American Heritage,* **14** (June 1963), 28–34; 89–92.

Fox, Florence Cornelia. "Personal Glimpses of Colonel Parker," *Progressive Education,* **9** (January 1932), 59–61.

Gale, Clarence Ross. "The Reconstruction of Cuba," *The Journal of Education,* **50** (December 21, 1899), 416.

Gary, Joseph E. "The Chicago Anarchists of 1886: The Crime, the Trial, and the Punishment," *Century Magazine,* **45** (April 1893), 803–837.

Gilmer, Carol Lynn. "Flora Cooke: Grand Old Lady of Education," *Coronet* (October 1947), 76–84.

Gladden, Washington. "Christianity and Popular Education," *The Century, Illustrated Monthly Magazine,* **31** (November 1885 to April 1886), 940–943.

Haley, Margaret A. "From the Funeral," *Journal of Education,* **55** (March 27, 1902), 205.

Harper's Weekly, **7** (July 18, 1863), 450.

Harris, William T. "Colonel Parker and the Quincy School," *Journal of Education,* **51** (June 7, 1900), 355.

Hefferan, Helen M. "Col. Francis Wayland Parker," *Chicago Schools Journal,* **18** (September 1936), 4–8.

Hoffer, Amalie. "The Chicago Manual Traning School—A Dream Come True," *Kindergarten Magazine.* **9** (November 1896), 170–197.

Illinois Society for Child Study **1–4** (1895–1899). Parker is listed as editor. The only copies available were at the University of Chicago, and the author was not able to avail himself of these periodicals. There is supposed to be F. W. Parker's "President's Report" in **3** (April 1898), 63.

Jackman, Wilbur S. "A Brief History of the School of Education," *University Record,* **9** (May 1904), 3.

————. "Francis Wayland Parker," *Review of Reviews,* **25** (April 1902), 448–452.

————. "Pensions for Teachers," *Journal of Education,* **39** (February 15, 1894), 100.

Journal of Education (New England), **3** (January 1, 1876) through **55** (March 27, 1902).

Koenig, Louis W. "The Most Unpopular Man in the North," *American Heritage,* **15** (February 1904), 12–14; 81–88.

McCaul, Robert L. "Dewey and the University of Chicago, September 1903–June 1904," *School and Society,* **89** (April 22, 1961), 202–206.

————. "Dewey and the University of Chicago, April 1902–May 1903," *School and Society,* **89** (April 8, 1961), 179–183.

————. "Dewey and the University of Chicago, July 1894–March 1902," *School and Society,* **89** (March 25, 1961), 152–157.

________. "Dewey's Chicago," *The School Review* (Summer 1959), 258–280.

McMaster, Rev. Richard K. "The Colonel Died with His Men," *New York State and the Civil War* (Emancipation Centennial Issue), II (September–October 1962), 26–35.

Parker, Francis Wayland. "Lectures and Lessons upon the Philosophy of Education and Bibliography," *Elementary School Teacher and Course of Study,* II (July 1, 1901–June 1902), 1–6.

________. "Function of Expression in Education," *Course of Study,* I. Chicago: The Lakeside Press, R. R. Donnelley and Sons. Co., 1901, pp. 398–400.

________. "Morning Exercises," *Course of Study,* I. Chicago: The Lakeside Press, R. R. Donnelley and Sons Company, 1901, p. 599.

________. "The Plan and Purposes of the Chicago Institute," *Course of Study,* I (July 1900), 9–24.

________. "The Quincy Method," *American Journal of Sociology,* **6** (July 1900), 114–120.

________. "Looking Backward," *The School Journal,* **59** (August 12, 1899), 118.

________. "Outlines of Pedagogies," *School Journal,* **31** (May 22, 1886), 325.

________. "Talks on Psychology, V," *School Journal,* **31** (June 26, 1886), 408.

________. "A Sketch of the Work in the Quincy Schools from 1875 to 1880, V," *School Journal,* **30** (August 1, 1885), 69–70.

________. "A Sketch of the Work in the Quincy Schools from 1875 to 1880, IV," *School Journal,* **30** (July 4, 1885), 5–6.

________. "A Sketch of the Work in the Quincy Schools from 1875 to 1880, III," *School Journal,* **29** (June 27, 1885), 407–408.

________. "A Sketch of the Work in the Quincy Schools from 1875 to 1880, II," *School Journal,* **29** (June 13, 1885), 374–375.

________. "A Sketch of the Work in the Quincy Schools from 1875 to 1880, I," *School Journal,* **29** (June 6, 1885), 357.

________. "Obstacles in Our Way," *Journal of Education,* **15** (May 18, 1882), 315.

________. "The Schoolroom as Workshop," *Journal of Education,* **5** (January 18, 1877), 32.

Parker, Franklin. "Francis W. Parker and Public Education in Chicago," *Chicago Schools Journal,* **42** (April 1961), 305–312.

"Pedagogical Works," *The Critic* (New Series), **23** (January–June 1895), 402.

Phillips, Wendell. "Wendell Phillips on the Quincy System," *Journal of Education,* **12** (December 16, 1880), 403.

Putnam, Alice H. "A Memorial Letter from Alice H. Putnam," *Kindergarten Review,* **12** (March 1902), 501–503.

Rice, J. M. "Our Public School System: A Summary," *The Forum,* **15** (June 1893), 504-518.

________. "The Public School System: A Summary," *The Forum,* **15** (March 1893), 200–215.

________. "Writers in the March Forum," *The Forum,* **15** (March 1893), 127.

School Journal, **29** (June 6, 1885)—**64** (April 5, 1902). F. W. Parker served as one of the editors from September 26, 1885 to October 16, 1885.

Scott, Thomas A. "The Recent Strikes," *The North American Review,* **125** (September 1877), 351–362.

Slade, James H. "The Finding of Colonel Parker," *Journal of Education,* **51** (April 26, 1900), 260.

Swearingen, James I. "The Institutional Heritage of Chicago Teachers College," *Chicago Schools Journal,* **43** (April 1962), 345–348.

Wainwright, Colonel Charles S. "So Ends the Great Rebel Army," Allan Nevins, (Ed.), *American Heritage,* **13** (October 1962), 33–47.

Washburne, Marion Foster. "The Educational Crisis in Chicago," *The Arena,* **15** (March 1896), 611–618.

"Week, The," *The Nation,* **67** (August 25, 1898), 139.

Wellers, Meta. "Chicago's Pension Law," *Journal of Education,* **44** (November 12, 1896), 331.

Wightman, S. K. "In Search of My Son," *American Heritage,* **14** (February 1963), 65–78.

Winship, Albert E. "Colonel Parker as a Leader (New Hampshire Memorial Service to F. W. Parker, Dover, May 2, 1902," *Journal of Education,* **15** (May 15, 1902), 314–317.

———. "The Finding of Colonel Parker, Quincy Celebration and Vendome Banquet, April 20, 21, 1900," *Journal of Education,* **51** (April 26, 1900), 259.

———. "Skirmishing in the West," *Journal of Education,* **43** (February 27, 1896), 144–145.

VII. Special Collections

Adams National Historic Site (Library). Quincy, Mass.
Adams Papers Microfilm. Part IV. Reels 594–597 (1874–1882).

Chicago Board of Education (Office of the Secretary). Chicago, Illinois:
Proceedings of the Board of Education of the City of Chicago. July 6, 1892–July 5, 1893. Chicago: Press of John H. Higgins, n.d.
Proceedings of the Board of Education of the City of Chicago. July 6, 1894–July 10, 1985. Chicago: Press of John H. Higgins, n.d.
Proceedings of the Board of Education of the City of Chicago. July 17, 1895–July 1, 1896. Chicago: Press of John H. Higgins, n.d.
Proceedings of the Board of Education of the City of Chicago. July 1, 1896–July 2, 1897. Chicago: Press of John H. Higgins, n.d.
Proceedings of the Board of Education of the City of Chicago. July 14, 1897–July 1, 1898. Chicago: Press of John H. Higgins, n.d.
Proceedings of the Board of Education of the City of Chicago. July 13, 1898–June 28, 1899. Chicago: Press of John H. Higgins, n.d.
School Histories (notebooks of typed pages of each school in Chicago).
School Report. Public Schools of the City of Chicago. Forty-second Annual Report of the Board of Education for the Year Ending June 26, 1896. Chicago: The J. M. W. Jones Stationery and Printing Co., 1896.
School Report. Public Schools of the City of Chicago. Forth-third Annual Report of the Board of Education for the Year Ending June 25, 1897. Chicago: The J. M. W. Jones Stationery and Printing Company, 1897.
School Report. Public Schools of the City of Chicago. Forty-fourth Annual Report of the Board of Education for the Year Ending June 25, 1898. Chicago: The J. M. W. Jones Stationery and Printing Company, 1898.
School Report. Public Schools of the City of Chicago. Forthy-fifth Annual Report of the Board of Education for the Year Ending June 30, 1899. Chicago: The J. M. W. Jones Stationery and Printing Company, 1899.

Chicago Historical Society (Library, Collections). Chicago, Ill.:

Parker, Francis Wayland, 1837-1902. Telegrams and Memoranda from nurse, physician, and undertakers regarding illness, death, and burial of Colonel Parker. Gift of Bayard Holmes, March 5, 1913.

Chicago Teachers College (South) (Historical Files, Main Office). Chicago, Ill.:

Alumni of the Chicago Normal School. A pamphlet published for the Officers of the Alumni Association, 1908–1909.

"Chicago Teachers College History." A typewritten manuscript, 10 pp., with corrections in ink, probably the work of Miss Sophia C. Camenisch of the Chicago Teachers College Faculty, as evidenced by a letter from Carleton Washburne to Miss Camenisch, July 21, 1941.

"The Colonel Francis W. Parker Memorial Fund" (Orville T. Bright, Chairman). A two-page printed statement requesting funds for a Parker memorial to be placed in the rotunda of the new building of the Chicago Normal School [1906].

"Extracts from the Deed to the Lots on which the Normal School is built."

Flynn, Polly. "The Early History of Chicago Teachers College in Its Relation to the Community." A scrapbook of newspaper clippings probably compiled in 1938 or 1939. Includes material on Wentworth and early Normal School notices and activities.

Parker, Francis W. (Ed.). "Englewood's Schools, Their Rise, Progress and Present Status Graphically Described. . . ." Typed copy from *Daily Evening Call,* Special Number, Englewood, Illinois, Thursday, October 9, 1890.

Preparations, Minutes, Activities surrounding the Dedication of a Plaque of Colonel Parker, Papers of Miss Camenisch.

Washburne, Carleton, Superintendent, Winnetka Public Schools. Letter to Miss Sophia C. Camenisch, July 21 1941.

________. Letter to Mr. Bartky, President of the Chicago Teachers College, September 18, 1940. This letter includes the letter from his mother, Marion Foster Washburne, about 1900, which describes her work in fighting for the transfer of the Cook County Normal School to the City of Chicago.

Cook County Board of Commissioners (Office of Comptroller and Clerk of Board of Commissioners). Chicago, Ill.:

Official Proceedings of the Board of Commissioners for the Year 1893–1894, Being from December 4, 1893 to December 3, 1894 inclusive. Chicago: J. M. W. Jones Stationery and Printing Co., 1895.

Official Proceedings of the Board of Commissioners for the Year 1895–1896, Being from December 2, 1895 to December 5, 1896. Chicago: Cameron, Amberg and Co., 1896.

Cook County Board of Education (Board Rooms). Chicago, Ill.:

Biennial Report of the County Superintendent of Schools from July 1, 1882 to June 30, 1884. Chicago: J. M. W. Jones Stationery and Printing Co., 1885.

Biennial Report of the County Superintendent of Schools from July 1, 1884 to June 30, 1886. Chicago: J. M. W. Jones Stationery and Printing Co., 1886.

Biennial Report of the County Superintendent of Schools from July 1, 1886 to June 30, 1888. Chicago: J. M. W. Jones Stationery and Printing Co., 1888.

Biennial Report of the County Superintendent of Schools from July 1, 1888 to June 30, 1890. Chicago: J. M. W. Jones Stationery and Printing Co., 1890.

Biennial Report of the County Superintendent of Schools from July 1, 1890 to June 30, 1892. Chicago: J. M. W. Jones Stationery and Printing Co., 1892.

Biennial Report of the County Superintendent of Schools from July 1, 1892 to June 30, 1894. Chicago: J. M. W. Jones Stationery and Printing Co., 1894.

Biennial Report of the County Superintendent of Schools from July 1, 1894 to June 30, 1896. Chicago: J. M. W. Jones Stationery and Printing Co., 1896.

Biennial Report of the County Superintendent of Schools from July 1, 1896 to June 30, 1898. Chicago: J. M. W. Jones Stationery and Printing Co., 1898.

Biennial Report of the County Superintendent of Schools from July 1, 1908 to June 30, 1910. Chicago: J. M. W. Jones Stationery and Printing Co., 1910.

Cook County Recorder of Deeds. Chicago, Ill.:

Records, document number 2,883,081, page 374 of Book 6764.

Dayton and Montgomery County Public Library (Dayton Room). Dayton, Ohio:

Dayton Directory, 1870–1871. Dayton, Ohio: A. Bailey, Publishers, 1870.

Dayton Public Schools. Annual Report of the Board of Education for the School Year Ending August 31, 1867. Dayton, Ohio: Journal Book and Job Rooms, 1868.

Dayton Public Schools. Annual Report of the Board of Education for the School Year Ending June 30, 1872. Dayton, Ohio: United Brethren Publishing House, 1873.

Dayton Public Schools. Annual Report of the Board of Education for the School Year Ending August 31, 1875. Dayton, Ohio: Journal Book and Job Rooms, 1876.

Dayton Public Schools. Annual Report of the Board of Education of the City of Dayton, Ohio for the School Year Ending August 31, 1904. Dayton, Ohio: The Groneweg Printing Co., 1904.

Williams' Dayton Directory for 1868–1869. Dayton, Ohio: Payne Holden and Co., 1868.

Williams' Dayton Directory for 1871–1872. Dayton, Ohio: Williams and Co., Publishers, 1871.

Francis W. Parker School (Library). Chicago, Illinois:

Catalogue of the Chicago Institute, Academic and Pedagogic, 1900–1901. Chicago: Published by the Chicago Institute.

Francis W. Parker, Educational Pioneer, Centennial, 1937. Chicago: Francis W. Parker Centennial Committee, n.d.

Preliminary Announcement, Chicago Institute, Academic and Pedagogic, January 1, 1900. Chicago: The Henry Shepard Co., n.d.

The Massachusetts Historical Society:

Adams, Charles Francis, Jr. Diaries. The years 1874 through 1880 were checked. Each year is a separate volume, handwritten. Daily entries average only a few lines.

National Archives (General Search Room, Record and Pension Office, and Records Division, Army and Air Corps Branch). Washington, D.C.:

Consolidated Morning Reports of 4th Regiment of New Hampshire Volunteers (October 4, 1861, through May 9, 1865).

Department of the Interior, Bureau of Pensions, Cert. N. 869791, Francis W. Parker, Soldier's Certificate, Can No. 17835, Bundle No. 22. This includes Parker's letters in regard to his wound in 1864, and his application for pension.

Muster Rolls, Company B, 7th Squadron Rhode Island Cavalry (3 months, 1902).

New Hampshire 4th Volunteers (box file) Circulars.

New Hampshire 4th Infantry Regimental Order Book.

New Hampshire Regiment Descript Book, 4th Infantry.

Parker, Francis W. Service Record. Record Group Number 94. (This includes Company muster-in and muster-out rolls, all orders, duty stations, commissions, leave petitions, etc.)

Proceedings of a General Court Martial Convened at Morris Island, South Carolina, August 5, 1865, by virtue of Special Oorder No. 48N, U.S. Forces Morris Island, South Carolina, Case 14, August 6, 1863, Captain Frank W. Parker, NN 383.

Record of a General Court Martial Held at St. Augustine, Florida, Convening July 30, 1862, Case of Frank W. Parker, Friday, August 8, 1862-August 9, 1862. KK260.

Regimental Letter Book, New Hampshire 4th Infantry.

Roster, Fourth Regiment New Hampshire Volunteers. Compiled and published by authority of the Fourth Regiment Veterans Association by John G. Hutchinson, First Sergt. Co. E. Historian. Manchester, N.H.: Printed by John B. Clarke Co., 1896.

New Hampshire Historical Society (Library). Concord, N.H.:

"Cemetery Inscriptions of Manchester, New Hampshire." Unpublished, copied by W.P.A., 1938.

Parker, Francis W. (A.M.) 1887. *Dartmouth College Necrology, 1901–1902.* Ernest Morten Hopkins (compiler).

New Hampshire State Library. Concord, New Hampshire:

Course of Study Adopted for the Public Schools of the City of Manchester —Adopted by the School Committee, June 5, 1868. Manchester, N.H.: Charles F. Livingston, Printer, 1868.

Little, William. *A Brief History of the Schools of Manchester, New Hampshire.* A bound volume of pamphlets, no publisher or date.

Manchester Directory, Containing the City Record of Names of the Citizens and a Business Directory with an Almanac for 1864. Manchester, N.H.: Adams, Sampson and Company, 1864.

Manchester Directory, 1866, Containing the City Record of the Names of the Citizens, and a Business Directory. Manchester, N.H.: Sampson, Davenport and Co., 1866.

Manchester Directory, 1869, Containing the City Record of the Names of the Citizens, and a Business Directory. Manchester, N.H.: Sampson, Davenport and Co., 1869.

Manchester School Reports. Eleventh Annual Report of the Superintendent of Public Instruction, Being the Twentieth Annual Report of the School Committee of the City of Manchester, 1865. Manchester, N.H.: Henry A. Gage, 1866.

Manchester School Reports. Twelfth Annual Report of the Superintendent of Public Instruction, and Reports of Sub-committees and Teachers, Constituting the Twenty-first Annual Report of the Board of Education of Manchester, 1866. Manchester, N.H.: William H. Fisk's Job Printing Establishment, 1867.

Manchester School Reports. Thirteenth Annual Report of the Superintendent of Public Instruction, Being the Twenty-second Annual Report of the Board of Education of the City of Manchester, 1867. Manchester, N.H.: John B. Clarke's Book and Job Printing Establishment, 1868.

Manchester School Reports. Fourteenth Annual Report of the Superintendent of Public Instruction, Being the Twenty-third Annual Report of the Board of Education of the City of Manchester, 1868. Manchester, N.H.: Henry A. Gage, Printer, 1869.

Regulations of the Public Schools in the City of Manchester Adopted by the School Committee, March 22, 1965. Manchester, N.H.: Printed by Charles F. Livingston, 16th and 17th Smyth's Block, 1866.

Piscataquog Cemetery, South Main Street, West Manchester, Manchester, N.H.:

Burial place of the Parkers and relatives.

School Committee Rooms, 70 Coddington Street, Quincy, Massachusetts:

Annual Report. School Committee. Town of Quincy, 1871–1872. Boston: Press of Rockwell and Churchill, 1872.

Annual Report. School Committee. Town of Quincy, 1874–1875. Boston: Press of Rockwell and Churchill, 1875.

Annual Report. School Committee. Town of Quincy, 1875–1876. Boston: Press of Rockwell and Churchill, 1876.

Annual Report. School Committee. Town of Quincy, 1876–1877. Boston: Press of Rockwell and Churchill, 1877.

Annual Report. School Committee. Town of Quincy, 1877–1878. Boston: Press of Rockwell and Churchill, 1878.

Annual Report. School Committee. Town of Quincy, 1878–1879. Boston: Press of Rockwell and Churchill, 1879.

Annual Report. School Committee. Town of Quincy, 1879–1880. Boston: Press of Rockwell and Churchill, 1880.

Annual Report. School Committee. Town of Quincy, 1880–1881. Boston: Press of Rockwell and Churchill, 1881.

"Record of the General School Committee for the Town of Quincy, March 25, 1849–February 8, 1903" (handwritten minutes).

"Scrapbook." Letters from high school students to Charles Francis Adams, Jr., 1877–1878. Their themes are all exercises in Autobiography.

State Library. The Commonwealth of Massachusetts, State House, Boston, Massachusetts:

Annual Report of the School Committee of the City of Boston, 1880. Boston: Rockwell and Churchill, City Printers, 1881.

Annual Report of the School Committee of the City of Boston, 1881. Boston: Rockwell and Churchill, City Printers, 1882.

Annual Report of the School Committee of the City of Boston, 1882. Boston: Rockwell and Churchill, City Printers, 1883.

Boston Directory 1881, No. 77, for Year Commencing July 1, 1881. Boston: Sampson, Davenport and Co., 1881.

Boston Directory 1882, No. 78, for Year Commencing July 1, 1882. Boston: Sampson, Davenport and Co., 1882.

Boston Directory 1883, No. 79, for Year Commencing July 1, 1883. Boston: Sampson, Davenport and Co., 1883.

Tolman Farm, Tolman Pond, Nelson, N.H.:

Cook County Normal Summer School . . . Englewood, Illinois. Francis W. Parker, Principal, Wilbur S. Jackman, Manager, Three Weeks, Beginning July 9th, 1894. (Eight-page announcement with symbol of the Theory of Concentration on the front. It is the "fundamental idea upon which the work of the Cook County Normal School rests." In addition to a sketch of the teachers and the program, there is an announcement of "excursions," which include the World's Fair Grounds and the "Pullman Car Works, at Pullman, a delightful suburb of Chicago.")

Cooke, Flora J. *Colonel Parker, As Interpreted Through the Work of the Francis W. Parker School.* Paper read before the Parents' Association of the Francis W. Parker School, December 6, 1910.

Parker, Francis W., (President, Chicago Institute, Academic and Pedagogic). Letter to "Dear Tersey," May 26, 1900.

Topping Collection (acquired by Helen F. Topping from Flora J. Cooke and Edna Shepard. The Collection is presently in the possession of the author at 1325 Stony Brook Lane, Mountainside, N.J.):

Armstrong, James E. Letter to Mr. E. P. Wilson, dated May 24, 1934.

Baker, Zonia. Letter to Mr. [E. P.] Wilson, dated June 4, 1934.

________. "Geography . . .," unpublished.

Bagley, William C. Letter to Miss Flora J. Cooke, dated April 14, 1936.

"Basic Tenets and Ideals of the Francis W. Parker School" (nine-page pamphlet).

Bass, Willard S. "Col. Parker's Influence in the Parker School" (seven pages, typed). Address given June 16, 1908.

________. "Col. Francis W. Parker as a Soldier" (six pages, typed), n.d.

Beck, Robert Holmes. Letter to Miss Helen F. Topping, dated October 25, 1945.

Blaine, Anita McCormick. Letter to Dear Miss [Zonia] Baber, dated March 4, 1901.

________. Letter to My Dear Miss Baber, dated September 7, 1900.

Brameld, Theodore. Letter to Helen F. Topping, dated September 6, 1956.

Chamberlen, Howard A., curator, Manchester Historic Association. Letter to Helen F. Topping, dated March 14, 1953.

Conover, Miss Charlotte O., librarian, New Hampshire Hist. Soc. Letter to Helen F. Topping, dated January 27, 1953.

Cooke, Flora J. "A Brief Sketch of a chapter in the early history of the Chicago Teachers College" (six pages), n.d.

________. "A Century of Progress in Education in a Democracy, 1833–1933" (thirteen pages), n.d.

________. "Childhood Education, 1833–1933" (twenty-four pages), n.d.

________. "After luncheon talk to tell college students about Chicago Teachers College in the Nineties" (three pages), n.d.

________. "Armistice Day Talk, November 12, 1945" (six pages), n.d.

________. "Colonel Parker in Chicago" (two pages), n.d.

________. "The Implications of Colonel Parker's Philosophy of Education for Today and Tomorrow" (eleven pages), n.d.

________. "1926 Statement, Miss Cooke taught under Colonel Parker" (two pages), n.d.
________. "Opportunities and episodes of a teacher's life in America during the last half century" (nine pages), n.d.
________. "Reminiscences of Colonel Francis W. Parker" (two pages), n.d.
________. "Speech . . . given before the Mayor's City Council Common School—1946" (two pages).
Cooley, Flora D. Letter to Mr. [E. P.] Wilson, dated January 12, 1938.
Death Notices (newspaper clippings).
Gossart, Paul, Superintendent of Schools, Quincy, Mass. Letter to Helen F. Topping, dated September 4, 1951.
Graduate Teachers College of Winnetka, Winnetka, Illinois, 1941–1943.
Heineman, Mrs. Cora de G. Letter to Mr. E. P. Wilson, dated March 4, 1938.
Jones, Marjorie. Letter to Miss Flora Cooke, dated July 15, 1950.
Kuh, Charlotte G., Nancy Blaine Harrison, Katherine Taylor. *Anita McCormick Blaine.* (No publisher or date, speeches were part of program in memory of Mrs. Blaine held at the Francis W. Parker School on the evening of April 22, 1955.)
Ludwig, Mrs. W. E. Letter to Mr. [E. P.] Wilson, n.d.
Melvin, A. Gordon to Miss Flora Cooke, dated December 13, 1938.
Mercier, Louis J. A. "A Pioneer in American Education: Col. Francis W. Parker, His Contributions to Educational Theory and Practice." 1910.
Morning Exercises—Memorial Day, dedication to Parker, May 28, 1909.
Parker, Francis W. Letter to Miss Zonia Baber, dated January 3, 1900.
________. (As President of the Chicago Institute.) Letter to Miss [Zonia] Baber, dated December 14, 1899.
________. Letter to "Dear Zony" [Zonia Baber], dated July 8, 1898.
________. Letter to "Dear Zonia [Baber]," dated June 30, 1898.
________. Letter to "Dear Zony" [Zonia Baber], dated June 23, 1898.
________. Letter to "Zony" [Zonia Baber], dated May 15, 1898.
________. Letter to "My Dear Zonia[Baber]," dated March 23, 1897.
________. Letter to "My Dear Zonia [Baber]," dated February 25, 1897.
________. Letter to "My Dear Zonia [Baber]," dated February 17, 1897.
________. Letter to Miss Zonia Baber, dated January 8, 1897.
________. Letter to "My Dearest Zonia [Baber]," dated August 3, 1896.
________. "Discussion of the Principles and Methods of Teaching Reading" 4 pp.
________. Unpublished Lectures:
1. "What Should be Taught in Our Schools?" (fourteen pages, typed).
2. "Froebel's Idea of Education" (eleven pages, typed).
3. "Departmental Instruction" (fourteen pages, typed).
4. "Order" (twelve pages, typed).
5. "Artists or Artisans? . . ." (sixteen pages, typed).
6. "Talks" (fifty-three pages, typed).
   a. "The study of the science and art of teaching is unlimited."
   b. "Reading."
   c. "What is the function of an oral or a written word?"
   d. "Learning to read is learning to think by the action of written and printed words upon consciousness."

e. "Script."
f. "Reading and Phonics."
g. Reading: Application of Principles.
h. Additional suggestions in regard to teaching reading.
i. Reading: application of principles concluded.
j. Spelling.
k. Writing.

7. "When we take into consideration the short time the common school system has been established. . . ." (twenty-one pages, typed).
8. "Upon the growth and development of the common school centers all the hopes of self-government . . ." (eleven pages, typed).
9. "That form of government is best which presents the highest conditions for self-effort in the direction of freedom, knowledge of the law and its application . . ." (fourteen pages).
10. "Methods of Quantity" (thirty-eight pages, handwritten).

Parker, Frank Stuart [Mrs. Parker]. Letter to "My Dear Zonia [Baber]," dated September 1, 1883 [1893?]

Roberts, W. M. Letter to Mr. [E. P.] Wilson, dated May 7, 1934.

Rugg, Harold. Letter to Miss Flora J. Cooke, dated May 10, 1933.

Skillin, Mrs. S. Dew. Letter to Flora Cooke, n.d.

Slade Scrapbook (copy). This was loaned to Miss Topping by Mary V. Hastings Slade, in 1945. Most of this includes clippings from the *San Francisco Chronicle* dealing with Slade's Parker crusade in California . . . includes one letter from Parker and one from C. F. Adams, Jr.

Walker, Hattie Adell. Letter to Mr. [E. P.] Wilson, dated April 28, 1935.

Wilson, E. P. "Colonel Francis W. Parker and Democracy in Education." 8 pp.

In addition, this collection contains numerous letters to Miss Topping in regard to a Parker Foundation, an interview with Miss Zonia Baber, and the following photographs:

Parker and Professional Training Class, n.d.

"Characteristic pose of the man we admire—eh?" Fl. Cooke, about 1898.

Colonel Parker with group of his grandnephews and nieces, n.d.

Colonel Parker in his old home library in Englewood, Ill., with comments by F. J. C. on back.

Photo inset of Parker at home, at school, at camp, in Hawaii, etc.

Photographs of Parker and relatives in New Hampshire on the farm (3).

University of Chicago (Archives, Harper Library). Chicago, Ill.

Colonel Francis Wayland Parker Materials and Special Collections. Eleven scrapbooks containing clippings of newspaper and magazine editorials and articles by and about Parker. The articles represent worldwide opinion covering the years 1873–1902; hundreds of journals and newspapers in this country and abroad are represented. Also contained in these scrapbooks are anniversary accounts, mementoes, and obituary notices, reviewing in detail Parker's contributions to education.

Wisconsin State Historical Society (McCormick Collections). Madison Wisconsin:

The Papers of Anita McCormick Blaine (1866-1954). Her papers are collected in 936 Archives boxes and 102 records center boxes, arranged chronologically, and there are 53 volumes, arranged alphabetically. (Mrs. Herbert Kellar, Curator.)

VIII. Special Correspondence to the Author

Hawkins, Paul B., State Board of Health, Jackson 5, Mo. Letter dated November 25, 1963.

Lang, Arthur W., Jr., Lang Funeral Home, Since 1884, 105 West Beach Street, Pass Christian, Mo. Letter dated March 7, 1964.

Lanyon, John B., Jr., The House of Lanyon Undertakers, 734 West 79th Street, Chicago 20, Ill. Letter dated June 19, 1963.

Melvin, Gordon, 963 Watertown Street, West Newton, Mass. Letter dated October 29, 1962.

Tolman, Newton F., Greengate, Nelson, N.H. Letter dated September 19, 1962.

Worthen, Mrs. John C., 2029 East 72nd Street, Chicago 49, Ill. Letter dated August 18, 1962.

IX. Unpublished Dissertations

Baylor, Ruth Markendorpff. "The Contribution of Elizabeth Palmer Peabody to Kindergarten Education in the United States." Unpublished Ed.D. dissertation, New York University, 1960.

Dangler, Edward. "Francis Wayland Parker's Educational Philosophy: Its Origins, Contents, and Consequences." Unpublished Ph.D. dissertation, New York University, 1939. This dissertation has been lost since 1951 but the abstract is available. *Abstracts of Theses, October 1939–June 1939, New York University*. New York: New York University, 1940.

Riley, Mary Agnes. "A History of the Chicago Normal School." Unpublished M.A. Thesis, University of Chicago, 1914.

Sollenberger, D. L. "The Development and Growth of the Public Secondary Schools of Dayton, Ohio from 1850 to 1935." Unpublished M.A. thesis, Ohio State University, 1935.

Tostberg, Robert Eugene. "Educational Ferment in Chicago, 1883–1904." Unpublished Ph.D. dissertation, University of Wisconsin, 1960.

White, William Bruce. "The Philanthropies of Anita McCormick Blaine." Unpublished M.S. thesis, University of Wisconsin, 1959.

X. Vital Statistics

Birth Records:

Parker, Ann E. September 9, 1865, Bedford, New Hampshire. [Daughter of F. W. Parker.] Bureau of Vital Statistics, New Hampshire State Department of Health, Concord, New Hampshire.

Parker, Robert. May 13, 1797. [Father of F. W. Parker.] Bureau of Vital Statistics, New Hampshire State Department of Health, Concord, New Hampshire.

Parker, Robert. August 6, 1827, Bedford, New Hampshire. [Half-brother of F. F. Parker.] Bureau of Vital Statistics, New Hampshire State Department of Health, Concord, New Hampshire.

Note: The Bureau of Vital Statistics in Concord, New Hampshire, contains all vital statistics for the whole state. The absence of birth, death, or other important notices in this bibliography, indicates that they were not filed or are missing from the state files.

Marriage Records:

Parker, Robert, to Charlotte Chamberlin, December 31, 1822, Pembroke, New Hampshire. [First marriage of F. W. Parker's father.] Bureau of Vital Statistics, New Hampshire State Department of Health, Concord, New Hampshire.

Parker, Robert, to Mille Rand, October 29, 1829, Coffstown, New Hampshire. [Father and mother of F. W. Parker.] Bureau of Vital Statistics, New Hampshire State Department of Health, Concord, New Hampshire.

Parker, Francis W., to Josephine E. Hall, December 1, 1864. (No place was indicated except that the groom resided in Bedford, New Hampshire, and the bride in Hancock, New Hampshire. The bride was born in Bennington, New Hampshire.) Bureau of Vital Statistics, New Hampshire State Department of Health, Concord, New Hampshire.

Parker, Francis W., to Mary F. Stuart, November 29, 1882, Boston, Massachusetts. Division of Vital Statistics (Vol. 336, p. 205, no. 3677), State House, Boston, Massachusetts.

Death Records:

Parker, Ann E., October 27, 1885, Normal Park, Englewood, Illinois. [Daughter of F. W. Parker.] Bureau of Vital Statistics, 130 North Wells Street, Chicago 6, Illinois.

Parker, E., December 6, 1870, Minneapolis, Minnesota. (This is undoubtedly Phenie E. Parker, as the place of residence was recorded as Dayton, Ohio, where Parker lived at that time. Minneapolis is engraved on her tombstone as the place of death.) Division of Public Health—Vital Statistics, Minneapolis, Minnesota. (Vol. I, p. 10.)

Parker, Frances Stuart, April 1, 1899, Chicago, Illinois. Bureau of Vital Statistics, 130 North Wells Street, Chicago 6, Illinois.

Probated Estates:

Parker, Francis W. File 17/7379, Docket 65, Probate Court of Cook County, Chicago, Illinois.

Parker, Nabby. [Grandmother of F. W. Parker.] No. O 7428, Probate Court, Hillsborough County, Nashua, New Hampshire.

Parker, Robert. [Father of F. W. Parker.] No. O 7406, Probate Court, Hillsborough County, Nashua, New Hampshire.

Parker, William. [Grandfather of F. W. Parker.] No. O 7109, Probate Court, Hillsborough County, Nashua, New Hampshire.

Index